Growth-oriented Women Entrepreneurs and their Businesses

NEW HORIZONS IN ENTREPRENEURSHIP

Series Editor: Sankaran Venkataraman
Darden Graduate School of Business
Administration, University of Virginia

This important series is designed to make a significant contribution to the development of Entrepreneurship Studies. As this field has expanded dramatically in recent years, the series will provide an invaluable forum for the publication of high-quality works of scholarship and show the diversity of issues and practices around the world.

The main emphasis of the series is on the development and application of new and original ideas in Entrepreneurship. Global in its approach, it includes some of the best theoretical and empirical work, with contributions to fundamental principles, rigorous evaluations of existing concepts and competing theories, historical surveys and future visions. Titles include original monographs, edited collections and texts.

Titles in the series include:

A General Theory of Entrepreneurship
The Individual–Opportunity Nexus
Scott Shane

Academic Entrepreneurship
University Spinoffs and Wealth Creation
Scott Shane

Economic Development Through Entrepreneurship
Government, University and Business Linkages
Edited by Scott Shane

Growth-oriented Women Entrepreneurs and their Businesses
A Global Research Perspective
Edited by Candida G. Brush, Nancy M. Carter, Elizabeth J. Gatewood,
Patricia G. Greene and Myra M. Hart

Growth-oriented Women Entrepreneurs and their Businesses

A Global Research Perspective

Edited by

Candida G. Brush
Babson College, USA

Nancy M. Carter
University of St. Thomas, USA

Elizabeth J. Gatewood
Wake Forest University, USA

Patricia G. Greene
Babson College, USA

Myra M. Hart
Harvard Business School, USA

NEW HORIZONS IN ENTREPRENEURSHIP

Edward Elgar
Cheltenham, UK • Northampton, MA, USA

Published by
Edward Elgar Publishing Limited
Glensanda House
Montpellier Parade
Cheltenham
Glos GL50 1UA
UK

Edward Elgar Publishing, Inc.
136 West Street
Suite 202
Northampton
Massachusetts 01060
USA

A catalogue record for this book
is available from the British Library

Library of Congress Cataloguing in Publication Data

Growth-oriented women entrepreneurs and their businesses: a global research
    perspective/edited by Candida G. Brush ... [et al.]
        p. cm. — (New horizons in entrepreneurship)
      1. Businesswomen. 2. Women-owned business enterprises. 3. New
    business enterprises. 4. Entrepreneurship. I. Brush, Candida G. II. Series.
    HD6053.G765   2006
    338.6'422—dc22

                                                            2005050166

ISBN-13: 978 1 84542 289 9
ISBN-10: 1 84542 289 9

Printed and bound in Great Britain by MPG Books Ltd, Bodmin, Cornwall

Contents

Contributors

Pia Arenius, PhD, is Assistant Professor of Technology Management at Ecole des Hautes Etudes Commerciales (HEC), University of Lausanne in Switzerland. Her research interests include entrepreneurship, social capital and innovation management.

Mary Barrett, PhD, is Professor and Director of the Graduate School of Business and Professional Development, and Sydney Business School, both located within the University of Wollongong, Australia. Her research focuses on gender issues in workplace communication; women business owners; and family business, including the role of women in family business.

Candida G. Brush, DBA, is Chair of the Entrepreneurship Division at Babson College, Wellesley, Massachusetts and holder of the President's Chair in Entrepreneurship. Her research investigates resource acquisition strategies in emerging organizations, the influence of gender in business start-up and growth strategies of women-led ventures.

Nancy M. Carter, PhD, is the Vice President of Research at Catalyst, in New York City, NY. In this role she leads Catalyst research teams in developing groundbreaking research and consulting on issues relating to building inclusive environments and women's advancement in the workplace. Dr Carter also holds the Richard M. Schulze Chair in Entrepreneurship at the University of St. Thomas, Minneapolis, Minnesota.

Sara Carter is Professor of Entrepreneurship in the Department of Management and Organization, University of Stirling, Scotland. Her research interests include gender, rurality and multiple business ownership. Her chapter was written when she was Professor of Entrepreneurship at the University of Strathclyde, Scotland.

Michelle Provorny Cash is an organizational consultant, editor and writer based in Edmonton, Alberta, Canada. Her research interests include social entrepreneurship, women's entrepreneurship, micro-finance and community economic development. She currently serves as Managing Editor for *Social Enterprise Reporter*, a monthly publication about social enterprise.

Anne de Bruin, PhD, is Professor of Economics in the Department of Commerce, Massey University at Albany, Auckland. Her research interests include entrepreneurship, career theory, labour market dynamics, non-standard work and pathways to sustainable employment.

Cristina Díaz is a lecturer in the Department of Business Administration at the University of Castilla-La Mancha (Spain). Her research interests are related to entrepreneurship, in particular with the resource mobilization and outcomes obtained by female entrepreneurs in comparison with their male counterparts.

Susan Flint-Hartle is Senior Lecturer in the Department of Finance, Banking and Property, Massey University at Albany, Auckland. Her research interests include franchising in the real estate agency sector, entrepreneurship and organizational learning.

Lene Foss, PhD, is Associate Professor in Entrepreneurship and Organizational Development at the University of Tromsø, Norwegian College of Fishery Science in Norway. She holds an Associate Professor II position at the Department of Industrial Economics and Technology Management at The Norwegian University of Science and Technology in Trondheim, Norway. Her research interests include women entrepreneurship and leadership, emerging industries and entrepreneurial networks.

Elizabeth J. Gatewood, PhD, is director of the University Office of Entrepreneurship and Liberal Arts at Wake Forest University, Winston-Salem, North Carolina. Her research interests include the factors influencing the success of women entrepreneurs, including access to resources for growing ventures, and entrepreneurial cognition.

Patricia G. Greene, PhD, is Dean of the Undergraduate School at Babson College, Wellesley, Massachusetts, where she holds the President's Chair in Entrepreneurship. Her research interests are the identification, acquisition and combination of entrepreneurial resources, particularly by women and minority entrepreneurs.

Angela Hamouda, MBS, is a research coordinator with the Centre for Entrepreneurship Research at Dundalk Institute of Technology, Ireland. Her research interests include female entrepreneurship, in particular financial and networking supports for female entrepreneurs.

Richard T. Harrison is Dixons Chair of Entrepreneurship and Innovation, and Director of Research, at University of Edinburgh Management School. His primary research interests include entrepreneurial finance (business angels, early stage venture capital), entrepreneurial learning and entrepreneurship and public policy.

Myra M. Hart, Professor of Management Practice in Entrepreneurship at Harvard Business School, Boston, Massachusetts, conducts research on entrepreneurship, venture capital and women business owners. Her experience as a founder of a large-scale public company informs her teaching in MBA, executive education and alumni programmes.

Colette Henry, PhD, is Head of Department of Business Studies and Director of the Centre for Entrepreneurship Research at Dundalk Institute of Technology, Ireland. Her research interests include entrepreneurship education and training – programme design and evaluation; female entrepreneurship and entrepreneurs in the creative industries.

Frances Hill is a senior lecturer in the School of Management and Economics, Queen's University Belfast. Her research interests include organizational change and innovation especially in relation to industry incumbents; the behavioural and interpersonal dimensions of technology transfer; inter- and intra-organizational learning; the education and training of aspiring/nascent entrepreneurs; issues surrounding the financing of new and growing business ventures; social entrepreneurship.

Jennifer E. Jennings, PhD (formerly Jennifer Cliff), is an Assistant Professor in the Department of Strategic Management and Organization at the University of Alberta. Her research interests include the differential experiences and outcomes of male and female entrepreneurs, the determinants and consequences of imitative versus innovative entrepreneurship, and issues at the nexus of entrepreneurship and family.

Juan J. Jiménez, PhD, is Academic Director of the Vicerrectorate of Albacete and Entrepreneurial Projects at the University of Castilla-La Mancha (Spain) where he holds a Chair in Business Administration. His research interests are entrepreneurship, SMEs and the promotion of an entrepreneurial culture.

Kate Johnston, PhD, is a Senior Researcher with the Centre for Entrepreneurship Research at Dundalk Institute of Technology, Ireland. Her research interests include entrepreneurship growth and funding strategies, applied financial economics and corporate governance.

John I. Kjeldsen holds an MSc in Economics and Business Administration and a Graduate Diploma in Business Administration and Marketing. He is Associate Professor at the Department of Marketing, Informatics and Statistics, Director of Study (Open University) and coordinator of the Diploma in Business Administration and Marketing at the Aarhus School of Business, Denmark. His research areas include Industrial Marketing Management, Buyer Initiative, Purchasing and Strategic Supplier Development, Entrepreneurship and Development of Small and Medium-sized Enterprises.

Anne Kovalainen, PhD, is Professor of Entrepreneurship at two Finnish Universities, at the Department of Management and Organization, Turku School of Economics and Business Administration, Turku, Finland and at the Swedish School of Economics and Business Administration, Helsinki, Finland. Her research interests range from entrepreneurship theory and economic sociology including non-standard work, self-employment, entrepreneurship and labour market restructuring to feminist theory and research methodology in social sciences.

Wing Lam, PhD, is Research Fellow in the School of Business and Management at the University of Glasgow, UK. Her research interests include new venture creation, family business, Chinese entrepreneurship, network and cross-cultural entrepreneurship.

Claire M. Leitch is a Senior Lecturer at Queen's University, Belfast. Her research interests include the company development process in the learning company; the application of action learning and other client-centred learning approaches, within entrepreneurial education; the dynamics of leadership in the process of organizational transformation; entrepreneurial learning, business development; and the technology transfer process.

Elisabet Ljunggren, PhD, is senior researcher and research manager at Nordland Research Institute, Bodø, Norway. Her research interests include gender aspects of entrepreneurship, the entrepreneurial process, the household dimensions in entrepreneurship and policy initiatives to enhance entrepreneurship and innovation.

Ann Mahuka is a Master of Finance student in Accounting and Finance at The University of Western Australia.

Tatiana S. Manolova is Assistant Professor of Management at Bentley University, Boston, MA. Her current research interests include competitive strategies for new and small companies, international entrepreneurship and organizational formation and transformation in transitional economies.

Helle Neergaard, MSc, PhD, currently holds an Associate Professorship in Entrepreneurship at the Department of Management and International Business, the Aarhus School of Business, Denmark. Her research interests include strategic and managerial aspects of entrepreneurship, female entrepreneurs, internationalization as well as qualitative methods.

Rick Newby is a Lecturer in Accounting and Finance at The University of Western Australia. His research interests include survey methodology and the relationship between SME owner goals and firm performance.

Kent T. Nielsen, PhD, is Associate Professor at the Department of Marketing, Information and Statistics at the Aarhus School of Business, Denmark. His research interests are within e-business, industrial policy and regional development, networking, internationalization of small and medium-sized enterprises and entrepreneurship.

Miroslav Rebernik, PhD, is Professor of Entrepreneurship and Business Economics at the University of Maribor, Slovenia. He holds the Entrepreneurship and Business Economics Chair, and is a Director of the Institute for Entrepreneurship and Small Business Management at the Faculty of Economics and Business. He is leading research teams for the Slovenian Entrepreneurship Observatory and for GEM Slovenia.

Eleanor Shaw, PhD, is Senior Lecturer in the Department of Marketing at Strathclyde Business School. Her research interests include the diversity of entrepreneurship, entrepreneurship under difficult conditions and the relationship between networks and small business development.

Polona Tominc, PhD, is an Associated Professor in the Department of Quantitative Economic Analysis at the Faculty of Economics and Business, University of Maribor, Slovenia. Her research is focused on statistical methods in economics, especially in the field of entrepreneurship and gender differences.

John Watson, PhD, is an Associate Professor in Accounting and Finance at The University of Western Australia. His research interests include SME performance, measurement and evaluation.

Friederike Welter is Professor for Management of SMEs and entrepreneurship at the University of Siegen, Germany, and holds the TeliaSonera Professorship for Entrepreneurship at the Stockholm School of Economics, Riga. Her research interests include entrepreneurship processes in various environments and media discourse about entrepreneurship.

Fiona Wilson is Professor of Organizational Behaviour in the School of Business and Management at the University of Glasgow in Scotland. She is currently researching banks' views on male and female business owners and their views on banks with Sara Carter, Eleanor Shaw and Wing Lam. The research is funded by the ESRC. Her research is mainly on gender relations at work.

PART ONE

Country Reports on Women's Entrepreneurship

1. Introduction: the Diana Project International

Candida G. Brush, Nancy M. Carter, Elizabeth J. Gatewood, Patricia G. Greene and Myra M. Hart

The Diana Project, named for the mythological goddess of the hunt, began as a US-based multi-university, multi-year project dedicated to the study of women business owners and their business growth activities. The project has grown to include more than 30 researchers from 20 countries. This chapter addresses the fundamental issues raised by a collaboration of scholars from around the world.

INTRODUCTION

Small firms drive economic growth. Research in the OECD countries consistently shows that job growth in the entrepreneurial sector is substantially higher than it is among established (corporate) incumbents (Audretsch and Thurik, 2001). More recently, the international buzz about entrepreneurship has become even more pronounced with the explosion of new technology, rise in the availability and use of equity capital and breaking down of economic and trade barriers. The Global Entrepreneurship Monitor (GEM) studies find that entrepreneurship is a central source for employment creation (Reynolds et al., 2001; Acs et al., 2005).

Collectively these studies reveal that location matters. The ways that people start and grow businesses vary substantially by country, depending on level of economic development, cultural factors, natural resources and industrial base. In developed countries, entrepreneurial ventures produce innovations and create wealth, as well as enhance economic development in challenging geographic or industrial sectors (Acs et al., 2005). In transitional economies entrepreneurship drives privatization by building market institutions, influencing monetary and fiscal policy, and affecting macroeconomic stabilization and growth. Economic development supporting new venture creation is an attractive public policy in most countries, but, as new firms are created in increasing numbers, policy emphasis turns to fostering growth of existing businesses. Regardless of location or country context, the increased attention to economic contributions of entrepreneurship, and, in particular, growing businesses, is reflected in the accelerated pace and variety of public and private sector policy initiatives at all levels – local, regional, national and super-national level (Hart, 2003).

How do women participate in this phenomenon? Recent statistics show that women are important drivers of growth in many of the world's economies (Minniti et al., 2005). However, while statistics recording small firm and entrepreneurship activity are available for many countries, there is far less documentation about the contributions women make to the process, particularly in non-OECD countries (Minetti et al., 2005). Further, almost no information is available about women's entrepreneurship as a global phenomenon, specifically, growth-oriented women-led businesses (Brush et al., 2005). Available information generally aggregates and studies all businesses together, without highlighting the sex of the founder or the business sector (Gatewood et al., 2003). Consequently, while entrepreneurship is viewed as a solution to economic development, we have little understanding of the gendered influences on the experience and subsequent contributions. This raises two important questions: Are the experiences similar or different for men and women? What country, venture and personal factors influence the growth experiences of women-led businesses?

Emerging research suggests that there are significant differences, especially with regards to the pathway to growth (Brush et al., 2004). Similarly, the GEM studies show variation across countries between men and women in motivations and business sector (Minetti et al., 2005). With increasing numbers of women starting new businesses worldwide, it is crucial to answer these questions to gain a better understanding of how to promote women's entrepreneurship, eliminate obstacles women may face in business creation, and facilitate the growth process of their businesses. A lack of understanding of the growth of women-owned businesses might ultimately inhibit competitiveness if a country does not understand, recognize and support contributions of all populations of entrepreneurs.

THE DIANA PROJECT

Since the mid-1980s, most research on women's entrepreneurship focused on factors influencing the start-up of ventures (Gatewood et al., 2003). Notably absent was an understanding of factors affecting growth. In 1999, we launched the Diana Project to study the phenomenon of women's entrepreneurship in the United States. Historically, women-led ventures were smaller than those of their male counterparts, whether measured by size of revenues generated or the number of people employed. The overarching question was: Why do women-owned businesses remain smaller than those of their male counterparts? A multi-method research effort was undertaken to examine supply of and demand for growth capital relative to women entrepreneurs. Our US research showed that women entrepreneurs seldom acquire sufficient funds to grow their businesses aggressively and to reach their full potential. This raised a new question: Do women face *unique* challenges in acquiring growth capital?

While the collective research documents demand by women entrepreneurs for equity capital, there was and still is a mismatch between the women, their ventures and sources of growth funding (Brush et al., 2001; Brush et al., 2004a). The Diana Project findings prompted great interest among the media, policy-makers, practitioners and educators wanting to learn more about ways to increase women entrepreneurs' receipt of growth capital by providing a better infrastructure of programs and curricula for women who wished to grow larger businesses (see for instance: Hart, 2003; Montandon, 2002; Hoover, 2002 and Henry, 2002). All these audiences shared the objective of facilitating the growth of new businesses that could produce innovation and wealth for the benefit of individual entrepreneurs, their families and, ultimately, their communities.

Simultaneous to the Diana Project research, interest in women entrepreneurs and growth of their ventures was rising in most countries around the world. To capture and leverage that interest, the Diana Project team, in partnership with ESBRI (Entrepreneurship and Small Business Research Institute, Sweden), convened an international gathering of scholars in 2003 to develop a shared research agenda (see Appendix 1.A for a listing of participants by country in 2003–04). The goal was to exchange ideas and learn from each other about the current state of research on creation and support for new women-led businesses, and particularly, support and development of growth-oriented businesses. Our purpose in creating the Diana International collaborative was twofold: 1) to provide a platform from which to develop, conduct and share a global research agenda; 2) to create an international community of scholars dedicated to answering the questions about women entrepreneurs and their growth-oriented businesses.

The first step in this collaborative effort was to document the status of women entrepreneurs and business growth in the home countries of each of the initial participants to identify where further research would be needed. Even a cursory search of existing secondary data by the participants quickly revealed that little systematic comparative data were available. Data from ILO, GEM and OECD as presented in Table 1.1 emphasize the disparity between men and women in self-employment and are useful for pinpointing rates of entrepreneurial activity and macro-environmental influences. For example, one of the GEM measures, TEA (total entrepreneurial activity), shows the number of people per 100 who are engaged in starting a business or who are owners/managers of a business less than 42 months old (Zacharakis et al., 2001). From their examination of start-up activity in 41 countries during 2003, GEM researchers found that men were almost twice as likely to be involved with a new business start-up as women (total entrepreneurial activity of women = 7.005; for men = 12.314 per 100) and that the rate differential varied across countries substantially (Minnetti and Byrave, 2003). Countries participating in both Diana International and GEM illustrate this point, with the TEA for women ranging from 2.79 (Sweden) to 12.02 (New Zealand) (Minnetti and Byrave, 2003).

Table 1.1   Statistics on women and business ownership

	Percent of women in population	Percent of women in workforce	Percent WOB	TEA country	TEA for women
Australia	50	29		8.7	7.76
Bulgaria	51	47	24.0	n/a	n/a
Canada	50	45	15.0	8.8	5.42
Chile					
China					
Denmark	49	47	30.0	6.5	3.62
Finland			33.0	4.6	2.90
Germany		43	27.0	5.2	3.66
Hungary					
Ireland	50	49	17.0	9.1	4.12
Korea				14.5	8.13
Northern Ireland	51	49		5.2	3.50
Netherlands			30.0	4.6	3.18
New Zealand	51	47	38.0	14.0	12.02
Norway			21.0	8.7	4.45
Slovenia		46	17.0	4.5	1.66
Spain		38	26.7	4.6	3.92
Sweden				4.0	2.79
United Kingdom			26.0	6.4	3.61
United States				11.3	8.34

Source: Brush et al., 2005.

While these statistics provided a foundation for our project, they were too generalized to permit a focus on growth activities of women-led businesses. Similarly, other secondary data provided only tangential information regarding growth-oriented women-led ventures. Statistics from around the world show size differences between men-led and women-led venture indicating that businesses led by women are universally smaller than those of men whether measured in terms of revenues generated or employees hired. Examples from countries participating in Diana International illustrate this point. In Norway, only 20 percent of women-led businesses (compared with 31 percent of men-owned business) have one or more employees, and businesses owned by men show stronger financial results. In the Netherlands, about 30 percent of entrepreneurs are female (approximately 250 000 female entrepreneurs), but their profile and that of their businesses are quite different from those of male entrepreneurs. In Canada, approximately 45 percent of SMEs have at least some degree of female ownership, but they are smaller in size by number of employees and average annual sales (approximately half were majority male-owned SMEs), and are younger and less likely to be in fast growth stage of business development (9 percent of majority female-owned versus 14 percent of majority male-owned).

The product of our first Diana International Conference in 2003 was a report discussing the importance of growth-oriented women-led businesses and summarizing the state of knowledge about these businesses in the initial countries involved. This report was released in spring of 2005 and provides a summary of the presentations about the state of women's entrepreneurship by country. For the second conference in 2004, participants presented working papers. Following the event, papers were peer reviewed, revised and finally submitted for consideration for this edited volume. This book is the product of our second Diana International Conference, which represents the hard work and dedication of an expanded community of scholars passionate about understanding growth of women's entrepreneurship. The next section presents the framework that organizes the chapters in this volume.

FACTORS INFLUENCING GROWTH OF WOMEN-OWNED BUSINESSES

Of all businesses launched each year, only a select few will grow rapidly. Why? Growth is a choice that is personal and strategic, and it is influenced by a variety of external factors including business sector and country context (Minetti et al., 2005). We organize these into a framework that includes four main constructs: the individual, venture concept, firm resources and financial resources that represent the factors influencing growth of individual women-led ventures (see Figure 1.1). These factors are contained in an industry sector and country context, within which supply of financial resources also resides. Following is a brief description of each of these concepts.

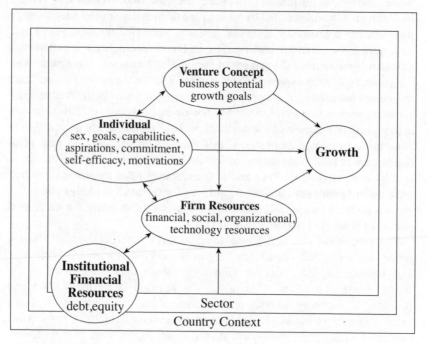

Figure 1.1   Research framework for women and growth businesses

Individual

All entrepreneurs start with a set of personal aptitudes, then add skills learned through formal education and on-the-job experience. This combination of natural talent and learned skills comprises 'human capital' (Becker, 1964). Each entrepreneur, whether they are starting alone or with a partner, has a unique bundle of human capital (Carter et al., 1997). Some bring years of college education and advanced professional degrees to their ventures, while others gain their knowledge through industry experience. Still others gain valuable expertise through specialized training. The package of capabilities that the entrepreneur or her team brings to the table is the foundation of the new venture (Brush, Greene and Hart, 2001). These capabilities are broad-ranging, from functional expertise in marketing, accounting or operations, to abilities in fund-raising, people management or negotiation, and they all make a difference in whether and how the business will grow (Hisrich and Brush, 1986; Schefczyk and Gerpott, 2001).

Another aspect of the individual is her personal aspirations and ambitions, which are translated into the vision of success for the business venture (Penrose, 1954; Bhide, 2000). Personal motivations for starting a business vary widely. For instance, some women entrepreneurs start a business because they want to meet a need that exists in the marketplace by providing a new service or product (Hisrich and Brush, 1986). Others become entrepreneurs because they want to work independently, make the decisions and take control of their work lives (Buttner and Moore, 1997). Still other entrepreneurs focus on creating their own work environment and providing family income. The motives for start-up are directly related to the goals for the business (Lau and Busenitz, 2001). Some women entrepreneurs intend to grow their businesses from the start, while others deliberately keep their companies small and manageable (Cliff, 1998; Du Reitz and Henrekson, 2000).

The Venture Concept

The venture concept is what the business does or the product or service it provides (Bhide, 2000). It starts from an idea, innovation or problem, which is transformed into a concept that is defined by the activities of the organization. The choice of business concept has a direct effect on potential growth. Those companies based on radically innovative ideas that solve a big problem have much greater potential for being scalable and attracting growth capital, while less innovative ideas serving small niche markets that are easily imitated have much lower growth potential (Bhide, 2000). The extent to which there is big demand for the product or service, and whether or not there are lots of substitutes, directly affect the potential for growth. Innovative concepts that are not easily imitable are more likely to attract growth capital for expansion (Timmons and Bygrave, 1997).

Firm Resources

Firm resources are applied to convert the concept to reality and take the goods and services to market (Penrose, 1954). Resources fall into several categories: social, financial, organizational, physical and technical (Brush, Greene and Hart, 2001). Social capital is a form of non-economic knowledge and emerges from norms, relationships and social structures in an individual's life (Coleman, 1988). This includes the network of contacts, reputation, as well as the skills and expertise that help entrepreneurs and their teams acquire the resources of the emerging organization (Aldrich, 1999).

Other resources include organizational resources, which are those relation-ships, structure, routines and information of the new venture (Dollinger,

1995). Physical resources include tangible and intangible assets needed for the operations of the business (Dollinger, 1995). These also may include technology and equipment as well as materials and other physical assets of the business. Financial resources are the cash and money assets of the business (Bygrave, 1992). Often personal savings of the entrepreneur and team are the first financial resources available to the firm.

Business Sector

The potential for business growth is also directly influenced by choice of industry sector (Carter et al., 1997). Highly competitive mature industries, such as restaurant, retail clothing or personal care services, are easy to enter and therefore easily imitated (Brush et al., 2004). Many women-led firms compete in saturated, highly competitive industries like consumer retailing and personal services, automatically limiting their growth potential (Brush et al., 2004).

Institutional Financial Resources

As Figure 1.1 reflects, institutional financial resources are outside the venture. These are the composite of external sources of venture financing, both debt and equity. Sources of growth capital include equity providers (angels, venture capitalists) and debt providers (banks, and other commercial lenders) (Mason and Harrison, 1999; Timmons and Bygrave, 1997). In the past, women most often sought debt financing (Riding and Swift, 1990; Coleman, 2000) but recent studies show that growth-oriented women-led firms pursue private equity as well (Brush et al., 2000).

  This framework provides a basis for the chapters that follow, which are of two types. First, a series of country reports provides an overview of the state of women's entrepreneurship in seven different countries. These include country labor force overviews that detail women's participation in the workforce and specifically in entrepreneurship. Second, other chapters explore the extent and nature of women's participation in entrepreneurship and their growth orientation relative to demand for resources to grow (social capital, personal goals, strategic choice and financing). Each chapter concludes with a discussion of sources of growth financing, issues and opportunities.

COUNTRY REPORTS ON WOMEN'S ENTREPRENEURSHIP

We begin with the country reports from Australia, Canada, Denmark, Finland, Germany, Norway and the US.

Mary Barrett presents a detailed overview of the state of women's entrepreneurship in Australia. She notes that women's participation in entrepreneurship is comparatively high at 33 percent, and women's total entrepreneurial activity (TEA) based on the GEM reports shows that their rate is increasing. Yet, women are less likely to be employers of other people even though they contribute nearly 40 percent of GDP (excluding general government) in Australia and about 20 percent of private sector net job creation. Barrett argues that even though the growth and contributions of women-owned business in Australia are significant, women are less likely to become entrepreneurs than their male counterparts because of socio-cultural norms, occupational segregation and migration patterns. Considering issues of importance for women, Barrett concludes that financial capital access, networks and strategic choice are challenges for women seeking to grow ventures, and offers research directions for the future.

Jennifer Jennings and Michelle Provorny Cash present a comprehensive overview of women's participation in entrepreneurship in Canada. Women entrepreneurs account for a sizeable proportion of Canada's total entrepreneurial activity and small business sector, but do not yet participate at the same rate as men. In terms of GEM's measure of nascent entrepreneurial activity, for example, the prevalence rate for women was only 3.7 percent in 2002, less than half the 9.7 rate for men in the same year. Jennings and Cash note that the growth and prevalence of women entrepreneurs is recognized by researchers and they present an overview of the relative performance of women-owned businesses and their growth orientation. They point out that the smaller size and slower growth rates of female-owned business in Canada may, to a certain extent, represent deliberate choices of many women entrepreneurs, but empirical substantiation of this causal inference does not yet exist. The authors present a detailed discussion of human and social capital factors, noting that industry context plays an important role in considering differences by gender. Motivations, goals and lower amounts of financial capital are also seen as factors influencing growth of women entrepreneurs in the Canadian context. They conclude this chapter with an exploration of strategic choice and access to financing, suggesting subtle perceptions may be a barrier to explore in the future.

A profile of the participation, growth and challenges of women entrepreneurs in Denmark is provided by Helle Neergaard, Kent Nielsen and John Kjeldsen. They show that Danish women have been actively involved in the labor market since the beginning of the 1960s at steadily increasing rates. Today, women constitute 47 percent of total employment. This development has been facilitated, in part, through liberal childcare facilities and state support of maternity leave. Though actively engaged in work outside the home, relatively few Danish women chose to become entrepreneurs. Only 30 percent of new enterprises are established by women and women account for a mere 25 percent of all self-employed. Neergaard points out that ventures owned by women in Denmark exhibit different growth patterns than those owned by men. Current research provides little information as to the causes of these patterns but there are indications that certain mechanisms such as socio-cultural norms and structures, as well as identity and role perceptions, may underlie the low rate of female entrepreneurship in Denmark.

Anne Kovalainen and Pia Arenius present women's participation and contributions to the Finnish economy. Using GEM data and labor force statistics, they find that approximately 33 percent of all self-employed are women and that their share has remained somewhat stable over past years. Despite public policy programs for day-care, a strong culture of work ethic and a tradition of gender equality, they find the share of women's entrepreneurship has declined over the past decade. Kovalainen and Arenius explore this issue by examining studies on access to start-up capital and growth intentions of women entrepreneurs. Finland does not offer special programs for women, and studies about access to venture capital and angel investors are scarce. Research shows that women on average earn less than men, and therefore it takes longer for them to accumulate start-up funding for a business. Social capital and social networking are essential to success of women-owned businesses, and women entrepreneurs overall are well educated. There is evidence of a glass ceiling in the corporate setting, which the authors suggest might contribute to entrepreneurial start-up. Of the Nordic countries, especially in Finland, the positive expectations of the family's future financial situation increase women's participation in new firm formation. The authors explore sectoral differences, finding that occupational segregation influences choice of women's businesses. The chapter concludes with discussion of education, perceived barriers and role models as influences to women's entrepreneurship in Finland.

The chapter on Germany, authored by Friederike Welter, presents a wide-ranging overview of the state of women's entrepreneurship. Welter documents that women account for approximately 28.5 percent of the East and West German labor force and that the percentage of women's entrepreneurship is growing. Overall, the 1990s saw an above average increase for women start-ups, but, the gender gap remains. Women tend to be clustered in services and retailing and compared with men, are less likely to have employees. Drawing from GEM data, Welter shows that the sector and size are related to lower turnover, profitability and growth. She explores the extent to which women may be 'dreamers' and 'doers' and considers factors that push and pull them into entrepreneurship. Importantly, family life and children are a factor in this decision. German women entrepreneurs with more education are more likely to be growth-oriented. Bank financing is most common for growth capital in

Germany, but little research explores gender differences. In a detailed discussion of financing programs Welter notes that the few studies of women's access to credit programs in Germany show women are less likely to apply for credit and those few who do, seek smaller amounts. Social networks of German women entrepreneurs tend to be both homogeneous and heterogeneous, but the extent to which these affect the likelihood of receiving capital is not well understood. The chapter concludes with an overview of the political and social context showing gender equality as essential in Germany, but nevertheless subject to subtle barriers rooted in traditional social roles and perceptions about women.

Lene Foss and Elisabet Ljunggren review women's labor force participation in Norway including women's rate of entrepreneurial activity. More than 37 percent of women work in the private sector, more than 66 percent work in the public sector, and their entrepreneurial rate is about 27 percent. Women entrepreneurs tend to be slightly older (30–40 years old), are well educated and experienced, but their businesses are typically smaller and they have lower growth aspirations than their male counterparts. The authors describe research findings showing women's growth aspirations in Norway related to motivation, education, industry and a number of organizational variables including previous growth in turnover and in the number of employees. But, another study they profile shows education as positively related to growth aspirations, while experience is not. Foss and Ljunggren find that research on women's access to financial capital is limited, while studies of women's networks are prevalent, and indicate that Norwegian women tend to include more family/kin and social contacts in their network. Women's goals in entrepreneurship are shown to be more opportunity- than necessity-oriented, and gender segregation by industry of women-owned firms is related to lower levels of investment by private investors and venture capitalists. While the venture capital industry and government programs are developing rapidly in Norway, the authors suggest that these are gender biased. They conclude with an overview of the challenges and suggestions for future changes as these relate to gendered-segregated labor market and education systems.

Candida Brush, Nancy Carter, Elizabeth Gatewood, Patricia Greene and Myra Hart profile the state of women business owners in the United States economy. Overall, the rate of women's entrepreneurship in the US is strong and the historical gap between men's and women's participation has narrowed to no longer being significantly different. Approximately 10.6 million privately-held majority-owned firms are women-led, and these employ 19.1 million people and contribute more than $2.46 trillion to the US economy. Nevertheless, a size differential between US men- and women-owned businesses continues. Women-owned businesses are, on average, still smaller than those owned by men, representing only 9 percent of all revenues for US businesses. Research shows that the size differential may be related to work and industry experience, women's social networks, especially as related to their ability to access financial resources, their financial reserves and strategies for funding their businesses, their choice of industry, and their reasons for starting businesses. US women frequently become business owners because it provides a way to balance career and family needs. The authors conclude that the number of women with higher aspirations is increasing. But for these women, institutional and cultural barriers provide challenges to successful growth. Specifically, education for women on the role of financing, and encouragement of financial providers to seek out and consider women-owned firms as investments is suggested.

RESEARCH TOPICS ON THE GROWTH OF WOMEN-OWNED BUSINESSES

Seven chapters from Australia, Bulgaria, Ireland, New Zealand, Northern Ireland, Slovenia, Spain and the UK offer focused empirical discussions of factors influencing growth of women-owned businesses. These chapters delve more deeply into relationships between social and human capital, access to financing, issues of risk and control, differences in skills and motivations of women, and subtle perceptions of bankers who make financing decisions about women-led ventures.

John Watson, Rick Newby and Ann Mahuka offer an analysis of demand-side issues related to external funding in Australian small businesses. Using a focus group methodology, they study the extent to which male and female owners are more risk-averse and therefore less inclined to use bank financing. This research finds that overall, risk is related to control of the businesses and that most prefer not to consider external funding if they risk losing control of their venture. Comparisons between men and women show that women are more risk-averse and less likely to access bank financing. However, when women access bank financing, they are inclined to repay it earlier than their male counterparts.

Tatiana Manolova presents an exploratory look at similarities and differences between men and women entrepreneurs in Bulgaria. This chapter examines the effects of human, social and financial capital on start-up and growth in the context of a non-traditional industry in a transitional economy. She posits that there are gender-based differences across human, social and financial capital that constrains growth. Using six case studies of male- and female-owned businesses in the Bulgarian construction industry, she finds that women are equally if not better educated than their male counterparts, and that financing is restricted for both groups. But, men do have more developed social networks that give them an advantage especially during start-up of their ventures.

Research in the Republic of Ireland reflects relatively lower female entrepreneurship for women than men compared with other developed countries, and therefore, women's entrepreneurship is considered a 'lost resource'. Reasons for this lower participation primarily focus on financial constraints. Colette Henry, Kate Johnston and Angela Hamouda investigate the role of banks, support agencies and venture capitalists in funding the development and growth of women's businesses in Ireland. They focus on supply-side issues, exploring the factors funding agencies look for in small businesses, and investigate the extent to which women are successful at obtaining financing or encounter barriers. The information technology (IT), pharmaceutical/medical and biotechnology sectors are the top three sectors most likely to attract VC funding in Ireland. Just over a third of the VCs surveyed identified the IT sector as the one in which they would 'most likely invest'. In contrast, the banks and support agencies are active across a range of sectors. Factors influencing likelihood of receiving funding include realism of financial projections, market knowledge, growth plans and experience. Women receive a small proportion of financing, which Henry, Johnston and Hamouda find to be caused by a limited capital pool, the sector of business and the nature of the ventures founded by women.

Anne de Bruin and Susan Flint-Hartle present findings of an in-depth study of the demand and supply of private capital for New Zealand women entrepreneurs. Their research explores the experiences of 'successful' women entrepreneurs, that is, those whose businesses had moved beyond the initiation phase and were commercially viable. Because the industry is somewhat undeveloped in New Zealand and research is sparse, the authors chose in-depth interviews using a story-telling methodology to explore the experiences of women in seeking financial capital. In addition, a detailed case study reflects the goals and challenges of a high-achieving woman entrepreneur. To complement the demand-side study, de Bruin and Flint-Hartle conducted a short survey with venture capitalists to explore their investments in women-led businesses. For the supply-side, information was gathered mainly through interviews of key informants especially from the venture capital industry. A simple e-mail questionnaire supplemented these interviews. Forty in-depth interviews with women entrepreneurs provided the principal material to comment on the demand for financial capital. The research specifically attempts to inform on finance-related issues of women's entrepreneurial activity.

Early findings from a study of the supply of finance to women-owned/led businesses in Northern Ireland is presented by Claire Leitch, Frances Hill and Richard Harrison. This research is based on semi-structured interviews conducted with senior representatives from the main banks and venture capital firms in the region. A number of issues emerging from the research to date are discussed: specifically, few women business owners in Northern Ireland seek funding from formal sources for the purposes of setting up and growing a business. Some possible reasons for this are discussed, and the implications for women's behaviors are identified.

Growth aspirations of women in Slovenia are explored in the chapter by Polona Tominc and Miroslav Rebernik. Considering the importance of economic growth in a transitional economy, they first provide an overview of the current state of female entrepreneurship in Slovenia, and show how business opportunities are perceived by male and female entrepreneurs. They hypothesize that men and women entrepreneurs will differ in their participation, perception of opportunities, capacity (skills) and aspirations for growth. Using data from the GEM study, they find that formal barriers are minimal and the climate is positive for women, yet there are significant differences in participation, involvement and aspirations for growth.

Cristina Díaz and Juan Jiménez explore the effects of gender on availability of resources in young and small firms in Spain. Drawing from current empirical research and theory, they develop a framework that explores the influence of human capital, social capital, financial capital and time, on both economic performance and perceptions of success. The initial sample was selected from CAMERDATA, consisting of new (between one to eight years old), small (with less than 100 employees) and service sector firms, and 112 usable responses were used in the analysis. The authors use parametric and non-parametric tests to examine differences by sex. Results show that female teams are less successful in terms of revenues, however, their owners seem to be more satisfied in a personal sense than other type of owners. Women do not intend to grow their firms to the same extent as men, and they highlight all the reasons for not growing to a greater level than men. Díaz and Jiménez find that for the male-owned firms, their size, the network size of the owner/s and his/their level of education, have a significant and positive effect on revenues. For female-owned firms, although not significant, having managerial experience and having invested their own savings in the firm help to obtain higher revenues.

The chapter by Sara Carter, Eleanor Shaw, Fiona Wilson and Wing Lam extends the investigation of financing of women-owned businesses by examining the influence of gender in the bank lending process in the UK. This chapter adopts a social constructionist perspective, considering the perceptions that are held by male and female entrepreneurs about banks, as well as the perceptions that are held by male and female bank officers about male and female entrepreneurs. The combined effects of these perceptions on the ability of entrepreneurs to mobilize financial resources are explored. The research presented outlines a comprehensive six-stage methodology that examines cognitive images and processes of bank lending officers using focus groups, interviews and a business plan assessment that replicates the business plan developed by Fay and Williams (1993) for their analysis of gender discrimination among bank lending officers in New Zealand. Carter et al. find that banks in the UK seek to make lending decisions in a bureaucratic and gender neutral manner to avoid biased decisions that may be made by individuals. Gender differences were evident with regard to size of firm and level of capitalization.

ADVANCING KNOWLEDGE ABOUT THE STATUS OF WOMEN'S ENTREPRENEURSHIP AROUND THE WORLD

Entrepreneurship is a critical tool for economic development around the world. Entrepreneurs seize opportunities to develop and deliver new goods and services and, in the process, create wealth for individuals, families, communities and countries. The chapters in this book show that women play an integral part in this economic progress across all countries. The data and insights from the Diana Project International reported here emphasize the need to better understand this important phenomenon. At a macro-level, the research highlights the challenges women entrepreneurs encounter in launching and growing their businesses, and how their experiences vary from country to country. The findings substantiate an apparent mismatch between the number of women-owned firms seeking resources to grow their businesses and the availability of those resources. The gap may represent rational economic decision-making or it may represent a significant market failure. At the micro-level the findings highlight the substantial similarities in the motivations, human capital, social capital and financial resources women bring to the creation and growth of their firms.

Despite the substantial contribution the chapters in this book make to advancing knowledge about women's entrepreneurship, there are still many questions waiting to be investigated. Exploring gender differences requires comparing subjective experiences just as it draws on objective data about revenues, employees and growth rates. There is a need to achieve an even greater understanding of the entrepreneurial dynamics within and across regions. Additional conceptual models need to be developed that account for country differences and that reflect the extent to which gender perceptions held by certain institutions, societal groups, or individuals, affect the entrepreneurial dynamics.

Finally, there is a need to determine the most important issues (from both the research and practical perspectives) for women's entrepreneurship in order to set an on-going research agenda. These issues are critical not only for theory development, but also for the development of more compatible methodologies. The projects described in this book make noteworthy progress toward this goal.

REFERENCES

Acs, Z., Arenius, P., Hay, M., Minniti, M. (2005), *2004 Global Entrepreneurship Monitor Executive Report*, Babson Park, MA and London, England: Babson College and London Business School.

Aldrich, H. (1999), *Organizations Evolving*, Thousand Oaks, CA: Sage Publications.

Audretsch, D.B. and Thurik, R. (2001), 'Linking Entrepreneurship to Growth', STI Working Papers 2001/2, OECD: Directorate for Science, Technology and Industry.

Becker, G. (1964), *Human Capital*, New York: Columbia University Press.

Bhide, A. (2000), *The Origin and Evolution of New Businesses*, New York: Oxford Publishing.

Brush, C.G., Greene, P.G. and Hart, M.M. (2001), 'From Initial Idea to Unique Advantage: The Entrepreneurial Challenge of Constructing a Resource Base', *Academy of Management Executive*, **15**(1), 64–80.

Brush, C., Carter, N., Gatewood, E., Greene, P. and Hart, M. (2000), 'Women and Equity Capital: An Exploration of Factors Affecting Capital Access', in Reynolds, P.D., Autio, E., Brush, C.G., Bygrave, W.D., Manigart, S., Sapienza, H. and Shaver, K.G. (eds), *Frontiers of Entrepreneurship Research*, Proceedings of the Babson Kauffman Entrepreneurship Research Conference, pp. 226–40.

Brush, C., Carter, N., Gatewood, E., Greene, P. and Hart, M. (2001), 'The Diana Project: Women Business Owners and Equity Capital: The Myths Dispelled', Report 1, Kansas City, MO: Ewing Marion Kauffman Foundation.

Brush, C., Carter, N., Gatewood, E., Greene, P. and Hart, M. (2004a), 'The Diana Project. Gatekeepers of Venture Growth: The Role and Participation of Women in the Venture Capital Industry', Report 2, Kansas City, MO: Ewing Marion Kauffman Foundation.

Brush, C., Carter, N., Gatewood, E., Greene, P. and Hart, M. (2004b), *Clearing the Hurdles: Women Building High Growth Businesses*, Englewood Cliffs, NJ: Prentice Hall.

Brush, C., Carter, N., Gatewood, E., Greene, P. and Hart, M. (2005), 'The Diana International Report: Research on Growth Oriented Women Entrepreneurs and their Businesses', Stockholm, Sweden: ESBRI.

Buttner, H. and Moore, D. (1997), 'Women's Organizational Exodus to Entrepreneurship: Self-reported Motivations and Correlates with Success', *Journal of Small Business Management*, **35**(1), 34–46.

Bygrave, W.D. (1992), 'Venture Capital Returns in the 1980s', in D.L. Sexton and J. Kasarda (eds), *The State of the Art of Entrepreneurship*, Boston, MA: PWS Kent, pp. 438–62.

Carter, N., Williams, M. and Reynolds, P. (1997), 'Discontinuance Among New Firms in Retail: The Influence of Initial Resources, Strategy and Gender', *Journal of Business Venturing*, **13**, 125–45.

Cliff, J. (1998), 'Does One Size Fit All? Exploring the Relationship between Attitudes Towards Growth, Gender and Business Size', *Journal of Business Venturing*, **13**(6), 523–42.

Coleman, J. (1988), 'Social Capital in the Creation of Human Capital', *American Journal of Sociology*, **94**, S95–2120.

Coleman, S. (2000), 'Access to Capital and Terms of Credit: A Comparison of Men and Women-owned Small Businesses', *Journal of Small Business Management*, **38**(3), 37–52.

Dollinger, M. (1995), *Entrepreneurship: Strategies and Resources*, Boston, MA: Irwin.

Du Reitz, A. and Henrekson, M. (2000), 'Testing the Female Underperformance Hypothesis', *Small Business Economics*, **14**, 1–10.

Fay, M. and Williams, L. (1993), 'Gender Bias and the Availability of Business Loans', *Journal of Business Venturing*, **8**(4), 363–76.

Gatewood, E.J, Carter, N., Brush, C., Greene, P. and Hart, M. (2003), *Women Entrepreneurs, their Ventures, and the Venture Capital Industry: An Annotated Bibliography*, Stockholm, Sweden: ESBRI.

Hart, D. (ed.) (2003), *The Emergence of Entrepreneurship Policy: Governance Start-ups and Growth in the U.S. Knowledge Economy*, Cambridge, UK: Cambridge University Press.

Henry, S. (2002), 'Women Fighting for Venture Capital Study: Study Cites Entrepreneur Networks', *Washington Post*, 13 February, p. E05.

Hisrich, R.D. and Brush, C.G. (1986), *The Woman Entrepreneur: Starting, Financing and Growing a Successful New Business*, Lexington, MA: Lexington Books.

Hoover, K. (2002), 'Women Entrepreneurs Push for Greater Access to Venture Capital', *Washington D.C. Business Journal*, 22 February.

Lau, C. and Busenitz, L. (2001), 'Growth Intentions of Entrepreneurs in a Transitional Economy: The People's Republic of China', *Entrepreneurship Theory and Practice*, **26**(1), 5–20.

Mason, C. and Harrison, C. (1999), 'Venture Capital: Rationale, Aims and Scope', *Venture Capital: An International Journal of Entrepreneurial Finance*, **1**(1), 1–47.

Minniti, M., Arenius, P. and Langowitz, N. (2005), *Global Entrepreneurship Monitor: 2004 Report on Women and Entrepreneurship*, Babson Park, MA and London: Babson College and London Business School.

Minnetti, M. and Byrave, W. (2003), *Global Entrepreneurship Monitor: National Entrepreneurship Assessment – United States*, Executive Report, Kansas City, MO: Kauffman Center for Entrepreneurial Leadership.

Montandon, M. (2002), 'The Ol' Gal Money Hunt', *Fortune Small Business*, http://www.fortune.com/indexw.jhtml?channel=artcol.jhtml&doc_id=207032.

Penrose, E. (1954), *Theory of Growth of the Firm*, New York: John Wiley.

Reynolds, P.D., Camp, S.M., Bygrave, W.D., Autio, E. and Hay, M. (2001), *Global Entrepreneurial Monitor: 2001 Executive Report*, London and Babson Park, MA: London Business School and Babson College.

Riding, A. and Swift, C. (1990), 'Women Business Owners and Terms of Credit: Some Empirical Findings of the Canadian Experience', *Journal of Business Venturing*, **5**(5), 327–40.

Schefczyk, M. and Gerpott, T. (2001), 'Qualifications and Turnover of Managers and Venture Capital-financed Firm Performance: An Empirical Study of German Venture Capital Investments', *Journal of Business Venturing*, **16**(2), 145–63.

Timmons, J. and Bygrave, W. (1997), 'Venture Capital: Reflections and Projections', in Sexton, D.L. and Smilor, R. (eds), *Entrepreneurship 2000*, Chicago, IL: Upstart Publishing, pp. 29–46.
Zacharakis, A., Neck, H., Bygrave, W. and Cox, L. (2001), *Global Entrepreneurship Monitor*, National Entrepreneurship Assessment – United States, Executive Report, Kansas City, MO: Kauffman Center for Entrepreneurial Leadership.

APPENDIX 1.A: FOUNDING PARTICIPATING RESEARCHERS AND HOST COUNTRIES

1) Australia
   a. Mary Barrett, University of Wollongong
   b. John Watson, The University of Western Australia
   c. Rick Newby, The University of Western Australia
2) Bulgaria
   a. Tatiana Manolova, Suffolk University
   b. Katia Vladimirova, University of National and World Economy
3) Canada
   a. Jennifer Jennings, University of Alberta
   b. Devereaux Jennings, University of Alberta
   c. Megan McDougald, University of Alberta
4) Chile
   a. Olga Pizarro Stiepovic, Universidad del Desarrollo
5) China
   a. Peilan Jane Guan, Wuhan University
6) Denmark
   a. Helle Neergaard, Aarhus School of Business
7) Finland
   a. Pia Arenius, Helsinki University of Technology
   b. Anne Kovalainen, Turku School of Economics and Public Administration
8) Germany
   a. Friederike Welter, RWI (Rheinisch-Westfälisches Institut für Wirtschaftsforschung) and JIBS (Jönköping International Business School, Sweden)
9) Hungary
   a. Éva Pintér, University of Pecs
10) Ireland
   a. Collette Henry, Dundalk Institute of Technology
   b. Kate Johnson, Dundalk Institute of Technology
   c. Angela Hamouda, Dundalk Institute of Technology
   d. Alison Hampton, University of Ulster
   e. Pauric McGowan, University of Ulster
11) Korea
   a. Bang Jee Chun, Hoseo University
12) Northern Ireland
   a. Claire Leitch, Queen's University of Belfast
   b. Frances Hill, Queen's University of Belfast
   c. Richard Harrison, University of Edinburgh

13) Netherlands
    a. Ingrid Verheul, Centre for Advanced Small Business Economics, Erasmus University
14) New Zealand
    a. Anne de Bruin, Massey University
15) Norway
    a. Elisabet Ljunggren, Nordland Research Institute, Bodø
    b. Gry Agnete Alsos, Nordland Research Institute, Bodø
    c. Lene Foss, Norwegian College of Fishery Science, University of Tromsø
16) Slovenia
    a. Polona Tominc, University of Maribor
    b. Miroslav Rebernik, University of Maribor
17) Spain
    a. Cristina Díaz, Universidad De Castilla – La Mancha
18) Sweden
    a. Magnus Aronsson, ESBRI
19) United Kingdom
    a. Eleanor Shaw, University of Strathclyde
    b. Sara Carter, University of Strathclyde
    c. Fiona Wilson, University of Glasgow
    d. Wing Lam, University of Strathclyde
    e. Rebecca Harding, London Business School
    f. Marc Cowling, The Work Foundation, London, UK
20) United States
    a. Candida Brush, Babson College
    b. Nancy Carter, University of St. Thomas
    c. Elizabeth Gatewood, Wake Forest University
    d. Patricia Greene, Babson College
    e. Myra Hart, Harvard Business School.

2. Women's entrepreneurship in Australia: present and their future

Mary Barrett

INTRODUCTION

This chapter provides an overview of the statistics on women's representation in the Australian workforce and as business owners, and of the indicators of their current and likely future status as entrepreneurs. It explores the Australian research on what these statistics show about how women and their businesses differ from their male counterparts, especially in terms of business size, motivation for entrepreneurship, access to start-up and growth finance, training and assistance, strategic choices about industry location of women-owned businesses, issues for special groups of entrepreneurs including indigenous people and people of non-English-speaking background, and other issues. The chapter hazards some answers to the many questions that this research provokes about the nature and future of women's entrepreneurship through a brief examination of some historical and cultural factors in Australia, and suggests some directions for future research to close the gaps in our knowledge of the nature, needs and future of Australian women entrepreneurs.

A. COUNTRY LABOR FORCE OVERVIEW

In December 2003, the estimated resident population of Australia was 19 997 800, of which 80 percent were aged 15 years or more (Australian Bureau of Statistics, 2003a). Figure 2.1 below indicates the proportions of the population by sex and by age groups, showing the changes from 1983 to 2003. From this figure, one can estimate that the percentage of women and men 15 years or more is 90.15 and 89.7 respectively.

Number of Women and Men in the Workforce

Figure 2.2 shows the distribution of full-time and total employment for men

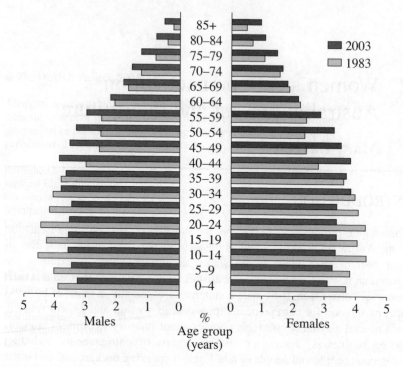

Source: Australian Bureau of Statistics (ABS), (2003b).

Figure 2.1   Population of Australia by age and sex – 1983 and 2003

and women and Figure 2.3 shows the number of men and women in employment. Taken together they indicate that 9.8 million people in Australia were employed either full-time or part-time in May 2004. Of these, 5.4 million (or just over 55 percent) were men and 4.4 million (or just under 45 percent) were women. This represents a participation rate of 71.9 percent for men and 55.9 percent for women.

These statistics show that Australia, like other Western countries since World War II, has a high percentage of women in the paid workforce. Increasingly, however, women are moving into business ownership from corporate ranks, as later sections will show.

Number of Business Owners

The Australian Bureau of Statistics, in its official data on the characteristics of small business in Australia, points out that there is no standard definition of a

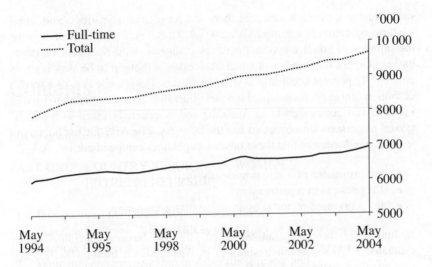

Source: Labour Force Survey. Australian Bureau of Statistics (ABS) (2004a).

Figure 2.2   Full-time and total employment in Australia

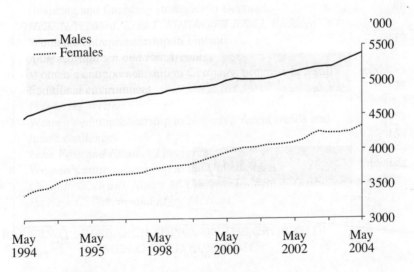

Source: Labour Force Survey. Australian Bureau of Statistics (ABS) (2004a).

Figure 2.3   Males and females in employment in Australia

small business operator and that there are no official statistics about small business operators as a group (ABS, 2003c). Thus it is impossible to determine the number of small business operators compared with operators of larger businesses, but the number of small businesses is thought to be very high, as much as 97 percent according to some estimates. Despite the lack of a formal definition, the expression 'small business operator' is one that is often used in research and policy debate in Australia and is generally taken to mean the person or persons who own and run the business. The ABS further points out in the same document that these business operators can be identified as:

- the proprietor of a sole proprietorship;
- the partners of a partnership;
- the working director(s) of an incorporated company.

In June 2003 there were an estimated 1 591 500 business operators of the estimated 1 179 300 small businesses in Australia. Of these, 1 063 000 (67 percent) were male and 528 600 (33 percent) were female at June 2003 (see Figure 2.4 below).

These statistics become more meaningful when they are considered in the context of Australian entrepreneurship as part of the world scene. As the next section points out, Australia currently ranks a respectable rather than a spectacular eighth in the world in terms of its total entrepreneurial activity

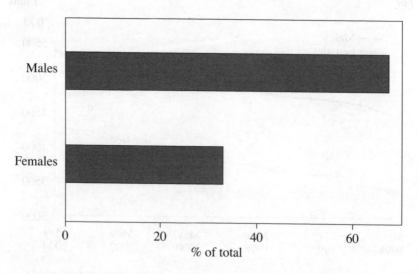

Source: Australian Bureau of Statistics (ABS) (2004b), Catalogue 8127.0.

Figure 2.4   Proportion of small business operators by sex at June 2003

(TEA) participation rate. (The TEA is an index of entrepreneurial activity formed from a national survey of GEM (Global Entrepreneurship Monitor) participating countries. It consists of two main elements: a measure of participation in genuine start-ups and a measure of participation in young firms.) Australia's increased rating is no doubt partly the result of a range of national policies and programs to encourage entrepreneurship, such as programs to support export development and the development of intellectual property protection (GEM Australia, 2003, p. 24).

Total Australian Entrepreneurial Activity Rates

Data on Australia's total entrepreneurial activity (TEA) participation rate is available commencing from 2000, the year in which Australia joined the Global Entrepreneurship Monitor (GEM). In 2003 Australia's TEA participation rate recovered from a low of 8.7 percent to 11.6 percent, and its rank improved from 15th to eighth among the countries participating. This is still not as high as it has been in the past, however, as Australia's TEA of 16.2 percent in 2001 makes clear (GEM Australia, 2003, p.1).

Total Women Entrepreneurial Activity Rates in Australia

Female participation in entrepreneurial activity in Australia rose sharply from 5.6 percent to 9.6 percent in 2003, which is not far below the 2001 high of 10.6 percent (GEM Australia, 2003, p. 6). The proportion of female entrepreneurs to male entrepreneurs rose from 48 percent to 71 percent, which is the highest proportion in the four years of Australia's participation in the GEM (GEM Australia, 2003, p. 6).

These statistics, especially considered together, show a growing rate of participation by both Australian women and men in entrepreneurship. But the profile of women's and men's entrepreneurship in Australia shows many contrasts beyond this initial similarity. The next section examines this profile more closely, and links it to the research that seeks to explain the gender differences it reveals.

B. PROFILE OF WOMEN'S ENTREPRENEURSHIP IN AUSTRALIA

Extent and Nature of Women's Entrepreneurship in Australia

Definitional issues
Australian researchers into women's entrepreneurship use varying definitions of this term. As noted earlier, the official statistics do not distinguish between

small and larger businesses and this is echoed by the fact that researchers and policy-makers do not distinguish between general business ownership and the ownership of growth-oriented firms. The size of women-owned firms often does not feature at all in much academic or public policy-oriented research. As well as this, the Australian definitions of large, medium, small and micro-firms differ from those used in the US, making comparisons with overseas findings about women entrepreneurship problematic.

Similar gaps are apparent in studies that include data on the form of women-owned businesses. Businesses in Australia are mostly small, with both predominantly male-operated businesses (59 percent) and predominantly female-operated businesses (75 percent) falling into the non-employing category (Australian Bureau of Statistics, 2004b). However, studies frequently treat women as if they were the sole owner-manager of the business, and do not indicate whether women are in partnership with others.

Some researchers, such as Still (1993), attempt to alleviate these research problems by including multiple 'layers' of definition of women-owned business. For example, Still allows five categories of self-employed women, which vary between size definitions (no employees, up to five employees, fewer than 20 employees) and goal definitions (personal, 'lifestyle' goals for being in business vs. growth aspirations).

Profile
The ABS distinguishes between small businesses operated 'predominantly' by men or by women, and businesses owned by equal numbers of men and women. In June 2003, of the 1 179 300 small businesses in Australia, 649 600 (55 percent) were operated by an individual male or predominantly by males. There were 299 600 businesses (25 percent), operated by equal numbers of males and females. The number of businesses in this group had declined, down an average annual rate of 3.9 percent, from the 324 600 businesses recorded in June 2001, reversing the average annual increase of 6.2 percent over the 1999 data. However, there were a further 230 200 businesses (20 percent) operated predominantly by females, up from 205 900 businesses in June 2001, an average annual growth of 5.7 percent (Australian Bureau of Statistics, 2004b).

Roffey et al. (1996), in an overview of research into women in small business, say that women business owners in Australia comprise about one-third of people working in their own business. (This is also evident from Figure 2.4 above.) They are more than twice as likely not to be employers as they are to employ one or more people. However, while this suggests that their contribution to Australian entrepreneurship is small, women are increasing their rate of increase of proprietorship (as a proportion of total business proprietors) at a faster rate than men. This trend has continued since Roffey's study, with ABS data from 2003 showing that of the total number of small businesses in Australia in 2003 (1 179 300), the number owned by one male or predominantly by males had increased at an average rate of 1.4 percent since June 2001. However, those run by equal numbers of men and women had declined, down an average annual rate of 3.9 percent since June 2001. By contrast, those operated predominantly by females had increased, with an average annual growth of 5.7 percent over the same period.

Women business owners contribute around 40 percent of GDP (excluding general government) in Australia and about 20 percent of private sector net job creation. According to Still and Guerin (1991, cited in Roffey et al., 1996), women business owners typically are aged between 30 and 45, are married, hold a degree or have had professional training. They are generally Australian born of Australian parents and are married. They are the sole owner of the business, which they started on their own, and were in full-time employment when they started the business. They operate the business themselves, with less than four employees, and rent business premises, rather than work from home. They started the business with less than A$10 000 and have been operating it for more than a year.

All of this suggests that, despite increases in the numbers of Australian women entrepreneurs, Australian women are still less likely than Australian men to become entrepreneurs. From the point of view of the general cultural context, this may be explainable in terms of the 'masculinist' Australian culture that has consistently appeared in studies such as those by Hofstede (1984). Specifically, according to Hofstede, both men and women in Australia (and in other 'masculinist' countries) have tended to accept a traditional division of roles between men and women, with men as breadwinners and women filling domestic roles. This would lead to a greater acceptance of entrepreneurship as an activity for men than for women. It is well known that, immediately following the end of World War II in Australia, and despite their having filled many traditionally male roles during the war, most Australian women 'retreated' to the domestic sphere, to re-emerge into the workforce in large numbers only in the 1960s and 1970s. Their re-entry to the workforce was influenced by the second wave of the women's movement as well as factors associated with the greater opening of the Australian economy to free trade forces, and the relative decline of the Australian manufacturing sector, which traditionally employs men (Mackay, 1997, pp. 51–5).

The traditional 'stay at home' role of women still applies in Australia, in the sense that women continue to carry out the bulk of the household's domestic duties even though they now typically also work outside the home after the early years of motherhood. Sex Discrimination Commissioner Pru Goward and other commentators on male–female relationships in Australia, have recently urged men to take on more of the domestic burden, arguing that women's 'dual role' is holding back their ability to fulfill their personal and economic potential. (Goward, 2005).

The fact that Australia is highly occupationally segregated by gender (Mackay, 1997, pp. 163–6), is important when we consider reasons for women business owners' choice of industry sector. (See 'Strategic Choices' below.) Australia women entrepreneurs, like their sisters in other countries, are most highly represented in service industries. Barrett (1997) found that in vocationally based business, this occupational segregation rigidity applied more to women than to men. That is, it seemed men were more likely to have established businesses in 'female image' industries than women were to have established businesses in 'male image' industries. Since women business owners are most likely to establish businesses in industries where they have been employed previously, their choice of industry sector is more restricted by their general occupational background than is the case for men. Moreover, women's service sector dominance is yet another manifestation of traditional gender divisions in the world of work.

Australia's migration patterns have also favored the traditional gender division in Australian entrepreneurship. The post-World War II years coincided with significant migration to Australia and entrepreneurship in Australia was boosted by migrant men – and women (Mackay, 1997, pp. 51–5). However, along with the post-World War II retreat to the domestic sphere mentioned earlier, this phenomenon could have contributed to Australian women of Anglo-Saxon backgrounds being less rather than more likely to become entrepreneurs, since this role was being filled by migrants from Europe or, later, Asian countries. The section on social capital says more about the contribution and barriers to entrepreneurship of women of non-English-speaking background in Australia.

Growth Orientation of Women Entrepreneurs in Australia

In general and as noted earlier, most businesses in Australia are small. In recent years Australian businesses have actually become smaller. That is, the percentage of non-employing businesses has increased and employing businesses has decreased, as the following figure, showing the average annual growth of small business from June 2001 to June 2003, makes clear.

In 2003, of all businesses in Australia:

- 666 200 (56 percent) were non-employing businesses, up by an average annual rate of 2.2 percent since June 2001;
- 389 100 (33 percent) employed 1–4 people, down by an average annual rate of 1.1 percent since June 2001;
- 124 000 (11 percent) employed 5–19 people, down by an average annual rate of 1.2 percent since June 2001.

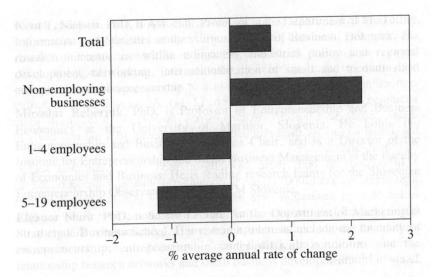

Source: Australian Bureau of Statistics (ABS) (2003c), Catalogue 8127.0.

Figure 2.5 *Average annual growth, small businesses – June 2001 to June 2003*

As is clear from the characteristics of women-owned businesses already cited and, by extrapolation from these statistics on small businesses generally, most businesses owned by women are also small. The majority of women business owners prefer to operate as a sole trader or a micro-business, that is, with less than four people. This is despite efforts by the Australian government and others to encourage women to 'grow their businesses' (Still, 2004). Still and Soutar (2001) have found that two significant reasons for the small size of women-owned businesses are 'lifestyle' (combining work and family), and 'wanting to make a difference' by providing quality products or services, being part of the community, looking after clients, and other more socially-oriented objectives. This contrasts with the pure economic objectives of growth and wealth creation that men prefer (Still and Timms, 2000; Still and Soutar, 2001). Still and Timms (2000) point out that women's businesses are not homogeneous enterprises, nor are women small business operators a homogeneous group (Still and Timms, 2000). Nevertheless, the 'lifestyle' and socially-oriented objectives of many women business owners mean that women's businesses do not necessarily follow the same growth trajectories as those of men.

GEM Australia (2003) points out the increase in the proportion of female to male entrepreneurs in the period that Australia has participated in the study

(GEM Australia, 2003, p. 6). However, this report also discusses factors affecting the likelihood that firms will expand, based on entrepreneurs' answers to questions about their perceptions of their customers' familiarity with their product or service, whether they thought they had many competitors, and whether their product or service was dependent on new technology (GEM Australia, 2003, pp. 12–14). As we will consider further under 'Strategic Choices', women-owned businesses' location in more traditional sectors for their products or services means they are less likely to be growth-oriented.

In contrast to both these 'socially-oriented' and 'traditional sector' arguments, Walker (2000) argues that younger women entrepreneurs, the so-called 'second generation', are more likely to be growth-oriented in their businesses and less risk-averse than their earlier counterparts. They are even seeking out venture capital and business 'angels'. Accordingly, changes to the current profiles of women small business operators and their businesses are likely in future.

C. DEMAND-SIDE ISSUES FOR WOMEN ENTREPRENEURS IN AUSTRALIA

Financial Capital

Roffey et al. (1996) report from their review of the international literature that, despite the public policy attention given to financing difficulties of small enterprises, specific financial institutions established for women typically receive little support. This is because their decision-making processes are at least partly based on non-commercial considerations. This in turn makes them unattractive to depositors, which restricts their lending base and their ability to grow.

The Australian experience echoes this finding. Australia's only experiment with loan guarantee schemes for women was seed funded by the Victorian state government and later operated by the Victorian Women's Trust. Like similar schemes in the US and the UK, it aimed to 'offset the lack of personal savings and/or traditional forms of collateral, isolation, lack of self-confidence, lack of credibility in the economic arena [and] lack of access to credit … which deter low-income women from choosing self-employment' (Victorian Women's Trust, 1987, p. 4). As in the US and the UK, it was a last resort scheme. It involved the State Bank of Victoria lending to women establishing a new business with the Victoria Women's Trust acting as loan guarantors. However, only two loans were made under the scheme. The Trust required women to raise their proposals to a high standard, with business plans backed by market research (see, for example, Ciastkowski, 1987). This had the effect of making the proposal sufficiently effective for it to receive bank finance by normal routes. The program was therefore terminated, and the Victorian Women's Trust subsequently provided assistance to women to develop their business proposals, improve their skills through training, and improve business information available to women.

According to some experts with long involvement in the area, the provision of financial advice and assistance in Australia has shifted from public sector institutions to the private sector arena in recent years (Amanda Ellis, *personal communication*, May 2004). Banks such as Westpac and the National Australia Bank (NAB) have been prominent in this area.

Beyond this, firm information is not available on how Australian women finance their businesses or how women differ from men in sourcing finance for their businesses. According to the GEM Report for Australia (2003, pp. 16–17), bank finance figures prominently as a source of finance for Australian business owners generally, followed by family, and then government programs. Australians, but especially women, generally make little use of business 'angels'. In fact, use of venture capital had declined for Australian entrepreneurs generally in the period before the latest GEM monitor data for Australia was released (GEM Australia, 2003, p. 25). However, Walker (2000) sees women seeking out 'angels' more actively in future as a younger generation of women entrepreneurs interested in wealth creation moves onto the scene. For now, however, it seems clear that Australian women business owners make more use than do men of their own financial resources, as well as the resources of family and friends when they start their businesses.

Social Capital

In Australia as elsewhere, social capital in the form of networks has been seen as crucial for securing necessary business knowledge, experience and contacts (Nelson, 1987, 1989; Meredith and Barrett, 1994). Formal research into business networking practices is usually based either on business owners' membership of formal organizations, or interviews with business owners to determine the sources, frequency and usefulness of contacts for business purposes. By implication then, although there is a lack of official data to confirm it, the most common business networking mechanisms – for male business owners at least – appear to be formal organizations such as chambers of commerce, along with service organizations such as Rotary.

For business women in Australia, research shows social capital in the form of networks is less available than for men. For example, Borzi (1994) has studied Australian business women's networks and the effects of this on women's ability to secure capital for their businesses. Borzi's findings are discussed further under 'Supply-side Issues for Women Entrepreneurs in Australia'. Calvert et al. (1994) in a study of Australian business women found that only half their sample belonged to networks. Business women most likely to belong to networks are generally Australian born with a post-secondary education. They run businesses in community services, manufacturing and finance, property and business services; or they run home-based businesses with no employees. Their firms have usually been in existence for less than ten years, and turn over less than A$100000 annually.

Still and Guerin's (1987) oral history study finds that women's networks are important sources of support, but not business credibility. Their 1991 study of 357 self-employed women in Sydney finds that two-thirds of the owners use neither women's organizations nor business associations.

Women in business in regional areas of Western Australia (Small Business Development Corporation of Western Australia, 1994) said they wanted access to informal and flexible networks for business discussion and professional development. They were dissatisfied with existing organizations saying they were either 'political' or 'service-oriented', and that they had little time for this type of involvement. Barrett (1997), in her study of women business owners in vocational education-based firms, found many owners distrusted the informal business information they were offered by men at meetings of professional bodies and organizations such as chambers of commerce. They believed such information was not always reliable, and was often derived from male colleagues wishing to inflate their view of themselves and their business influence and acumen. This study as well as other Australian studies found that women's access to potential investors or business partners via networks is conditioned by the level of their caring responsibility, the degree of comfort they felt in handling Anglo-masculine modes of interaction such as alcohol and sport, workforce contacts and gendered perceptions of their capacities.

In Australia, networks have also been examined in the context of ethnic minority businesses (Ip and Lever-Tracy, 1992). The Ip and Lever-Tracy study of Indian and Chinese businesses in Australia highlighted the importance of kinship networks in providing skills and resources to family enterprises. These and other studies have found that the networks of ethnic minority business may be needed to negotiate racism in the wider society. Their study also showed non-English-speaking background is perceived as a strong barrier to participation in chambers of commerce.

These findings about networks for ethnic minority businesses and for women business owners in Australia suggest some common issues. Racism, whether perceived or actual, and the feeling by many women that they are uncomfortable with male ways of interacting and exchanging information, suggest that both women and people of non-English-speaking backgrounds are excluded, not from business ownership itself, but from ways of developing contacts and skills, which would allow their businesses to grow. Public policy-makers and business people themselves should consider this situation carefully. Recommending that women or people from business groups of a specific ethnic background form their own networks may do little to make them part of the main business action.

Human Capital

Research into human capital for Australian business owners generally, as pointed out earlier, suggests that all of them are most likely to start businesses in industries they are familiar with through having worked in them before. In addition, men have a human capital 'edge' in that they are more likely to have owned businesses previously (Barrett, 1995b). The latest GEM data for Australia (GEM Australia, 2003) points to some other fundamental concerns about human capital for Australian entrepreneurs. Australian entrepreneurs perceive that the education system, while generally excellent, is too theoretically-oriented, particularly at school level and at all levels before the entrepreneur starts their first business. For example, even business students typically learn about the theory of accounting rather than finding funds and using them to leverage a business (GEM Australia, 2003, p. 27).

Adequate, willing role models are also lacking. Entrepreneurs in Australia, while plentiful and ethical, hesitate to present themselves as role models. The GEM monitor recommends that business skills be introduced as a regular part of the school curriculum and that Australians give thought to publicly endorsing those aspects of the national character – the value placed on opportunity and enterprise ('a fair go'), creativity and self-reliance – that help entrepreneurship and wealth creation (GEM Australia, 2003, p. 55).

Australian research into human capital for women business owners, in the form of training and assistance for existing or intending business owners, seems to vary greatly in its focus. This variability includes the stage of business development at which owners seek access to business training or assistance. Some of the usual research difficulties appear here. For example, many studies do not differentiate between owners (or aspiring owners) who are contemplating start-up, in the process of start-up, in the operational phase, or in the early growth phase of the business. Studies also vary in the extent to which they focus on owners' use, need for, or simple awareness of the training and assistance programs available to them. Furthermore, most studies do not explicitly define what they mean by training programs and business assistance programs. A training program is usually assumed to be a reasonably formal educational class, in which any woman owner and/or manager in any stage of business development might be taking part. Business assistance programs, by contrast, tend to be organizations or individuals providing verbal or published advice and assistance on any area of concern a woman business owner and/or manager may have. They could include accountants, bank loan officers, tax agents and Small Business Development Corporations.

The Australian research findings include a number of recurring themes on women entrepreneurs' use of training and business assistance programs. First, women typically make low use of government services, with the most used sources of assistance being Small Business Development Corporations (findings of between 20 percent and 35 percent) and University or Technical and Further Education (TAFE) colleges (16 to 20 percent) (Western Australian Department of Employment and Training, 1988; Victorian Women's Consultative Council, 1988; MacDiarmid and Thomson, 1991; Meredith and Barrett, 1994; Barrett, 1995a, 1995b). Women tend to favour independent sources of assistance over government sources (Victorian Women's Consultative Council, 1988; MacDiarmid and Thomson, 1991; Meredith and Barrett, 1994; Barrett, 1995a, 1995b).

Possible reasons for these findings are that women are sometimes unaware of the services available, or women's perceptions that their businesses, being small and often sole trader businesses, do not come into the categories of businesses to which government provides services. The perception by some women that assistance is only for people who want to grow their businesses can also hold some women back from seeking out government sources (Barrett, 1995a, 1995b). A further restrictive perception is held by some women in vocationally-oriented firms in which their partner provides the product or service. They often see themselves as 'not really business people' and merely providing support. This is despite their responsibility for ordering, pricing and a range of strategic decisions for the business (Barrett, 1997).

The most frequently used independent professional sources of assistance to women in business are accountants, followed at some distance by lawyers, bank loan officers and tax specialists (Western Australian Department of Employment and Training, 1988; Still and Guerin, 1991; MacDiarmid and Thomson, 1991; Peacock, 1994; Calvert et al., 1994; Meredith and Barrett, 1994; Barrett, 1995a, 1995b; Still and Chia, 1995). The most frequently used independent non-professional (that is, personal, family or community) sources of assistance are family and friends and colleagues. Business associates rank relatively poorly compared with the previous categories (Western Australian Department of Employment and Training, 1998; Still and Guerin, 1991; MacDiarmid and Thomson, 1991; Peacock, 1994; Calvert et al., 1994; Meredith and Barrett, 1994; Barrett, 1995a, 1995b; Still and Chia, 1995).

Women tend to use similar sources of assistance when they are starting a business as when they are in the operating stage (Western Australian Department of Employment and Training, 1988; Still and Guerin, 1991; Still and Chia, 1995). Women are most likely to cite financial management, marketing and promotion, and confidence-building as the areas of business assistance they most need and actually undertake training in (Victorian Women's Consultative Council, 1988; MacDiarmid and Thomson, 1991; Meredith and Barrett, 1994). In terms of these issues, and from the little research available, there appear to be few differences in patterns of men's and women's use of sources of business advice (Meredith and Barrett, 1994; Barrett, 1995a, 1995b).

These observations seem to be linked to differences in women's and men's social and human capital. In the section on social capital, we saw that women's lesser access to male-dominated networks implied less capacity to grow their businesses. Similarly, people from non-English-speaking backgrounds tended to confine their networks to people from their own ethnic backgrounds, for fear of actual or perceived racism, limiting their businesses' potential as a result. For women and other special groups to rely more than men on non-professional, independent sources of business advice such as family and friends, suggests they are missing out on the more broadly based, complete and customized knowledge that would help them expand their businesses. Professional business advisers would be more likely than non-professionals to take account of the business's stage in its business life cycle, which is crucial information for nurturing the business through the next growth stages. And, unless family members are also financial management experts, they can probably do no more than provide 'general wisdom' about the financial side of running the business, the very management area in which women feel least confident.

Finally, and intriguingly, the education variable – an important aspect of human capital – appears to have an ambiguous influence in men's and women's entrepreneurship. A New Zealand study by Fay and Williams (1991, 1993) found that educational qualifications increase the likelihood of women's business loan applications being approved, but that the same effect was not apparent for male business loan applications. This suggests on the one hand that men do not need as high an education level for their loan applications to be approved, but also that education is a way women may reduce gender-related prejudice against them in small business. This result is confusing, but perhaps the *type* of education is important here. In a later section we discuss what the GEM Report for Australia describes as a lack of business-oriented education (as opposed to more theoretically-based education) for Australian entrepreneurs generally.

Personal Goals

GEM Australia (2003, p. 8) distinguishes between necessity- and opportunity-based entrepreneurship, pointing out that in 2003 in Australia, the proportion of female participants in entrepreneurial activity who were motivated by opportunity rather than necessity was much higher than that of male entrepreneurs (see Figure 2.6 below).

The necessity–opportunity distinction echoes the distinction between 'push' and 'pull' entrepreneurial factors in other research. Push factors include the need to earn additional income to support oneself or one's family, lack of skills to enter other areas of worklife, or dissatisfaction with corporate life, for example because the firm allows few opportunities to advance or because its culture is unsupportive of women. Pull factors, by contrast, include the desire for achievement, for independence and the recognition of a business opportunity. Push factors, according to Still (2005) are associated with more constraints around the time of starting the firm, such as gaining the necessary confidence to start the business, finding adequate sources of assistance, including start-up capital and business advice, such as mentors and advisors to sole traders. At a personal level, a sense of isolation and difficulty in adapting from organizational to self-employment, gaining acceptance from suppliers, other businesses and clients, difficulties in managing a home as well as business, and simply managing one's own time and trying to build confidence, can all add further burdens, sap entrepreneurial spirit and turn risk-taking into risk aversion.

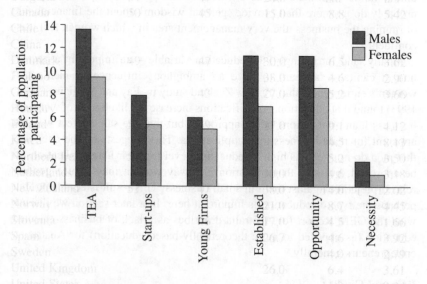

Source: GEM Australia, 2003, p. 9.

Figure 2.6   Australian entrepreneurial activity participation: males–females

On balance, Australian research suggests that 'pull', or opportunity-based factors are still outweighing 'push' or necessity factors for women. Still points out in the same chapter that Australian research from the 1970s through to the early 1990s concluded that women entered self-employment to gain autonomy and independence, escape the corporate glass ceiling, and gain more flexibility and balance in their lives (Still and Guerin, 1991; Still and Chia, 1995; Still and Timms, 2000). Still also points to US research suggesting that women over 40 are more likely to want to escape the 'glass ceiling', while those under 40 pursue wealth creation and want to have an impact on strategy. She believes these factors are also likely to hold in Australia.

Still's work echoes the findings of the GEM Report for Australia cited earlier in this section, namely that women are proportionately more motivated by opportunity-based entrepreneurship than men. The earlier, more negative findings were possibly affected by limitations in the samples of women entrepreneurs used in the research. In Still's view, research into the factors behind women's entrepreneurship needs to take more account than in the past of multi-faceted models of women's entrepreneurship. Research should also be more skeptical of assumptions about women entrepreneurs that are founded on samples of sole traders, home-based business owners, part-time entrepreneurs and those who are 'buying' employment (Still, 2005).

In all, research and public-policy development needs to take account of the diversity of women themselves, their businesses, and avoid too rigid a distinction between 'push' and 'pull' factors, and simplistic definitions of business success. After all, policies that define success only in terms of substantial growth will miss the small, profitable, sustainable, even socially conscious businesses that appeal to many women.

Strategic Choices

The strategic choices of Australian women entrepreneurs have, at least in the past, included the decision to keep the business small. The reasons for this, according to Australian research, were discussed in the section on the characteristics of women-owned businesses. They included lifestyle factors, and many women's desire to have an influence on strategy and make a difference in their immediate communities. We included the caveat that a younger generation of female business owners appeared to be more interested in growing their firms.

The industry distribution of women-owned businesses in Australia is a further aspect of their owners' strategic choices. Table 2.1 below looks at persons working in their own small business by sex and industry. While this table is from 1995, there is no reason to assume that major changes in terms of the proportions of men and women have taken place.

Table 2.1   Persons working in their own business, by sex and industry
*   1994–95*

Industry	Females		Males		All
	'000	%	'000	%	'000
Mining	0.4	10.0	3.6	90.0	4.0
Manufacturing	25.4	35.6	46.0	64.4	71.4
Construction	28.9	13.6	184.3	86.4	213.4
Wholesale Trade	13.0	30.9	29.1	69.1	42.1
Retail Trade	86.4	40.2	124.4	57.9	214.8
Accommodation, Cafes					
and Restaurants	16.4	47.8	17.9	52.2	34.3
Transport and Storage	10.8	17.9	49.5	52.2	34.3
Finance and Insurance	2.2	21.4	8.1	78.6	34.3
Property and Business					
Services	44.2	32.1	93.4	67.9	127.6
Education	9.7	61.0	6.2	39.0	15.9
Health and Community					
Services	25.2	55.0	20.6	45.0	45.8
Cultural and Recreational					
Services	12.7	42.9	16.9	57.1	29.6
Personal and Other Services	33.0	52.1	30.3	47.9	63.3
Total all Selected Industries[a]	310.6	32.7	638.9	67.3	949.5

Note: [a] Includes the Electricity, Gas and Water Supply and Communication Services industries.

Source: Survey and Employment and Earnings, unpublished data; Labour Force Survey, unpublished data. Adapted from Table 1.3 in *Small Business in Australia*, 1995 (Australian Bureau of Statistics, 1995, Catalogue 1321.0).

The table shows that the industries in which most women ran businesses were Education; Health and Community Services; Personal and Other Services; Accommodation, Cafes and Restaurants; and Cultural and Recreational Services.

Table 2.2 below shows employment in small business by sex and industry. This table shows that the industries in which most women worked were Retail Trade; Property and Business Services; and Health and Community Services. Significant numbers were also employed in Accommodation, Cafes and Restaurants; Personal and Other Services; Manufacturing, and Wholesale Trade. The industries in which women represent the greatest proportion of employment are Education; Health and Community Services; Personal and Other Services; Accommodation, Cafes and Restaurants; and Cultural and

Table 2.2   *Employed persons in small business, by sex and industry*
1994–95

Industry	Females		Males		All
	'000	%	'000	%	'000
Mining	1.4	14.7	8.1	85.3	9.5
Manufacturing	74.6	31.2	164.3	68.8	238.9
Construction	58.7	16.2	303.4	83.8	362.1
Wholesale Trade	72.8	33.7	143.2	66.3	216.0
Retail Trade	231.7	45.7	275.3	54.3	507.0
Accommodation, Cafes					
and Restaurants	83.0	55.9	65.4	44.1	148.4
Transport and Storage	29.1	23.7	93.9	76.3	123.0
Finance and Insurance	24.0	47.4	26.6	52.6	50.6
Property and Business					
Services	174.5	46.2	203.3	53.8	377.8
Education	30.4	69.6	13.3	30.4	43.7
Health and Community					
Services	123.1	69.1	55.0	30.9	178.1
Cultural and Recreational					
Services	37.7	52.8	33.7	47.2	71.4
Personal and Other Services	74.8	57.7	54.8	42.3	129.6
Total all Selected Industries[a]	1019.4	41.3	1450.6	58.7	2470.0

Note: [a] Includes the Electricity, Gas and Water Supply and Communication Services industries.

Source: Survey and Employment and Earnings, unpublished data; Labour Force Survey, unpublished data. Adapted from Table 1.3 in *Small Business in Australia*, 1995 (Australian Bureau of Statistics, 1995, Catalogue 1321.0).

Recreational Services. Clearly, women's employment is concentrated in the services sector of the economy rather than the goods-producing sector.

A comparison of Tables 2.1 and 2.2 shows that the industries in which women run their own businesses are the same as those in which they represent the highest proportion of employment.

This bears out findings of research based on surveys and interviews (for example, Still and Guerin, 1987; Barrett, 1995a, 1995b). Women business owners themselves say work experience in the same or similar businesses is a strong influence on the types of industry they will select for their own businesses. In addition, given the frequent findings on women's broad range of motivations for business ownership, including 'lifestyle' and 'balance' factors, service industries are seen as good strategic choices to support those goals.

D.   SUPPLY-SIDE ISSUES FOR WOMEN ENTREPRENEURS IN AUSTRALIA

Issues Related to Sources of Finance for Women Entrepreneurs in Australia

The small firm finance gap has a long history of public policy concern and investigation, in Australia as elsewhere. It could be assumed to affect business owners of both genders, especially since recent data from GEM Australia suggests that virtually all owners of small businesses continue to make the major contribution to start-up funding from personal sources. Figure 2.7 below illustrates this.

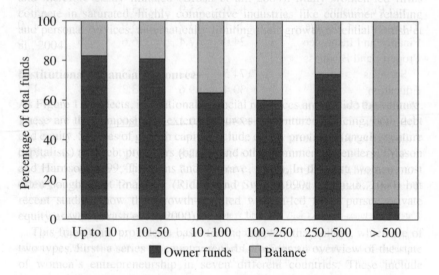

Source: GEM Australia Report, 2003, p. 17.

Figure 2.7   Percentage of owner contribution to start-up funds compared with amount of start-up funds (in A$) required

As the latest GEM Report for Australia says:

> The majority required only a modest investment, with 42 percent of startups requiring $10,000 or less and 67 percent requiring $50,000 or less. ... Of the 61 participants who disclosed the amount of their own money they expected to invest, 58 percent expected to fund the entire venture themselves. 85 percent expected to fund at least half the venture themselves. The more money was required to launch the venture, the less likely the owner was to provide all of it. ... All expected to invest at least some of their own money (GEM Australia, 2003, pp. 16–17).

Given that Australian women are more likely than men to be using small amounts of start-up capital, they are also more likely to be contributing larger proportions of start-up funds from their personal resources.

Globally, the issue of sources of finance for women entrepreneurs continues to surface in anecdotal evidence including in 2004 web-published discussion forums of bodies such as the World Bank (World Bank, 2004) and in studies of lending to women for other purposes such as housing (Taylor and Jureidini, 1994).

However, firm evidence from Australia on whether women are disadvantaged or not in financing their businesses is limited in its quality and has yielded mixed results. Borzi (1994) argued that women have both less personal wealth and more limited networks for raising capital, and so are disadvantaged from the outset in seeking finance to start a business. According to his analysis, women's active networks typically include women partners and close friends rather than business associates and male friends who have greater wealth and access to finance. As a result, women are disadvantaged in their prospects of finding investors, business partners and commercial information. The same author also argues that the banking sector is least competitive in the small business lending sector so that competition among banks is unlikely to overcome any possible gender finance gap. Breen et al. (1995) also argue that the range of funding options for female owners of small to medium-size enterprises is more limited than for men.

Yellow Pages Australia (1994), a gender comparative study, made a contrary finding that women who applied for finance were, on average, more successful than their male counterparts (p. 1) with a 94 percent success rate compared with 85 percent for men. Women reported finance as less of a factor limiting their success in business than did men. Even so, women proprietors still felt that banks were less sympathetic in their dealings with women than with men. From this study, we might conclude that there is a disparity between women's actual success rates and their perceptions of the experience of dealing with banks. However, other factors may be relevant for explaining the different success rates. Smaller proportions of women may seek bank finance in the first place and, as noted earlier, fewer women may be seeking to expand their businesses. Non-response bias could also be a factor in the Yellow Pages Australia study. Barrett (1995b) finds that men regarded access to external financing as a greater problem than did women, and that men report encountering most difficulties more frequently than do women. A similar finding was made by Meredith and Barrett (1994) for finance and interest rates, with men rating them as greater problems than women did. Roffey et al. (1996) in their overview of research point to the lack of quality research on this issue and conclude that, while women and men face difficulties in obtaining capital for small business, it is not clear that this problem is more serious for women.

Access to finance generally is likely to be affected by trends in the availability of venture capital. The latest GEM Report for Australia points out a recent decline in the availability of venture capital, but argues that the long-term trend is upwards (GEM Australia, 2003, pp. 23–4).

E.   GROWTH OF WOMEN'S ENTREPRENEURSHIP EMBEDDED IN THE AUSTRALIAN CONTEXT

This chapter has already mentioned the close correlation between the industry sectors in which most Australian women are employed and those in which they start their businesses. This is also linked to the country context for women's entrepreneurship in another way, namely that Australia is characterized by a high level of gender segregation in employment. That is, there tends to be little 'cross-over' from women into traditionally male industries, either in terms of employment or as business owners. This, combined with the observation that women are typically employed in traditional service industries, means in turn that women's firms are less likely to be in some high-technology growth areas.

This division between 'women's industries' and 'men's industries' is also echoed in studies of the values of Australian women business owners, and linkages between values and the broader industry context. Admittedly, there are few such studies, but Barrett (1995a), in a study of 792 Queensland business owners distributed amongst four industries – 'traditional male' manufacturing, 'traditional male' service, 'traditional female' manufacturing and 'traditional female' service – found significant differences in owners' values that related to the reasons for going into business in the first place, and the degree to which owners felt themselves disadvantaged by the various types of problems business owners encounter around the time of starting the firm.

Women's progress towards the upper echelons in management in general has been slower in Australia than in other Western countries, with the possible exception of the public sector. Even in the public sector, recent work by Barrett and Hede (2002) indicates that the desired effects of equal employment opportunity policy to increase women's representation in the executive ranks is extremely slow in being realized. On the one hand this may help swell the ranks of women business owners as women leave the public sector and large corporations in a well recognized trend to start their own businesses. On the other hand, the same trend may suggest complacency on the part of Australia's larger organizations, and this may be echoed in a reluctance on the part of the wider community to accept women as managers of their own businesses, especially if these businesses are growth-oriented.

In general, as the latest GEM Report for Australia points out (2003, p. 29) there are many factors in the Australian ethos that enhance entrepreneurial capacity, such as the belief in equality, 'a fair go', and a support for enterprise, that is, 'having a go'. However, Australia's 'tall poppy syndrome' – the Australian enjoyment of seeing high achievers cut down to an average level – contributes to an absence of empathy and identification with people who achieve a great deal on their own behalf. Australians dislike arrogance and the flaunting of wealth. On the positive side, Australians only want to cut their tall poppies back to an average level, not back to the lowest level, which would reduce entrepreneurial capacity. Australians also expect high standards of their entrepreneurs and others who achieve notable success. They are more punitive towards people who are perceived as having cheated to become wealthy than those who became wealthy through honest entrepreneurship (GEM Report for Australia, 2003, pp. 25, 29). The publicity given to a number of high profile corporate failures recently, several of which have been followed by the jailing of the associated entrepreneur, could be contributing to a distrust of the entrepreneurial process, and even a feeling that 'entrepreneur' is a derogatory term.

F. PROGNOSIS

In Australia, the future for women's entrepreneurship is mixed. While it will certainly continue to grow and to contribute to the Australian and world economies, the predictions of the Australian Bureau of Statistics' (1997) *Special Report on Women in Small Business* that women would soon make up half the business population, have not been realized. The ABS reported on 28 April 2004 that the growth of the small business sector as a whole had slowed by 0.4 percent (ABS, 2004b). South Australia reported a decrease of 6 percent in the growth rate of female business operators. In other states such as Victoria, however, the growth rate of small businesses was up by 6 percent, which included a 13 percent increase in women operators.

To continue and enhance the potential for business creation, and the sustaining and growing of businesses by women, it would be helpful to know more about their needs, interests, distinguishing features, and so on. To do this, of course, the gaps in research on enterprising women in Australia should be filled, wherever possible, by more and better studies of the issues confronting Australian women in business. For this to happen, more work needs to be done on the various research deficiencies surrounding women and business ownership outlined here and elsewhere in this book. This will enable better comparisons between the Australian situation and the situation of women in business worldwide. Specific research issues and questions arising from this chapter include: definitional issues, the nature of the link between women's career development (or lack of it) in corporate life and women's training for entrepreneurship; the disentangling of mixed results in comparisons of men and women on pre-start-up business planning and preparation; men's and women's access to finance (including the effect of the education variable); entrepreneurship of special groups, and other issues. We will deal with each of these briefly in turn.

Definitional Issues

As well as the lack of adequate official data mentioned at the start of this chapter and, sometimes, the conflation in official statistics of various categories of entrepreneurs, academic research has sometimes contributed to definitional confusion in research on women's entrepreneurship. In many research studies, firm size often does not feature at all. Indeed, most refer simply to women 'entrepreneurs', that is, women are specified as business owners or managers, but without indicating, or analyzing as a research variable, the size of their firm. Equally, studies frequently to do not indicate whether women are in partnership with others, but simply treat them as if they were the sole owner-manager of the business. All this means that the problems arising from the dearth of data generally on women's entrepreneurship are made even more complex. Including information about the type of contribution women business owners make to their firms, and differentiating between their goals, would make a lot of difference to the usefulness of future research.

The Link Between Women's Corporate Career Development and Women's Training for Entrepreneurship

It would be useful to know more about the large firms that experienced women managers are increasingly leaving as a result of industry structural change or other factors (Still, 1994), to understand the extent to which this trend is likely to have on women-owned business. After all, the firms these women leave are typically large, and the firms they start are small. What happens to women if the firms they start fail? Do they return to corporate life and if so, are they then even more marginalized? Should women entrepreneurs build a path back to corporate life as part of a small business exit strategy?

The Disentangling of Mixed Results in Comparisons of Men and Women on Pre-start-up Business Planning and Preparation

We saw earlier in this chapter that research results were unclear about the extent to which women and men entrepreneurs in Australia have similar or different access to human and social capital, especially in terms of business education, planning and preparation. There is probably some truth in each of the varying conflicting results. So it would be useful to understand more about the business planning and preparation areas where women feel less confident – financial management appears to be one likely area – and address this. The issue could also be linked to motivations for entrepreneurship and for the future of the business, for example, entrepreneurs with growth aspirations and those without. As Still's work in Australia and Carter's (1989) work in the UK show, training programs need to be informed by an awareness that business owners' motivations may change. As we said in the previous point, training should take account of business exit strategies as well as entry strategies.

Men's and Women's Access to Finance

Despite the long history of investigation of whether women have a harder time than men in getting access to finance for their businesses, the issue remains a very cloudy one in Australia. Quality empirical evidence of the kind carried out in the US in studies such as Coleman (2000) has generally been difficult to locate in Australia. While results in many studies in the international arena are also conflicting (Baydas and Meyer, 1994) more insights would be achieved if there were less use of convenience samples solely comprising women business owners. The participants often respond in a group environment, from which findings are derived that report a 'percentage' of women having experienced difficulty in accessing finance. These results are virtually impossible to interpret. Also, the fact that these are often single gender studies means they provide no direct basis for comparison with male-owned enterprises. Survey studies that aim to study the extent of 'bias' or 'discrimination' against women in business need to ensure their conclusions are based on comparative evidence using both genders' experience. Non-response bias also needs to be avoided, by including people who have *not* started businesses as well as those who have, in studies of the effect of finance access on business start-up.

Entrepreneurship of Special Groups

The chapter briefly examined some contributions and obstacles to entrepreneurship of special groups, such as women from non-English-speaking backgrounds and migrant women. More minority or special groups should be studied to better appreciate both their needs and their contributions. These should include indigenous entrepreneurs, entrepreneurs in rural and remote areas, and 'co-preneurs', that is, husband and wife entrepreneurial teams.

Other Issues

There are also some general factors that the Australian and other research literature have tried to investigate in terms of their relationship to business success or failure. Many of these rely on self-report data and thus may be subject to social desirability response bias. For example, Yellow Pages Australia (1994) finds that successful women small business owners attribute their business success to (in order of importance) having a pleasant personality, business experience, communication skills, good customer service and hard work. Males rated experience and hard work ahead of communication skills and customer service as factors contributing to business success. Studies of gender difference in business managerial and leadership style indicate that women managers tend to be more collaborative, consultative and participatory in their style of operating. However, non-self-report evidence on the relationship between managerial style, gender and small business survival or growth is also inconclusive. To avoid these issues, the Australian research approach could benefit from the use of more methodologically sophisticated studies of factors associated with business success or failure such as have been undertaken in the US (for example, Cuba et al., 1983; Denison and Alexander, 1986; Neider, 1987; Brush and Hisrich, 1988; Miskin and Rose, 1990; Brush and Hisrich, 1991; Dodge and Robbins, 1992). Although no clear predictor of business success or failure emerges from these studies, success seems to be associated with financial management ability and prior experience in the industry, but *not* necessarily with level of previous formal education.

However, more than research is needed. More discussion and awareness are needed in policy-making and business arenas about those elements of the business environment that seem to affect women differently from men, the Australian public policy initiatives that seem to have been most effective, and which public policy initiatives from elsewhere in the world are likely to translate well to the Australian environment.

As well as a better understanding of women's place in the business environment, the most recent GEM Report for Australia (2003) points to a number of problems in the business environment generally, which could be expected to affect women's business ownership along with men's, when these businesses are high-growth, high-impact businesses. These factors include culture, education, government policy support, financial support and entrepreneurial capacity. While these same group of five weaknesses have been reported in previous years, 'financial support' topped the most recent list of weaknesses. Specific 'financial support' issues reported by the GEM include the relative unavailability of equity capital, especially for early stage ventures, and a continuing lack of access to debt capital; and the concentration of capital in the major population centres of Sydney and Melbourne.

The burden of compliance with government policy is reported by GEM Australia (2003) to be severe enough to be forcing some businesses to close down. This burden, which includes tax rules that change too often, the need to collect Goods and Services Tax (GST) on behalf of the government, the complexity of employment regulations and the growing expense of professional indemnity insurance, particularly affects the productivity and growth potential of small businesses. This is only partly counterbalanced by the fact that it is not expensive to set up a business in Australia – a factor that nevertheless should help women, who may have less access to capital through their own sources – and the fact that there are well-directed government policies supported by well-developed programs such as export development and IP Australia, which improve the environment for entrepreneurship (GEM Australia, 2003, p. 24).

In the area of education, the problem is seen as too great a focus on qualifications and employment to the detriment of true learning, including 'experiential' learning, and developing the potential for self-employment. The basic education system is good though perhaps in need of more investment, and there are excellent business programs available in schools, universities and elsewhere, with increasing involvement from industry associations. However, education needs to be more focused on 'business' rather than its component elements such as accounting, legal issues, human resource management, and so on. There is little taught about how to grow businesses (as opposed to start-ups and the management of established businesses) and insufficient vocational education such as trade apprenticeships. These factors may disproportionately affect women who, the evidence suggests, lack networks that would teach them how to grow their businesses. The system favours the academic type of student; the others – including the entrepreneurs – tend to drop out for lack of alternatives – a waste of talent (GEM Australia, 2003, p. 24).

There are some encouraging signs as well, however, according to the latest GEM Report. At the level of general culture, and including Australia's general entrepreneurial capacity or human capital, the potential in Australia for entrepreneurship is large. Australians are known to be creative, inventive and adaptable, hardworking and resilient, competitive and natural networkers who are always aiming to improve. Australians have plenty of success stories, although they are shy about talking about them. However, there are also important skill deficits, some of which appear to affect women even more than men, including the knowledge of how to turn an idea into an opportunity, financial literacy, knowledge of the market, risk management and team-building. As noted earlier, there is some discomfort with perceptions about entrepreneurs and this makes successful entrepreneurs reluctant to act as role models. Corporate Australia discourages entrepreneurial activity within its ranks, and the short-term, comfortable, individualistic Australian culture discourages the sacrifices needed in the early stages of an entrepreneurial venture. A major recommendation for improvement of Australia as an entrepreneurial nation is that its education system should focus more on developing the ability to think and learn, to collaborate and be creative, and close the skill gaps mentioned earlier. These changes would do a great deal to lift the potential of women to start and grow new enterprises.

REFERENCES

Australian Bureau of Statistics (ABS) (1995), *Catalogue 1321.0, Small Business in Australia, 1994*, at http://www.abs.gov.au/ausstats. Accessed 16 September 2004.

Australian Bureau of Statistics (ABS) (1997), *Special Report on Women in Small Business*, at http://www.abs.gov.au/ausstats. Accessed 16 September 2004.

Australian Bureau of Statistics (ABS) (2003a), *Catalogue 3101.0, Australian Demographic Statistics*, at http://www.abs.gov.au/ausstats. Accessed 16 September 2004.

Australian Bureau of Statistics (ABS) (2003b), *Catalogue 3201.0 Population Trends and Estimates*, at http://www.abs.gov.au/ausstats. Accessed 16 September 2004.

Australian Bureau of Statistics (2003c) (ABS), *Catalogue 8127.0, Characteristics of Small Business in Australia*, at http://www.abs.gov.au/ausstats. Accessed 16 September 2004.

Australian Bureau of Statistics (ABS) (2004a), *Catalogue 6105.0, Labour Force Statistics*, at http://www.abs.gov.au/ausstats. Accessed 16 September 2004.

Australian Bureau of Statistics (ABS) (2004b), *Catalogue 8127.0, Characteristics of Small Business in Australia*, at http://www.abs.gov.au/ausstats. Accessed 16 September 2004.

Barrett, M.A. (1995a), *Comparisons of Women and Men Business Owners in Queensland – Business Problems, Strategies and Values*, Report to the Queensland Department of Small Business Development, Brisbane.

Barrett, M.A. (1995b), 'The Learning Experience of Entrepreneurs: Some Gender and Industry-Related Effects', in *Frontiers of Entrepreneurship Research*, Babson College, MA.

Barrett, M.A. (1997), *Women Training for Transitions: Enhancing VET for Women's Business Involvement*, Queensland University of Technology, Brisbane.

Barrett, M.A. and Hede, A. (2002), 'Principles and Practice of Gender Diversity Management in Australia', in Marilyn Davidson and Sandra Fielden (eds), *Individual Diversity in Organisations*, Chichester, UK: John Wiley.

Baydas, M.M. and Meyer, N.A. (1994), 'Discrimination Against Women in Formal Credit Markets: Reality or Rhetoric?', *World Development*, **22**(7), 1073–82.

Borzi, A.M. (1994), *The Gender Finance Gap*, Sydney: Smythe Pty Ltd.

Breen, J., Calvert, C. and Oliver, J. (1995), 'Female Entrepreneurs in Australia: An Investigation of Financial and Family Issues', *Journal of Enterprising Culture*, **3**(4), 445–61.

Brush, C.G. and Hisrich, R.D. (1988), 'Women Entrepreneurs: Strategic Origins' Impact on Growth', in *Frontiers of Entrepreneurship Research*, Babson College, MA, pp. 612–25.

Brush, C.G. and Hisrich, R.D. (1991), 'Antecedent Influences on Women-Owned Businesses', in *Journal of Managerial Psychology*, **6**(2), 9–16.

Calvert, C., Oliver, J. and Breen, J. (1994), *Investigation of Issues Affecting Women in Small Business*, Melbourne: Small Business Research Unit, Victorian University of Technology.

Carter, S. (1989), 'The Dynamics and Performance of Female-owned Entrepreneurial Firms in London, Glasgow and Nottingham', *Journal of Organizational Change and Management*, **2**, 54–64.

Ciastkowski, J. (1987), *How to Assess Your Business Idea, a Victorian Woman's Guide to a Preliminary Business Plan*, Melbourne: The Victorian Women's Trust Ltd.

Coleman, S. (2000), 'Access to Capital and Terms of Credit: A Comparison of Men- and Women-owned Small Businesses', *Journal of Small Business Management*, **28**(3), 37–53.

Cuba, R., Decenzo, D. and Anish, A. (1983), 'Management Practices of Successful Female Business Owners', *American Journal of Small Business*, **8**(2), 40–46.

Denison, D.R. and Alexander, J.M. (1986), 'Patterns and Profiles of Entrepreneurs: Data from Entrepreneurship Forums', in *Frontiers of Entrepreneurship Research*, Babson College, MA, pp. 578–93.

Dodge, H.R. and Robbins, J.E. (1992), 'An Empirical Investigation of the Organizational Life Cycle Model for Small Business Development and Survival', *Journal of Small Business Management*, **30**(1), 27–37.

Fay, M. and Williams, L. (1991), 'Sex of Applicant and the Availability of Business "Start-up" Finance', *Australian Journal of Management*, **16**(1), 65–72.

Fay, M. and Williams, L. (1993), 'Gender Bias and the Availability of Loans', *Journal of Business Venturing*, **8**(4), 363–76.

Global Entrepreneurship Monitor (GEM) Australia (2003), at http://www.swin.edu.au/ agse/research/gempapers/WestpacGEMO203.pdf. Accessed 29 August 2005.

Goward, P. (2005), 'Men at Work', *The Weekend Australian Magazine*, 5–6 February.

Hofstede, G. (1984), *Culture's Consequences: International Differences in Work-Related Values*, Newbury Park, CA: Sage.

Ip, D. and Lever-Tracy, C. (1992), 'Asian Women in Business', *Asian Migrant*, **5**, 12–23.

MacDiarmid, J. and Thomson, L. (1991), *Women in Business: A Local Enterprise Development Project*, Melbourne: Economic and Employment Branch, City of Melbourne.

Mackay, H. (1997), *Generations: Baby Boomers, their Parents and Their Children*, Sydney: Macmillan.

Meredith, G.G. and Barrett, R.G. (1994), *Women Self-Employed Entrepreneurs in Queensland*, Lismore, NSW: Southern Cross University.

Miskin, V. and Rose, J. (1990), 'Women Entrepreneurs: Factors Related to Success', in *Frontiers of Entrepreneurship Research*, Babson College, MA, pp. 27–38.

Neider, L. (1987), 'A Preliminary Investigation of Female Entrepreneurs in Florida', *Journal of Small Business Management*, **25**(3), 22–9.

Nelson, G.W. (1987), 'Information Needs of Women Entrepreneurs', *Journal of Small Business Management*, **25**(3), pp. 38–44.

Nelson, G.W. (1989), 'Factors of Friendship: Relevance of Significant Others to Female Business Owners', *Entrepreneurship Theory and Practice*, **13**(4), 7–18.

Peacock, R.W. (1994), *Home-based Enterprises in South Australia*, Small Enterprise Series No. 26, Adelaide: University of South Australia.

Roffey, B.S., Stanger, A., Forsaith, D., McInnes, E., Petrone, F., Symes, C. and Xydias, M. (1996), *Women in Small Business: A Review of Research. A Report by The Flinders University of South Australia to The Department of Industry, Science and Tourism*, Canberra: The Australian Government Publishing Service.

Small Business Development Corporation of Western Australia (1994), *Women and Small Business in Regional Western Australia*, SBDC (WA), Perth, November.

Still, L. (1993), *Where To From Here? – The Managerial Woman in Transition*, Sydney: Business and Professional Publishing.

Still, L. (1994), 'Women in Management and Self-employed Women', *Canberra Bulletin of Public Administration*, **76**, 170–73.

Still, L. (2004), 'Women in Management in Australia', in Marilyn J. Davidson and Ronald J. Burke (eds), *Women in Management Worldwide: Facts, Figures and Analysis*, Aldershot, UK: Ashgate.

Still, L. (2005), 'The Constraints Facing Women Entering Small Business Ownership', in Marilyn J. Davidson and Sandra L. Fielden (eds), *International Handbook of Women and Small Business Entrepreneurship*, Cheltenham, UK and Northampton, MA: Edward Elgar.

Still, L. and Chia, B. (1995), *Self-Employed Women: Four Years On*, Women and Leadership Series, Paper No. 1, Perth: Edith Cowan University.

Still, L. and Guerin, C. (1987), 'Enterprising Women: Australian Women Managers and Entrepreneurs – A Comparison of their Career Paths and Futures', Sociological Association of Australia and New Zealand Annual Conference, Sydney.

Still, L. and Guerin, C. (1991), *Typologies of Enterprising Women: Managers Versus Entrepreneurs*, Sydney: Faculty of Commerce, University of Western Sydney.

Still, L. and Soutar, G. (2001), 'Generational and Gender Differences in the Start-Up Goals and Later Satisfaction of Small Business Proprietors', *Proceedings of Australian and New Zealand Academy of Management Conference*, Auckland, New Zealand, December.

Still, L. and Timms, W. (2000), 'Women's Business: The Flexible Alternative Workstyle for Women', *Women in Management Review*, **15**(5/6), 272.

Taylor, J. and Jureidini, R. (1994), 'The Implicit Male Norm in Australian Housing Finance', *Journal of Economic Issues*, **28**(2), 543–54.

Victorian Women's Trust (1987), *Second Annual Report*, 1986–87.

Victorian Women's Consultative Council (1988), *Women and Small Business – Overview*, Melbourne: Victorian Women's Consultative Council.

Walker, E. (2000), *The Changing Profile of Women Starting Small Businesses*, Paper no. 6, Centre for Women and Business, Graduate School of Management, The University of Western Australia.

Western Australian Department of Employment and Training (1988), *The HUB Report 1988*, Perth, July.

World Bank (2004), Online discussion: Hot topics for a global community at http://rru.worldbank.org/Discussions/Topics/Topic28.aspx. Accessed 29 August 2005.

Yellow Pages Australia (1994), *Small Business Index – A Special Report on Women in Business*, Pacific Access Pty Ltd.

3. Women's entrepreneurship in Canada: progress, puzzles and priorities

**Jennifer E. Jennings and
Michelle Provorny Cash***

OVERALL ENTREPRENEURIAL ACTIVITY IN CANADA

Women's entrepreneurial activity in Canada occurs within the context of a strong national culture of entrepreneurship and small business ownership. In the 2002 Global Entrepreneurship Monitor (GEM) study of nascent entrepreneurship rates,[1] Canada ranked eighth out of the 37 countries surveyed, up from its thirteenth place ranking only one year earlier (Riverin, 2003: 7). The country's nascent prevalence rate in 2002 was 5.9 percent – a rate that was superior to the G7 average of 3.7 percent and the GEM 37 mean of 4.7 percent, on par with that of Korea, and only slightly behind the US rate of 7.1 percent (Riverin, 2003: 7). In addition, the study estimated Canada's new firm rate[2] at 3.6 percent during the same year (Riverin, 2003: 12). Although both of these rates were lower than those reported for 2001, Canada's five-spot jump in the rankings indicates that, relative to other countries, the nation has not been as severely affected by the global decline in entrepreneurial activity (Riverin, 2003: 12).

Canada also has a vibrant small business sector. According to the most recent Statistics Canada data available,[3] approximately 2.4 million Canadians were self-employed in 2003, representing 14 percent of the Canadian labor force. These individuals own approximately 2.2 million business establishments, of which 1 million have employees and 1.1 million do not. The vast majority of those that employ others – 98 percent – are 'small businesses'; that is, firms with less than 100 employees. Just over half of those that employ others – 54 percent – would actually be classified as 'micro-enterprises', as they employ fewer than five workers. Collectively, however, these small businesses provide employment for 47 percent of the nation's labour force, with 'medium-sized firms' – that is, those with 100 to 499 employees – providing employment for an additional 16 percent of the nation's workers. Entrepreneurs and their businesses are thus vital contributors to the Canadian economy.

A PROFILE OF WOMEN'S ENTREPRENEURSHIP IN CANADA

The Prevalence and Economic Significance of Women's Entrepreneurship

Women entrepreneurs account for a sizeable proportion of Canada's total entrepreneurial activity and small business sector, but do not yet participate at the same rate as men. In terms of GEM's measure of nascent entrepreneurial activity, for example, the prevalence rate for women was only 3.7 percent in 2002, less than half the 9.7 rate for men in the same year (Riverin, 2003: 7). The gender gap in nascent entrepreneurial activity is particularly wide in the 24–35 year old age category, where the 2002 rate for Canadian women was only 3 percent while that for Canadian men was 10.7 percent – a gap most likely attributable to women's focus on raising families during those years of their lives (Riverin, 2003: 7). There is some evidence to suggest, however, that these gaps may narrow in the future.

Consider the statistics for women's self-employment. As indicated in Figure 3.1, the number of self-employed women in Canada has risen dramatically since the mid-1970s. Between 1981 and 2001, their numbers increased by 208 percent. Between 1991 and 2001, the rate of self-employment amongst Canadian women grew by 43 percent, which was double

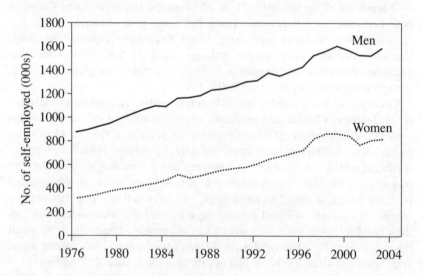

Source: Statistics Canada, CANSIM, Table 282-0012 and catalogue no. 89F0133XIE.

Figure 3.1   Trends in the self-employment of men and women in Canada

the rate for men's self-employment. Moreover, in the five-year period from 1996 to 2001 alone, the number of self-employed women grew by 8 percent compared with only 0.6 percent for self-employed men (Prime Minister's Task Force on Women Entrepreneurs, 2003: 25). In 2003, approximately 826000 Canadian women were self-employed, constituting 34 percent of the 2412700 self-employed individuals in the country. According to a recent report, 'women in Canada make up a greater share of the self-employed than in any other country' (Prime Minister's Task Force on Women Entrepreneurs, 2003: 26).

Just as women constitute 34 percent of all self-employed workers in Canada, Figure 3.2 indicates that they hold at least 50 percent ownership in 34 percent of all Canadian small and medium-sized enterprises (SMEs). Only 15 percent of these enterprises, however, are majority female-owned. Moreover, over half of SMEs in Canada – 55 percent – have no female ownership whatsoever (Statistics Canada, 2000a). Although women do not yet participate in entrepreneurial activity and small business ownership to the same extent as men in Canada, those that do have an undeniable impact on the nation's economy.

According to a very recent report: 'Almost 570,000 people were employed by majority women-owned businesses in 2001 and an additional 404,000 people were hired through contract. Majority women-owned SMEs brought in combined annual revenues of $72 billion in 2000, representing approximately

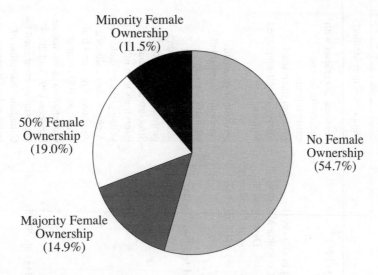

Source: Statistics Canada, 2000a.

Figure 3.2   Ownership of Canadian SMEs in the year 2000

Table 3.1 Methodological details of cited empirical studies of women's entrepreneurship in Canada

Study	Data Collection Method	Region	Sample Size
Belcourt (1990)	Personal interviews with successful female entrepreneurs	Convenience sample	No. of F entrepreneurs = 36
Belcourt et al. (1991)	In-depth interviews	Nationwide	No. of F entrepreneurs = 193
British Columbia Ministry of Economic Development, Small Business and Trade (1991)	Survey of self-employed women	British Columbia	No. of F self-employed = 600
Cliff (1998) and Cliff et al. (2005)	Structured personal interviews with small business owners	Greater Vancouver Regional District (GVRD)	No. of M-headed firms = 141 No. of F-headed firms = 88
Cliff and Jennings (2004)	Structured personal interviews with young professional service firms	Greater Vancouver Regional District (GVRD)	No. of maj M-headed firms = 38 No. of min F-headed firms = 15 No. of maj F-headed firms = 7
	Structured personal interviews with other young privately-held firms	Greater Vancouver Regional District (GVRD)	No. of maj M-headed firms = 32 No. of min F-headed firms = 10 No. of maj F-headed firms = 41
	Archival data collected on young firms that had issued an IPO on any Canadian stock exchange between 1997 and 2003	Nationwide	No. of maj M-headed firms = 102 No. of min F-headed firms = 33 No. of maj F-headed firms = 5
Fabowale et al. (1995)	Mail survey conducted by Canadian Federation of Independent Business	Nationwide	No. of M-headed firms = 1891 No. of F-headed firms = 756

Study	Method	Location	Sample
Fischer (1992)	Mail survey	Nationwide	No. of M-headed firms = 323 No. of F-headed firms = 49
Fischer et al. (1993)	Mail survey	Nationwide	No. of M-headed firms = 448 No. of F-headed firms = 60
Haines et al. (1999)	Archival data drawn from bank loan files	Nationwide	No. of M-headed firms = 835 No. of F-headed firms = 105
Hughes (2003; forthcoming)	In-depth interviews with self-employed women	Alberta	No. of F self-employed = 61
Lee-Gosselin and Grisé (1990)	Questionnaires and in-depth interviews with female business owners	Quebec	No. of questionnaires from business owners = 400 No. of in-depth interviews with F business owners = 75
Orser and Hogarth-Scott (2002)	In-depth interviews	Western Canada	No. of M-headed firms = 106 No. of F-headed firms = 33
Orser and Riding (2004)	Telephone survey	Western Canada	No. M business owners = 219 No. F business owners = 107
Riding and Swift (1990)	Mail survey conducted by Canadian Federation of Independent Business	Nationwide	No. of M-headed firms = 153 No. of F-headed firms = 153
Staber (1997)	Mail survey	Atlantic Canada	No. of M-headed firms = 147 No. of F-headed firms = 141
Statistics Canada (2000a)	Telephone interviews and faxed questionnaire	Nationwide	No. of majority M-headed firms = 4754 No. of majority F-headed firms = 1080
The Research Institute for SMEs, Université du Québec à Trois-Rivières (2002)	Mail and telephone survey	Nationwide	No. of M entrepreneurs = 510 No. of F entrepreneurs = 505

57

8 percent of all revenues from Canada's SMEs' (Industry Canada, 2004: 2).
Moreover, according to a study conducted by Deloitte & Touche, the 100
largest women-headed companies in Canada alone generated revenues of $2.1
billion in the year 2000 – up from $1.2 billion in 1999 (as reported in Ramsay,
2002).[4]

The growth, prevalence and economic significance of women's
entrepreneurship in Canada has not gone unrecognized by researchers.
Numerous essays, policy-oriented papers and empirical articles have been
written on the topic. Table 3.1 summarizes the key methodological details of
the empirical studies that we reviewed for this chapter.

The Relative Performance of Male and Female Entrepreneurs and their Firms

Female entrepreneurs and their business ventures are becoming much more
prevalent within Canada and are thus increasingly important contributors to
the Canadian economy. But how does their performance compare with that of
male entrepreneurs and their firms? Empirical research provides evidence of a
clear performance differential, with female entrepreneurs and their businesses
performing less well on standard indicators such as firm size, revenues,
income level and rates of growth.

With respect to firm size, for example, the latest Statistics Canada data
indicates that majority women-owned firms are disproportionately represented
in the smallest employment size categories. The vast majority of female-
owned SMEs – 85 percent – are actually micro-businesses, employing fewer
than five individuals. Only 14 percent of female-owned SMEs would be
categorized as small businesses, employing between five and 99 individuals.
In comparison, 79 percent and 20 percent of male-owned SMEs would be
classified as micro-businesses and small businesses respectively (as reported
in Industry Canada, 2004: 2). The studies by Cliff (1998); Cliff et al. (2005);
Fischer (1992); Fischer et al. (1993) and Orser and Hogarth-Scott (2002)
provide corroborating evidence, revealing that, on average, firms headed by
women tend to be less than one half the size of those headed by men, as
measured by number of employees.[5]

Female-owned businesses in Canada also tend to generate significantly less
revenue than male-owned businesses. In the year 2000, majority female-
owned firms generated average annual sales of $334542 – less than half the
$705793 average for male-owned firms (Statistics Canada, 2000a). The
studies by Fischer (1992); Fischer et al. (1993) and Orser and Hogarth-Scott
(2002) once again provide corroborating evidence: in these investigations, the
average annual sales level reported by female-headed firms was closer to one-
third the amount reported by male-headed firms. Fischer's studies also

revealed that the female-headed businesses tended to generate significantly lower sales per employee (Fischer, 1992; Fischer et al., 1993).

A corresponding gap exists in the income levels of male and female entrepreneurs and their firms. A mere 17 percent of self-employed women earn over $30000 per year, compared with 42 percent of self-employed men (Prime Minister's Task Force on Women Entrepreneurs, 2003: 26). Other Statistics Canada data indicates that the annual profits generated by majority female-owned firms are approximately half those generated by majority male-owned firms, averaging $33834 versus $64809 respectively (Statistics Canada, 2000a). Fischer's (1992) study provides corroborating evidence. Notably, however, neither Fischer (1992) nor Fischer et al. (1993) found any significant differences in the profitability ratios of male and female-headed firms, as measured by either income per owner or income per sales. Similarly, Statistics Canada's 'Survey on Financing of Small and Medium-sized Enterprises' (2000a) revealed that the ratio of net profit to total revenues was almost identical for majority male-owned and majority female-owned firms, averaging 9.2 and 10.1 percent respectively.

Some research also suggests that businesses headed by women in Canada tend to grow more slowly than those headed by men. One recent nationwide study, for example, found that 58 percent of the 505 female entrepreneurs surveyed, but only 49 percent of the 510 male entrepreneurs surveyed reported that their firms were in a slow-growth stage of business development; in contrast, only 9 percent of the women, but 14 percent of the men, reported that their firms were in a fast-growth stage (The Research Institute for SMEs, 2002: 32). Orser and Hogarth-Scott (2002) provide corroborating evidence: between 1991 and 1995, the 33 female-headed firms in their study grew at a significantly slower pace in terms of both revenue and employment growth than the 106 male-headed firms. In contrast, Fischer et al. (1993) found that although the female-headed firms in their sample exhibited significantly slower income growth than male-headed firms, they did not exhibit significantly slower sales or employment growth. Likewise, Staber (1997) found no statistically significant differences in the financial or employment growth of the male and female-owned businesses in his Atlantic Canada study.

Interpreting these mixed findings regarding the rate at which male and female-owned firms tend to grow is difficult. On the one hand, the findings reported by The Research Institute for SMEs at the Université du Québec à Trois-Rivières (2002) are based on a very large, nationally-representative sample, but the operationalization of business growth is fairly crude (that is, a self-reported categorical measure). On the other hand, Fischer et al. (1993), Orser and Hogarth-Scott (2002) and Staber (1997) used much more objective and finer-grained indicators of business growth, but their sample sizes were much smaller and not as representative. Nevertheless, there is at least some evidence to indicate that firms headed by women in Canada exhibit slower growth than those headed by men.

The Growth Orientations of Male and Female Entrepreneurs

The above-noted evidence clearly demonstrates that female-headed businesses in Canada tend to be smaller than male-headed businesses, whether size is measured in terms of number of employees, revenues or income level. There is also some evidence to suggest that they tend to grow more slowly. What can help explain these consistent findings? Several Canadian scholars have called attention to the growth orientations of male and female entrepreneurs, arguing that many women business owners *deliberately* choose to keep their companies small and to shy away from fast-paced expansion (Belcourt et al., 1991; Cliff, 1998; Lee-Gosselin and Grisé, 1990; Orser and Hogarth-Scott, 2002).

On balance, empirical research conducted within Canada provides a base of support for the deliberate choice argument. Lee-Gosselin and Grisé (1990), for example, noted that although revenue growth was the most frequently-cited success criteria mentioned by the 400 female entrepreneurs surveyed for their Quebec study, in-depth interviews with 75 of these women revealed that most possessed only modest financial expectations and were satisfied with the slow growth of their business revenues. In fact, the majority emphasized that they had deliberately limited the growth of their firms, viewing a small company as a 'desirable and stable state – rather than as a transitory phase' (Lee-Gosselin and Grisé, 1990: 432). Belcourt et al. (1991) reported a similar pattern in their study of 193 women business owners from across Canada. Although 93 percent of these women reported sales growth as a business objective, only 45 percent reported that their firms' revenues were actually growing beyond the rate of inflation. Moreover, although 60 percent intended to hire more employees over the next three years, only 45 percent had done so in the previous three years and only 20 percent reported intentions of moderate to high growth. These two pioneering studies clearly reveal that while most women entrepreneurs in Canada have goals of increasing business revenues, only a minority have ambitions of heading large, high-growth enterprises. Hughes's more recent Alberta-based study corroborates this conclusion. Of the 61 self-employed women interviewed, slightly less than one-third (32 percent) reported being interested in 'significantly expanding their business – either by developing new products, targeting new clients, or entering new markets nationally or internationally' (Hughes, forthcoming: 233).

Cliff (1998) examined whether women business owners' attitudes towards growth differ from those of their male counterparts, and could thus provide a plausible explanation for the observed performance differential between male-headed and female-headed firms. Data collected through personal interviews with 229 small business owners in the Greater Vancouver Regional District (GVRD) revealed that although male and female entrepreneurs appear to be *equally* desirous of business growth, there are important differences in terms of *how* they wish to grow. More specifically, female business owners are more likely to establish maximum business size thresholds beyond which they would prefer not to expand, and these thresholds tend to be smaller than those set by their male counterparts. Female entrepreneurs also appear to be more concerned about the risks associated with fast-paced growth and, as such, tend to deliberately adopt a slow and steady pace of expansion. Cliff's (1998) qualitative analysis revealed intriguing reasons for women's more cautious attitudes towards growth, including: the wish to maintain control over the organization, a lack of time or energy to devote to business expansion, the desire to achieve a balance between work and personal life, and a concern that growth would interfere with other valued business objectives like product quality, customer service and employer–employee relationships.

Orser and Hogarth-Scott (2002) recently corroborated and extended the essence of Cliff's (1998) findings through a study of 106 male and 33 female business owners in Western Canada. These scholars reported that the women in their study scored significantly lower than the men when asked to rate the likelihood, value and importance of business growth. Moreover, although both sexes tended to weigh financial and non-financial factors in the growth/no-growth decision, women tended to accord more weight to the need for spousal support before embarking upon expansion. The women were also discouraged to a greater degree by the anticipated demands that growth would place on their time and the consequent deleterious effects for their stress level and ability to achieve work–family balance.

In contrast to Cliff (1998) and Orser and Hogarth-Scott (2002), Statistics Canada data indicate that, in the year 2000, 49 percent of majority female-owned businesses – but only 30 percent of majority male-owned businesses – anticipated growing by more than 60 percent over the next two years (Industry Canada, 2002b). Likewise, The Research Institute for SMEs at the Université du Québec à Trois-Rivières (2002) found that 43 percent of the female entrepreneurs but only 30 percent of the male entrepreneurs in their study predicted growth over the same time period. On the surface, these findings seem to suggest that women entrepreneurs may actually possess *higher* growth expectations than their male counterparts. It would be interesting to analyze both of these datasets further, though, to determine whether such differences remain after controlling for the significantly smaller size and younger age of female-headed firms (Statistics Canada, 2000a). It could be that the data primarily reflect the influence of firm size and age (with the owners of smaller and younger firms likely to report higher expected growth rates expressed in percentage terms), rather than true differences in the growth orientations of male and female entrepreneurs. We thus encourage readers to exercise caution in drawing inferences from these studies, the findings of which run counter to those reported by Belcourt et al. (1991), Cliff (1998), Hughes (forthcoming), Lee-Gosselin and Grisé (1990) and Orser and Hogarth-Scott (2002).

One further caveat should be raised at this point. Although the studies by Lee-Gosselin and Grisé (1990), Belcourt et al. (1991), Cliff (1998) and Orser and Hogarth-Scott (2002) suggest that the smaller size and slower growth rates of female-owned business in Canada may, to a certain extent, represent deliberate choices of many women entrepreneurs, empirical substantiation of this causal inference does not yet exist. Through their longitudinal analysis, Orser and Hogarth-Scott (2002) demonstrated that owners' growth intentions actually do impact the subsequent growth of their firms, but these scholars did not examine the extent to which the observed differences in the growth orientations of the male and female entrepreneurs in their study could help account for the observed differences in the subsequent growth of their firms. Longitudinal investigations of the deliberate choice argument thus represent one of the top priorities for future research on women's entrepreneurship in Canada.

DEMAND-SIDE ISSUES FOR WOMEN ENTREPRENEURS IN CANADA: HOW DO MALE AND FEMALE BUSINESS OWNERS DIFFER?

The Human Capital of Male and Female Entrepreneurs

The human capital argument attributes the performance differential between male and female-owned firms primarily to differences in the education and experience of male and female entrepreneurs. More specifically, the argument here is that the comparatively poorer performance of female-owned firms can be explained by the tendency of women entrepreneurs to possess less relevant education, less managerial and industry experience, and less prior business start-up experience, on average, than their male counterparts. Given its intellectual roots in liberal feminist theory, the human capital argument's main inference is hopeful: once women entrepreneurs possess educational and work experiences equal to those of men, then the business performance differential will disappear.

Canadian research attests that, on average, female business owners do possess less human capital than their male counterparts. For example, although most studies have not found any significant differences in the education *level* of male and female entrepreneurs (Fischer, 1992; Fischer et al., 1993; Staber, 1997), the studies by Cliff and her colleagues (Cliff, 1998; Cliff et al., 2005) did reveal significant differences in the *nature* of their educational backgrounds. Although almost one-quarter (23 percent) of the 141 male business owners in this GVRD-based study possessed a business degree, less than one-tenth (9 percent) of the 88 female business owners did so. Research also suggests that, in comparison to their male counterparts, women business owners tend to possess: fewer years of overall work experience (Staber, 1997), less industry experience (Fischer, 1992; Fischer et al., 1993; Industry Canada, 2002b; The Research Institute for SMEs, 2002)[6] and less management experience (Fischer, 1992; Fischer et al., 1993).[7] They are also less likely to have previously owned or started up their own business (Cliff, 1998; Fischer, 1992; Fischer et al., 1993).[8] These differences may partially be explained by their relatively younger age: an average of 43 years for women and 49 years for men (The Research Institute for SMEs, 2002).

Cliff and Jennings (2004) pointed out, however, that much of the work in this area has been based on studies of privately-held firms in the retail/ wholesale, manufacturing and personal service industries. These scholars suggested that the observed pattern of gender differences may not be as apparent in certain settings that have not yet received as much attention from entrepreneurship researchers; namely, in knowledge-intensive companies, such as professional service firms, where the credentialing of practitioners is common practice. In support, these scholars found that while the male and female owners of 60 recently-established professional service firms in the GVRD possessed *equivalent* levels of human capital, the female owners of 83 other recently-established privately-held firms in the same regional district did, in fact, score lower than their male counterparts on this dimension. In general, then, while it is certainly the case that many women entrepreneurs in Canada may be disadvantaged by their comparatively lower human capital, this is not necessarily the case for all women entrepreneurs. In particular, those heading knowledge-intensive companies such as professional service firms may not be at as great a disadvantage in this regard.

Moreover, even if the average Canadian woman entrepreneur possesses less human capital than her male counterpart, some research suggests that this apparent shortcoming may not be all that detrimental to her firm's relative performance. The nationwide studies conducted by Fischer and her colleagues, for example, revealed that observed differences in the education and experience level of male and female entrepreneurs explained 'an almost negligible portion of the variance in firm performance' (Fischer, 1992: 11; Fischer et al., 1993: 163), whether performance was measured in terms of size, growth or productivity. Reported R-squared values in the Fischer (1992) and Fischer et al. (1993) studies, for instance, ranged from only 0.01 to 0.07.

Likewise, Staber's (1997) analysis of 288 firms in Atlantic Canada did not reveal many significant associations between an owner's education level, years of work experience, or prior business ownership and the growth of his or her firm. Staber thus concluded that: 'Differences in employment outcomes that are often attributed to differential human capital endowments ... may therefore not be generalizable to business performance' (1997: 16).

Cliff and Jennings (2004) reached a very different conclusion based upon their research findings. These findings revealed that, in the case of professional service firms, male and female owners not only possessed equivalent levels of human capital but their firms were similar in size, average revenues and revenues per employee; in contrast, in the case of other privately-held firms, female owners not only possessed lower levels of human capital but their firms were smaller in size, average revenues and revenues per employee. Cliff and Jennings (2004) thus inferred that their results provided empirical support for the continued development and resourcing of programs designed to enhance the human capital of female entrepreneurs. Given the very different conclusions reached by these sets of scholars, further research is obviously needed within Canada to substantiate the human capital argument that equal access to education and work experience opportunities will help eradicate the performance gap between male and female-owned businesses.

The Social Capital of Male and Female Entrepreneurs

Proponents of the social capital perspective believe that the observed performance differential between male and female-headed firms can be partially explained by key differences in the social network structures of male and female entrepreneurs. More specifically, female-headed firms may under-perform relative to male-headed firms because women business owners are not part of the 'right' social networks – they are not as well connected to individuals capable of providing the instrumental resources particularly relevant to business performance (such as information, access and financing).

Staber's (1997) study of 147 male-owned and 141 female-owned firms in Atlantic Canada represents the first effort to investigate some of these arguments in the Canadian context. The findings provide strong support for the existence of gender differences in business owners' social network structures. As anticipated, the women entrepreneurs reported a higher proportion of kin in their discussion networks (24 percent kin for women versus 15 percent kin for men) and were more likely to mention their spouse as their first network affiliate (23 percent of women versus 9 percent of men). Unexpectedly, the women reported a marginally *greater* number of weak ties in their discussion network: that is, their networks were more likely to consist of strangers to one another who might thus be a superior source of non-redundant information and other resources.

In contrast to Staber (1997), Cliff and Jennings (2004) did not find *any* significant differences in the social capital of the male and female business owners in their investigation, regardless of whether these men and women were heading professional service firms or other privately-held companies. These scholars operationalized social capital by an index of social status and social tie indicators, such as memberships in business or professional organizations. These differences in measurement may help explain the discrepant results obtained from the two Canadian studies.

To date, Staber's (1997) study is the only one conducted in Canada that reports explicit tests of the relationship between an entrepreneur's social capital and the performance of male and female-owned firms. The findings are somewhat complex and rather surprising. For example, Staber (1997) found that the proportion of kin in an entrepreneur's discussion network was actually associated with an *increase* in the financial growth of both male-owned and female-owned firms (as well as with an increase in the employment growth of the former). Spousal centrality in an entrepreneur's discussion network, however, was related to financial performance in very different ways for male and female-owned businesses. In the case of male-owned firms, spousal centrality was *negatively* associated with financial and employment growth; in the case of female-owned firms the opposite was the case, with spousal centrality being *positively* related to both of these performance indicators. Network tie strength also operated in different ways for firms headed by men versus women, with weak ties being *positively* associated with employment growth in the former yet *negatively* associated with employment growth in the latter (network tie strength, however, was not associated with the financial growth of either male or female-owned firms). Given this mixed set of findings, which are difficult to interpret from a theoretical standpoint, further research on the performance effects of entrepreneurs' social capital seems warranted.

The Financial Capital of Male and Female Entrepreneurs

Another reason why female-owned firms tend to be smaller and grow less quickly than male-owned firms may be that women entrepreneurs possess less financial capital to invest into their business. Their smaller personal financial investments may, in turn, influence the amount of tangible assets that they are able to secure; as such, they may have less collateral available to obtain the debt financing that is often required for fast-paced expansion (Webber, 2004). Some descriptive evidence exists to support such an argument. Statistics

Canada's 'Survey on Financing of Small and Medium-sized Enterprises' (2000a), for example, found that majority female-owned firms tend to have less than one-half the owner's equity of majority male-owned firms, averaging $58 200 versus $141 746 respectively. Likewise, the same study found that majority female-owned firms tend to have less than one-half the total assets of majority male-owned firms, averaging $269 182 versus $586 922 respectively. Further details on the financing of male-headed and female-headed firms are presented in a later section. The main point here is that female entrepreneurs tend to have less owner's equity invested in their firms than male entrepreneurs.[9]

Gender Differences in Motivations, Goals and Success Criteria

A number of Canadian women's entrepreneurship scholars point to differences in the motivations, goals and success criteria of male and female entrepreneurs as a possible explanation for the observed performance differential between male and female-headed firms (Belcourt et al., 1991; Cliff, 1998; Fischer, 1992; Fischer et al., 1993; Lee-Gosselin and Grisé, 1990; Orser and Hogarth-Scott, 2002; Orser and Riding, 2004). On balance, research conducted within Canada provides an empirical basis for continued work consistent with this argument. Studies by Belcourt (1990); the British Columbia Ministry of Economic Development, Small Business and Trade (1991); HRDC and Statistics Canada (2000); Hughes (2003) and Lee-Gosselin and Grisé (1990), for example, provide interesting insights into women's reasons for pursuing an entrepreneurial career.

Some of these motivating factors are similar to men's. For instance, in analyzing the in-depth interviews conducted with 36 of Canada's most successful female entrepreneurs at the time, Belcourt found that 67 percent cited 'independence and control of their own destinies as the primary motivation for opening their own business' (1990: 437). This was also the most frequently-mentioned motivating factor of the 600 self-employed women surveyed by the British Columbia Ministry of Economic Development, Small Business and Trade (1991). Similarly, 80 percent of the 61 women in Hughes' (2003) Alberta-based study rated this factor as a very important reason for becoming self-employed (this was the third most highly-rated factor, behind the desire for challenging work and a positive work environment). Belcourt noted that a desire for independence and control 'largely support[s] the data emanating from studies of male entrepreneurs' (1990: 437). As noted by Hughes (2004), however, the recent HRDC and Statistics Canada (2000) 'Survey of self-employment in Canada' found that women were much less likely than men to cite independence as their main reason for becoming self-employed, at 24 and 42 percent respectively.

Belcourt (1990) also identified two motivational factors that she considered to be unique to women. First, 45 percent of the successful female entrepreneurs in her study reported that they were impelled to pursue an entrepreneurial career because they were 'unable to fit into the corporate world', with many explicitly citing 'sexual discrimination in pay and promotion policies within organizations' (1990: 437). Second, Belcourt (1990) observed that of the 29 married women in her sample, 45 percent reported that they had started their own businesses because they could not rely upon their husbands for a number of reasons (including chronic under-employment, addictions and abuse). The overarching portrait that emerges from Belcourt's research in particular, then, is one of women turning to entrepreneurship because others – fathers, husbands, workplaces – were 'unwilling or unable to support them' (1990: 437).

Belcourt's (1990) theme of women being pushed into entrepreneurial careers resonates throughout Lee-Gosselin and Grisé's (1990) analysis as well. These scholars, however, identified a somewhat different underlying driver of this 'necessity'. More specifically, their survey findings revealed that many of the 400 women in their Quebec sample had turned to entrepreneurship 'not so much by choice but to adapt to the demands of the parent and spouse/partner roles while also responding to their needs for identity and status' (Lee-Gosselin and Grisé, 1990: 425). As such, these scholars concluded that the phenomenon of women's entrepreneurship 'can be viewed as an innovative response to some sociological constraints' that face women in general (1990: 425).

Hughes' (2003) analysis also highlights the importance of 'push factors' beyond job loss or a lack of job opportunities as motivators of self-employment. In particular, the results of her in-depth interviews revealed that: 'Negative work environments, overly bureaucratic organizations and a lack of independence and decision-making ability' can 'clearly operate as a powerful "push"' (2003: 450). The British Columbia Ministry of Economic Development, Small Business and Trade (1991) study provides corroborating evidence, revealing that many of the women who had turned to self-employment in the province at the time had done so out of frustration with the inflexible work styles of their employing organizations. Interestingly, a flexible schedule, work–family balance and the ability to work from home were deemed very important reasons for becoming self-employed by 63 percent, 41 percent and 35 percent of the women in Hughes' (2003) study. As noted by Hughes (2004), the HRDC and Statistics Canada (2000) 'Survey of self-employment in Canada' revealed that women were much more likely than men to cite work–family balance and flexible hours as their main reasons for becoming self-employed.

Although the specific factors either pulling or pushing women into entrepreneurship are diverse – and may be subject to debate (Hughes, 2003) – one striking similarity across the five above-noted studies is the relative silence regarding such motivations as the desire for financial gain or the pursuit of identified market opportunities. Such factors were mentioned by only 9 percent and 8 percent, respectively, of the 600 women surveyed in the British Columbia Ministry of Economic Development, Small Business and Trade (1991) study. Likewise, in Hughes' (2003) study, only 32 percent of the women surveyed rated 'better income' as a very important reason for becoming self-employed (this reason ranked 9th out of the 13 motivating factors presented). Women's lack of emphasis on financial gain and the pursuit of identified market opportunities is particularly noteworthy given the implicit assumption of such motivations in many theoretical models of entrepreneurial processes and decision-making.

In sum, then, some Canadian evidence exists to suggest that women are motivated to become entrepreneurs for reasons both similar to men yet unique to their gender. But do these motivating factors for launching a business venture become manifested in different operating goals and success measures? The findings presented thus far certainly seem to suggest that personal criteria would figure more prominently than financial criteria in women's measures of entrepreneurial success. Lee-Gosselin and Grisé (1990), however, found the opposite to be the case. When asked what criteria they used to assess their success as entrepreneurs, the three most frequently-cited measures included increasing revenue, increasing profits and attaining an adequate income level: only 7 percent of the 400 women surveyed mentioned personal success criteria (Lee-Gosselin and Grisé, 1990). Lee-Gosselin and Grisé (1990) noted that these findings seemed contradictory not only to the findings from these women's accounts of why they had started their own business, but also to the qualitative findings that emerged from their in-depth interviews with 75 of the women. During these interviews, personal objectives were once again prevalent. In attempting to reconcile the discrepant quantitative and qualitative findings, Lee-Gosselin and Grisé (1990) speculated that perhaps the survey respondents did not feel free to express personal success criteria to researchers associated with a business school because they were concerned about presenting themselves as credible businesspeople.

Lee-Gosselin and Grisé's (1990) 'social desirability bias' explanation may also help reconcile the contradictory results reported by Fischer and her colleagues (Fischer, 1992; Fischer et al., 1993), which were based on studies conducted in the early 1990s, with those reported by Cliff (1998) and Orser and Riding (2004), which were conducted in the late 1990s and early 2000s. Fischer (1992) found very few gender differences in the importance attached to financial, lifestyle and social/recognition goals by 156 retail establishment owners and 216 service firm owners: the only significant difference was that the female service firm owners attached greater importance to lifestyle goals (such as achieving work–family balance, spending more time on leisure activities and avoiding stress) than their male counterparts. Moreover, in the full dataset of 506 business owners in the manufacturing, retail and service sectors across Canada, Fischer et al. (1993) found that female entrepreneurs actually reported a *higher* emphasis on financial goals than male entrepreneurs.

In contrast, Cliff (1998) found that in her sample of 141 male business owners and 88 female business owners, the women were significantly *less* likely to report measures of business size and growth as success criteria: almost one-third of the men (32 percent) but only one-fifth of the women (20 percent) mentioned such criteria as sales level, number of customers, number of employees, market share or business growth. Most recently, Orser and Riding (2004) found that the 107 female business owners in their study valued success criteria associated with work–life balance and personal fulfillment significantly more highly than the 219 male business owners, with work–life balance being the most highly-rated success measure for these women. Moreover, Orser and Riding (2004) found no significant gender differences in the value that entrepreneurs attached to financial outcomes as indicators of success.

Overall, then, empirical research does seem to suggest that the motivations, goals and success measures of male and female entrepreneurs in Canada do differ in some important ways. But to what extent do these differences impact the decision-making of entrepreneurs and the performance of their firms? This question is far from resolved in the Canadian context. Although Orser (2004) reported that business owners' success criteria were related to their growth intentions, with those rating financial outcomes more highly being more likely to indicate that they wished to grow their business and those rating work–family balance more highly being less likely to do so, she has not yet investigated the consequent implications for firm performance. Hughes (2003) observed an association between women's motivations for becoming self-employed and their satisfaction with various outcomes, with those being pushed into being self-employed by job loss or a lack of job opportunities being much less satisfied with their level of personal income, job security and ability to save for retirement. However, she did not report any correlations between the motivating factors and any objective financial indicators. Fischer et al. (1993) examined the direct effect of entrepreneurs' financial goal emphasis on numerous indicators of firm performance, but observed only limited effects. Further research is thus clearly needed to disentangle the direct and indirect effects – if any – of gender differences in business owners' motivations, goals and success criteria on the performance of their firms.

The Strategic Choices of Male and Female Entrepreneurs

The strategic decisions made by male and female entrepreneurs may also help account for the discrepancy in the relative performance of their firms. The fundamental decision of which industry to enter is likely to be particularly influential. As with women's employment in general, evidence of industry segregation is clear and unsurprising. Although data indicate that the fastest growing industries for women's self-employment between 1991 and 2001 included management services, at 140 percent, educational services, at 120 percent, and professional/scientific/technical, at 105 percent (Hughes, 2004), female-headed firms in Canada are still highly clustered in the service and retail/wholesale industries. According to a recent report, nearly half – 49 percent – of service sector businesses are women-owned, as are 30 percent of retail/wholesale trade businesses, 27 percent of finance/insurance businesses, 24 percent of agriculture businesses and only 21 percent of manufacturing businesses (Industry Canada, 2002b: 9).

Although certainly a contributing factor, some research indicates that women's tendency to establish service and retail/wholesale businesses cannot fully account for the comparatively poorer performance of their firms. When Fischer (1992) and Fischer et al. (1993) conducted within-industry comparisons of male-headed and female-headed firms, they still found an overall pattern of sex-based differences in performance. Moreover, Staber (1997) found that the industry in which a male or female-owned firm operated was rarely related to its financial or employment growth. Most recently, Cliff and Jennings (2004) reported that several of the performance differentials between privately-held male- and female-controlled firms in the manufacturing, retail/wholesale and personal/business services industries remained even after controlling for the effects of industry.

Interestingly, however, Cliff and Jennings (2004) research also revealed that male- and female-controlled firms in the *professional* services sector exhibited *no* significant differences in performance, as measured by average revenues and revenues per professional. This finding holds promise for the 31 percent of knowledge-based firms that are apparently now at least 50 percent owned by women (Industry Canada, 2002a: 15). Taken together, Cliff and Jennings' (2004) results suggest that the environment in which male and female-headed firms are operating should not be dismissed as an unimportant determinant of differences in their performance: in certain environments, the sex-based performance differential may actually disappear completely. Moreover, as will be discussed in the following section, other research indicates that industry plays a key role in the financing of Canadian SMEs.

One other strategic difference is worth mentioning at this point: the lower exporting rates of women-owned businesses. In the year 2000, 13 percent of majority male-owned firms while only 7 percent of majority women-owned firms engaged in exporting (Statistics Canada, 2000a). This may be partially a function of firm size and industry. As noted by Riding (2004), however, existing research indicates that the costs associated with developing foreign markets, a lack of knowledge about such markets, and a lack of understanding regarding customs, duties and border taxes deter many business owners from exporting. A lack of time, production capacity and qualified personnel may further inhibit women-owned businesses in particular from engaging in export activities (Fischer and Reuber, 2004). Further research is needed on the relationship between exporting and the smaller size and slower growth of firms headed by women in Canada.

THE FINANCING OF MALE- AND FEMALE-OWNED BUSINESSES IN CANADA: ARE THERE ANY DIFFERENCES?

It is commonly assumed that differences in the financing of male- and female-owned firms can help account for differences in their performance. To help shed some light on this argument, we first present data on how SMEs tend to be financed in Canada. Then, in the 'supply-side' section, we review Canadian studies that have empirically examined the extent to which a business owner's sex influences an SME's ability to secure financial capital relative to other considerations. While some of the findings should come as no surprise, others are quite intriguing.

Start-up Financing

Figure 3.3 presents Statistics Canada data comparing the sources of start-up financing utilized by majority male-owned and majority female-owned SMEs, as summarized in Industry Canada's 'Small business financing profiles – women entrepreneurs' (2004: 6). These findings reveal that both types of firms tend to rely primarily on personal sources of financing to capitalize their firms during the start-up phase. As illustrated in Figure 3.3, during the start-up period very few differences are observable between male- and female-owned firms in the use and importance attached to such financing instruments as: personal savings, personal credit cards and lines of credit, personal loans and loans from family and friends (that is, 'love money'). Commercial loans and lines of credit also represent an important source of start-up financing for SMEs, but less so for female-owned firms than male-owned firms. Moreover, female-owned firms appear to be less likely than male-owned firms to rely on

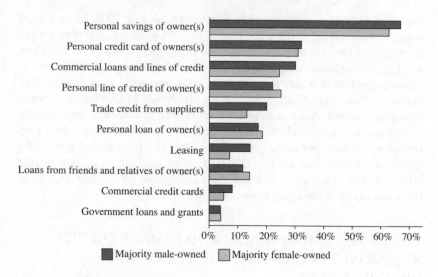

Source: Statistics Canada, 2000a.

Figure 3.3   Top ten sources of financing used during start-up by Canadian SMEs

trade credit, leasing and commercial credit cards as sources of financial capital during start-up.

A number of financing sources are notably absent from Figure 3.3, which suggests that they are much less frequently used by Canadian SMEs in general during the start-up period. These include venture capital, informal angel investments and the public equity accessible through the issuance of an initial public offering (IPO). Unfortunately, we could not find any reported analyses of the Statistics Canada dataset regarding the extent to which majority male-owned and majority female-owned differ in their under-utilization of these financing sources during start-up. According to a 2001 survey conducted by Deloitte & Touche, however, firms headed by women received less than 5 percent of the $4.9 billion of venture capital invested in 818 Canadian enterprises in that year (as reported by the Prime Minister's Task Force on Women Entrepreneurs, 2003). Similarly, Cliff and Jennings (2004) found that of the 140 firms less than nine years old that had issued an IPO on any Canadian stock exchange between 1997 and 2003, only 4 percent were female-controlled (that is, the majority of the top management team members were female or the firm had a female CEO).

On balance, the data presented thus far seem to suggest that women entrepreneurs are less likely to be financed by formal, external sources of capital during the start-up phase than their male counterparts. Cliff and

Jennings' (2004) study provides preliminary corroborating evidence. In their sample of privately-held firms in the GVRD, the female-controlled firms reported starting up with a significantly lower proportion of formal, externally-raised funds than the male-controlled firms, at 5 percent and 11 percent respectively.

Financing Ongoing Operations

Figure 3.4 presents Statistics Canada data comparing the financial instruments utilized by majority male-owned and majority female-owned SMEs to capitalize their ongoing operations, as summarized in Industry Canada's 'Small business financing profiles – women entrepreneurs' (2004: 6). As in the case of start-up financing, some differences between firms headed by men versus women can be observed. For instance, Figure 3.4 illustrates that although both types of firms tend to rely primarily on commercial loans and lines of credit to finance their ongoing operations, majority female-owned firms appear less likely to do so. Firms owned by women also appear less likely to utilize the second and fifth most important sources of ongoing financing utilized by male-owned firms – trade credit and commercial credit cards, respectively. Instead, female-owned firms appear more likely than

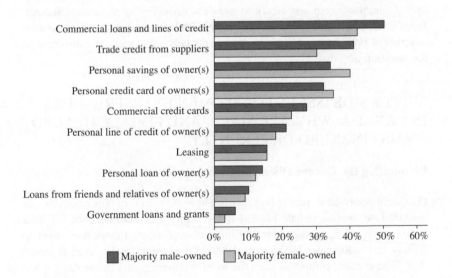

Source: Statistics Canada, 2000a.

Figure 3.4   Top ten sources of financing used for ongoing operations by Canadian SMEs in the year 2000

male-headed firms to finance their ongoing operations through the owners' personal savings and personal credit cards.

On balance, the patterns evident in the Statistics Canada data seem to suggest that women entrepreneurs are less likely to use debt financing for capitalizing the ongoing operations of their firms. Other Statistics Canada data provide preliminary support for this inference: on average, the total liabilities of majority female-owned firms in the year 2000 were less than half those of majority male-owned firms, at $152300 and $351400 respectively (Statistics Canada, 2000a). It should be noted, however, that in the same year, female-owned firms also had less total equity invested in their businesses, averaging only $116882 in comparison with the average of $236622 invested in majority male-owned firms (Statistics Canada, 2000a).

Overall Differences in the Financing of Male and Female-owned Firms

Two observations are worth highlighting at this point as a way of summarizing the preceding material. First, the available evidence does seem to suggest that male and female-owned firms in Canada tend to rely on slightly different mixes of financial instruments to capitalize both their start-up activities and their ongoing operations: during start-up, women business owners appear less likely to utilize financing provided by formal, external sources; for ongoing operations, they seem less likely to use debt financing in particular. Second, firms headed by women appear to operate with less financial capital overall – in terms of both debt and equity – than firms headed by men. We turn now to the question of 'why?'.

SUPPLY-SIDE ISSUES FOR WOMEN ENTREPRENEURS IN CANADA: WHY ARE MALE- AND FEMALE-HEADED FIRMS FINANCED DIFFERENTLY?

Discounting the Gender Discrimination Argument

One commonly-held perception is that the suppliers of financial capital discriminate against female-headed firms, which can help account for their lower levels of financing. Many women entrepreneurs themselves seem to believe this is the case. In the early 1990s, for example, Belcourt et al. noted that: 'The greatest complaint from the women entrepreneurs in our sample had to do with their treatment by financial institutions. About one-quarter reported discrimination by creditors' (1991: 20). Ten years later, a higher proportion of the women than the men in Statistics Canada's 'Survey on financing of small and medium-sized enterprises' (2000a) reported that they had not bothered requesting financing in 2000 – even though they required greater financial capital for their business operations. The women in this study were more likely than the men to provide the following rationales to justify their decision: first, they believed that the application process would be too difficult, and second, they believed that even if they were to apply, they probably wouldn't end up being approved.

To what extent are these perceptions based on fact or fiction? A 1995 study conducted by the Canadian Federation of Independent Business (CFIB) found that firms owned by women were 20 percent more likely to be turned down for financing by banks than firms owned by men (as reported in Industry Canada, 2002b: 9). But is this supposed 'financing double standard' primarily attributable to the business owner's sex or to other characteristics of female-headed firms? This question fuelled a line of very rigorous research conducted by Riding and his colleagues.

In the first of these studies, Riding and Swift (1990) found that, after matching 153 male-owned and female-owned firms on the basis of size, location, age, sector and form of business, no statistically significant differences remained in five out of six terms of credit: rates of loan approvals, co-signature requirements, requirements for loan collateral and interest rates on loans and lines of credit.[10] In the second of these studies, a large-scale investigation of 1891 male and 756 female business owners, Fabowale et al. observed that: 'after accounting for structural differences between male and female business owners, no difference remained in the rate of loan rejections; nor did any differences persist in other objective measures of terms of credit' (1995: 57). These other objective terms included the ratio of the dollar value of loans approved to the total dollar value of loans sought, the requirement of a co-signature and the interest rate on loans. Finally, upon analyzing the bank loan files associated with 835 male-owned and 105 female-owned firms, Haines et al. concluded that: 'The results are very clear. After allowing for size of firm, age of firm and sector, gender is not associated with the size of loan or with the interest rates charged by lenders' (1999: 304). Their data also suggested that 'the demands for collateral are no greater for women' (1999: 304).

This line of research clearly discredits the gender-based discrimination argument, demonstrating instead that 'female-owned firms are more frequently below the threshold of bankability that lenders arguably require of all borrowers' (Haines et al., 1999: 305). Although this may be the case, recent Statistics Canada data reveal that women entrepreneurs are actually *just as likely* (if not slightly more so) to have their requests for financing approved. According to Statistics Canada's 'Survey on financing of small and medium-sized enterprises' (2000a), 82 percent of majority female-owned firms and 80 percent of majority male-owned firms that requested debt financing in that year were approved. Even better, 87 percent of majority female-owned firms but only 70 percent of majority male-owned firms that requested equity financing that year were approved.[11] In addition, the same study found that female applicants were not required to provide more documentation than male applicants, nor were they more likely to have been required to pledge personal assets as collateral. In fact, 23 percent of majority female-owned firms but only 15 percent of majority male-owned firms did not have to provide any documentation whatsoever. As summarized in Figure 3.5, the nationwide study conducted by The Research Institute for SMEs (2002) found a similar set of results.

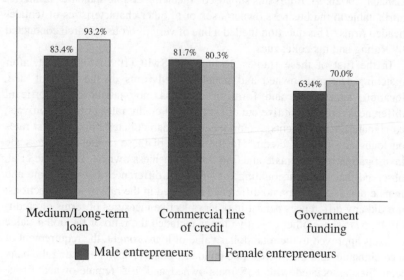

Source: The Research Institute for SMEs, 2002.

Figure 3.5   Proportion of Canadian entrepreneurs' requests for financing approved

Considering the Case for Gendered Preferences in Financial Strategies

If Canadian financial suppliers aren't discriminating against female-headed firms on the basis of their owner's sex, why, on average, do these enterprises tend to operate with relatively lower amounts of debt and equity than male-headed firms (Statistics Canada, 2000a)? Some evidence suggests that differences in the financing preferences of male and female business owners may be playing a role.

For example, the findings presented in Figure 3.6, from the nationwide study conducted by The Research Institute for SMEs, clearly show 'that female entrepreneurs make requests from fewer different external financing sources than their male counterparts, regardless of the type of financing' (2002: 92). Such a conclusion could also be reached by analyzing the results of Statistics Canada's 'Survey on financing of small and medium-sized enterprises' (2000a). The data presented in Figure 3.6 indicate that female entrepreneurs appear to be especially uninterested in approaching external suppliers for *equity* financing. In fact, only 5 percent of the firms in the Research Institute study that had sought equity infusions from informal angel investors (excluding family, friends and employees) during the previous three years were headed by women. Even more striking, absolutely *none* of the firms that had sought equity from either venture capital firms or crown corporations during the same time period were female-owned (The Research Institute for SMEs, 2002: 69).

Given that female-headed firms are just as likely to be approved as male-headed firms when they apply for external financing, why is it that women entrepreneurs are apparently so reluctant to seek this form of capital? We have already discussed one possible reason: the (unfounded) perception that they will be more likely to be turned down because of their sex. Here, we raise two additional possibilities. The first stems from our earlier analysis of gender differences in entrepreneurs' growth orientations. If, as the research on this

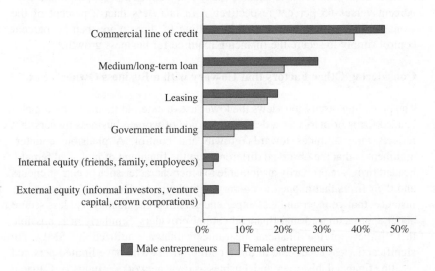

Source: The Research Institute for SMEs, 2002.

Figure 3.6   Proportion of Canadian entrepreneurs requesting various types of financing

topic suggests, women prefer to head more slowly growing firms, perhaps they simply perceive less need for raising large amounts of external financing. Some evidence exists to support such an argument. In the Research Institute study, just over one-fifth of the female entrepreneurs (21 percent) but almost one-third of the male entrepreneurs (32 percent) reported that they would be requesting financing in the upcoming year. Moreover, only 22 percent of the female entrepreneurs (versus 27 percent of the male entrepreneurs) considered insufficient financing an obstacle to business growth (The Research Institute for SMEs, 2002).

A second possible reason why women appear more reluctant to seek external financing also stems from our earlier analysis of entrepreneurs' growth intentions. Cliff's (1998) analysis in particular revealed that female business owners seem more concerned than their male counterparts about maintaining control over their firms. As such, perhaps they are less willing to give up even partial ownership control in exchange for an infusion of external equity. Some of the data collected by The Research Institute for SMEs at the Université du Québec à Trois-Rivières (2002) provide suggestive support for such an argument. Although a larger proportion of the female entrepreneurs than the male entrepreneurs in the study were already equal co-owners of their businesses (45 percent versus 40 percent respectively), of the sole proprietors, a much larger majority of the women than the men expressed an unwillingness to share control in order to finance their firm's expansion (approximately 80 percent versus 65 percent respectively). In fact, less than 2 percent of the women admitted that they would be willing to share more than 50 percent control simply to secure the financing required for business growth.

Considering Other Factors that Co-vary with a Business Owner's Sex

The preceding discussion views the lower use of external financing by female-headed firms primarily as a deliberate choice of women business owners that reflects their attitudes towards growth and control. A plausible counter-argument is that the observed differences in the financing of male and female-headed firms are primarily attributable to other characteristics of entrepreneurs and their firms that happen to co-vary with their sex. One could imagine, for instance, that younger and less experienced entrepreneurs may feel less secure about approaching formal financial capital providers. Similarly, it is possible that '[m]any of the financial instruments that are utilized by SMEs are significantly less accessible to those entrepreneurs who have limited personal wealth, financial histories and business-savvy networks' (Industry Canada, 2002b: 8). These arguments attribute the financing differences to women's lower human, social and personal financial capital rather than to their personal preferences. One could also speculate that the type of firms headed by women

– those that are smaller, slower-growing, service-based and not engaged in export activities – simply have less need to raise external financing.

The multivariate analyses conducted by The Research Institute for SMEs (2002) provide support for this counter-argument. In these analyses, owner sex was not significantly associated with the probability of requesting either short or medium/long-term debt financing when other factors that co-vary with owner sex were entered simultaneously into the statistical models. Rather, the analyses revealed that the firms more likely to request debt financing were those that were: operating in the construction rather than the service sector, larger in size (in terms of both employees and assets), already more in debt, investing more heavily in R&D, and headed by younger entrepreneurs. Similar analyses may be presented in Statistics Canada's 'Survey of the suppliers of business financing' (2000b). Thus, the available evidence suggests that it is factors that co-vary with a business owner's sex (such as industry choice, firm size and owner age), rather than his or her sex per se, that influence the decision to request external financing.

Raising Another Supply-side Puzzle

Our objective for this 'supply-side' section was to present research findings that could help explain the puzzle of why male and female-headed firms in Canada tend to be financed differently. During the process of reviewing these research findings, another puzzle emerged: why are female-headed firms just as likely to have their requests for financing approved (Statistics Canada, 2000a; The Research Institute for SMEs, 2002) even though, on the surface, they don't seem to fit the profile of an 'ideal' investment opportunity? After all, such firms tend to be younger and smaller, tend not to grow as quickly, and tend to be over-represented in the services and retail/wholesale industries. Moreover, female owners tend to be younger, less experienced, and to have invested less of their own equity into their businesses. So why are they just as likely (and sometimes even more likely) to be approved when they request financing?

One possibility may be that financial providers consider female-headed firms to be better investments despite their apparent, more superficial, shortcomings. Earlier, we reported data indicating that the profitability ratios of male and female-headed firms tend to be similar (Fischer, 1992; Fischer et al., 1993; Statistics Canada, 2000a). As such, female-headed firms may be perceived as equally able to meet their financial obligations. Fabowale et al.'s (1995) data are suggestive in this regard. Of the 1899 male and 756 female entrepreneurs surveyed who had applied for credit in the three years prior to the study, very few differences were apparent in the proportion reporting a history of defaulting on a loan. Moreover, the female entrepreneurs appeared somewhat less likely to have a history of exceeding their line of credit limit.[12] Interestingly, Haines et al.'s (1999) analysis of the bank loan files associated with 835 male-owned firms and 105 female-owned firms revealed that the latter were not deemed significantly more risky than the former. In fact, it was the *male*-owned firms that were deemed 'problematic' more frequently than the female-owned firms. Thus, some preliminary Canadian evidence exists to suggest that financial capital providers may actually perceive women entrepreneurs as better clients – as long as they and their firms meet minimum thresholds of creditworthiness in the first place. This intriguing speculation warrants further research within the Canadian context. Statistics Canada's 'Survey of the suppliers of business financing' (2000b) may be illuminating in this regard.

The recent strong financial performance of Canadian banks themselves may also help explain why, at present, female-owned businesses are just as likely as male-owned businesses to have their requests for financing approved despite their structural differences.[13] When their own performance is strong, financial institutions may be more willing to 'take a risk' on investments deemed to be socially important. Given the increased attention paid to the phenomenon of women's entrepreneurship in the late 1990s, female-headed firms may have been specifically targeted as a group deserving of increased access to financing. Statistics Canada's 'Survey of the suppliers of business financing' (2000b) may include data to ascertain the validity of this possible explanation.

THE CANADIAN CONTEXT FOR WOMEN'S ENTREPRENEURSHIP: IS IT SUPPORTIVE?

The Canadian government is very supportive of entrepreneurship in general and of women's entrepreneurship in particular. As noted in Industry Canada 'Presentation to the Prime Minister's task force on women entrepreneurs' (2002a), the country's small business policy agenda is designed to create an entrepreneurial economy that supports the growth of SMEs. This agenda encompasses four types of assistance: 1) financing, 2) management training and advisory services/mentoring, 3) networking and 4) strategic information/ research and analysis. Recently, the Canadian government has cut back on subsidies and has focused instead on providing small businesses with information about market trends, best practices, emerging opportunities and new technologies that can help them better understand their competitive environments.

During the past five years, the Canadian government has demonstrated a particularly strong commitment to investigating the impact of gender on SME growth and development. In June of 1999, the government launched the *SME Financing Data Initiative*, a collaborative data collection and information dissemination project headed by Industry Canada, Statistics Canada and the Department of Finance. As part of this initiative, Industry Canada commissioned reports on the barriers to financing faced by women entrepreneurs (for example, Heidrick and Johnson, 2002; Heidrick and Nicol, 2002) as well as nationwide empirical research on the financing of SMEs that specifically included data on female ownership (for example, The Research Institute for SMEs, 2002; Statistics Canada, 2000a, 2001). Industry Canada presented many of its preliminary gender-related findings to the Prime Minister's Task Force on Women Entrepreneurs (see below) in December of 2002, and released its specialized report, 'Small business financing profiles – women entrepreneurs', in November of 2004.

In November of 2002, 'the Prime Minister of Canada announced the creation of the first Prime Minister's Task Force on Women Entrepreneurs to provide advice on how the federal government can enhance the contribution of women entrepreneurs to the Canadian economy' (Prime Minister's Task Force on Women Entrepreneurs, 2003: 27). This task force consulted with 'thousands of women entrepreneurs across Canada, their organizations, and other interested stakeholders including officials from government departments and agencies, financial institutions, non-governmental organizations, and leading academics' (Prime Minister's Task Force on Women Entrepreneurs, 2003: 1). In October of 2003, just one year after its inception, the task force presented its report and recommendations to the Canadian parliament, in the meantime gaining recognition as 'a best practice internationally' (Prime Minister's Task Force on Women Entrepreneurs, 2003: 134).

Recognizing the importance of sustaining the momentum that currently exists about women's entrepreneurship in Canada, Industry Canada and the Eric Sprott School of Business at Carleton University co-chaired an Economic Forum on Women Entrepreneurs in October of 2004. Held in the nation's capital, this forum brought together academics, policy-makers and members of advocacy groups from across the country. A summary report of the deliberations and resultant policy recommendations, entitled 'Sustaining the momentum: an economic forum on women entrepreneurs', was released in March 2005 (Industry Canada, 2005).

In addition to these data collection and information dissemination initiatives, a variety of organizations exist across Canada that provide financing, training, networking and advisory services specifically for women entrepreneurs. Details can be found in the report prepared by the Prime Minister's Task Force on Women Entrepreneurs (2003). In sum, the Canadian government is clearly dedicated to fostering women's entrepreneurship as a means of attaining the Prime Minister's objective of making Canada 'one of the most innovative countries in the world by 2010' (Prime Minister's Task Force on Women Entrepreneurs, 2003: 1).

PRIORITIES FOR THE FUTURE

The progress made by women entrepreneurs in Canada over the past 30 years is undeniable. So too is the contribution made by Canadian researchers to our understanding of these women and their firms, as is the Canadian government's commitment to creating an environment that facilitates their success. But there is still more work to do. For academics, there are puzzles to be solved. For policy-makers, there are recommendations to be prioritized. And for the entrepreneurs themselves, there are important signs of progress to be acknowledged, embraced and built upon.

Priorities for Academics

In our view, one of the most important near-term priorities for academics is to solve the puzzle of why female-headed firms tend to be smaller and grow more slowly than male-headed firms. As indicated in this chapter, scholars have accumulated a solid base of empirical research demonstrating that, for the most part, male and female entrepreneurs *do* differ in some fundamental ways with respect to their: human and social capital; motivations, goals and success criteria; growth orientations; strategic choices and use of financial capital. What we need now are longitudinal studies capable of testing the causal inference that these observed differences actually affect firm-level outcomes, and can thus account for the consistently-reported performance differential between male-headed and female-headed firms. We need to understand which of the plausible factors are the strongest determinants and we need to estimate the combined explanatory power of the entire set of factors. We also need to explore whether the possible determinants differ for male-headed and female-headed firms: it could be, for example, that many of the hypothesized determinants can account for a large proportion of the variation in the performance of male-headed firms but not necessarily for female-headed firms. Such knowledge is critical to the ability of policy-makers to make informed decisions regarding the prioritization of recently-proposed policy initiatives.

Our speculation that the above set of commonly-identified determinants may not account for much of the variation in the performance of female-headed firms underlies our primary mid-term recommendation for scholars of women's entrepreneurship. We need to consider new research paradigms – particularly those more grounded in the realities of female entrepreneurs' everyday experiences. These realities typically involve challenges attributable to the embeddedness of entrepreneurs in two distinct spheres: that of business ownership and that of family membership. In recent conceptual work, for example, we explicate how differences in the work–family interface experiences and coping strategies of male and female entrepreneurs can help account for the observed performance differential between their firms (Cliff and McDougald, under review). For us, then, a top mid-term priority for academic research on women entrepreneurs is to consider theoretical constructs and approaches beyond those that currently dominate mainstream entrepreneurship research.

Finally, we believe that the longer-term success of women's entrepreneurship research rests on much greater attention being paid to the heterogeneity that exists amongst women entrepreneurs (Cliff and Jennings, 2004; Hughes, forthcoming). To date, much of our knowledge derives from comparisons between the 'average' male and female entrepreneur. In order to best help female entrepreneurs, we need to identify and understand any systematic differences *between* them. Otherwise, we risk the danger that our policy initiatives will be based upon a theoretical 'prototypical' female entrepreneur that, in reality, does not capture the essence of many women business owners at all.

Priorities for Policy-makers

In Canada, policy-makers have recently been presented with an extremely comprehensive set of policy recommendations explicated within the 2003 Prime Minister's Task Force Report on Women Entrepreneurs. An equally detailed set of recommendations appears in the 2005 summary report 'Sustaining the momentum: an economic forum on women entrepreneurs'. In our view, the most pressing near-term priority for policy-makers is to prioritize all of these recommendations. To do this, we strongly encourage policy-makers to base their choice (at least partially) on the inferences that can be drawn from the existing body of academic research. For example, some of this research clearly indicates that female entrepreneurs possess very different attitudes towards growth than their male counterparts, due to time constraints, the desire to achieve work–family balance, a wish to remain in control over the operational side of the business and other considerations. As such, we would caution policy-makers against committing large amounts of resources to initiatives that would likely run counter to some of these expressed concerns (such as, for example, a heavy investment in programs designed to increase the proportion of female entrepreneurs engaged in exporting or those designed to provide women with the business skills for managing fast-paced growth).

Above all, then, we would like to see policy-makers make a more concerted effort – in the near, mid and longer term – to tap the wealth of knowledge being produced by academics. To do so effectively might require the creation of a liaison-type job position at the national level, in which an individual is specifically designated to be responsible for such activities as: commissioning (and funding) specific research projects on women's entrepreneurship, soliciting and interpreting the results of non-commissioned studies of women's entrepreneurship, identifying the policy implications contained within academic research (as it cannot be assumed that academics are necessarily trained or motivated to derive such implications), and disseminating the policy implications to the appropriate agents. In sum, we believe that a more concerted exchange of knowledge – possibly attained through the means proposed here – will be of the greatest longer-term benefit to policy-makers (and ultimately female entrepreneurs themselves).

Priorities for Entrepreneurs

As alluded to at the beginning of this final section, in our view the top near-term priority for female entrepreneurs themselves is to acknowledge and embrace the progress that has already occurred. For instance, it is very important that existing (and nascent) women business owners in Canada recognize the very clear evidence that financial providers are *not* discriminating against them because of their sex – and that they may, in fact, have a higher chance of having their request for financing approved in spite of the fact that their firms typically fall short of the criteria established by financial providers. It is also very important for nascent entrepreneurs in particular to recognize the growing number of women who are establishing businesses in non-traditional industries, so that they do not shy away from doing so.

   In the mid to longer term, it is important for female entrepreneurs to sustain and build upon the progress that has already occurred. This will likely be best achieved through more collective efforts in which these women can share experiences and 'best practices' that may be unique to their sex, act as role models for the next generation, build an even stronger presence in the national economy, and thus stimulate further economic and social development. We look forward to sharing the progress made by Canadian women entrepreneurs, policy-makers and academics in the future.

NOTES

*   We would like to acknowledge the helpful comments provided by P. Devereaux Jennings, the research assistance provided by Christina Zschocke, and the financial support provided by a Social Sciences and Humanities Research Council of Canada grant awarded to the first author.

1. The nascent entrepreneurship rate represents the percentage of the adult population (from 18–64 years of age) that actively took part in creating a business in the previous year, owned (or would own) that business in whole or in part, and had not earned a salary from that business in over three months.
2. The new firm rate represents the percentage of the adult population (from 18–64 years of age) that was active in managing a business 42 months of age or less that the individual owned in whole or in part.
3. http://cansim2.statcan.ca.
4. In this chapter, we distinguish between *majority women-owned businesses* (that is, those in which women hold greater than 50 percent ownership) and *women-headed businesses* (that is, those that are led by a woman – such as those with a female CEO – but in which women may or may not hold majority ownership).
5. It should be noted that Staber (1997) found no significant differences in the size of the 147 male-owned and 141 female-owned firms in his Atlantic Canada sample, as measured by number of employees.
6. Cliff (1998) found that although 71 percent of the male business owners but only 63 percent of the female business owners in the GVRD sample possessed prior industry experience, the difference was not statistically significant at $p<0.05$.
7. Cliff (1998) and Cliff et al. (2005) found that although 79 percent of the male business owners but only 73 percent of the female business owners in their GVRD sample possessed prior management experience, the difference was not statistically significant at $p<0.05$.
8. Staber (1997) found that although 28 percent of the male business owners but only 23 percent of the female business owners in his Atlantic Canada sample possessed prior business ownership experience, the difference was not statistically significant at $p<0.05$.
9. As pointed out by one of the reviewers, it should be noted that the value of equity ownership may also be a function of the size of the enterprise. As such, the amount of equity invested may be related as much to the entrepreneur's growth intentions and industry choice as to his or her personal access to financial resources.
10. The only remaining statistically significant difference was the higher collateral required for lines of credit requested by female-headed firms (Riding and Swift, 1990).
11. These differential approval rates for equity financing may partially be explained by differences in the *type* of equity providers typically approached by female-owned and male-owned firms. According to Statistics Canada's 'Survey on financing of small and medium-sized enterprises', in the year 2000 majority female-owned firms were more than three times as likely as male-owned firms to have asked family and friends for equity investments (37 percent versus 11 percent, respectively). Moreover, the same study found that the majority female-owned firms were relatively less likely than the majority male-owned firms to have approached venture capitalists (2 percent versus 9 percent), angel investors (10 percent versus 12 percent) or crown corporations and government institutions (33 percent versus 41 percent) for equity financing.
12. Unfortunately, Fabowale et al. (1995) did not report tests of the statistical significance of the reported differences in the entrepreneurs' histories of defaulting on a loan or exceeding line of credit limits.
13. We would like to thank Dev Jennings for raising this intriguing hypothesis.

REFERENCES

Belcourt, Monica (1990), 'A family portrait of Canada's most successful female entrepreneurs', *Journal of Business Ethics*, **9**(4/5), 435–8.

Belcourt, Monica, R. Burke and H. Lee-Gosselin (1991), 'Women business owners in Canada', Ottawa: Canadian Advisory Council on the Status of Women.

British Columbia Ministry of Economic Development, Small Business and Trade (1991), 'Profile of women business owners in British Columbia'.

Cliff, Jennifer E. (1998), 'Does one size fit all? Exploring the relationship between attitudes towards growth, gender, and business size', *Journal of Business Venturing*, **13**(6), 523–42.

Cliff, Jennifer E. and P.D. Jennings (2004), 'Closing the gap? The relative performance of male-headed and female-headed firms across different capital environments', Ottawa: Presented at Sustaining the Momentum: Economic Forum on Women Entrepreneurs, 27–29 October.

Cliff, Jennifer E., N. Langton and H.E. Aldrich (2005), 'Walking the talk? Gendered rhetoric vs. action in small firms', *Organization Studies*, **26**(1), 61–89.

Cliff, Jennifer E. and M.S. McDougald (under review), 'Work–family interface experiences and strategies: Consequences for entrepreneurship research and practice', under review at the *Academy of Management Review*.

Fabowale, Lola, B. Orser and A. Riding (1995), 'Gender, structural factors, and credit terms between Canadian small businesses and financial institutions', *Entrepreneurship Theory and Practice*, **19**(4), 41–65.

Fischer, Eileen M. (1992), 'Sex differences and small-business performance among Canadian retailers and service providers', *Journal of Small Business and Entrepreneurship*, **9**(4), 2–13.

Fischer, Eileen M. and A.R. Reuber (2004), 'Exporting activities in women-owned firms: A research agenda', Ottawa: Presented at Sustaining the Momentum: Economic Forum on Women Entrepreneurs, 27–29 October.

Fischer, Eileen M., A.R. Reuber and L.S. Dyke (1993), 'A theoretical overview and extension of research on sex, gender, and entrepreneurship', *Journal of Business Venturing*, **8**(2), 151–68.

Haines, George H., Jr, B. Orser and A.L. Riding (1999), 'Myths and realities: An empirical study of banks and the gender of small business clients', *Canadian Journal of Administrative Sciences*, **16**(4), 291–307.

Heidrick, Ted and S. Johnson (2002), 'Financing SMEs in Canada: Barriers faced by women, youth, aboriginal, and minority entrepreneurs in accessing capital – Phase 2 gap analysis and recommendations for further research'. Report commissioned by Industry Canada.

Heidrick, Ted and T. Nicol (2002), 'Financing SMEs in Canada: Barriers faced by women, youth, aboriginal, and minority entrepreneurs in accessing capital – Phase 1 literature review'. Report commissioned by Industry Canada.

HRDC and Statistics Canada (2000), 'Survey of self-employment in Canada'. Available at www.statscanada.ca.

Hughes, Karen D. (1999), 'Gender and self-employment in Canada: Assessing trends and policy implications', *CPRN Study No. W04 Changing Employment Relationship Series*.

Hughes, Karen D. (2003), 'Pushed or pulled? Women's entry into self-employment and small business ownership', *Gender, Work and Organization*, **10**(4), 433–54.

Hughes, Karen D. (2004), 'Women, self-employment and the "new economy": What policy can do', Ottawa: Presented at Sustaining the Momentum: Economic Forum on Women Entrepreneurs, 27–29 October.

Hughes, Karen D. (forthcoming), *Risky Business? Women, Self-Employment and Small Business in Canada*, University of Toronto Press.

Industry Canada (2002a), 'Presentation to the Prime Minister's task force on women entrepreneurs'. Available at www.strategis.ic.gc.ca/fdi.

Industry Canada (2002b), 'SME financing in Canada'. Available at www.strategis.ic.gc.ca/fdi.

Industry Canada (2004), 'Small business financing profiles – women entrepreneurs'. Available at www.strategis.ic.gc.ca/fdi.

Industry Canada (2005), 'Sustaining the momentum: an economic forum on women entrepreneurs – summary report'. Available at www.strategis.ic.gc.ca.

Lee Gosselin, Helène and J. Grisé (1990), 'Are women owner-managers challenging our definitions of entrepreneurship? An in-depth survey', *Journal of Business Ethics*, **9**(4/5), 423–33.

Orser, Barbara (2004), 'Perceptions of success and public policy', Ottawa: Presented at Sustaining the Momentum: Economic Forum on Women Entrepreneurs, 28 October.

Orser, Barbara and S. Hogarth-Scott (2002), 'Opting for growth: Gender dimensions of choosing enterprise development', *Canadian Journal of Administrative Sciences*, **19**(3), 284–300.

Orser, Barbara and A.L. Riding (2004), 'Examining Canadian business owners' perceptions of success', Regina: Presented at the Canadian Council for Small Business and Entrepreneurship Conference.

Prime Minister's Task Force on Women Entrepreneurs (2003), 'Report and recommendations'. Available at www.liberal.parl.gc.ca/entrepreneur.

Ramsay, L. (2002), 'A league of their own', *Globe and Mail*, 29 November.

Riding, Allan L. (2004), 'Gender and SME exporters', Ottawa: Presented at Sustaining the Momentum: Economic Forum on Women Entrepreneurs, 28 October.

Riding, Allan L. and C.S. Swift (1990), 'Women business owners and terms of credit: Some empirical findings of the Canadian experience', *Journal of Business Venturing*, **5**(5), 327–40.

Riverin, Nathaly (2003), 'Global entrepreneurship monitor: 2002 Canadian report'. Available at www.gemconsortium.org.

Staber, Udo (1997), 'Entrepreneurial network structures: Gender differences and performance outcomes', Boston: Presented at the Academy of Management Meetings, 10–13 August.

Statistics Canada (2000a), 'Survey on financing of small and medium-sized enterprises'. Available at www.statscanada.ca.

Statistics Canada (2000b), 'Survey of the suppliers of business financing'. Available at www.statscanada.ca.

The Research Institute for SMEs, Université du Québec à Trois-Rivières (2002), 'Financing SMEs: Satisfaction, access, knowledge and needs', Research report commissioned by Industry Canada.

Webber, Peter (2004), 'Capitalization of women-owned businesses (WOBs)', Ottawa: Presented at Sustaining the Momentum: Economic Forum on Women Entrepreneurs, 27–29 October.

4. State of the art of women's entrepreneurship, access to financing and financing strategies in Denmark

Helle Neergaard, Kent T. Nielsen and John I. Kjeldsen

INTRODUCTION

In the beginning of the 1990s, Danish policies directed towards spawning entrepreneurship were primarily a means to reduce unemployment, among other things through income support to individuals who started a new business (Blenker et al., 2003). However, the political efforts towards increasing entrepreneurship saw a change in the middle of the 1990s and approaching the millennium. There was new emphasis on developing entrepreneurship via education at various levels and stimulating technology transfer from universities to industry. There was added support for knowledge and technology-based entrepreneurship with the establishment of incubator environments, in particular, ICT and biotechnology, and the provision of seed capital in the form of government guaranteed loans (see reports from The Danish Government, 2003a and b). Though not discriminatory, neither were these initiatives proactive in terms of supporting women or minority groups. In Denmark there are no affirmative action initiatives directed towards such groups; politicians apparently perceive that women in particular will not welcome such initiatives. This perception is based on anecdotal research that indicates that women would rather compete on the same terms as men in order not to be stigmatized.

Until the end of the 1990s, very little was known about entrepreneurship in Denmark, with even less attention to the subset of entrepreneurs who are women. Notable exceptions include *Women Entrepreneurs: Now and in the Future* (Nielsen and Kjeldsen, 2000), which focused on elucidating the general pattern of entrepreneurship, and *The Circumstances of Women Entrepreneurs* (Kjeldsen and Nielsen, 2000), which included a section on the demand side of financing women-owned enterprises. Both were commissioned by the Ministry of Economics and Business Affairs as was a study of the supply side that followed a year later, *The Relation of Banks to Women Entrepreneurs* (Sidenius and Bauer, 2002). However, research investigating women's entrepreneurship and ownership of business remains rather sparse, and mostly takes the form of statistical probes that are part of larger government reports on entrepreneurship in general.

This chapter gives an overview of extant knowledge concerning female entrepreneurs in Denmark. The chapter is divided into six sections. The first provides a historical account of statistical data on the situation concerning entrepreneurial activity in general. The second section gives a profile of women's entrepreneurship describing the extent and nature of their entrepreneurship and their growth orientation. The third and fourth sections address the demand- and supply-side issues for women entrepreneurs respectively. The fifth section discusses the institutional issues that may influence women's entrepreneurship. Finally, the sixth section concludes with an overview of the type of research needed in the future.

1. PROFILE OF WOMEN ENTREPRENEURS IN DENMARK AND KEY STATISTICS

The following provides up-to-date statistics on the adult population in Denmark with regard to labour participation rates for both men and women. It also gives gendered information about the number of business owners and provides figures concerning the entrepreneurial activity rates as presented by the Global Entrepreneurship Monitor (GEM).

1.1 Labour Force Overview

In comparison with other European countries, Denmark has the highest labour participation rate in total and the participation of women has increased significantly in the period 1981–2002 (Statistics Bureau Denmark, 2003). Most of the increase took place in the 1980s, however, with a small decline in the 1990s, after which women are again gaining ground. In a European comparison, Denmark is in second place after Sweden with regard to the participation of women (Statistics Bureau Denmark, 2003).

The Danish population in 2004 is divided almost equally between the sexes 50.5 per cent women and 49.5 per cent men (Statbank Denmark). As shown in Table 4.1 below, women also make up almost half of the labour force, but only 25 per cent of the self-employed. Whereas female self-employment as the ratio of women active in the labour market has remained relatively stable, women's share of self-employment has grown. Male self-employment as the ratio of men active in the labour market, on the other hand, has actually decreased substantially over the past 20 years.

Table 4.1   Male and female labour force and self-employment (in 000s)
            1983–2002

Year	Male			Female			Female share of	
	Labour force	Self-employed	Ratio %	Labour force	Self-employed	Ratio %	Labour force %	Self-employed %
1983	1407	221	15.7	1135	46	4.0	44.6	17.1
1984	1410	215	15.3	1130	47	4.2	44.5	17.9
1985	1442	210	14.6	1157	48	4.1	44.5	18.5
1986	1482	206	13.9	1192	49	4.1	44.6	19.3
1987	1499	205	13.7	1222	52	4.3	44.9	20.3
1988	1500	202	13.5	1241	53	4.3	45.3	20.8
1989	1468	196	13.4	1224	53	4.3	45.5	21.3
1990	1454	188	12.9	1219	51	4.2	45.6	21.3
1991	1438	180	12.5	1212	49	4.1	45.7	21.5
1992	1426	187	13.1	1200	54	4.5	45.7	22.4
1993	1412	184	13.1	1198	55	4.6	45.9	23.0
1994	1396	179	12.9	1189	55	4.6	46.0	23.3
1995	1425	172	12.1	1192	52	4.4	45.6	23.2
1996	1444	170	11.8	1205	52	4.3	45.5	23.3
1997	1453	168	11.6	1217	51	4.2	45.6	23.3
1998	1465	162	11.1	1234	50	4.0	45.7	23.4
1999	1475	161	10.9	1263	51	4.0	46.1	23.9
2000	1474	161	10.9	1276	51	4.0	46.4	24.2
2001	1478	159	10.8	1287	51	4.0	46.5	24.4
2002	1477	158	10.7	1298	52	4.0	46.8	24.7
2003	1466	160	10.9	1293	55	4.3	46.9	25.7

Source: Labour Force Statistics Denmark. Bank of Statistics (2003).

In the past two decades women's share of self-employment has grown substantially, primarily because the number of men who have chosen entrepreneurship has declined by 20 per cent while the number of self-employed women has increased by almost 20 per cent. The numbers can be compared over a long period of time because the same method of calculation has been used. Based on a review of this 20-year period, we can see a positive development in female entrepreneurship.

The figures in Table 4.1 do not correspond directly to those provided in the Global Entrepreneurship Monitor because GEM figures are based on survey data from a sample of 2008 Danish adults (Hancock and Bager, 2003), whereas the data provided by the Bank of Statistics are census data, counting the whole population. According to the 2003 report, 1 in 17 Danes were involved in starting a new venture. The total entrepreneurial activity rate amounted to 5.88 (Hancock and Bager, 2003: 43) whereas the total female entrepreneurial activity rate was only 2.87 (male 8.82). In comparison, in the GEM 2000 report, the entrepreneurial activity rate for men was lower, whereas the rate for women has remained constant. However, the most recent GEM report (Bager and Hancock, 2004: 144) reveals that the actual rate of female involvement has risen by 11 per cent in the last year whereas that of men has fallen by 25 per cent, which corresponds more directly to the figures from the Bank of Statistics.

2. PROFILE OF WOMEN'S ENTREPRENEURSHIP IN DENMARK

This section has two subsections. The first focuses on the extent and nature of women's entrepreneurship in Denmark, providing details on the peculiarities and distinguishing characteristics that need to be understood when comparing the entrepreneurial activities of Danish women to those in other countries. The second focuses on entrepreneurs' growth orientations in general and on women's intentions specifically.

2.1 Definitions of a Newly Founded Business and an Entrepreneur

Broadly defined, entrepreneurship involves the creation of a new economic entity that sells a novel product or service, or a product that differs significantly from those hitherto offered in the market (Deakins and Freel, 1999) and an entrepreneur is an individual who creates a new business in the face of risk and uncertainty for the purpose of achieving a profit. However, a number of definitions include the qualifying term 'growth' (see, for example, Zimmerer and Scarborough, 2004). As the following will show, few of the businesses started by Danish women fall into either of these categories. Indeed, most products or services offered by women-owned and led businesses are neither novel, nor do they differ significantly from existing products or services, nor do Danish female entrepreneurs have an explicit purpose to obtain growth (Kjeldsen and Nielsen, 2000).

The figures presented in this chapter are dependent on the definition of both a newly founded business and the term entrepreneur. First, in Denmark, a *newly founded business* is defined as one that has not previously been VAT registered. An additional requirement is that the business needs to have either purchases or sales in the first four quarters of its existence. The latter of these requirements ensures that the businesses included in the statistics as new businesses are actually active businesses and not just pro forma ventures. Second, an *entrepreneur* is defined as a person who establishes a personally owned firm. A personally owned firm may be an own account worker or have employees. Eighty per cent of all new enterprises are personally owned. However, it is necessary to distinguish between being an entrepreneur and being self-employed. Self-employment is often equated with entrepreneurship. However, in Denmark in order to be self-employed an individual has to run a business as the primary occupation. In other words, the Danish definition of an entrepreneur excludes, for example, women who are self-employed as a secondary occupation (for example, consultancy, advisory or educational activity) even if they are VAT registered and have volume in their business.

The major advantage of fine-grained statistics is that a very precise picture of the dynamics and renewal of Danish business conditions can be achieved. The first drawback is connected to merging the individual with the firm and constitutes a particular problem with regard to enterprises operated in company form. It means that a team of entrepreneurs appears in the statistics as one entrepreneur only. Thus, the picture becomes blurred, because one or more individuals in a team of founders may be a woman. Data from the SNE project[1] shows that approximately 5 per cent of the technology-based entrepreneurs were women, but often in joint ownership with men (Christensen et al., 2001). Indeed, five growth ventures in biotech founded in the last decade have a female CEO, who was also a co-founder. Secondly, ventures in industries not covered by the VAT system, especially the health sector (dentists, veterinaries, dieticians etc.) are never registered as new enterprises. This may distort the statistics, because these industries are traditionally dominated by women. Third, ownership does not necessarily equate active involvement in the business, for example, many Danish men who have gone bankrupt have registered a new business in their wife's name, but in reality she is not actively involved in the business. Therefore, it is very difficult to produce a true statistical picture of the situation concerning Danish female entrepreneurs. Finally, just to complicate matters even further, it is almost impossible to compare Danish data on newly established enterprises with data from other nations, because Danish businesses are registered at a much earlier stage in the foundation process than businesses in, for example, the UK and USA.

2.1.1 Defining the female entrepreneur

Because of the differences concerning the statistical definitions of entrepreneurs and self-employed it may be an advantage to focus on the ownership of the enterprise and the factors that influence the establishment of a new enterprise. Hence, Nielsen and Kjeldsen (2000: 13–15) use the generic term of 'new enterprise owner' for an individual who has either established a new enterprise or who has taken over an existing one. On the basis of the statistics on new enterprise owners it is possible to identify six different types of new venture owners:

1. the self-employed entrepreneur;
2. the traditional, self-employed worker;
3. the growth-oriented entrepreneur;
4. the leisure or hobby entrepreneur;
5. the family-owned business, and
6. the networked entrepreneur.

The first type establishes a new venture as her primary occupation and is often an own account worker. In the year of establishment she therefore counts both as entrepreneur and self-employed. Women in this category are concentrated in industries traditionally dominated by women such as retail, hotels and restaurants and services. The second type has taken over and is running an existing company – and is therefore statistically not an entrepreneur. The third type founds a limited company and does not count as an entrepreneur in the Danish statistics because founders of limited companies are registered as salaried employees. The fourth type typically starts a business to generate a second income and are as such VAT-registered. Although these entrepreneurs proliferate, they typically do not figure in the statistics as they generally have a very low level of activity. The fifth type inherits the company, typically from her father. She does not appear in the statistics as an entrepreneur because she is also a salaried employee. Finally there is the networked entrepreneur. These entrepreneurs are typically free agents working from project to project and assignment to assignment. These entrepreneurs are in essence self-employed, own account workers. However, they may form ad hoc partnerships with other free agents.

2.1.2   Profile of Danish women entrepreneurs

According to Boegh Nielsen (2001) Danish women are generally older, and they are more often married than men when they start their own business. The chart below indicates relatively little difference in the percentage of female and male self-employed between over 35 and early retirement. However, if we compare self-employed women with women in general, we see a noticeable difference in the age group of 40–59. Men stay longer in the workforce – self-employed and employed – than women. In knowledge- and technology-based sectors (ICT and biotechnology/health science), the difference is pronounced with an average age of 49.2 years for women compared with 37.1 years for men (Neergaard et al., 2003). Table 4.2 shows the general age distribution of employed as well as the age distribution of entrepreneurs in per cent.

Table 4.2   Total employment and self-employed distributed by age and gender

	Total employment		Self-employed	
	Women %	Men %	Women %	Men %
15–24 years	14.9	14.6	2.1	2.5
25–29 years	11.0	10.7	5.4	5.4
30–34 years	11.9	11.7	9.4	8.4
35–39 years	13.3	12.8	13.0	11.5
40–44 years	12.0	11.2	12.6	11.2
45–49 years	11.7	10.8	13.0	11.1
50–54 years	11.6	10.9	15.1	12.7
55–59 years	9.7	10.2	14.4	13.9
60–66 years	3.0	4.6	8.0	10.8
67+ years	1.0	2.6	6.9	12.5
In figures	1 298 682	1 483 624	51 806	157 647

Source: Bank of Statistics (2002).

Women generally have different explanations for starting their own business depending on whether they start early or later in life: when they are young they start a business because they want to have more flexibility that enables them to spend time with their children; when they are older they do it because the children have grown and they now have the time to devote to their own interests. This seeming paradox can be explained by the choices of business that each group makes. The results from the SNE-study indicate that those starting later in life are founding businesses with a greater technology-content and businesses that cannot be run from the home, whereas those starting from an early age are typically businesses in areas characterized by a lower technology content, for example, hairdressers, cleaners etc. This may partly explain the pattern noted above.

If we look at the family circumstances of the entrepreneurs, it is characteristic that the proportion of singles is about the same as in the population generally, while on the other hand the somewhat older self-employed typically live in couplehood, and the great majority are married. Hence women entrepreneurs are like their employed 'sisters' in the whole population.

In comparison with men, however, fewer women are single when they establish an enterprise, probably because men are relatively younger. In

Table 4.3　*Marital status of entrepreneurs, the total population*
　　　　　(16–66 years), employers and other self-employed 1996

	The total population		Newly started enterprises		Employers		Other self-employed	
	Men	Women	Men	Women	Men	Women	Men	Women
Singles	37	32	36	29	14	24	22	24
Married couples	48	52	42	51	75	63	64	64
Unmarried couples	15	16	22	22	11	13	14	12
Total	100	100	100	100	100	100	100	100

Source:　Kjeldsen and Nielsen (2000).

comparison with individuals who are employers the picture is the opposite: 86 per cent of male employers live in a permanent relationship as opposed to only 76 per cent of all female employers. Although we can surmise why relatively fewer female employers are in a permanent relationship, we do not have any exact knowledge about the reasons for this picture. However, it would be interesting to investigate if 1) women choose career over family or 2) they have been divorced somewhere along the way.

2.2　Growth Orientation

According to an international comparison, the growth rate of newly started ventures in Denmark ranks 7th behind the UK, USA, Belgium, Germany and Portugal (Kjeldsen et al., 2003). Only 1 in 20 start-ups can be categorized as a growth enterprise (minimum annual turnover of DKK 1 million, which has been doubled within the first five years). The growth rate for technology-based ventures is even lower (Neergaard et al., 2003). In comparison, in the US, new ventures grow between three to four times faster (Kjeldsen et al., 2003).

　　According to Koch et al. (2003) Danish entrepreneurs can be divided into four groups with regard to growth:

1.　Businesses with no employees and a very small turnover. These are typically 'part-time entrepreneurs' who want a second income. These businesses do not fulfil the criteria provided above. Some 952, equalling 22 per cent of the businesses in this group created in 1994 survived until 2000.

2.   Businesses with no employees and controlled growth – also termed 'full-
     time' or 'lifestyle entrepreneurs'. In other words being an entrepreneur is
     a lifestyle. These individuals generate enough income to live from and
     their most important motive for starting a new business is the ability to
     decide their own work and living conditions. Some 1807 businesses
     equalling 41 per cent of those founded in 1994 still existed in 2000. Data
     on gender distribution exist but are at present inaccessible.
3.   Those businesses that are 'employers' have had employees for six years
     and nine employees at the most in year 2000. Some 1553 businesses
     founded in 1994 equalling 35 per cent of the entrepreneurs were part of
     the business population in 2000.
4.   The last type of business is characterized by the business having increased
     the number of employees to at least ten between 1994 and 2000. This
     criteria is quite high as only 14.6 per cent of the total number of private
     businesses have 10 employees and above. Therefore, it is possible to
     assume that growth and turnover constitute the driving forces behind this
     type of 'growth-oriented entrepreneur'. However, only 1 per cent or 63 of
     these businesses survived from 1994 till 2000.

If this categorization is compared with the former in section 2.1.1, businesses
belonging under the heading 'self-employed entrepreneurs', 'leisure/hobby
entrepreneurs' and 'networked entrepreneurs' are most likely to be found in
the second group and there are relatively more women among these than men
compared with the other groups (see also Kjeldsen and Nielsen, 2004).
Notably these businesses seem to have the highest survival rate of the four
groups with 41 per cent, whereas the growth-oriented businesses are very poor
survivors indeed. Further, more than 25 per cent of these entrepreneurs are
found in the knowledge-service sector, which is also one of the sectors with
the highest survival rate and highest level of income. However, there is not a
significant gender difference in the survival rates after six years.

   Although no publicly available data exists about the gender distribution of
growth versus no-growth or low-growth businesses, women seem to be less
growth-oriented than men (Nielsen and Kjeldsen, 2000). Studies also show
that women are no less ambitious, although they prioritize the ability to
combine family life and work. Indeed, this is supported by statistical evidence
showing that female entrepreneurs have a higher income than women in
general (Koch et al., 2003).

   Further, recent interviews with a group of female entrepreneurs in the
knowledge-service sector reveal that they do not interpret growth in the
traditional way. They talk about growing through their networks as opposed to
organic growth or other types of growth. The latter involves responsibility
for other people's livelihood, whereas the former avoids this whilst

simultaneously affording the female entrepreneurs significant flexibility. Hence their growth intentions in traditional terms is low, but growing through their networks means that each woman has her own firm, thus keeping the fixed costs low and they pool together individual resources to provide complex project solutions. All members of a network gain a growth in profits, but none has organic growth. The drawback is that such growth does not reflect anywhere in statistics and therefore these businesses are counted as non-growth or low-growth.

3. DEMAND-SIDE ISSUES FOR WOMEN ENTREPRENEURS

The profile of women entrepreneurs would not be complete without addressing the various types of capital that they need in order to start a business. Most theoretical contributions operate with three types of capital: human, social and financial, although other forms of capital may also be included. However, 'capital' is here interpreted as a factor with a value that may be increased by the proactive action of the entrepreneur and needs maintenance in order to provide a rent return, tangible or intangible.

3.1 Financial Capital

On the demand side, one study interviewed self-employed women about their perception of difficulties encountered in obtaining capital and a survey was undertaken comparing the perceptions of men and women (Kjeldsen and Nielsen, 2000). The results of this study show that 25 per cent of the men report difficulties in obtaining the necessary capital compared with only 18 per cent of the women. The amount being sought might, however, be influential, unfortunately there are no statistics to help clarify this. However, the results do reveal that 50 per cent of women who gave up the idea of starting their own business gave difficulties in obtaining the necessary capital as the reason.

Approximately 30 per cent of the entrepreneurs in general used their own savings to start the new business. Nevertheless, for women, problems associated with access to finance seemed more pronounced in industries that were typically male-dominated, such as construction and transportation. Another influential factor was that bankers find the areas in which women want to start a business more risky. Bankers may perceive traditionally male-dominated industries as more risky for women due to the experience component, for example, women may be expected to have insufficient experience in these areas or they may be perceived as being unable to compete on male terms. Further, the areas in which women traditionally choose to start a business are potentially low-growth areas and banks are generally more interested in backing ventures with an export potential (which could be due to the small home market). Enterprises that do not have growth as an explicit objective are not popular with bankers (Kjeldsen and Nielsen, 2000). The implication is that women may be discriminated against because they choose industries and areas in which the growth potential may be limited.

More women entrepreneurs start businesses in areas where the need for investment is low (Kjeldsen and Nielsen, 2000). They often make a small beginning and do not take out huge loans. This may present a problem of under-reporting women's actual use of debt, because only loans over a certain amount are typically referred to the business department of the bank. Lower amounts remain with the private customer department, and more often than not these advisors are unable to provide sufficient guidance on business-related matters.

Further, in the opinion of bankers, women are not good at selling themselves and their ideas. They are often too modest, and they do not negotiate or shop around between banks to get the best deal. On the other hand, women come better prepared than men and in the bankers' view they work at least as hard as men. Further, their goals are more realistic and they tend to have more financial flair and common sense. This represents a paradox, since it should then be easier for women to obtain loans. However, the bank's evaluation of a business proposal often depends on its knowledge of the applicant as a stable payer with a good financial situation (Sidenius and Bauer, 2002) and since women are rarely in charge of the family's finances and have little to do with the bank, this may present an obstacle. Further, smaller bank branches lack employees who possess the capability to assess a business proposal and the personal and professional competencies of the applicant, man or woman (Kjeldsen and Nielsen, 2000). Therefore, they often have rigid guidelines for providing loans for founding a new business.

Interviews undertaken in the demand-side study revealed that many women tend to think that it makes a difference whether it is a man or a woman who steps into the bank (Kjeldsen and Nielsen, 2000). The women interviewed were convinced that if they were men, they would not be put through the wringer in the same way. A woman, they felt, has to prove herself, time and again. She has to earn the banker's (who is most often a man) respect through her success. However, real-time studies need to be undertaken in order to explore whether this constitutes a real obstacle or whether it is merely a perceived one.

Women in general are not disposed to use the various types of public support schemes available. The primary reason is that the majority of these are associated with unemployment assistance and this tends to blot the users.

Thus, social acceptability plays a major role for Danish women and they do not find that it is socially acceptable to be 1) unemployed and 2) receive support from the state. In fact, one study shows that women reject affirmative action concerning financing of new ventures because they feel that such an initiative will stigmatize them in the public domain (Kjeldsen and Nielsen, 2000).

3.2   Social Capital – Women's Networks

Social capital can be defined in a number of ways. The definition used here is based on Baron and Markman (2000) who suggest that it consists of *social networks* (formal and informal ties), *social skills* (interpersonal and communicative ability) and *social identity* (status, identity and reputation).

The findings of studies on social networks all concur that extensive networks are critical for the growth of an entrepreneurial venture because they provide access to a variety of resources held by other actors (Shaw, 1997; Shaw and Conway, 2000). In other words the larger the network, the better access to resources that the entrepreneurs do not possess themselves. However, there are inconsistent findings with regard to whether gender differences exist in the way that networks are built and maintained (Carter, 2000). With a few exceptions little research on gender differences in networking patterns have been carried out in Denmark. A quantitative study of female managers' networks showed that they were less active builders and users of business networks (Waldström, 2003). Further, a qualitative study of self-employed women provided evidence that women did not seem to engage heavily in developing their professional networks since they were very satisfied with their personal network, which generally consists of their husband, extended family and friends (Nielsen and Kjeldsen, 2000). This means that women may encounter a homophily constraint (Ruef et al., 2003) and not obtain the advice necessary to access various types of angel and venture finance or grow their business. Although the women participating in the study were aware that they needed a professional network they found it difficult to find time to network and some described the purposes of networking as 'a sharing of mutual problems, which was impossible to achieve with men'. Nevertheless, as the section on growth reveals, women often use networks in a very different way to achieve the capabilities of a much larger organization by pooling their individual business resources to provide complex project solutions. However, so far no studies have focused on exploring the content, structure and interaction of the networks of entrepreneurial women in Denmark. Based on the results of extant studies, it seems likely that there will be significant differences between the networks of male and female entrepreneurs and that there are also differences between various types of female entrepreneurs depending on, for example, their choice of industry.

The importance of the two other components of social capital, social skills and social identity, needs yet to be explored. The results from the supply-side study cited above suggests that social skills play a role in women's access to financial capital. Further, a recent preliminary study of the importance of women's perception of their identity and role as entrepreneurs shows that if women's identity perception is strongly anchored in their role as entrepreneur the propensity to start and grow a business is greater than if their identity perception is anchored in their role as a wife and mother (Graversen, 2004).

3.3 Human Capital

The number of years, as well as level and type of education, including courses and languages, constitute part of the human capital at the disposal of the entrepreneur. Further, the extent of an individual's experience also influences the stock of human capital. Human capital is likely to increase over time. Therefore, such variables as age tend to influence the amount of human capital an individual possesses.

Human capital is often divided into two categories: general and specific human capital. Different interpretations of the content of these categories exist. Becker (1975) defines experience and education as general capital if it is not specifically related to the business sector and entrepreneurial activity undertaken. Becker's (1975) categorization is explicated in Table 4.4.

Table 4.4   Categorization of elements in human capital

	General	Specific
Education	College, university or business education	Specialist training within a certain area, e.g. textiles, design
Experience	Experience from previous jobs (non-managerial positions)	Previous entrepreneurship and management positions within a specific area

Source: Madsen et al., 2003.

Human capital is thus defined as the total sum of education and experience, general and specific, that an individual possesses.

Women's education is generally at the same or even higher level than men (see Table 4.5), in particular short- and medium-cycle long-term educations, mainly directed at the public teaching, health and care sector (nurses, teachers

Table 4.5   Total employment and self-employed distributed by educational level and gender, 2002

	Total employment		Self-employed	
	Women	Men	Women	Men
Total	1276822	1482486	51267	160796
Basic school and unknown %	30	32	35	36
General upper secondary school %	8	5	5	4
Vocational upper secondary school %	3	2	1	1
Vocational education and training %	34	40	38	43
Short-cycle higher education %	5	4	5	4
Medium-cycle higher education %	16	9	8	5
Bachelor and higher education %	5	8	8	8

Source: Statistics Denmark. Bank of Statistics.

etc.) and recent figures reveal that female entrepreneurs have a higher education than women in general.

Danish women are generally very well educated, indeed, in recent years women have overtaken men in completing further education. In 2001, 94801 women and 80474 men completed further education. However, in the age group in which most entrepreneurs are found only 49 per cent of women had completed a further education. Further, in 1998 women dominated the studies in, for example, law and medicine with as much as 15 per cent and 40 per cent respectively. Table 4.6 shows the type of degree and the number distributed according to gender. The main differences are found in languages and theology, the technical sciences and health. Women are particularly found within pedagogy, language, theology and health sciences, whereas they are under-represented in the technical sciences (for example, engineering). However, women are making headway into the natural sciences, although if the numbers are further broken down, they show that women tend to choose, for example, biology over physics (Statistics Bureau Denmark, 2003). Given the growth in new biotechnology-based ventures this may provide a unique opportunity for women.

A large number of women are found in the health sector; most of these are

Table 4.6   Gender distribution in highest completed education, 2002

	Bachelor level (3 years)		Master level (5 years)		PhD (8 years)	
	Men	Women	Men	Women	Men	Women
Pedagogy	1904[a]	6608[a]	9	30	N/A	N/A
Languages	194	232	725[b]	1626[b]	65[b]	60[b]
Art	45	135	120	106	16	11
Natural sciences	N/A	N/A	663	437	135	83
Social sciences	102	538	1980	1727	80	36
Technical	1467	538	898	340	144	42
Agriculture	23	5	134	156	62	53
Health	212[c]	2761[c]	371	602	145	142

Notes:
[a] Most types of pedagogical education only have a duration of three years.
[b] These figures include theology.
[c] These figures include nurses of whom very few go on to a longer education.

Source: Statistics Denmark. Bank of Statistics.

nurses, but there are now as many women as men who train as medical practitioners and surgeons. Approximately 40 per cent of those who completed a Masters or PhD degree were women, but fewer women generally obtain a PhD degree apart from in languages, art, agriculture and health sciences where numbers are about equal.

The inference is that women's choice of education allows them to establish an enterprise in a broad spectrum of lines of business. However, the industries and sectors in which women are most likely to start their own business generally do not require a very high degree of education, and those that are in self-employment generally have a shorter education. However, as Table 4.6 shows, there are relatively many highly educated, (bachelor and higher education) self-employed women, compared with both men and total employment. This is mainly due to the strong presence of women in, for example, medical, dental and veterinary areas, but more female self-employed have a short further education or vocational training (Statistics Bureau Denmark, 1998). Most women establish a business in the service sector (48 per cent) and most of these are found mainly within knowledge-services (Koch et al., 2003: 72 and 77). These also have the highest income of all female entrepreneurs.

With regard to the second component of human capital, experience, industry-related experience has been found to be one of the most important success factors, as has professional experience (Koch et al., 2003). Some

57 per cent of female entrepreneurs have more than six years' professional experience, which compares favourably with that of male entrepreneurs (63 per cent).

On average, women have a smaller gross annual income than men at the same age and professional stage before starting business (Koch et al., 2003), which may influence their ability to invest their own funds and to access financial capital, for example, bank loans and credits. However, this does not apply to the small group of innovative female entrepreneurs, many of whom have a university degree and a long experience in research (the SNE project). These entrepreneurs generally have no difficulty in procuring financing for their business.

Finally, the number of women in managerial positions is quite low (15 307 out of 63 584 or approximately one-quarter of top management positions are occupied by women). Therefore, women entrepreneurs may be at a disadvantage, lacking general managerial and business administration skills.

3.4 Women's Personal Motives and Goals

The motives for entering into self-employment can be either extrinsic or intrinsic. Extant research has found that women tend to choose to become self-employed primarily for intrinsic reasons, for example, the most important factor to women who have a family is the possibility of being able to obtain a holistic balance between family and work commitments and achieve a greater flexibility in structuring the workday. However, work satisfaction also ranks highly (Kjeldsen and Nielsen, 2000). Although family issues may act as a motivating factor, they may also constitute a hindrance. In Denmark, pregnancy and maternity leave have been major obstacles to running your own business, as, until recently, legislation has prevented the female business owner from deciding how much she wants to be involved with her business during maternity leave. New legislation has, however, relaxed the former rules and female business owners are now allowed to work part-time on their business whilst on maternity leave.[2] Being forced to take time away from an entrepreneurial venture is tantamount to shutting it down. This may partly explain why statistics reveal that women are comparatively older than men when they start their own business. Women may be brought into a situation where the work–family role system reinforces the traditional gender division of labour in the workplace and in the home, even though Denmark has a reputation for being extremely equality-oriented. Another intrinsic motive is that many women have a desire to exploit their creativity to a higher extent than they are able to as employed labour (Kjeldsen and Nielsen, 2000; Moos, 2002).

Extrinsic motives such as a perceived glass ceiling (and poor promotion chances) also play a role for some women. Studies show that Danish women see themselves as better managers, and better at cultivating customer relations and it is more likely that if they perceive these aspects of a business as mismanaged in an existing job then this will motivate them to establish their own business (Moos, 2002). In Denmark today, it is the norm that women earn their own money and some women also mention economic independence as an important motivating factor. Generally, more women than men come from an unemployment situation or from outside the labour force when they start their own business (Kjeldsen and Nielsen, 2000). They often find unemployment to be unacceptable, and therefore choose to start their own business. However, on average only approximately 8 per cent of women and 6 per cent of men come from unemployment into entrepreneurship (Koch et al., 2003). On the other hand, 18 per cent come from outside the workforce into entrepreneurship. Hence, entrepreneurship may act as a catalyst for getting women into the workforce.

A final aspect is that there are more self-employed women in rural areas. The pattern is reversed for self-employed men who are concentrated in the cities. This indicates that it may be easier for rural women to carry out their dual role as wage earners and mothers by working from home, or that they may have fewer alternatives for earning their own money (Koch et al., 2003).

3.5 Strategic Choices

Women tend to establish their own business within those sectors that are traditionally dominated by women, such as retail (typically clothing and art) and services (for example, auditing, cleaning) and when they establish a manufacturing company the dominant industries are textiles and ceramics. Women in these industries are also often characterized by coming from an unemployment situation and their financial basis is generally less stable compared with men. Administration including book-keeping and auditing constitute a heavy workload particularly for small businesses and many women have education and competence within this area. This is shown in the 'Top 12' list in Table 4.7 of industries 'dominated' by women entrepreneurs.

In comparison there are few women in construction, transport and agriculture, which are traditionally male-dominated industries. Table 4.8 shows that the share of women in the different sectors has remained relatively stable from 1997–2002, apart from the financial and business services, in which the number of women has increased by approximately 5 per cent.

Table 4.7   Top 12 list of industries 'dominated' by self-employed women, ranked by women's relative share

1.	Manufacturing of wearing apparel; dressing etc. of fur	78%
2.	Service activities (e.g. hairdressers, sun centres etc.)	75%
3.	Retail sale of clothing, footwear etc.	67%
4.	Manufacturing of glass and ceramic goods etc.	57%
5.	Social institutions etc. for adults	55%
6.	Social institutions etc. for children	53%
7.	Retail sale of pharmaceutical goods, cosmetics art. etc.	52%
8.	Manufacturing of textiles and textile products	50%
9.	Accounting, book-keeping, auditing etc.	43%
10.	Hotels etc.	42%
11.	Medical, dental, veterinary activities etc.	41%
12.	Retail sale in other specialized stores, etc.	40%

Source: Special runs, Statistics Denmark.

Table 4.8   Percentage of self-employed women in various sectors, 1997–2002

	1997	1998	1999	2000	2001	2002
Total women self-employed %	23.3	23.4	23.8	24.2	24.4	24.7
Agriculture, fishing and quarrying %	9.7	9.6	10.5	10.8	10.7	10.8
Manufacturing %	20.9	20.7	20.9	21.0	20.9	20.9
Electricity, gas and water supply %	17.3	14.8	15.2	15.3	15.2	16.9
Construction %	3.3	3.3	4.5	4.5	4.4	4.2
Wholesale and retail; hotels, restaurants %	29.5	30.4	29.9	30.4	29.8	29.9
Transport, post and communication %	8.0	7.8	9.0	9.1	8.7	8.7
Financial and business services %	24.8	24.7	28.0	28.6	28.9	29.2
Public and personal services %	51.0	51.6	52.4	51.5	51.4	51.6
Activity not stated %	54.7	53.1	49.1	46.8	47.5	45.2

Source: Statistics Bureau Denmark, 2003

In general, very few ventures are founded by individuals who have previous employment in the public sector. As twice as many women (628811, which constitutes approximately 50 per cent of all women in employment) as men (317835) work in the public sector, it may not be surprising that the rate of women's entrepreneurship is not as high as that of men (Statistics Bureau Denmark, 2003). Table 4.9 shows women's share of employment distributed in the public and private sectors and the self-employed.

Table 4.9   Women's share of employment distributed by sector, 2000

	Total employment	Public sector	Private sector	Self-employed
Total	46%	69%	36%	24%

Source: Statistics Denmark. Bank of Statistics.

As Table 4.6 shows women are primarily educated in subject areas that result in employment in the public sector. Contrary to other countries in which such tasks as caring for the elderly or children take place either in the home (family-oriented) or in the private sector, in Denmark such provisions are made by the state. Hence, the institutional structure in Denmark may constitute a barrier to women's entrepreneurship within these areas. However, if the public sector starts to be privatized this picture might change (Holmquist and Sundin, 1985).

4.   SUPPLY-SIDE ISSUES FOR WOMEN ENTREPRENEURS IN DENMARK

On the supply side, very little data exists. The only existing study interviewed 15 bank advisors and consultants and conducted a focus group meeting[3] (Sidenius and Bauer, 2002).

For innovative, knowledge- and technology-based female entrepreneurs access to capital generally presents a lesser problem than for female entrepreneurs in traditional industries, as venture capitalists are keen to invest in such enterprises regardless of the gender of the founder. In fact, in some instances the SNE study showed that it was easier for female entrepreneurs to find venture capital than it was for their male counterparts (Neergaard et al., 2003). Some women even reported that they had offers of investment way beyond their immediate capital needs and had to turn away venture capitalists. However, the easy access to finance was also associated with the high education and fine reputation of these women.

These findings should be seen in the light of the fact that Denmark has one of the lowest levels of seed and venture capital investment as a share of GDP among OECD countries (Baygan, 2003) averaging about 0.1 per cent in 1998–2001. Danish venture capital is further primarily focused on investing in relatively new industries, ICT and medical and health-related sectors, sectors in which there are fewer start-ups established by women (approximately 5 per cent) than in more traditional manufacturing and service sectors (approximately 30 per cent).

It is estimated that in 2001, Denmark had around 1700 potential business angels willing to invest on average DKK 1 million per year (Vaekstfonden, 2002). Total annual investments by business angels constituted approximately DKK 1.7 billion, representing some 40 per cent of all venture investments. Further, Christensen (2002) highlighted that small firms in Denmark seemed unaware of financing sources and found the venture market confusing. According to a survey in which 76 questionnaires were returned, representing a response rate of 48.4 per cent, none of the business angels were female (Vaekstfonden, 2002). The Danish Business Angel Network reports that only two of their 200 members are women. There is, however, no data available as to the extent to which women receive angel capital or their experiences with such capital infusion, nor on whether female business angels are more likely to invest in ventures founded by women.

Taking into consideration the young and immature market for seed financing, women's access to risk capital, whether bank financing, business angel, venture or unit trust capital, is indeed very limited.

5. GROWTH OF WOMEN'S ENTREPRENEURSHIP

A number of new initiatives have been instigated by the government. However, so far none of these have been directed towards women. For example, the Bankruptcy Act is being relaxed making it easier to start afresh (The Danish Government, 2003b). Another initiative is going to reduce the administrative burden for new companies in the first three years of their existence. Improved access to financing for service industries may inadvertently be a particular help to women, seeing that many female entrepreneurs are found in the knowledge-service sector. In order to increase the amount of risk capital flowing to small firms, the government has allowed the establishment of SME unit trusts operating under more liberal investment rules (Baygan, 2003). There is currently no knowledge of the pattern of investment by these unit trusts, but since these are also primarily focused on the new industries, the pattern is likely to be the same as that found in venture capital investments.

Further, entrepreneurship is going to be introduced earlier and to a greater extent in the curriculum. A special body is also being set up for local ethnic entrepreneurs, but there is not a similar initiative for women (The Danish Government, 2003a). Most recently, minor local initiatives have been taken to promote entrepreneurship among female academics, particularly within the arts.

Finally, although women's entrepreneurship is supposedly supported by liberal childcare support from when the child is six months old, the lack of flexibility in the public childcare system may influence female entrepreneurship negatively, for example, opening hours are very rigid, and it is impossible to obtain public childcare prior to the baby's sixth month. Further, whilst Danish women are provided with some of the best conditions in the world concerning maternity leave, the fact that they not allowed to work full-time whilst on maternity leave makes it impossible to fulfil a role as entrepreneur (Nielsen and Kjeldsen, 2000). Therefore, a major improvement for women who are business owners would entail that they be allowed more liberal conditions for maternity leave and childcare.

6. FUTURE PERSPECTIVES AND RESEARCH AGENDA

Despite these experiences and earlier reports published by the government, the most recent government report on a future growth strategy takes few of the recommendations from previous studies into account (The Danish Government, 2003a). Further, all entrepreneurs are bundled into one category, even though previous studies show that there are vast differences based on sector and gender.

Danish women are generally very well educated and dominate many university study programmes that were previously male dominated such as medicine. They are also making a fast move into other areas such as engineering and business studies. This presents a challenge for the future, if indeed women are less oriented towards starting their own businesses. Thus, if we are going to promote entrepreneurship among women we need to find out more about what triggers or hinders their entrepreneurial activity. We may make suppositions, but firm evidence is needed if we are to influence policy towards women's entrepreneurship.

The 1999 GEM report revealed that Denmark was the only country where the share of women entrepreneurs was the same in the group of 18–25 year olds and the group of 26–44 year olds (Warhuus and Christensen, 1999). This is particularly interesting in the light of the Danish equal rights policies. Thus, certain socio-cultural factors might be underlying the low participation of women in entrepreneurship and lead to an assumption that by far the most inhibiting factor may indeed be women's own perception of what it entails to be an entrepreneur and how the role as an entrepreneur can interact with the role as wife and mother. This perception may be compounded by several factors: for example, is it possible that the discourse in society concerning the needs of children and how difficult these demands may be to combine with running your own business influences the low number of women entrepreneurs? Indeed, the discourse in the popular media does stress how important it is for a female entrepreneur to, for example, have a supportive husband and the necessity of being extremely organized. Is it possible that women reject the notion of starting a business because they have created a social construction of circumstances associated with entrepreneurship that they wish to avoid? In order to explore these issues further, a comprehensive research project is being initiated. One part of this research project is to establish a database including articles from the printed media over a 20-year period 1985–2005. The aim is to establish whether the discourse on female entrepreneurs has increased in this period, if it has changed, and how it compares with the discourse on male entrepreneurs. The underlying assumption of this project is that the public discourse influences how women perceive entrepreneurship. Therefore, the second part sets out to explore how identity and role construction influence women's career choice as entrepreneurs and business owners. Do women perceive that they have to balance several roles and to which extent do they identify with the identity as an entrepreneur? Which women see themselves first and foremost as entrepreneurs and which prioritize family? The third part of the project sets out to explore women's networking behaviour. International research disagrees whether gender plays a role in the establishment and maintenance of networks. The research proposed takes the view that it is possible that extant research has overlooked certain dimensions and leans towards social support theory in order to produce new insights. Last, but not least, the supply- and demand-side studies undertaken so far have produced contradictory evidence. Therefore, the fourth part of the project introduces real-time studies to test the extent to which female entrepreneurs and business owners encounter credit discrimination based on gender. A research project directed at this issue is in planning stages. In sum, the four parts of the project are supposed to result in evidence concerning women's propensity to start and grow a new business. On a policy level, this information can then be used to start educational initiatives to aid potential and existing female entrepreneurs.

As a final comment, it should be noted that it may be necessary to educate Danish women about the positive sides of affirmative action. In order to introduce equal opportunities and treat individuals in the same way, it is sometimes necessary to treat them differently and give some groups preferential treatment.

NOTES

1. The SNE project (Social Networks and Entrepreneurship) is a longitudinal research project involving more than 100 businesses in the Danish ITC, biotechnology and pharmaceuticals industries, which participated in two surveys (2000 and 2002). All the founders in a subgroup of 24 ventures participated in personal interviews. The results from the project have been reported in a number of conference papers and articles.
2. This information has been obtained from various female entrepreneurs. However, the legislative jungle has made it impossible to verify it.
3. Focus group composition: seven heads of lending departments, two registered accountants, one state-authorized accountant, eight other consultants (one trade promotion officer, one head of corporate department, one industrial promotion officer, two establishment consultants and three entrepreneur consultants).

REFERENCES

Bager, T.E. and Hancock, M. (2004), *Global Entrepreneurship Monitor Denmark 2003*, Boersens Forlag, Copenhagen.
Baron, R.A. and Markman, G.D. (2000), 'Beyond Social Capital: How Social Skills can Enhance Entrepreneurs' Success', *The Academy of Management Executive*, **14**(1), 106–15.
Baygan, G. (2003), *Venture Capital Policies in Denmark*, STI Working Paper Series, OECD.
Becker, G.S. (1975), *Human Capital*, National Bureau of Economic Research, New York.
Blenker, P., Dreisler, P. and Nielsen, K. (2003), 'Promoting Entrepreneurship – Changing Attitude or Behaviour?', *Journal of Small Business and Enterprise Development*, **10**(4), 383–92.
Boegh Nielsen, P. (2001), 'Statistics on Start-Ups and Survival of Women Entrepreneurs: The Danish Experience', in *Women Entrepreneurs in SMES – Realising the Benefits of Globalisation and the Knowledge-based Economy*, OECD, Paris.
Carter, S. (2000), 'Gender and Enterprise', in Carter, S. and Jones-Evans, D. (eds), *Enterprise and Small Business*, Prentice Hall, pp. 166–81.
Christensen, J.L. (2002), *Effects of Venture Capital on Innovation and Growth*, Division of Economic Analysis, Ministry of Economic and Business Affairs.
Christensen, P.V., Neergaard, H., Bollingtoft, A., Fisker, S., Ulhoi, J.P. and Madsen, H. (2001), *Etablering og udvikling af nye innovative virksomheder: erfaringer og udfordringer*, Nyt fra Samfundsvidenskaberne, Copenhagen.
Deakins, D. and Freel, M. (1999), *Entrepreneurship and Small Firms*, McGraw-Hill Education.
Erhvervsfremmestyrelsen (1999), *Gratis Raadgivning 1997–1999*, Danish Ministry of Trade and Industry.
Graversen, A. (2004), *The Influence of Identity and Role Perception on Women's Choice of an Entrepreneurial Career*, Master Thesis, The Aarhus School of Business.
Hancock, M. and Bager, T. (2003), *Global Entepreneurship Monitor Denmark*, Boersens Forlag, Copenhagen.
Holmquist, C. and Sundin, E. (1985), *Kvinnor som foeretagare – Kartlaeggning av Sveriges kvinnliga foeretagare aar 1980* (Report No. 9), Umeaa.

Kjeldsen, J.I. and Nielsen, K.T. (2000), *The Circumstances of Women Entrepreneurs*, Danish Agency for Trade and Industry, Copenhagen.

Kjeldsen, J.I. and Nielsen, K.T. (2004), *Growth Creating Entrepreneurs: What are their Characteristics and Impact, and Can They Be Created?*, in Hancock and Bager (eds), Global Entrepreneurship Monitor: Denmark 2003, Boersens Forlag, Copenhagen.

Kjeldsen, C., Kristensen, M.D. and Rosted, J. (2003), *Et benchmark studie af iværksaetteraktivitet – hvad kan Danmark laere?*, Centre for Economic and Business Research, Ministry of Economic and Business Affairs.

Koch, D., Lundstrøm, B., Andersen, A. and Kjeldsen, C. (2003), *De nye virksomheder – 4. statistiske portræt af ivaerksaettere*, Ministry of Economic and Business Affairs.

Madsen, H., Neergaard, H. and Ulhoi, J.P. (2003), Knowledge-intensive Entepreneurship and Human Capital, *Journal of Small Business and Enterprise Development*, **10**(4), 426–34.

Moos, H. (2002), 'An Analysis of the Competencies of Female Entrepreneurs', Competence House.

Neergaard, H., Fisker, S., Jensen, B., Madsen, H. and Ulhoi, J.P. (2003), *Udvikling og Vaekst i nye Innovative Virksomheder*, Nyt fra Samfundsvidenskaberne, Copenhagen.

Nielsen, K.T. and Kjeldsen, J.I. (2000), *Women Entrepreneurs: Now and in the Future*, Danish Agency for Trade and Industry, Copenhagen.

Ruef, M., Aldrich, H.E. and Carter, N.M. (2003), 'The Structure of Founding Teams: Homophily, Strong Ties and Isolation among U.S. Entrepreneurs', *American Sociological Review*, **68**, 195–222.

Shaw, E. (1997), 'The Real Networks of Small Firms', in Deakins, D., Jennings, P. and Mason, C. (eds), *Small Firms: Entrepreneurship in the 1990s*, Paul Chapman Publishing, London.

Shaw, E. and Conway, S. (2000), 'Networking and the Small Firm', in Carter, S. and Jones-Evans, D. (eds), *Enterprise and Small Business*, Prentice Hall, Harlow.

Sidenius, L. and Bauer, C. (2002), *The Relations of Banks to Women Entrepreneurs*, Danish Agency for Trade and Industry, Copenhagen.

Statistics Bureau Denmark (1998), *Statistical Ten-year Review*.

Statistics Bureau Denmark (2003), *Statistical Ten-year Review*.

The Danish Government (2003a), *Promoting Entrepreneurship: A Plan for Action*, The Ministry of Economic and Business Affairs.

The Danish Government (2003b), *New Ways of Interaction Between Research and Industry – Turning Science into Business*, Ministry of Science Technology and Innovation.

Vaekstfonden (2002), *Business Angels in Denmark*.

Waldström, C. (2003), *Understanding Intra-organizational Relations through Social Network Analysis*, unpublished PhD dissertation, The Aarhus School of Business.

Warhuus, J. and Christensen, P.R. (1999), *Global Entrepreneurship Monitor: Country Report Denmark*, Danish Agency for Development of Industry and Trade.

Zimmerer, T.W. and Scarborough, N.M. (2004), *Essentials of Entrepreneurship and Small Business Management*, Prentice Hall.

5. Women's entrepreneurship in Finland

Anne Kovalainen and Pia Arenius

A. FINLAND LABOR FORCE OVERVIEW

In 2004 the total population of Finland is 5214051, of which 79 percent are older than 18 years of age (US Census International Database, 2004). Of the adult population, 2122805 (52 percent) are women and 1985686 (48 percent) are men. The size of the labor force, that is, people between 15 and 74 years, is 2594000. Of these, 1247000 (48 percent) are women and 1346000 (52 percent) are men. In 2004 there were 301000 employers and own-account workers in Finland, of which 32 percent were women (97000) and 68 percent men (204000) (2004 Labor Force Survey, Statistics Finland). In 2004, the rate of unemployment was 8.8 per cent, having been 9.0 percent one year earlier (Statistics Finland, 2004).

According to the Global Entrepreneurship Monitor (GEM) study, the total entrepreneurial activity (TEA) rate in Finland in 2004 was 4.4 percent compared to 6.9 percent in 2003 (Global Entrepreneurship Monitor (GEM), 2004). The female entrepreneurial activity rate in 2004 was 2.8 percent compared with 5 percent of men (GEM Finland, 2004). Men are more active than women in all age cohorts. The entrepreneurial activity rate of men also peaks earlier than that of women. Men are entrepreneurially most active during the age of 25 years to 34 years, whereas women are entrepreneurially most active during the age of 35 to 44 years.

B. PROFILE OF WOMEN'S ENTREPRENEURSHIP IN FINLAND

Extent and Nature of Women's Entrepreneurship in Finland

The most extensive data on women's entrepreneurship is to be found from employment and labor force statistics in Finland. The business statistics do not currently classify the gender of the business owner, nor do they classify the percentages of and changes in the ownership position according to gender. In the following, the figures are based on the labor force statistics, which classifies the occupational and employment status of an individual according to the register basis and also according to survey data. Those classified as self-employed persons include farmers, small employers, other employers, own-account workers, self-employed persons in liberal professions and other self-employed persons.

According to the Finnish Labor Force Survey, about 32 percent of those 301 000 persons who are classified as self-employed in 2004 were women (Statistics Finland, 2005). The share of women of all entrepreneurs has remained relatively stable over time, while the total number of entrepreneurs has slightly declined during the last decade, the 1990s. The decline in the overall entrepreneurial activity during the 1990s is due to two things prevalent in Finnish society: on the one hand the deep economic recession of the 1990s generally caused a large number of business failures and bankruptcies, and all these processes hindered and delayed the start-up processes of new firms and caused decline in the overall number of active businesses. The recession peaked the number of bankruptcies, which was almost three times higher for three consecutive years in the mid-1990s when compared with figures of today. On the other hand the relatively large share of agriculture in Finnish entrepreneurship, and long-term, structural decline in the number of agricultural businesses, has caused decline that affects the general entrepreneurially active population's figures. If agriculture is excluded from the figures, the curve of decline flattens to some extent. However, today the share of agriculture is only 3.4 percent of the number of all businesses (Statistics Finland, 2004).

Even if Finland has strong historical traditions in general equality issues between genders, being the first country in Europe to give women the right to vote in 1906 and eligibility to stand as candidates in general elections for Parliament that same year, women's participation in entrepreneurship has always been clearly lower than women's participation in the labor force. Finnish women have been active in labor markets, first in agrarian societies because of economic necessity and later on as a 'natural' continuation of the strong cultural pattern of working women. The proportion of women (aged 15–74) of the labor force is currently 50.1 percent whereas the proportion of men is 49.9 percent (Statistics Finland, 2004). For women, the labor force participation rate, which is the proportion of those belonging to the labor force (employed + unemployed) in the population aged 15–74, is 71.2 percent. For men the respective figure is 74.5 percent (Statistics Finland, 2004).

Even before the public subsidized daycare system was universally available in Finland (in the early 1970s), women's labor force participation was already very high, well over 50 percent. When the publicly provided daycare system was introduced, women's labor force participation remained at its high level even for those women who are on maternity leave or on leave with a children's home care allowance scheme, indicating that these women stay in the active labor force and do not withdraw from the labor markets or leave their jobs permanently or even temporarily (Kovalainen, 2003). This refers to a strong working culture for women in Finnish society. When we look at the employment rate (that is, the employment of the age group between 15–64), of the 15 EU countries, Finland ranks as third with the percentage of 65.2 percent for women and 71.1 percent for men (Eurostat, 2002). The age group between 15–64 is important for inspection and gives a fuller picture as the formal retirement age is currently 65, and only a very small fraction of age cohorts over 65 are actively in employment, often only by special arrangement with employers. The unemployment rate for men is 8.7 percent and for women 8.9 percent (Statistics Finland, 2004).

Today in Finland (2004) women comprise 51 percent of the total labor force. When we compare the share of women in entrepreneurship, 32 percent, and the profile, extent and nature of women's entrepreneurship, with women's share of the total labor force, profile, extent and nature of it, and divisions within the labor force according to industries, we find plausible reasons for the relatively low figures for entrepreneurial women, which we will take up later in the chapter.

The overall development of entrepreneurship and division between genders over the last ten-year period can be seen in Table 5.1. The table is based on register data and includes both self-employed persons and assisting family members. The decline in women's share over time is partly due to the decline in the number of women belonging to the category of 'assisting family members' that is, 'unpaid family members who assist in the business activities'.

Table 5.1   Entrepreneurs and assisting family members by gender in Finland, years 1990–2004

Year	Women	Men	Total	% Women
1990	151000	237000	388000	39
1995	114000	211000	325000	35
1998	110000	206000	317000	35
2000	105000	214000	319000	33
2003	103000	201000	304000	34
2004	97000	204000	301000	33

Source: Statistics Finland. Register data.

As in other countries, in Finland, women entrepreneurs are generally invisible in the statistics. Little has been done up until now to increase the presentation of gender-disaggregated statistics on women-owned businesses in Finland, even if the technical possibilities for that have existed. The main problems in generating gendered statistics concerning business activities center around the problems of identifying gender of the business ownership, combining individual-level data and business-level data and creating gendered statistical knowledge also on new business activities and business intentions (see, for example, Kyrö and Torikka, 2002).

The availability of statistical information on women and entrepreneurship in Finland has been addressed in the Finnish Entrepreneurship Project, launched by the government in 2000 and managed by the Ministry of Trade and Industry. In new business activities where women are participating, the formation process and financial structure of these new firms, etc. is not yet fully known, except when women entrepreneurs apply for publicly available support, loan schemes, etc. and their gender becomes noticed. The fragmentary nature of the information on gendered business activities becomes visible when gender-specific issues, such as women's start-up loans is being discussed. Even if information on women-specific loan-systems exists, other forms of government-supported loan schemes do not report on the gender of the owner of those businesses who have received other financial support instruments available for new business start-ups, or investments of other kinds. Therefore, we receive information that might, in general, give a fragmented or even one-sided picture of the women's entrepreneurial activities. Only by using several sources, such as register data, statistical information, survey data and government offices figures can we identify the most prominent features in women's entrepreneurship in Finland.

Growth Orientation of Women Entrepreneurs in Finland

We do not have specific data concerning business activities or the extent or nature of exports or growth, but we can assume from several data sources, that women's business activities are not growth-oriented as such, but that in the sector where business activity is established, the general dynamics within that sector and EU development all play crucial roles in the growth orientation.

Despite the general growth models for businesses offered in the literature, one of the starting points for the growth intentions and possibilities is closely related to the economic sector of the business. Even if the business activities might aim for global growth, the nature and process of, and possibilities for, the growth are very different in services and in the technology-intensive manufacturing sector. While the majority of Finnish women-owned businesses are in the service sector, even in high-tech industries, and most women-owned businesses offer business-related services, it is self-evident that the growth orientation of these companies does not follow the growth model and logic of technological or high-tech companies with global openings. We argue that the strong gender division according to industries thus creates different settings for the growth orientation of men and women. Instead of directing the growth to the global markets, the possibilities for growth in the labor-intensive industries have to be sought from the internal or geographically close markets. The high labor cost differences between Baltic countries (Estonia, Lithuania, Latvia) and Finland have already resulted in the shift of much of the labor-intensive production industry, such as the clothing industry to cheaper labor cost countries, and have thus changed the business ownership structures in Finland as well. The small and medium-sized garment and clothing industries have disappeared from Finland, and several companies have either shifted their production and/or ownership to Baltic States.

C. DEMAND-SIDE ISSUES FOR WOMEN ENTREPRENEURS IN FINLAND

Financing has a key role in giving access and possibilities not only for growth but for the existence and development of women's entrepreneurship. However, financial capital does not alone create entrepreneurial activities, but human and social capital inputs are also needed.

Financial Capital

Traditional bank financing is the most commonly sought source of funding for women entrepreneurs. The private banking system does not formally provide women entrepreneurs with women-only services to meet women customers' needs, but it is assumed that banks target women entrepreneurs as clients as they form growth potential and as indicated by researchers (Hyrsky, 2005), their balance sheets tell convincingly of sound economic basis for business activities.

The rapid growth of the equity markets and specifically in venture capital took place at the end of 1990s and early 2000 globally. In Finland, the comprehensive information on women's access to venture capital and angel investment funding is still lacking. What we know is that in Finland the venture capital industry is well male-dominated with 84 percent of all employees being men (Finnish Venture Capital Association, 2004). From the GEM research, we know that, in addition to traditional venture capital, informal business angel investments also play a major role in business start-ups. According to GEM, 2004 only 2.1 percent of the adult population invest their own capital into other people's businesses. We have no specific data on women's business financing structure, but early research results indicate that in those businesses owned by women, the financial structure of the company is very sound (Hyrsky, 2005). It is possible to analyze this when the register data from taxation officials is combined with company register data, but this form of data is not usually given to individual researchers due to data protection legislation reasons.

Women's comparatively low waged earnings are reported to affect the time it can take to accumulate sufficient financial capital for business start-up (Renzulli et al., 2000). In Finland, women are, on average, paid less than men. When we compare the monthly earnings of employees by sector (private sector, central government, municipalities) earned in Finland in 2002, we find that at municipal level women's earnings are 84 percent of men's earnings, in the private sector women's earnings are 83 percent of men's earnings, while in the government sector, women earn only 81 percent of men's earnings (Statistics Finland, 2004). Thus, in Finland it may also take longer for women to accumulate necessary start-up capital. On the other hand, women tend to start businesses with lower start-up capital than men do (GEM Finland, 2004).

Social Capital

One of the aspects of successful business formation and development during the last few years has been the social capital of the entrepreneur. The elasticity of the term 'social capital' across disciplinary fields has led to a situation where it is used very differently, depending on the context and research purpose in question. What is common to much research is the use of the concept of 'social capital' to refer to a set of norms, networks, institutions and organizations through which access to specific elements such as power, or resources embedded within or available through these elements, is gained (Kovalainen, 2004a). According to Coleman (2000: 23), 'all social relations and social structures facilitate some forms of social capital; actors establish relations purposefully and continue them when they continue to provide benefits'. Coleman introduces social capital into social theory as paralleling the concepts of financial capital, physical capital and human capital – 'but embodied in relations among persons' (2000: 36). The personal networks that are open, and not based on family ties, exemplify the social capital embedded in networks. The elements of social capital: trust, networks and norms create dense and loose constructs, where knowledge as well as enabling contacts are embedded (Kovalainen, 2004a). In business start-up, all these elements can be crucial.

Several studies show that this is also the case for women's businesses (Arenius and Kovalainen, 2006), whether or not they are self-employed, run by women businesses or family businesses, where women have a prominent co-partner role (Kovalainen, 2004b). In order to develop and establish such networks and increase social capital of women entrepreneurs through networking, several associations and activities backed up by government exist. One example is 'Women Entrepreneurship Centers', where locality, specific female-dominated sectors and questions are being dealt with and taken into consideration. These centers are run locally by the Ministry of Trade and Industry. Another example of these activities are mentoring projects, where women entrepreneurs mentor and give tuition to start-up women entrepreneurs. This model is extended beyond the country borders, and exists today as government-funded bilateral collaboration between Finland and Estonia. The creation of social capital can be extended, but as it most often is locally created and renewed, strong local ties seem to be important for women-owned service sector firms.

Is social capital easily measured? We can use several proxies for measuring social capital, such as structure of the networks, network density, reciprocity and forms of trust, and indeed, more detailed knowledge of the workings of social capital in gendered business formation is needed.

Human Capital

Finland is characterized by a very high education level among the population. More than 50 percent of women have a higher-level education degree in higher-level education. In general, women have a higher education level than men in Finland. Only at the doctoral level are men still in the majority (their share is about 60 percent). Women and men dominate different fields in education, and this model of strong gender segregation in the education institutes is later on repeated both in paid employment and in self-employment. The strong segregation of the educational institutions is partly related to the strong role of the welfare state in Finland: the growth in the education system has taken place partly due to the public sector needs. The educational fields related to the strong public sector are teaching, nursing, care and medical occupations, where the expansions of the education system during the 1970s and 1980s did increase possibilities especially for women. Men concentrate on the technical education fields, trade, craft and various industrial and manufacturing education programs. Women are predominant in the humanistic and social science fields, education, nursing, medicine and service-related educational fields.

Today, women in entrepreneurship have a higher level of education in comparison to male entrepreneurs when same-age groups are being compared (Statistics Finland, 2004). The comparison tells us also about segregated positions in the economic arena: even if in business consulting business activities women and men have a similar level of education, this field does not cover the majority of the business activities of women and men. The vast majority of women and men concentrate on business activities other than B-to-B.

Personal Goals

Several research reports in the 1980s and 1990s indicate that women start their businesses later in life on average in comparison to men (Kovalainen, 1995; Holmqvist and Sundin, 1989). The national GEM 2004 research also shows how the age difference exists between genders in entrepreneurial start-up activity (total entrepreneurship activity): women are more interested in entrepreneurial activities later on in their lives, in comparison to men. Reasons for this are manifold: the need to acquire work experience and build networks before the business start-up is crucial especially within the service sector. Personal life situation affects this as well: the research results (Arenius and Kovalainen, 2006) show that for women it is beneficial to be in paid employment as maternity leave benefit is based on salary income. While we know that few entrepreneurs are able to pay a high salary for themselves during the early period of business start-up phase, the start-up phase might be postponed until after the children are born. Entrepreneurial activity may, however, offer greater flexibility to combine family and work responsibilities, in comparison to paid employment in many countries, thus increasing the interest of women to start new businesses once they have children. Being entrepreneurially active may offer the possibility to arrange working hours conveniently for childcare.

Highly educated women still meet obstacles in their careers in larger corporations in Finland, hence being more prone to participate in new firm formation processes to overcome the glass ceiling effect. Also, young women have not benefited from their high educational intellectual capital, in comparison to young men with similar academic degrees. During the 1990s, young highly educated women were prone to be employed only for fixed-term employment contracts, while men of their age and with similar degrees were employed for permanent positions (Järnefelt and Lehto, 2002). Finland appears as a country that does have a gendered nature of corporation recruitment and personnel policy, and at the same time one where formal gender equality is a priority of the national agenda (see, for example, Hearn et al., 2002).

GEM Finland has addressed the issue of gender-based differences in entrepreneurial behavior (for example, Galloway et al., 2002; Arenius and Kovalainen, 2006) in several papers and articles. Arenius and Kovalainen (2005) used logistic regression to estimate structural and personal factors that influence women's participation in new firm formation process. The results show that the factors affecting women's participation in the new firm formation differ across the four Nordic countries, in spite of economic, legal, cultural and societal similarities between the Nordic countries. The most important factor affecting women's participation in new formation is the individual perception of skills referring to an individual's personal ability to reflect and compare her own skills in relation to other people's skills and surrounding business opportunities. The ability to perceive one's own skills requires self-esteem and an ability to put a value on one's own competences. In the Nordic countries, especially in Finland, the positive expectations of the family's future financial situation increase women's participation in new firm formation (Arenius and Kovalainen, 2006). We assume this reflects, contrary to other Nordic countries, a slightly lower standard of living, which puts pressure on family finances. As most of the Finnish household wealth creation and accumulation takes place through house ownership, which is most often funded with bank loans, it is realistic to assume that a positive future for the family's financial situation gives more of a possibility of obtaining new funding for new challenges, such as business start-up.

Strategic Choices

The types of businesses owned by women reflect on the one hand the strong gender division that exists not only in the labor markets but also within the education system. It is therefore of interest to shed some light on the division in the labor markets, not only to be able to understand the entries and exits among women in business ownership, but also the dynamics and future business sectors for women in Finnish society.

As can be seen in Table 5.2, women's employment is concentrated in the service industries, while men's employment is more dispersed over sectors. This as such is not exceptional but seems to follow a global model

Table 5.2   Employed persons by gender and by industry, 2003

Industry	Women	%	Men	%
Agriculture and forestry	38 000	3	83 000	7
Manufacture, construction	143 000	13	478 000	39
Services	954 000	84	662 000	54
Industry unknown	4 000	0	5 000	0
Total	1 138 000	100	1 227 000	100

Source: Statistics Finland, 2004.

of gender segregation, with entrepreneurship being no exception to this pattern.

Historically, women's participation in entrepreneurship has been active, as has women's participation in paid employment: historical studies show the activity of women in sewing, baking and even wholesale in the 18th and early 19th centuries, as widows, taking care of the spouse's business. Women gained economic opportunities that were connected to their home and family tasks: before 1747 women did not have the right to economic activities in Sweden (of which Finland was part at that time), and after that, they were able to run bed and breakfast types of services and sell clothes in cities such as Stockholm (Sweden) and Turku (Finland) (Bladh, 1999). With industrialization in the early part of the 20th century and after World War II, women's entrepreneurship followed to a large extent the production mode of the modern industrialized society: women were active as entrepreneurs within the clothing and textile industries, and with the growth of the standard of living, the service industries grew in importance. There appears to be no great difference between women in self-employment and women in paid employment according to marital status in Finland.

The overall view and sector development on women's self-employment and business activities during 1960 and 1990 is available in Kovalainen (1995), where the notion of women's marginality in business activities is taken up. The entrepreneurial activities are strongly embedded and intertwined in educational and labor market segregation. The sector segregation to men's and women's separate economic arenas is even more strongly present in business ownership than in paid employment. Even new fields of business activities in Finnish society are gender-segregated (Kovalainen, 2003; Kovalainen and Simonen, 1998). The research also reveals the higher threshold for women to enter entrepreneurship in the traditionally male sectors.

It still seems to be predominantly through marriage and family businesses that women gain entry to the very traditional male sectors in the economy, such as the transport business or manufacturing industry. The high level of education for women does not change the situation, as women predominantly acquire their education in fields other than technical and natural science. Women's entry into IT businesses has not been large, but their share in the business-related service sector has grown. The sector division between men and women indicates that women entrepreneurs dominate in 'traditionally female' activities such as personal services, retail trade and restaurants businesses. Women entrepreneurs are active in business sectors where the tradition of women's paid employment and also entrepreneurship is long. In manufacturing industries women-owned companies are active in textiles, clothing and food products industries. Overall, men have clear dominance in manufacturing and construction businesses, as well as in the transport, financial and rental industrial sectors. New entries in the service sector, such as new businesses within care (social care and health care), are women-dominated, and this field of business is inevitably breaking new ground for women-owned and run businesses (Kovalainen, 2004b). Traditional personal services with relatively low human capital investments into education and low investments in the start-up phase, such as hairdressing, beauty therapy, etc. are dominated by women. New entries and innovative business ideas in the personal service sector are found, but the overall impact, durability of and width of these businesses is largely dependent on the economic development in general. Estate agencies, legal services and these types of personal services that require high human and social capital are relatively equally divided between genders, while men dominate in specific fields (for example, legal services for consumers), women have gained entry within these fields of businesses through education and the relatively low start-up capital needed.

Table 5.3   Sector division of entrepreneurs, by gender, 2002

	Women (%)	Men (%)
Primary production	34.6	33.3
Construction	1.1	12.6
Manufacturing	5.5	8.7
Transport, incl. IT	2.0	10.7
Hotels and restaurants	4.8	1.7
Business services	8.2	8.3
Education, health care	8.8	2.2
Retail trade	12.7	13.3
Other personal services	15.5	4.4
Other	6.8	4.8
	100.0	*100.0*

Source: Statistics Finland, 2004.

As Table 5.3 indicates, the sector division in the share of women and men respectively reveals the gender segregation that offers less sector openings for women and gives a more even picture of men's entrepreneurial activities in Finland. When looking at individual sectors, this picture gets blurred, as we find new innovative businesses started by women in traditional male sectors and vice versa. It is therefore of importance to give the overall sector division, even if the businesses do not always follow the sector division, especially when more knowledge-intensive businesses are being classified under one sector only. As a schematic overall picture, however, Table 5.3 is indicative.

D. SUPPLY-SIDE ISSUES FOR WOMEN ENTREPRENEURS IN FINLAND

The sectoral segregation of business activities has called for specific actions of support to enhance women's interest in business activities. One of these actions of support is the supply side of finance, in the form of targeted funding instruments for women entrepreneurs, but also other forms of supply-side support are available. One is a government-funded loan scheme for women entrepreneurs, another is the mentoring program for new business start-ups by women, also funded and enabled by the government.

In 1997 the Finnish government launched a targeted loan scheme for women entrepreneurs, as one instrument for women-specific needs in entrepreneurial activities. The key aim was to increase access to financial services for those women entrepreneurs with low income from business activities. Hokkanen et al. (1998) examined the bank shopping patterns and loan characteristics of 74 female-owned and 62 male-owned business service companies. The study found little difference between male and female entrepreneurs in terms of banking practices, and this most probably has remained the same. This tells us about the relative equality between genders in economic terms and activities.

The loan scheme offered by the Finnish government for women entrepreneurs is targeted at enterprises in which women are majority shareholders and which are managed and run by a woman. This form of lending extends to start-ups as well as already operating businesses. The size of the company is defined as one employing a maximum of five persons. Loans are granted for investments in machinery and equipment relating to an enterprise's business. Funding is also granted for working capital requirements, expansion phase and company development phase. This loan scheme is sometimes combined with start-up money, which is granted by the Ministry of Labor, on the grounds of unemployment and business start-up. A loan for women entrepreneurs is available to a maximum of 35000 euros for a five-year period. Normal business analysis is carried out to judge whether the business has potential for profitable activities. The evaluations take into consideration the competitive situation in various economic sectors and compare the activities according to, for example, local demand–supply situations. The loan scheme is a very popular one, and has a success rate (fully paid-back loans) of close to 99 percent.

E. GROWTH OF WOMEN'S ENTREPRENEURSHIP EMBEDDED IN FINLAND

Does the educational background of women restrict available business opportunities?

Women are either the majority or equal in educational areas such as medical, nursing and social services, nursery and elementary teaching, personal service-related fields, humanities and arts, and social sciences, business and law. Most of these educational fields are geared towards public sector paid employment. Close to 90 percent of those graduated within the field of education are women, and close to 75 percent of humanities and arts graduates are women. Over or close to 60 percent of graduates are women also within the health and welfare fields of education, services, as well as in social sciences, business and law faculties. Women also start their businesses in these areas. In 1993, 76 percent of all women-owned business operated in these areas. These areas are far from being opportunity poor. The health and welfare sector has been forecast to be the major source of business in the future. Within engineering, manufacturing and construction, only 22 percent of university graduates are women. Therefore, the figures of the sector division of entrepreneurs by gender are no surprise (Table 5.3).

Are women lacking entrepreneurial role models?

Social learning can occur through the observation of behavior of others, often referred to as role models. Analysis of the GEM data has shown that knowing someone who has started a new business during the past two years is positively and significantly related to being a nascent entrepreneur (Arenius and Minniti, 2005). The GEM surveys in Finland have revealed that women have less immediate role models than men have. Almost 54 percent of the male respondents personally knew someone that had started a business in the past two years. Only 42 percent of the women reported similarly (GEM Finland, 2004). Perhaps the mentoring projects, where women entrepreneurs mentor and give tuition to start-up women entrepreneurs, should be enlarged to a wider public.

How to increase women's earnings from self-employment

Being an entrepreneur does not, on average, pay off in Finland. In Finland, for self-employed women who have been self-employed for seven years, their earnings are approximately 7 percent less in comparison to their prior earnings, that is, in paid employment (Hyrkkänen, 2003). The possible explanations for this can be partly found from the strong sector division between genders, which causes the segregation of the business activities as well, resulting in the concentration of women into relatively lower productive services; the heavy taxation structure that raises the price of the labor-intensive services and results thus in the decline in the demand of the consumptions of various services.

How to lower the perceived barriers to women's entrepreneurial activities
Vesalainen et al. (1999) found that on average women find the obstacles for starting a business of one's own higher than men do. In the GEM 2001 study, 37 percent of women reported that fear of failure prevents them from starting a business compared with 25 percent of men. The difference between men and women is statistically highly significant in the GEM 2001 Finnish data. Both studies report on perceptual variables, which are powerful predictors of entrepreneurial activity (Arenius and Minniti, 2005). Perceptional variables do change over time, but to alter the way in which individuals think about themselves and their entrepreneurial career takes a long time. In the long run, increased information flows, targeted programs and increased general interest towards entrepreneurship may contribute towards lower perceived barriers.

F. PROGNOSIS FOR THE FUTURE

It is evident that the structural changes, such as changes in the educational gender division, or the changes in the public services, taxation, etc., take a long time. These changes would most probably bring in a major shift in the present gender division of entrepreneurial activities in Finland, and increase the general level of entrepreneurship in society. However, these structural changes are not to be seen within a short-term perspective, and they would most probably also include major shifts in the economic structure of Finnish society in general.

In Finland, one of the important issues in increasing women's entrepreneurial activities is the question of funding possibilities. Even if the lack of funding or resources might not be a problem as such, women's access to finance might be hampered by the fact that many women-owned firms are either micro-enterprises or small businesses in the service sector. As many of the government programs target high-tech and high-growth industries – as wishes for both wealth and job creation are high – women-owned businesses may be indirectly suffering from this one-sided policy emphasis.

It is most probable that we come to see slight and steady growth of women-owned and women-run businesses in the future Finland. While no dramatic changes or structural shifts are to be expected, the increased information flows, targeted programs and increased general interest towards entrepreneurship continue to promote gender awareness in economic issues, and entrepreneurship is one of the most crucial of them.

REFERENCES

Arenius, P. and A. Kovalainen (2006), 'Similarities and differences across the factors associated with women's self-employment preference in the Nordic countries', *International Small Business Journal*, **24**(1).

Arenius, P. and M. Minniti (2005), 'Perceptual variables and nascent entrepreneurship', *Small Business Economics*, **24**(3), 233–47.

Bladh, C. (1999), 'Women and family structure in late 18th-century Stockholm', in M. Hietala and N. Larsson (eds), *Women in Towns. Studia historica*, Finnish Historical Society, Stockholm.

Coleman, J. (2000), 'Social capital in the creation of human capital', in E. Lesser (ed.), *Knowledge and Social Capital: Foundations and Applications*, Woburn, MA: Butterworth Heinemann, pp. 17–41.

Eurostat (2002), *The Life of Women and Men in Europe*.

Finnish Venture Capital Association (2004), *The Finnish Venture Capital Association*, available at: http://www.altassets.com/pdfs/FVCA04.pdf (accessed 3 September 2005).

Galloway, L., W. Brown and P. Arenius (2002), 'Gender-based differences in entrepreneurial behavior: A comparative examination of Scotland and Finland', *The International Journal of Entrepreneurship and Innovation*, **3**(2), 109–20.

GEM Finland (2004), unpublished press release of the key results of GEM 2004 data in Finland, GEM Team Finland.

Hearn, J., A. Kovalainen and T. Tallberg (2002), *Gender Divisions and Gender Policies in Top Finnish Corporations*, Swedish School of Economics and Business Administration, Helsinki.

Hokkanen, P., A. Lumme and E. Autio (1998), 'Gender-based differences in bank shopping and credit terms', Babson-Kauffman Conference in Research in Entrepreneurship, Gent, Belgium, 20–23 May.

Holmquist, C. and E. Sundin (1989), *Kvinnor som företagare – osynlighet, mångfald, anpassning – en studie' (Women as Entrepreneurs – Invisibility, Multidimensionality, Coping)*, Liber, Malmö.

Hyrkkänen, R. (2003), *Uusien yrittäjien työtulon kehitys*, Eläketurvakeskus, Helsinki.

Hyrsky, K. (2005), 'Oral information on forthcoming report on the assets and liabilities of women owned businesses in Finland', Ministry of Trade and Industry.

Järnefelt, N. and A.-M. Lehto (2002), *Työhulluja vai hulluja töitä. Tutkimus kiirekokemuksista työpaikoilla*, Tilastokeskus, Helsinki.

Kovalainen, A. (1995), *At the Margins of the Economy. Women's Self-Employment in Finland 1960-1990*, Ashgate, Avebury.

Kovalainen, A. and L. Simonen (1998), 'Neo-entrepreneurship in Finland in welfare services', *Transfer*, **4**(3), 462–90.

Kovalainen, A. (2003), 'Finland', in L. Walter (ed.), *The Greenwood Encyclopedia of Women's Issues Worldwide. Part Europe*, Greenwood Press. Westport, CT and London, pp. 189–204.

Kovalainen, A. (2004a), 'Rethinking the revival of social capital and trust in social theory: Possibilities for feminist analysis', in Barbara L. Marshall and Anne Witz (eds), *Engendering the Social. Feminist Encounters with Sociological Theory*, Open University Press, pp. 155–70.

Kovalainen, A. (2004b), 'Yrittäjyyden sukupuolen mukaiset jaot 2000-luvulla' (in Finnish only: 'Gender divisions in self-employment and business ownership in 2000'), in *Hyvinvointikatsaus (Welfare Review)*.

Kyrö, P. and J. Torikka (2002), 'Naisyrittäjyyden tiedonkeruun kehittäminen. Jyväskylän yliopisto', Jyväskylä.
Renzulli, L.A., H. Aldrich and J. Moody (2000), 'Family matters: Gender, networks and entrepreneurial outcomes', *Social Forces*, **79**, 523–46.
Statistics Finland (2002), *Labour Force Survey*, http://www.stat.fi/index_en.html (accessed 15 February 2005).
Statistics Finland (2004), www.stat.fi. Published and unpublished statistical data (accessed 15 February 2005).
Statistics Finland (2005), www.stat.fi. Published and unpublished statistical data (accessed 10 December 2005).
US Census International Database (2004), http:www.census.gov/cgi-bin/ipc/idbsum.pl?cty=F1 (accessed 3 September 2005).
Vesalainen, J., T. Pihkala and T. Jokinen (1999), Yrittäjyyspotentiaali Varkaudessa sekä Kotkan', Haminan ja Tampereen seutukunnissa. Vaasan yliopisto, johtamisen laitos, 11/99 (in Finnish).

6. Women's entrepreneurship in Germany: progress in a still traditional environment

Friederike Welter

A. INTRODUCTION: ENTREPRENEURSHIP IN GERMANY

Whilst support policies for small and medium-sized enterprises (SMEs) have a long tradition in Germany going back to the 1950s, the late 1990s saw a particular concentration on start-ups in an attempt to push new businesses and create new employment possibilities. Both federal and the state governments initiated a number of new approaches to support new and existing enterprises and entrepreneurship from the mid-1990s onwards, without this initiative losing its momentum after the elections in September 1998, which ended the 13-year government of the Christian Democratic Union (CDU) and Chancellor Kohl. On the whole, women have gained in importance in the overall labor force and their share increased during the 1990s. However, women still account for less than half of the total workforce. Current statistical data for mid-2003 show the numbers of women and men in the overall workforce amounting to 16 176 millions (44.7 percent) and 19 996 millions (55.3 percent) respectively.

Despite the ongoing support focus on new businesses, the late 1990s saw a decrease in business start-ups,[1] mainly due to an overall economic decline. Start-up rates, which reached their highest level with a total number of 531 000 in 1991, have been decreasing more or less continuously since 1998, dropping to 455 000 in 2001, whilst the rates of market exits increased until 1999. Only in 2000 and 2001 the trend was reversed, although business closures in 2001 were still considerably higher compared with the early 1990s. Nowadays, the total entrepreneurial activity rate of the Global Entrepreneurship Monitor, which includes both nascent and young entrepreneurs, amounted to 5.2 percent in 2003, whilst the prevalence rate for the share of nascent entrepreneurs in the German population accounted for 3.4 percent in total and for 2.1 percent for women (Sternberg et al., 2003).

B. WHAT IS KNOWN ABOUT WOMEN'S ENTREPRENEURSHIP IN GERMANY?

As said above, only since the mid-1990s did politics focus more and more on women's entrepreneurship. The Federal Action Program on 'Innovation and employment in the knowledge society of the 21st century' pursues the aim to increase the share of female entrepreneurs in entrepreneurship to 40 percent. This is accompanied by an ongoing subtle shift in support policies for women entrepreneurs (see Welter et al., 2003). The underlying support paradigm on the federal level concentrates more and more on an organization-based support approach. This is aimed at integrating gender-specific support topics not only into support agencies, but also into organizations such as chambers of commerce and business associations, although support policies are slow(er) to adapt.

The increasing importance of women's entrepreneurship is also reflected in a recent upswing regarding systematic studies. The first such project, financed by the Federal Ministry of Education and Research (BMBF) and carried out by the author of this chapter and colleagues (for an overview of results see Leicht and Welter, 2004), analyzed patterns and characteristics of women's entrepreneurship, growth potentials and development trends for the past ten years (Fehrenbach, 2004; Fehrenbach and Leicht, 2002; Fehrenbach and Lauxen-Ulbrich, 2002; Lauxen-Ulbrich and Leicht, 2002; Lauxen-Ulbrich and Leicht, 2004) as well as looking at nascent women entrepreneurs, growth intentions, the institutional environment and support policies for women entrepreneurs (Welter, 2002b, 2004a, 2004b; Welter et al., 2003).[2]

Extent and Nature of Women's Entrepreneurship: Gender Boom, but Gender Gap Remains

Women's entrepreneurship in Germany is growing, alongside an increasing share in the overall labor force. Today, small entrepreneurs (that is, self-employed businesspersons)[3] account for a total of 3744 million in both West and East Germany, and 28.5 percent are women. Overall, the 1990s have seen an above average increase for women start-ups, although the gender gap remains, and we can still observe differences between West and East Germany.

In West Germany,[4] female entrepreneurship has been rising slowly, but continuously from 757000 (men: 2.55 million) self-employed persons in 1960 to 1.01 million in mid-2003 (men: 2.67 million), representing a growth rate of 33 percent for women and a 'mere' 4.7 percent for men. Most of this growth occurred during the past decade. From 1991–2003, the total West German female labor force (including self-employed persons) grew by 10.7 percent, the male labor force decreased by 6.3 percent, whilst female entrepreneurship increased by nearly 29.6 percent, which is considerably higher compared with the 13.5 percent increase in male entrepreneurship. Nowadays women entrepreneurs account for 6.7 percent of all the West German female labor force and 27.9 percent of all entrepreneurs. On the other hand, women still constitute the majority of all family help in small enterprises.

In East Germany, total female entrepreneurship has increased considerably by 85.7 percent, amounting to 182000 (men: 401000; +60.4 percent) in mid-2003; but this growth started from a very low level with 98000 women entrepreneurs and 250000 male entrepreneurs existing in 1991. However, the positive development of women's entrepreneurship went hand in hand with an overall loss in female wage employment, which decreased by 21.6 percent to 2.7 million. This appears to indicate a push towards entrepreneurship, especially as women were the first to be fired and the last to find new employment after transition started. On the other hand, the share of female entrepreneurs to all entrepreneurs in East Germany has been high since the reunification averaging 28 percent in 1991 and 31 percent in 2003, which can also be attributed to the tradition of a high labor participation of women in the former GDR and not only to their rising unemployment after 1991.

Sectorwise, women entrepreneurs (similar to female wage employees) cluster in trade and services. They are still more likely to enter entrepreneurship in consumer-oriented and personal services such as laundry, cosmetics, hairdressing and personal care (Fehrenbach and Lauxen-Ulbrich, 2002). In 2002, the top four sectors for women entrepreneurs were trade (19.9 percent of female entrepreneurs), personal services (18.2 percent), social and health services (15.5 percent) and business-oriented services (14.9 percent) (Lauxen-Ulbrich and Leicht, 2004). Business-oriented services and trade also rank first (17.9 percent of male entrepreneurs) and second (16.7 percent) respectively for men entrepreneurs, followed by construction (14.0 percent) and manufacturing (11.8 percent). Some female-dominated business fields such as social and health services offer women less possibilities for entering entrepreneurship, obviously due to these fields being dominated by public employers and large organizations (Lauxen-Ulbrich and Leicht, 2004).

With regard to size, statistical data confirms also for Germany, that women entrepreneurs more frequently work without employees, compared with men. Generally, the 1990s observed a trend towards micro-firms, that is, enterprises without any employees (Welter, 2002a), which is even more pronounced for women entrepreneurs. Whilst in 1991 55.1 percent of all women entrepreneurs worked without any employees, compared with 42.2 percent of all men entrepreneurs, in 2003 this share had increased to 61.5 percent for women and 48.7 percent for men respectively.

Could this dominance of micro-enterprises explain differences in characteristics and performance between female and male entrepreneurs? A popular hypothesis in research on women's entrepreneurship states that women enterprises are not only smaller, but they also perform less well than men-owned firms. In this context, Fehrenbach (2004) used panel data from a regular survey on firms with employees (the so-called 'IAB-Betriebspanel')[5] to analyze both firms' characteristics and their performance in more detail. Women-led firms accounted for 9 percent of all employees in owner-led firms, with an average of seven employees compared with 15 in firms led by men or with mixed ownership; less than 5 percent of the women firms, but 12 percent of men firms employ more than 20 employees. Moreover, and partly due to their smaller size, women-led firms have a considerably lower turnover. Forty percent of the women firms, but only 18 percent of the men firms earn less than 128 000 euros per year. Not surprisingly, this is reflected in lower average turnover per year and low investment activities in women firms. The average yearly turnover and investment sums amount to 661 000 euros and 26 000 euros for women entrepreneurs and to 4.9 million euros and 105 000 euros for men respectively. When asked how they assessed their firm's profitability, women entrepreneurs showed less confidence with only one-quarter of the women assessing their profitability as 'very good' or 'good', compared with 35 percent of the men. Again, this differs across enterprise sizes, with the smallest firms showing the worst assessment.

'Dreamers' and 'Doers': Thinking about and Entering Entrepreneurship

What do we know about nascent female entrepreneurs in Germany? These concepts have emerged from recent studies focusing on the business formation process and especially the so-called pre-stages and differentiating between 'dreamers' and 'doers'. A 'dreamer' is interested in entrepreneurship, (s)he might have already perceived a business opportunity without having undertaken any steps to realize the idea. A 'doer' represents the nascent entrepreneur as defined by the Entrepreneurial Research Committee (ERC, nowadays, Panel Study of Entrepreneurial Dynamics/PSED, Reynolds, 1997). (S)He has already taken first steps to realize the business start-up. Other types of would-be entrepreneurs include those persons who abandoned their project or who never got started so far, that is, discontinued (or probably even disappointed) entrepreneurs. Moreover, there is the dormant entrepreneur who temporarily has given up any work on the planned project, or the discouraged/discontinued entrepreneur who made the transition to nascent entrepreneur but gave up completely (Carter et al., 1996).

A gender gap is also apparent when looking at these would-be entrepreneurs, as illustrated by a pilot study researching nascent entrepreneurship in Germany in 1999 (Figure 6.1): 16 percent of all men as

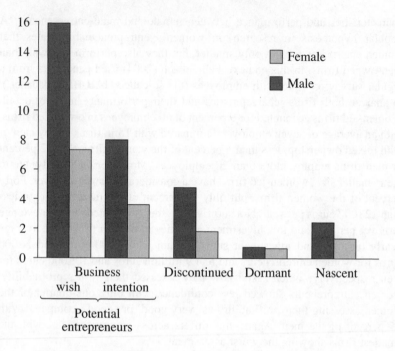

Source: Sample B, Infratest 1999.

Figure 6.1   Would-be entrepreneurs in Germany: gender (in % of population)

compared with only 7 percent of the women were interested in starting their own business, whilst the rate for female nascent entrepreneurs amounted to only 1.3 percent, compared with 2.4 percent for men (Welter et al., 2003).[6] Although the rate of female nascents has increased since, reaching 2.1 percent in 2003, the gender gap remains, as the rate for male nascents was 4.8 percent in the same year (Sternberg et al., 2003).

This raises the question where there are gender differences with respect to who makes the transition from a 'dreamer' to a 'doer'. An analysis for the transition from business wish to nascent entrepreneurship illustrates that German women have a 4 percent lower probability to express a business wish (see Engel and Welter, 2004 for more details). Interestingly, a sensitivity analysis done in the same paper shows that this only applies to West German women, confirming that women employment and consequently entrepreneurship is more accepted in East German society (Welter, 2002a).

Research for Germany also appears to confirm a 'push' hypothesis for women towards entrepreneurship. Unemployment or fears of job loss are considered main push motives for entering entrepreneurship; and push motives play a more important role for unemployed business founders, pull motives such as personal independence or attractive business opportunities for employed ones (Hinz and Jungbauer-Gans, 1999). In a study asking self-employed persons in 1997 for their objectives, nearly two-thirds of the female entrepreneurs would never consider giving up entrepreneurship compared with 57 percent of male entrepreneurs (Welter, 2001a). Although this may partly indicate entrepreneurship as an attractive employment possibility for women, allowing them to balance work and household or family responsibilities (as well as showing learning experiences and growing self-confidence), entering entrepreneurship was often a necessity for those women in order to be able to participate in the labor market, especially after child-rearing periods.

An overall push towards entrepreneurship is confirmed by statistical data. A large share of women who changed or obtained employment in the year 2000 (47 percent, men: 39 percent), were previously unemployed, another 32 percent (men: 21 percent) held a non-wage position, that is, they were studying or at home as a 'housewife' before setting up their venture (Lauxen-Ulbrich and Leicht, 2002: 30). This appears to confirm recent GEM results for Germany, which indicate a higher share of necessity-based female entrepreneurship, compared with men (women: 28 percent, men: 17.4 percent; see Sternberg et al., 2003: 15). Case studies add to this, illustrating that women oftentimes set up their own business when re-entering the labor market after a period of child raising (Welter, 2000c), although there remains doubt whether this reflects genuine 'necessity-based' entrepreneurship, the more so, as concepts such as necessity- and opportunity-based entrepreneurship neglect the fact that most entrepreneurs set up their business for a variety of reasons.

Growth Intentions of Nascent Entrepreneurs

Do women entrepreneurs want to grow their business? At a first glance, results from the pilot study of German nascent entrepreneurs confirm a well-known story, that is, women nascents are less interested in growing their business, whilst male nascents are more inclined to plan for growth (Welter, 2001a, 2001b). When asked for their business aims, 18 percent of male and 28 percent of the female nascents had plans to work on their own without employees, and, regardless of gender, most aimed at moderate employment growth, planning an enterprise with some employees. Less than 7 percent of female nascents, but nearly 25 percent of male nascents intend to have a large enterprise.

This differs when taking into account the education level and current job status (Figure 6.2). Interestingly, higher educated women nascents are more

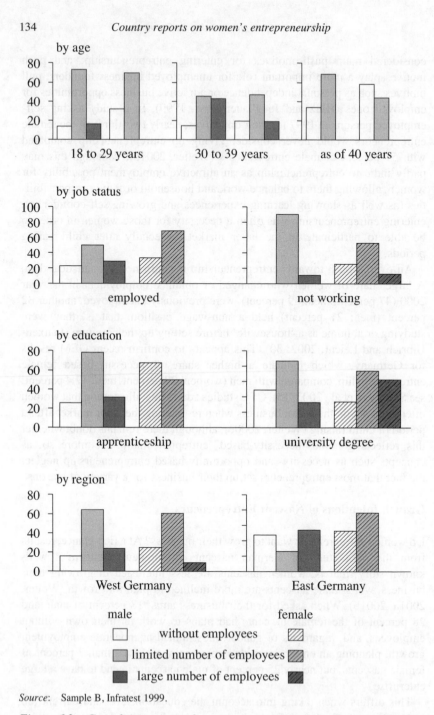

Source: Sample B, Infratest 1999.

Figure 6.2   Growth intentions of nascent entrepreneurs in Germany (in %)

interested in growing their enterprise to a large size, compared with both women with apprenticeship and highly educated male nascents, which might indicate growing confidence going hand in hand with higher qualifications. Growth intentions in terms of limited employment growth are also more pronounced for women nascents starting from wage employment.

Recent GEM results show a similar picture. When asked how many employees their enterprise will have five years after having been set up, 56 percent of the female nascents planned for a firm with one or two employees, whilst 51 percent of the male nascents aimed to have an enterprise with more than six employees (Sternberg et al., 2003: 37). On the other hand, the majority of female entrepreneurs in Germany have micro-enterprises without employees, as shown above.

On the whole, the results from these various studies and statistical sources cannot confirm a popular hypothesis, namely, that women entrepreneurs are less inclined to grow their enterprises, although the picture is a static one, as research on changes in growth intentions is lacking. Instead, the discrepancies between growth aims and growth realization[7] may indicate gender-specific access to external resources (especially capital). Additionally, more women entrepreneurs start a part-time business compared with men, which in general have lower growth potentials. Statistical data show that in 2002 nearly 23 percent and 16 percent of self-employed women worked up to 20 hours and 39 hours respectively, compared with only 5 and 7 percent of the self-employed men (Lauxen-Ulbrich and Leicht, 2003). Finally, the differences between business aims and realized growth might also hint at self-perceived and objective barriers (availability of growth finance) arising during venture creation and business development, preventing women entrepreneurs from realizing their growth plans.

C. DEMAND-SIDE ISSUES FOR WOMEN ENTREPRENEURS IN GERMANY

Human Capital of German Entrepreneurs

Are differences in enterprise characteristics and performance due to differences in human capital of women and men entrepreneurs? This section takes a closer look at empirical evidence with regard to the level of human capital of German entrepreneurs. Older studies for Germany demonstrated a positive influence of human capital on the economic success of new firms and an increase in their probability to survive (Brüderl et al., 1996), whilst Jungbauer-Gans and Preisendörfer (1992) showed that a lower survival rate for women entrepreneurs was also due to their lower level of human capital.

Other studies, cited in Strohmeyer (2004a) and based on the Socio-Economic Panel, a longitudinal household study for Germany, confirmed that a higher qualification of women had a positive effect on their entrance into self-employment.

Nowadays, women entrepreneurs are often highly qualified, which goes hand in hand with a growth in 'non-traditional' business fields and sectors such as consultancy or business-oriented services. Using data from the micro-census,[8] Strohmeyer (2003, 2004a, 2004b) analyzed the influence of human capital on the probability of entering entrepreneurship, asking whether the extent and nature of human capital could explain gender differences in entrepreneurship. The data clearly illustrate the influence of human capital on self-employment and entrepreneurship. The growth in women's entrepreneurship during the 1990s as outlined in the first section can be mainly attributed to the considerable increase in the number of female university graduates entering self-employment (Strohmeyer, 2003). Between 1991 and 2001, this number increased by 114 percent (+147000) and a 'mere' 58 percent (+249000) respectively (Strohmeyer, 2004a). Twenty-seven percent of the women entrepreneurs (and 26 percent of the men entrepreneurs) nowadays have a university degree, compared with 17 percent in 1991. Most of these entrepreneurs create ventures within knowledge-intensive services, which trend can be observed for both women and men. This boom in academic entrepreneurship goes hand in hand with less and less persons starting self-employment without any qualification.

Not surprisingly, self-employment of university graduates is also strongly related to the subject choice, with different subjects offering different opportunities for entrepreneurship and self-employment (Strohmeyer, 2003, 2004b). Interestingly, women studying female-dominated or male-dominated subjects show a lower probability to enter entrepreneurship compared with those who graduated in integrated fields of study. Here, Strohmeyer (2004b) tested whether the gender gap in entrepreneurship would be reduced if female students selected the same subjects as men. His shift-share analysis demonstrated a negative result, confirming an overall lower inclination for women to enter entrepreneurship regardless of their field of study. This result is particularly important in terms of recent policy measure attempting to increase the female share in engineering and science (see Welter et al. 2003).

Finally, Strohmeyer (2004b) showed that women entrepreneurs managed to reach higher 'professional' levels compared with women employees who had graduated in the same subjects. This is interesting in as far as it demonstrates that women's entrepreneurship is obviously one way for highly qualified women to break through the 'glass ceiling' still dominating in wage employment.

Financing a Business in Germany

An enabling environment for women's entrepreneurship includes a gender-neutral access to resources such as capital. Bank financing is by far the most common source to finance a business in Germany (see section on supply side for more details), and when starting, most entrepreneurs, regardless of gender, rely on own savings or informal credits from family. Access to finance has received surprisingly little attention in German research, given the changing conditions for business financing (Basle II accord). An extensive literature review confirms that research analyzing access to financing for small companies in Germany as a rule does not include gender variables. Yearly surveys show smaller and micro-firms experiencing increasing difficulties in accessing external finance, in particular bank credits (for example, Hansmann and Ringle, 2001, 2002; Hansmann et al., 2003; IfM, 2000; KfW, 2001, 2002, 2004). A recent study illustrates that especially the smallest firms complained of difficulties in obtaining short-term (43 percent) and long-term (40 percent) loans, compared with 37 percent and 26 percent of medium-sized companies (Hommel and Schneider, 2003).

However, evidence for a systematic credit rationing by German banks is not conclusive, as studies also show that loan rejections differ across types of banks. Here, recent research indicates a particular restrictive lending policy by the large commercial banks such as Deutsche or Dresdner Bank, which apparently restrict their loan supply regardless of the profitability of the firms and their projects (Nehls and Schmidt, 2003). This goes hand in hand with results of smaller surveys illustrating that new and small entrepreneurs rank savings and smaller banks higher with regard to their credit services (Hölscher et al., 1998).

With regard to women entrepreneurs and access to finance, there are even fewer studies, most of which are based on small regional or local samples (for example, Döbler, 1998; Kehlbeck and Schneider, 1999) or on case study evidence (for example, Janssen and Nienhaus, 2003; Welter, 2000b, 2000c). Most of the results, however, hint at gender-related differences in access to finance. For example, Döbler (1998) cites a study for Baden-Württemberg from 1992, where every fourth out of 59 surveyed women entrepreneurs mentioned difficulties with banks. A large company survey conducted in 2003 did provide gender-specific data on financing problems, but the question whether credit institutions discriminate against women entrepreneurs was not included (IfM, 2003). Here, experts were interviewed, and not surprisingly results show an ambiguous picture. Half of the experts confirmed gender-specific difficulties for women in accessing credits, two experts assessed this as being an attitude problem of single bank officials, and the remaining experts (interestingly all of them regionally concentrated in the larger Munich area) negated any gender discrimination (IfM, 2003: 132–33).

Recent research (Piorkowsky, 2002; Welter, 2002b) analyzed whether the 'classical' financial support programs in Germany discriminated against women entrepreneurs. Female participation rates in mass programs appear to indicate a restricted access to financial support. Female take-up rates (on average 21 percent) are considerably lower than the overall share of female entrepreneurs in Germany (30 percent). Moreover, they have been decreasing over the past years, although the amounts of credits approved within most programs have been rising over the same period (Welter, 2002b). However, lower participation rates for women entrepreneurs do not allow us to generally conclude that these programs discriminate against women entrepreneurs. This would need data on both applications and rejections, which is not available. Interestingly, the program designs reflect an implicit gender discrimination of financial support. According to Kehlbeck and Schneider (1999) and Piorkowsky (2002), programs suitable for female entrepreneurs would need to take into account a small business size, lower credit needs, less guarantees and a higher need for working capital. They should, moreover, ideally allow for applications of part-time entrepreneurs, services and academic professions. Most German programs, even more so those offering capital to high-tech firms, show flaws with respect to one or more of these criteria, thus implicitly restricting the access of women entrepreneurs.

In the late 1990s, micro-credit programs were introduced, namely the 'Startgeld', which offers credits amounting up to 50000 euros, and the 'Mikrokredit', which offers 25000 euro credits for starting and new entrepreneurs (up to three years). Both programs show a higher participation rate for female entrepreneurs. Within the 'Startgeld', it amounts to 36 percent for all of Germany, nearly 43 percent in East and 34 percent in West Germany, demonstrating regional differences in take-up. On the whole, these programs are better suited to providing for women entrepreneurs' financial needs, as they acknowledge the fact that women entrepreneurs need smaller amounts of credits, and/or they frequently start as part-time ventures (Piorkowsky, 2001). A critical point could be that both programs only support temporary part-time entrepreneurship. Moreover, an initial assessment for the Startgeld pointed out higher failure rates (www.enterprising-women.de/docu2002/down/WS percent207percent20Tchouvakhina.ppt), indicating that supported enterprises appear to be undercapitalized.

Kehlbeck and Schneider (1999) found interesting differences in financing strategies, which appear to indicate a gender-specific access of women to external financing, although they rely on a very small sample of 35 women start-ups and 45 men start-ups in Hamburg. Less women entrepreneurs than men approached banks, and they more often (nearly two-thirds, but only slightly more than 50 percent men) felt as petitioners. When preparing for a credit application and a conversation with her bank, women entrepreneurs preferred informal advice, whilst men entrepreneurs mainly used advice from either chambers of commerce, consultants or the support agency for start-ups in Hamburg. Interestingly, more credit applications of men were refused. On the other hand, the majority of surveyed women entrepreneurs implicitly mentioned a restricted access to credit, because they could not find adequate financial support for their business idea and/or their capital needs.

In general, women entrepreneurs tend to apply for smaller credits, compared with men. When starting their venture, women entrepreneurs tended to use their own capital, informal credits from friends and relatives or investments in kind (Kehlbeck and Schneider, 1999). The recent GEM illustrated that a similar share of women (64 percent) and men nascents (66 percent) turn to external sources, although there are differences in the type of sources they approach. Women rely more frequently on informal sources such as family credits (30 percent, men: 21.7 percent), whilst a larger share of men approach banks (50.4 percent, women: 30.8 percent); see Sternberg et al., 2003: 41. Own capital and bank credits are generally the most common forms of financing for German SMEs (Mittelstandsmonitor, 2003). Most small firms named independence (51 percent) and readily available other sources of finance (45 percent) as reasons for not turning to venture capitalists (IfM, 2000).

The 'housebank' relationship is a distinctive characteristic of the German banking and financing system. It is reflected in the fact that most German SMEs rely on one bank for financing their business (and also their personal life). This system goes back to the industrialization in the 19th century. Whilst on the one hand long-term relationships between bank and client facilitate the customer's access to loans (Friderichs et al., 1999; Lindner-Lehmann et al., 1998), there is a danger of restricting access to external finance in those cases where commercial banks take on a negative gatekeeper function, screening out applications.

This might be of particular importance for women entrepreneurs, especially where small enterprises are set up at home, which could constrain their legitimacy towards creditors (Mirchandani, 1999). In this context, Swire (1995, cited in Kehlbeck and Schneider 1999: 10) points out that female entrepreneurs might pursue a rational strategy in not investing in their credit legitimacy if they expect gender-based credit refusals. Moreover, the OECD (2000: 54) draws attention to the fact, that a 'non-traditional thinking' of female entrepreneurs and innovative business ideas play an additional role in restricting their access to external finance: 'Financial intermediaries ... may not have the skills necessary to evaluate innovative business ideas for which there are no benchmark values to use for credit assessment'. In such situations, a financing system based on close relationship banking could involuntarily restrict access to credit.

As stated above, venture capital generally plays a less important role for German entrepreneurs. Where entrepreneurs turn to venture capital, they name growth financing as their major reason (76 percent), followed by preparations for going public (46 percent) (IfM, 2000). However, the same survey also reveals that only a minority of German SMEs (30 percent) have engaged venture capitalists. Moreover, this mainly applies to stockholding companies, which were founded between 1996 and 2000. Here, 40 percent work with venture capital (IfM, 2000: 45). Again, no gender-specific data is available. Taking into account that most women-owned firms are sole proprietorships (for example, 75 percent of women who received start-up support from the former DtA, but only 59 percent of the men, see Tchouvakhina, 2001: 10), we might assume that considerably less women entrepreneurs use venture capital.

Although some of the empirical evidence appears to indicate a restricted access to finance, we cannot deduct systematic gender discrimination by banks and/or other financing institutions. Nevertheless, this poses the important question whether or not a (perceived) lack of financing possibilities has an impact on growth and development of women-owned firms in Germany. Again, empirical evidence is lacking. General survey data show an ambiguous picture. In 1999, less than 15 percent of German SMEs considered access to finance a major business constraint. Empirical data from various other countries suggest that other factors such as a lack of skilled labour might be more important for business performance (Wagenvoort, 2003: 34). However, a survey of European SMEs also indicates that finance constraints might impede innovation, thus acting as an obstacle to growth (Eurostat, 2002).

Social Capital and Women's Entrepreneurship

It is not financing alone, but also access to other resources such as social capital, that have an impact on business development and growth. Many research studies have demonstrated that networks and network contacts are important during the establishment, development and growth of business. With regard to women entrepreneurs, different network structures (for example, less outreaching and more homogeneous networks) and a different networking behavior (for example, a focus on emotional support and less on strategic networking) may influence both the decision to start and to grow a business as well as business survival and success, as women entrepreneurs' networks and their networking tactics might offer less possibilities for access to business-relevant resources. In this context, this section takes a brief look at social capital on the micro-level, discussing the use of and usefulness of women associations and networks for women entrepreneurs. Data come from an online survey of women (nascent) entrepreneurs, which was carried out by Sozialforschungsstelle Dortmund (sfs) and RWI within a research project committed by the Federal Ministry of Economics and Labour (see Welter et al., 2004).

Results of the online survey show that women on average are engaged in 1.7 networks, but most are involved passively (64 percent have no task). The Internet ranks first, when asking where women (nascent) entrepreneurs heard about women associations and networks. This is followed by press media and family and friends for nascent entrepreneurs and other (women) entrepreneurs for established entrepreneurs.

What are the advantages women entrepreneurs themselves see in joining networks and business associations? Two-thirds of the respondents mentioned mutual strengthening of women (entrepreneurs) as the main advantage for networking, whilst 54 percent referred to specific advice, and another 50 percent to the possibilities for mutual exchange with women (entrepreneurs) in similar situations.

More than half of the respondents named reciprocity (give and take) as the most important element in creating a good network, followed by networks restricted to women (45 percent). Network heterogeneity in terms of members' business fields and industries (42 percent) and broad experiences (40 percent) were the third and fourth most important criteria, which, according to the respondents, help create network identity. These results are interesting, as they indicate that women entrepreneurs value both homogeneous and heterogeneous networks, the former in terms of the sex of its members and the latter in terms of business fields across members. Moreover, this differs across early stages of business development, reflecting different needs: contrary to established women entrepreneurs, nascent women entrepreneurs are looking for more homogeneous networks in terms of sector and sex, whilst those interested in starting a venture (that is, being in a very early stage of entrepreneurship) valued networks with a heterogeneous sector membership highest.

In which ways do networks and business associations foster women's entrepreneurship? When asked which role networks play in creating, establishing and growing a business, only 12 percent of the respondents conceded a considerable impact of the network on their decision to set up a business, which is also reflected in the low number of nascent women entrepreneurs participating in the online survey. Networks play a more important role in overcoming difficult stages during business development, thus obviously being able to contribute to the growth of women businesses. Here, 37 percent concede a large role and 24 percent a minor role for networks. The same applies to expanding into new business fields, where 31 percent of the respondents see a large impact and 33 percent a minor impact.

Thus, networks apparently assist women entrepreneurs in growing their enterprises in as far as they provide information, emotional assistance and role models. Whether network membership also facilitates access to debt or equity finance remains an open question and a possible interesting avenue for further research.

D.   SUPPLY-SIDE ISSUES FOR WOMEN ENTREPRENEURS IN GERMANY

Where Does Financing Come From? Sources of Finance for Women Entrepreneurs

Besides bank loans, which type of finance is available in Germany to start and grow a business? In general, the German financing system is dominated by banks, although the supply of venture capital has increased over the past years. In 2003 (1993), the major association (BVK), which was founded in 1988, had 187 (72) full members, investing 2.5 billion euros and managing 5497 portfolio enterprises. Overall, the German market has entered a phase of consolidation, after the shake-up experienced by the collapse of the new economy. This is reflected in the number of VC companies in the BVK, which decreased by 53 over the past three years. Moreover, members received 38 300 requests for capital in 2003, which is less than half of the requests coming in the year before (68 500). Seventeen percent of the members of the association are corporate VCs (that is, subsidiaries of large companies), 63 percent are independent ones and 20 percent are publicly supported and/or oriented specifically towards small and medium-sized ventures (KfW, 2003).[9] How many women are involved in the venture capital industry? This needs further in-depth research, as gender-specific data on employment in the VC industry is not readily available. In 2003 (1993), the VC companies employed 1445 persons (508), 905 (310) of whom were professionals. Beginning of 2001, a total of 182 VC companies had 424 directors, a mere 23 (5 percent) were women.

Informal venture capital, that is, business angels, is a relative new phenomenon in Germany. A recent study analyzed both the personal and the investment profile of German business angels, including some information on women angels (Stedler and Peters, 2002).[10] The typical German business angel is male, occupied at upper management level with a background in company leadership and mainly business management; investment preferences are IT enterprises. Only 11 of the sample (4.7 percent) are women. Both women (55 percent) and men (52 percent) prefer investments in IT firms. Whilst men are more active in life science (23 percent, 9 percent women) and media/entertainment (12 percent, 9 percent women), both of which represent growth sectors in Germany, women more frequently invest in women-dominated sectors such as services (27 percent, 17 percent men). Most angels invest less than 0.5 billion euros, but 9 percent of the women angels (3 percent and 4 percent men) claimed investments between 1 and 2 billion and above each. Although the empirical results are not statistically significant because of the very small sample, they illustrate interesting gender-specific trends in the investment behavior of German business angels, which definitely ask for in-depth research with a larger stratified sample.

With regard to financial support we can distinguish between three types: 'mass programs', programs for a specific group, and group-specific regulations within 'mass programs'. The majority of financial support programs in Germany address all start-ups and/or existing enterprises. Programs that are exclusively for female entrepreneurs include small credit lines in some of the German states. All such programs only support a small number of female entrepreneurs, for example, in Mecklenburg-Western Pomerania, 322 female entrepreneurs received credits during the period 1996–2002. State governments also frequently introduce specific regulations into mass credit programs, especially where federal and state governments jointly finance these programs. One such example refers to a credit program in North-Rhine Westphalia where the state government allows credit applications of female nascent entrepreneurs without previous industry knowledge, which otherwise is required in order to receive a credit. Another such regulation is to be found in Mecklenburg-Western Pomerania, where the state investment bank hands out credits directly to female entrepreneurs, provided they previously were rejected by banks (Kehlbeck and Schneider, 1999: 29). These regulations try to level out the possibly negative effects of the German 'housebank system', that is, all applications for financial support programs are processed by commercial banks.

Social Capital from a Supply-side Perspective: Business Associations and Women's Networks

The 1990s saw a considerable increase in gender-specific public-private and wholly private networks for women entrepreneurs in Germany. Women entrepreneurs appear to be more reluctant to address chambers of commerce and industry and chambers of crafts, which traditionally play a major role in the German (support) system with obligatory membership. The overall dominance of male entrepreneurs in business associations and chambers is reflected in the low shares of women entrepreneurs in boards and committees. For example, only one out of 82 chambers of commerce and industry is presided by a woman, another four have female CEOs, whilst there are one female president, one female vice-president and six female CEOs across the 55 chambers of crafts (Welter et al., 2003).

Women-related organizations fall into different categories: those organizations or networks aiming at working women in general (for example, the Business and Professional Women Organization, which was originally founded in the 1920s in the USA, and in the 1930s in Germany) and specific associations/networks for female entrepreneurs or female business founders. The latter category includes, for example, the oldest, and with 1700 members, also largest female entrepreneur association in Germany, the 'Verband Deutscher Unternehmerinnen' (VdU), which was set up in 1954. It still remains the only women entrepreneur association on federal and regional level, whilst most of the other organizations either have a mainly sectoral focus (such as 'Schöne Aussichten' with 700 members, which is concentrated on female entrepreneurs in professions, or 'Webgrrls', which focuses on women entrepreneurs in new media) or an explicit regional and local orientation respectively. This overall increase and the focus on regions or sectors reflect a general shift in the organizations' philosophies from general lobbying towards providing direct membership benefits in order to acquire new clients (Frerichs and Wiemert, 2002).

Data from a recently finalized project on women networks allow a closer look at the supply side (see Welter et al., 2004). Within this study, nine typical networks were selected, using a classification of 1) organization structures (real structures, virtual), 2) outreach (national, local), 3) target group (start-ups/existing firms, potential entrepreneurs), 4) gender (exclusive women, non-exclusive). Results show some distinctive characteristics of women (entrepreneurs) networks. Networks mainly originate in urban areas; this can be explained through factors of institutional thickness and a critical mass of women entrepreneurs in urban areas who can be recruited as members. The study also showed that the older the networks are, the smaller their share of young and nascent entrepreneurs. Apparently, networks grow old with their founders and members, which is partly a result of shifting interests when businesses grow and mature. Although the 1990s saw a pronounced trend towards more and more virtual networks, this appears to be a temporary phenomenon. Networking obviously needs face-to-face contacts and geographical proximity to work effectively, which is reflected in the fact that most virtual networks and Internet communities today are complemented by 'real' regional and local groups meeting regularly.

Networks and business associations today experience several problems, two of which will be briefly mentioned here (for more details see Welter et al., 2004), as they might have a considerable impact on women entrepreneurs and business development. The first difficulty is to decide on network structures in terms of membership, which refers to heterogeneity versus homogeneity.

Whilst a homogeneous membership assists in creating network identity, a heterogeneous membership adds more value for members, although this might foster free-riding and opportunism as well. Moreover, most network promoters interviewed within this particular study claimed enormous and growing difficulties in involving (more) members on a voluntary basis, whilst more and more networks have been set up since the mid-1990s. The resulting vicious circle of 'networking' (few members, few finances, small range of services, not attractive for new members) clearly illustrates the dilemma German networks and business associations have to solve in the near future.

E.   POLITICAL AND SOCIETAL CONTEXT IN GERMANY: (NO) ROLE MODELS FOR STARTING AND GROWING A BUSINESS?

Whilst gender equality is codified in the German Constitution, its implementation throughout economy and society might still lead to open and subtle discrimination (Holst, 2002). Open discrimination could be observed until the early 1970s concerning legal regulations where women needed their husband's signature on a labor contract to become valid, or regulations with respect to bank accounts where husbands were required to countersign a woman's application. Nowadays, hidden constraints, expressing themselves through the institutional environment, might play an even more important role in restricting women's entrepreneurship.

Childcare facilities play a role in supporting or constraining female entrepreneurship in practice. Here, Germany is still characterized by a rather traditional labor distribution, where men contribute incomes and women are mainly responsible for childcare. In addition, social and tax policies could influence women entrepreneurs with respect to the level of social security connected to entrepreneurship. This is an important factor for potential women entrepreneurs who might also consider entrepreneurship for family reasons or in order to improve household income. Moreover, Holst (2002) refers to the gender-restrictive role of the German tax system that mainly favors male participation in the formal labor market and informal, unpaid work of women through discriminating against married women.

Female entrepreneurship is also influenced to a large extent by the value society attaches to women employment. Evidence for East Germany demonstrates that the decreasing labor market participation of East German women following re-unification can only partly be attributed to higher unemployment rates for women, but it also reflects an overall conservative trend in Germany, ascribing a housebound role for women as well as the decrease in childcare facilities. Moreover, (West) German society still defines women mainly through roles connected to family and household responsibilities, thus conveying female entrepreneurship as less desirable (Welter et al., 2003, also IfM, 2003). The role distribution is one where men contribute incomes and women are mainly responsible for childcare. A reluctant attitude of German women towards entrepreneurship is reinforced through the ambivalent image of entrepreneurs (*Unternehmer*),[11] which is still attributed with male characteristics. Since the turn of the 19th century entrepreneurs had been identified as 'heroic lone fighters' (*heroische Einzelkämpfer*), which led to entrepreneurship being understood as a male task (Schmidt, 2002). German society even nowadays tends to rate male characteristics higher than female ones (Holst, 2002: 92).

All this is reflected in the way German media discuss women entrepreneurs and construct their identity. Achtenhagen and Welter (2003, 2005) have been researching the discourse on women's entrepreneurship in selected German newspapers, concluding that they often paint a 'restricted' picture of women entrepreneurs. This applies both to implicit role models and traditional values. For example, several articles discuss the double burden of work and family for women, sometimes stating explicitly that this particular female entrepreneur chose not to have a family and children because of her entrepreneurial role. Moreover, women entrepreneurs are mainly understood as being hard-working power-women, showing enthusiasm, energy, firmness and cleverness, in short: they are superwomen in a male-dominated business world.

All this clearly illustrates the traditional role model for (West) German women. Thus, societal values implicitly assess female entrepreneurship as less desirable, which in turn affects the self-perceptions and individual attitudes of potential female entrepreneurs. Interviews with women entrepreneurs in Germany demonstrate that most women entrepreneurs, especially those having set up a venture in the professions (for example, as doctors or lawyers), do not see themselves as '*Unternehmerin*', which term they attribute to those women who lead larger industry firms (Welter et al., 2003). Here, research also confirmed that professional choices of women take into account what society deems desirable and 'correct' for their sex (Holst, 2002). If (West) German society values for women a housebound role higher than a professional one, it is not surprising that women often deny their entrepreneurial identity. All this in turn could restrict both the inclination of women to set up a business as well as their attitudes towards business growth.

F.   CONCLUSIONS AND OPEN QUESTIONS: WHAT DO WE KNOW, WHAT WOULD WE LIKE TO KNOW?

Much is already known about women entrepreneurs in Germany, especially with regard to their characteristics, the businesses they own and the overall development of women's entrepreneurship over the past decades. To sum up: women's entrepreneurship has developed positively over the past decade, although the gender gap remains; women businesses are smaller and concentrate on few sectors and business fields, although there is a growth in 'non-traditional' fields; they perform differently and less compared with men-owned firms, although the differences are often negligible when controlling for sector and size; women are interested in growing a business, although less women own large firms; more and more women entrepreneurs today are highly qualified, often using entrepreneurship to break through the glass ceiling; women value business networks and associations as one source for assistance when developing their business; there is anecdotal evidence for gender discrimination with regard to access to finance; and finally the overall political and societal environment in Germany can be characterized as a traditional one (sometimes) impeding women's entrepreneurship as role models are lacking,

There are also gaps in our knowledge, indicating interesting research questions, which so far have not been thoroughly researched in the German context:

- One such question concerns growth constraints for women entrepreneurs. Research obviously demonstrates less women enterprises with employees, although female nascents claim to be interested in growing their firm, even if less so than men. This questions the assumption that women entrepreneurs are generally less interested in business growth. Here, we need research on why fewer women nascents appear to be able or interested in realizing their growth intentions.
- Finance is often said to be a critical issue for women entrepreneurs in Germany, and hidden discrimination by bank clerks might be one explanation for women not accessing (or not being able to access) external financing sources. So far, there is no conclusive empirical evidence to research this question. Instead, we have to rely on either studies with very small samples or on anecdotal evidence from single case interviews with women entrepreneurs. In this context, we need much more substantive research.
- Moreover, the supply side of finance has been neglected in the German context as well. One particular interesting question here concerns the differences in investment behavior of business angels, which became apparent from a preliminary investigation. Again, this would ask for a systematic approach in order to answer the question whether women business angels are more inclined to finance women growth businesses.

Finally, the question remains how best to foster women's entrepreneurship in Germany. There is an ongoing debate as to the best way to stimulate women's entrepreneurship that contributes to both economic competitiveness and social inclusion. Most support for women entrepreneurs today addresses existing start-ups, either through specific programs directed at women only, or through the overall support structures for start-ups. Mirchandani (1999) draws attention to the fact that a barrier-focused approach towards female entrepreneurship 'makes it seem as though the barriers women face are removable through individual action ... what is needed, it is therefore suggested, is for women to train or educate themselves better, develop more appropriate networks and mentoring relationships, and re-assign domestic work'. The author stresses that this shifts the attention of policy-makers away from environment constraints towards the woman entrepreneur. Whilst individual support is an important element in an overall policy strategy for fostering women's entrepreneurship, an enabling environment takes on special importance, given the fact that the (West) German society still understands entrepreneurship as a male phenomenon and ascribes a housebound, traditional role to women.

All this indicates a specific role for government in creating adequate political and socio-economic framework conditions. In the German context, an integrated strategy for fostering female entrepreneurship obviously needs to take into account that there are shortcomings in the institutional (political and societal) environment, possibly restricting women's interest in and entry into entrepreneurship as well as their options for growing their businesses.

NOTES

1. The statistics on business registrations (*Gewerbemeldungsregister*) is used as an indicator to determine business start-up rates, although these statistics show a number of flaws such as double registration, under coverage of professions. So far, Germany has no enterprise register.
2. The project Web page contains short papers for downloading, as well as the final workshop presentations and policy recommendations. Another project financed by the Federal Ministry of Labour and Economics (BMWA) and carried out by the IfM in Bonn, concentrated on existing women entrepreneurs (IfM, 2003). Additionally, the European initiative 'Equal' now supports statistical reports on women entrepreneurs within its project 'Women's Way of Entrepreneurship (WWOE)', see Lauxen-Ulbrich and Leicht (2003); Lauxen-Ulbrich and Fehrenbach (2003).
3. This is a category in the micro-census, a yearly 1 percent-representative survey of the German population, conducted by the Federal Statistical Office. The classification of entrepreneur refers to the question regarding employment positions. If the respondent answers '*selbständig*', (s)he is classified as entrepreneur. '*Selbständige*' include both self-employed persons (that is, genuine self-employed persons) as well as small business owners with employees. Data cited in this section are taken from the micro-census, percentage and growth rates are calculated by the author, if not cited otherwise.
4. Longitudinal data are only available for West Germany; for East Germany we can observe the developments since 1991.

5. The 'IAB-Betriebspanel' does not cover micro-enterprises, where the entrepreneur works on his/her own, as it only includes firms with employees for whom social security is paid by the employer. However, this is the only representative survey collecting performance data and gender of entrepreneurs. The data reported here are for the year 2000.

6. The data come from a pilot study on nascent entrepreneurs in Germany. Two random and representative samples of 1945 persons (sample A) and 1909 persons (sample B) out of the residential population over 18 years were interviewed by phone (computer-assisted telephone interviews) between February and April 1999. Nascent entrepreneurs were identified based on screening criteria developed by the ERC. We used the same wording for previous, current, nascent, discontinued and discouraged entrepreneurs, although the questions were translated into German and slightly reworded in the case of nascent entrepreneurs. We also included questions asking for a more general business wish. For more details on the methodology and results, see Welter (1999, 2000a, 2001a), Welter and Bergmann (2002).

7. Of course, the differences between nascents with growth intentions and entrepreneurs who did grow in terms of employment could be a result of the fact that mainly nascents with growth intentions give up throughout the process of business formation, although this is not very realistic. Data on nascents for other countries confirm that between 30 percent in the Netherlands, 33 percent in Sweden and 14 percent in Norway manage to set up a business (Van Gelderen and Bosma, 2000; Alsos et al., 2000). With respect to the realization of growth intentions, our pilot study thus only allows for very basic reasoning because we do not know how many nascents will make it through the formation process.

8. Strohmeyer based his analysis on a 70 percent sub-sample of the micro-census, which is available as raw data for scientific analysis from the Federal Statistical Office, but which covers only certain years.

9. This study surveyed members of the German Association of Venture Capitalists (BVK). The questionnaire was sent out to all members in autumn 2002. Some 107 members of the 196 participated.

10. This study is the first large-scale survey of German business angels. Business angels were identified through matching events, which accompanied large fairs in Hannover (CeBIT, Industry Fair), and through contacting business angels networks. Approximately 500 business angels were contacted in summer 2001, 232 (46 percent) participated. Another survey on angel networks has been conducted by BAND in late 2003, but unfortunately detailed results are not available. Many business angels are organized in networks, 20 of which are members of BAND (Business Angels Netzwerk Deutschland).

11. The German language distinguishes between '*Unternehmer*' (men entrepreneur) and '*Unternehmerin*' (women entrepreneur). In daily life, most people as well as the media, unless specifically reporting about women entrepreneurs, use the male term, meaning this to include women as well.

REFERENCES

Achtenhagen, L. and F. Welter (2003), 'Female entrepreneurship as reflected in German media in the years 1995–2001', in J. Butler (ed.), *New Perspectives on Women Entrepreneurs*, Greenwich: Information Age Publishing, pp. 71–100.

Achtenhagen, L. and F. Welter (2005), '"The attractive blond lady in a pink business suit" – analyzing the discourse on female entrepreneurship in German newspapers between 1997 and 2003', Paper presented at the IECER Conference, 2–4 February, Amsterdam.

Alsos, G.A., E. Ljunggren and B. Rotefoss (2000), 'Who makes it through the business formation process? – A longitudinal study of entrepreneurs', Paper presented at the Babson College–Kauffman Foundation Entrepreneurship Research Conference, Babson, 8–10 June.

Brüderl, J., P. Preisendörfer and R. Ziegler (1996), *Der Erfolg neugegründeter Betriebe – eine empirische Studie zu den Chancen und Risiken von Unternehmensgründungen*, Berlin: Duncker & Humblot.

Carter, N., W.B. Gartner and P.D. Reynolds (1996), 'Exploring start-up event sequences', *Journal of Business Venturing*, **11**: 151–66.

Döbler, T. (1998), *Frauen als Unternehmerinnen: Erfolgspotentiale weiblicher Selbständiger*, Wiesbaden: DUV.

Engel, D. and F. Welter (2004), 'Dreamers and doers – who succeeds in the process of venture creation?', Paper presented at the Interdisciplinary European Conference on Entrepreneurship Research (IECER), Regensburg, 18–20 February.

Eurostat (2002), *SMEs in Europe: Competitiveness, innovation and the knowledge-driven society – Data 1996–2001*, Luxembourg: Eurostat.

Fehrenbach, S. (2004), 'Charakteristika der von Frauen und Männern geführten Betriebe', in R. Leicht and F. Welter (eds), *Gründerinnen und selbständige Frauen – Potenziale, Strukturen und Entwicklungen in Deutschland*, Karlsruhe: Loeper, 170–92.

Fehrenbach, S. and M. Lauxen-Ulbrich (2002), 'A gender view on self-employment in Germany', BMBF Project, Download-Paper Nr. 4, http://www.rwi-essen.de/pls/portal30/url/page/PAGE_GRUENDERINNEN.

Fehrenbach, S. and R. Leicht (2002), *Strukturmerkmale und Potentiale der von Frauen geführten Betriebe in Deutschland*, Veröffentlichungen des Instituts für Mittelstandsforschung der Universität Mannheim, Grüne Reihe Nr 47. Mannheim: Universität Mannheim.

Frerichs, P. and H. Wiemert (2002), '"Ich gebe, damit Du gibst": Frauennetzwerke – strategisch, reziprok, exklusiv, Soziale Chancen'. Schriftenreihe des ISO-Instituts Köln, 2, Opladen: Leske + Budrich.

Friderichs, H., B. Paranque and A. Sauvé (1999), 'Structures of corporate finance in Germany and France: A comparative analysis for West German and French incorporated enterprises with special reference to institutional factors', in A. Sauvé and M. Scheuer (eds), *Corporate Finance in Germany and France*, Frankfurt am Main and Paris, pp. 64–137.

Hansmann, K.-W. and C.M. Ringle (2001), *Finanzierung Mittelstand: Eine empirische Untersuchung*, Institut für Industriebetriebslehre und Organisation, Arbeitspapiere Industrielles Management, 6, Universität Hamburg.

Hansmann, K.-W. and C.M. Ringle (2002), *Finanzierung Mittelstand 2002: Eine empirische Untersuchung*, Institut für Industriebetriebslehre und Organisation, Arbeitspapiere Industrielles Management, 8, Universität Hamburg.

Hansmann, K.-W., M. Höck and C.M. Ringle (2003), *Finanzierung Mittelstand 2003: Eine empirische Untersuchung*, Institut für Industriebetriebslehre und Organisation, Arbeitspapiere Industrielles Management, 11, Universität Hamburg.

Hinz, Th. and M. Jungbauer-Gans (1999), 'Starting a business after unemployment', *Entrepreneurship & Regional Development*, **11**(4): 317–33.

Hölscher, R., S. Daferner, R. Bonn and J. Alsfasser (1998), *Finanzierung von Existenzgründungen in Rheinland-Pfalz – Eine empirische Analyse unter besonderer Berücksichtigung der Rolle der Kreditinstitut*, Studien zum Finanz-, Bank- und Versicherungsmanagement des Lehrstuhls für Finanzierung und Investition, Universität Kaiserslautern.

Holst, E. (2002), 'Institutionelle Determinanten der Erwerbsarbeit', in F. Maier and A. Fiedler (eds), *Gender Matters: feministische Analysen zur Wirtschafts- und Sozialpolitik*, Fhw-Forschung, 42/43, Berlin: Edition Sigma, pp. 89–109.

Hommel, U. and H. Schneider (2003), 'Financing the German Mittelstand', *EIB Papers* (2), 52–90.

IfM (2000), *MIND – Mittelstand in Deutschland – Finance*, edited by Gruner + Jahr and Dresdner Bank, Köln and Frankfurt am Main.

IfM (2003), *Unternehmerinnen in Deutschland*, Dokumentation 522, Bonn/Berlin: BMWA.

IfM Bonn (2001), *Gender-spezifische Aufbereitung der amtlichen Statistik: Möglichkeiten respektive Anforderungen*, Materialien zur Gleichstellungspolitik, 82/2001, Bonn: BMFSFJ.

Janssen, M. and M. Nienhaus (2003), 'Wege in die "neue" Selbständigkeit: Erfahrungen und Handlungsempfehlungen von Akteuren im regionalen Gründungsgeschehen', Berichte des ISO 69, Köln: ISO.

Jungbauer-Gans, M. and P. Preisendörfer (1992), 'Frauen in der beruflichen Selbständigkeit: Eine erfolgversprechende Alternative zur abhängigen Beschäftigung?', *Zeitschrift für Soziologie*, **42**(1), 61–77.

Kehlbeck, H. and U. Schneider (1999), *Frauen als Zielgruppe von Existenzgründungen unter besonderer Berücksichtigung der Finanzierungsaspekte*, eine Untersuchung im Auftrag des Senatsamtes für die Gleichstellung, Hamburg.

KfW Bankengruppe (2001), *Unternehmensfinanzierung im Umbruch – die Finanzierungsperspektiven deutscher Unternehmen im Zeichen von Finanzmarktwandel und Basel II*, Frankfurt am Main: KfW.

KfW Bankengruppe (2002), *Unternehmensfinanzierung in schwierigem Fahrwasser: Wachsende Finanzierungsprobleme im Mittelstand, Auswertung der Unternehmensbefragung 2002*, Frankfurt am Main: KfW.

KfW Bankengruppe (2003), *Beteiligungskapital in Deutschland: Anbieterstrukturen, Verhaltensmuster, Marktlücken und Förderbedarf*, Frankfurt am Main: KfW.

KfW Bankengruppe (2004), *Unternehmensfinanzierung: Noch kein Grund zur Entwarnung … aber Fortschritte bei der Anpassung an neue Spielregeln des Finanzmarkts, Auswertung der Unternehmensbefragung 2003/2004*, Frankfurt am Main: KfW.

Lauxen-Ulbrich, M. and S. Fehrenbach (2003), *Zur Verfügbarkeit von Daten über Gründerinnen und selbständige Frauen – Eine Bestandsaufnahme*, Institut für Mittelstandsforschung, Universität Mannheim.

Lauxen-Ulbrich, M. and R. Leicht (2002), *Entwicklung und Tätigkeitsprofil selbständiger Frauen in Deutschland: Eine empirische Untersuchung anhand der Daten des Mikrozensus*, Veröffentlichungen des Instituts für Mittelstandsforschung, 46, Universität Mannheim.

Lauxen-Ulbrich, M. and R. Leicht (2003), *First Statistical Overview – National Report on Women (Start-up), Entrepreneurs and Female Self-Employment in Germany*, Small Business Research Institute, University of Mannheim.

Lauxen-Ulbrich, M. and R. Leicht (2004), 'Wirtschaftliche und berufliche Orientierung von selbständigen Frauen', in R. Leicht and F. Welter (eds), *Gründerinnen und selbständige Frauen - Potenziale, Strukturen und Entwicklungen in Deutschland*, Karlsruhe: Loeper, 72–96.

Leicht, R. and F. Welter (eds) (2004), *Gründerinnen und selbständige Frauen – Potenziale, Strukturen und Entwicklungen in Deutschland*, Karlsruhe: Loeper.

Lindner-Lehmann, M., E.E. Lehmann and D. Neuberger (1998), *Kreditvergabe der Banken an kleine und mittelständische Unternehmen: Ergebnisse einer schriftlichen Befragung deutscher Banken*, Wirtschafts- und Sozialwissenschaftliche Fakultät, Universität Rostock.

Mirchandani, K. (1999), 'Feminist insight on gendered work: New directions in research on women and entrepreneurship', *Gender, Work and Organization*, **6**(4), 224–35.

Mittelstandsmonitor (2003), *Jährlicher Bericht zu Konjunktur- und Strukturfragen kleiner und mittlerer Unternehmen*, Published by Creditreform, IfM Bonn, ZEW, DtA, Die Mittelstandsbank and KfW Bankengruppe.

Nehls, H. and T. Schmidt (2003), 'Credit crunch in Germany?', RWI: Discussion Paper, 6, Essen: RWI.

OECD (2000), *The OECD Small and Medium Enterprise Outlook*, Paris: OECD.

Piorkowsky, M.-B. (2001), *Existenzgründungsprozesse im Zu- und Nebenerwerb von Frauen und Männern: Eine empirische Analyse der Bedingungen und Verläufe bei Gründungs- und Entwicklungsprozessen von Unternehmen unter besonderer Berücksichtigung genderspezifischer Aspekte*, Bonn: BMFSFJ.

Piorkowsky, M.-B. with assistance of S. Scholl (2002), *Genderaspekte in der finanziellen Förderung von Unternehmensgründungen. Eine qualitative und quantitative Analyse der Programme auf Bundesebene – unter besonderer Berücksichtigung der Gründung durch Frauen*, Bericht im Auftrag des BMFSFJ. Universität Bonn.

Reynolds, P.D. (1997), 'Who starts new firms? – Preliminary explorations of firms-in-gestation', *Small Business Economics*, **9**(5): 449–62.

Schmidt, D. (2002), 'Im Schatten der "großen Männer": Zur unterbelichteten Rolle der Unternehmerinnen in der deutschen Wirtschaftsgeschichte des 19. und 20. Jahrhunderts', in F. Maier and A. Fiedler (eds), *Gender Matters: feministische Analysen zur Wirtschafts- und Sozialpolitik*, Fhw-Forschung, 42/43, Berlin: Edition Sigma, pp. 211–29.

Stedler, H.R. and H.H. Peters (2002), *Business Angels in Deutschland*, empirische Studie der FH Hannover im Auftrag der tbg Technologie-Beteiligungs-Gesellschaft mbH der Deutschen Ausgleichsbank, Hannover and Bonn.

Sternberg, R., H. Bergmann and I. Lückgen (2003), *Global Entrepreneurship Monitor: Länderbericht Deutschland*, Köln: Universität zu Köln.

Strohmeyer, R. (2003), 'Gender differences in self-employment: does education matter?', Paper presented at the ICSB 48th World Conference, 15–18 June 2003, Belfast, BMBF Project, Download-Paper 8, http://www.rwi-essen.de/pls/portal30/url/page/PAGE_GRUENDERINNEN.

Strohmeyer, R. (2004a), 'Berufliche Ausbildung und Gründungsaktivitäten im Geschlechtervergleich', in R. Leicht and F. Welter (eds), *Gründerinnen und selbständige Frauen – Potenziale, Strukturen und Entwicklungen in Deutschland*, Karlsruhe: Loeper, pp. 97–118.

Strohmeyer, R. (2004b), 'Studienfachwahl und berufliche Platzierung von selbständigen Akademikerinnen', in R. Leicht and F. Welter (eds), *Gründerinnen und selbständige Frauen – Potenziale, Strukturen und Entwicklungen in Deutschland*, Karlsruhe: Loeper, pp. 119–37.

Tchouvakhina, M. (2002), *'Small is Beautiful' – aber auch finanzierbar?*, Vortrag auf der Konferenz Enterprising Women II, Frankfurt, 7 March, available at: http://www.enterprising-women.de/docu2002/down/WS%207%20Tchouvakhina.ppt.

Van Gelderen, M. and N. Bosma (2000), 'Setting up a business in the Netherlands: Who gets started, who gives up, who is still organizing', Paper presented at the RENT XIV, Prague, November.

Wagenvoort, R. (2003), 'Are finance constraints hindering the growth of SMEs in Europe?', *EIB Papers*, **8**(2), 22–50.

Welter, F. (1999), 'Wege in die Selbständigkeit – Anmerkungen zu Gründungsfähigkeit, Gründungsneigung und Gründungsengagement', *BISS-Public*, **9**(27), 169–83.

Welter, F. (2000a), *Gründungspotenzial und Gründungsprozess in Deutschland – Eine konzeptionelle und empirische Betrachtung*, Schriften und Materialien zu Handwerk und Mittelstand, 4, Essen: RWI.

Welter, F. (2000b), 'Germany: Is the outcome desirable? Quality of work in self-employment', a contribution to the ILO Action Programme: *Enterprise Creation by the Unemployed – Microfinance in Industrialized Countries*, Geneva: ILO; Reprint als Schriften und Materialien zu Handwerk und Mittelstand, 7, Essen: RWI.

Welter, F. (2000c), '*Einmal im Leben darf jeder etwas Risikoreiches tun' – Fallstudien von Gründern und Gründerinnen*, Schriften und Materialien zu Handwerk und Mittelstand, 9, Essen: RWI.

Welter, F. (2001a), *Nascent Entrepreneurship in Germany*, Schriften und Materialien zu Handwerk und Mittelstand, 11, Essen: RWI.

Welter, F. (2001b), 'Who wants to grow? – growth intentions and growth profiles of (nascent) entrepreneurs in Germany', *Frontiers of Entrepreneurship Research 2001*, 91–100.

Welter, F. (2002a), 'Entrepreneurship in West and East Germany', Paper presented at the Babson College-Kauffman Foundation Entrepreneurship Research Conference, Boulder/USA, 6–8 June 2002.

Welter, F. (2002b), 'The environment for female entrepreneurship in Germany', Paper presented at the RENT XVI, 21–22 November 2002 in Barcelona, BMBF Project: Download-Paper 5, http://www.rwi-essen.de/pls/portal30/url/page/ PAGE_GRUENDERINNEN.

Welter, F. (2004a), 'The environment for female entrepreneurship in Germany', *Journal of Small Business and Enterprise Development*, **11**(2), 212–21.

Welter, F. (2004b), 'Rahmenbedingungen für Gründerinnen und Unternehmerinnen in Deutschland', in R. Leicht and F. Welter (eds), *Gründerinnen und selbständige Frauen – Potenziale, Strukturen und Entwicklungen in Deutschland*, Karlsruhe: Loeper, pp. 193–212.

Welter, F. and H. Bergmann (2002), '"Nascent Entrepreneurs" in Deutschland', in J. Schmude and R. Leiner (eds), *Unternehmensgründungen – Interdisziplinäre Beiträge zum Entrepreneurship Research*, Heidelberg: Physica, pp. 33–62.

Welter, F., U. Ammon and L. Trettin (2004), *Netzwerke und Unternehmensgründungen von Frauen*, RWI: Schriften, 76, Berlin: Duncker & Humblot.

Welter, F. and B. Lageman with assistance of M. Stoytcheva (2003), *Gründerinnen in Deutschland: Potenziale und das institutionelle Umfeld*, Untersuchungen des Rheinisch-Westfälisches Institut für Wirtschaftsforschung, 41, Essen: RWI.

7. Women's entrepreneurship in Norway: recent trends and future challenges

Lene Foss and Elisabet Ljunggren

A. LABOR FORCE OVERVIEW

The total population in Norway of persons aged 16 years and above is 3 607 184. Of this, 50.9 percent comprises women and 49.1 percent men (*Befolkningsundersøkelsen*, 2004). Six out of ten women hold part-time positions, giving Norway the highest percentage of part-time employees in Europe (OECD, 2001, *Employment Outlook*). The gender difference between the private and public sector in Norway is pronounced. In 2001, 63 percent of men and 37 percent of women are working in the private sector. The gender structure in the public sector is quite the opposite: 66 percent women and 34 percent men. There is a clear discrepancy between women's management positions in the private and public sectors. Women occupy a steady 40 percent of managerial positions in the public sector, compared with 21–22 percent in the private sector.

Compared with other industrialized countries the Norwegian labor market has a higher proportion of part-time work among women. Women put fewer hours into paid work than men. High female employment rate, in fact, 'conceals' low actual hours at work (Ellingsæter, 1999). In a study using aggregate data from nine advanced industrialized countries Rosenfeld and Birkelund (1995) show that the organizational power of labor and the proportion of employed women in the public sector have some of the strongest and most consistent effects on a country's part-time female labor force. The authors argue that this is due to the large public sector in the Scandinavian countries, which, together with the family-friendly policy, tends to favor part-time work among women. In the US, Canada, Germany, Australia and to some extent the UK, countries with weak unions and centrist or right-wing governments tend to have less beneficial family policies and a smaller public sector. This leaves women with the choice of unemployment or full-time employment. In this study Norway emerged as the country with the highest proportion of part-time employed women, which was also more extreme than the other Scandinavian countries. Recent data confirms this: Norway still has the highest part-time share (35 percent) compared to 20–25 percent in Sweden and Denmark (Skjeie and Teigen, 2003).

With regard to management positions a steady 6 percent of Norwegian women are in senior executive positions in the private sector, while in both the US and the UK the corresponding proportions have increased to 15.7 percent (Catalyst Inc., 2002) and 9 percent respectively (Fortune 500). Of Norway's 300 largest companies in 1997, only three (1 percent) were headed by a woman. This can be compared with the 5000 largest companies in the US, where 11 percent were headed by a woman. The proportion of female managers in Norway declined from 24 percent in 1999 to 21 percent in 2002 (Colbjørnsen, 2004).

Norwegian women are also marginally represented in the boardrooms. Three reports indicate that the number of female board members is decreasing (*Økonomisk Rapport*, 1999). In seven out of ten corporations on the stock exchange, no women are represented on the management. Women occupy just 69 (5.9 percent) of a total of 1164 board memberships. In 30 of these, women represent the quota accorded to the employees. Female shareholders constitute only 3.4 percent of the total. The larger corporations have a 6.6 percent female share in the boardrooms, whereas the small and medium-sized corporations have 4.75 percent women.

Of the total employment in Norway in 2004 (2291414) 92 percent were employed and 8 percent were self-employed. The pattern of men and women in ordinary employment and self-employment differs. There is 50.8 percent men and 49.2 percent women in employment. The share in self-employment is 74.6 percent men and 25.4 percent women.

Statistics show that education in Norway is also gender segregated. Of all students graduating in 1999/2000 women constituted 94 percent of the pre-school teachers, 90 percent of the nurses, 70 percent of the teachers, 65 percent of the degrees in social sciences and 64 percent of the degrees in humanities. Men constituted 82 percent of the engineers, 78 percent of the chartered engineers, 58 percent in the natural sciences and 56 percent of the economists (Statistics Norway, 2001d). This gender segregation in education seems to structure the entrance into the labor market. The most widespread occupations for women are sales staff, nurse, enrolled nurse and teacher (Statistics Norway, 2002). Eight out of ten women work in the health sector and in teaching. The largest occupational groups for young men are information technology-related occupations, carpenter and joiner/cabinetmaker. Eight out of ten men work in commodity production and administration. This occupational narrowness makes Norway the fifth most gender-segregated labor force in the OECD. A report of the difference in range between the occupational choices of men and women show that Norway ranks as number 23 of the 27 most industrialized countries in the world (OECD, 2000). While

Norwegian women tend to choose among 30 different occupations, men choose among 300. Norwegian women fill a larger share of the positions in the service sector than women in other Western countries: of the total workforce of 1057 million women, 87 percent work in service-related occupations across all sectors, compared with 49 percent of the male workforce. This fact makes it structurally difficult to break the glass ceiling, as women are grouped together in typically female-related service sectors (Hansen, 1995). Table 7.1 showing employees in managerial occupations in the private and public sectors underlines the gendered work pattern in Norway. The majority of women work in the public sector, while men are recruited into the private sector.

Table 7.1   Employees in managerial occupations in private and public sectors (in '000s; percentages in parentheses)

	Private sector		Public sector	
	Men	Women	Men	Women
2000	115 (79)	30 (21)	21 (57)	16 (43)
2001	98 (78)	28 (22)	21 (60)	14 (40)

Source: Statistics Norway, 2000, 2002.

This difference in recruitment to the public and private sectors in Norway seems to repeat itself concerning women entrepreneurship. Here, Norway lags behind other Western countries (Kolvereid et al., 2004). The total entrepreneurial activity rate (TEA) in Norway for women is 3.5; the average in all 34 European countries is 7.2, whereby Norway ranks as 19th (Global Entrepreneurship Monitor, 2004). The female proportion of the total TEA is lower: the Norwegian women's proportion of the total entrepreneurial activity rate is 26 percent. This places Norway at the lower end of the ranking, with only Croatia and Greece having lower proportions.

Among Norwegian men, the entrepreneurial activity rate is 10.3 percent. The average for men in other countries is 11.6 percent, where Norway ranks 14th. Female entrepreneurship has always been at a lower rate than the average for women in GEM countries, whereas Norwegian male entrepreneurship typically has been at a higher rate, with the exception of 2003 and 2004.

B. PROFILE OF WOMEN'S ENTREPRENEURSHIP IN NORWAY

Extent and Nature of Women's Entrepreneurship in Norway

Norwegian studies show that women account for approximately 25 percent of the business start-ups (Ljunggren, 1998; Alsos and Kolvereid, 2005). This number has been stable for the last decade. One study (Ljunggren, 1998) indicates that women are present in 16 out of 23 industries while men are present in 22. This is a result of more men than women establishing businesses, but it is also a result of Norway's gender-segregated educational and labor market.

The extent of women's entrepreneurship in Norway in 2004 is presented in Table 7.2. It shows the distribution of self-employment by gender and organizational form. The following three categories of organizational form are used: general partnerships, general partnerships with shared liability and sole proprietorships. These forms account for three-quarters of all new establishments in Norway.

Table 7.2 shows that the pattern between the three different organizational forms in self-employment seems somewhat equal between men and women. Women account for about a quarter of the total businesses in each of the organizational forms. It is interesting that the pattern is similar across various organizational forms is interesting as the general understanding has been that women are mainly represented in sole proprietorships. In fact, every third sole proprietor-ship in 2003 was started by a woman. That means that this organizational form has the highest proportion of women. This might be an

Table 7.2   Self-employment by organizational form and gender (percentage in parentheses)

Organizational form	Self-employed		
	Actors total	Men	Women
General partnership	19977 (100)	14727 (74)	5250 (26)
General partnerships with shared liability	14195 (100)	10740 (76)	3455 (24)
Sole proprietorships	157488 (100)	117464 (75)	40024 (25)

Source: Statistics Norway, Structure and Business register, Table 05215.

indication of the uneven distribution of capital between men and women in Norway (Jensen, 2005).

Data on persons receiving an *Etablererstipend* (entrepreneurial grant) show that women who establish businesses are between 30 and 40 years of age and that they are married or cohabiting. Two-thirds of the women have children living at home. Approximately 40 percent have a high-school certificate, while 40 percent have a university degree. This is a somewhat higher educational level than in the general population. Five out of ten women have work experience from the public sector and six out of ten have work experience from the private sector (Pettersen et al., 1999).

Growth Orientation of Women Entrepreneurs in Norway

According to Brun (1998) there is a gender difference between the size of men's and women's businesses measured in total employees. Women establish smaller businesses that remain small over time more so than male-owned businesses. Brun also claims that women have lower growth ambitions than men. Table 7.3 can be interpreted as growth ambitions.

Recent research by Isaksen and Kolvereid (2005) supports Brun's findings about gender differences in aspirations for business growth. In their study of Norwegian new businesses they found that although there were no gender differences in the expectation that the business would provide full-time employment for the founder (50 percent expected it would provide full-time employment), there were differences between expectations regarding having employees. Male founders had significantly higher ambitions to hire staff than did female founders (27.1 percent of male founders, and 17.9 percent of women founders).

Ljunggren (2002) suggests that these kinds of results need to be considered in the labor market context where a high degree of Norwegian women work part-time. It may be that women who establish a business may have an idea with part-time employment in mind.

In a survey using data from 250 Norwegian entrepreneurs Kolvereid (1992) concludes that growth aspirations are related to motivation, education, industry and a number of organizational variables including previous growth in turnover and in the number of employees. Growth aspirations were not significantly related to experience, sex, location, or the size of the firm as measured by the number of employees. The results indicate that entrepreneurs with no growth aspirations tend to have high school as their highest level of education. The reason for starting their business seems to be more connected with opportunity rather than as a means of fulfilling their achievement and welfare motives. Entrepreneurs with only revenue growth aspirations tend to have a low level of education and to have started their business for welfare and

Table 7.3 Economic results, employment and plans for employment among entrepreneurs

	Women (%)	Men (%)
Financial results		
Large profit[a]	12	15
Some profit	52	44
Balance	21	20
Some deficit	12	18
Large deficit	2	4
No turnover	2	1
	100	100
Employment		
0–1 years	65	46
2–4 years	30	34
5–9 years	4	11
10+ years	1	9
	100	100
Plans for employment		
Increase	26	41
As today	68	51
Reduced	2	4
Plan to close down	2	1
No plans	3	3
	100	100
Total	(N = 133)	(N = 528)

Note: [a] Whether this is profit or surplus is not stated.

Source: Brun, 1998: 163.

tax considerations. Entrepreneurs who want their firm to grow and intend to hire additional employees seem to have strong achievement motives and a higher level of education than other entrepreneurs. This study indicates that education is positively related to growth aspirations, while experience is not. Whereas highly educated entrepreneurs have easier access to alternative employment and are therefore more willing to face the risks involved with growth, experienced entrepreneurs may have developed more firm-specific human capital that does not increase the chances for alternative employment.

Norwegian entrepreneurs seem to have lower growth aspirations compared with entrepreneurs in other countries such as Great Britain and New Zealand (Kolvereid et al., 1991). However, differences between aspiration levels of Norwegian men and women seem to parallel findings in other countries (Singh et al., 2001). Norwegian female entrepreneurs, like those in other countries, are more concentrated in traditional industries where the prospects of growth are limited (Berg and Foss, 2002) and similar to other countries (see Anna et al., 1999; Clark and James, 1992; Devine, 1994) generate more moderate profits and hire fewer employees than male businesses (Berg and Foss, 2002).

C.   DEMAND-SIDE ISSUES FOR WOMEN ENTREPRENEURS IN NORWAY

Financial Capital

There is little knowledge on how women finance their businesses in Norway. Pettersen et al. (1999) report that one in ten women entrepreneurs claim not to have put equity into the business, although the researchers assume that this level is higher as the women do not count their own labor in the total investment estimates. Other research shows that 31.9 percent of Norwegian new businesses have no equity invested (Isaksen and Kolvereid, 2005). Between 50 percent (Pettersen et al., 1999) and 74.2 percent (Isaksen and Kolvereid, 2005) have no bank loans. We find no studies reporting primary data on the demand side: the sources of financing for women entrepreneurs. There are some indications that government funding by grants is very important. This is followed by government loans, bank loans, private funding and also financing by the Graemen bank system (Pettersen et al., 1999). A recent study (Jensen, 2005) indicates that ownership of capital and real property is unevenly distributed among men and women in Norway. Women might not necessarily have the possibility to mortgage and thereby get a bank loan.

Social Capital

Social capital is defined as the resources entrepreneurs have through their networks (see Burt, 1997). Research on entrepreneurial networks in Norway is more prevalent. Foss (1994) investigated how networks affect resource acquisition and the likelihood of establishing a business. Networks had a strong indirect effect on the likelihood of starting a business because these provide access to essential resources. Once resources were acquired however, networks had no additional effect. Sample characteristics in the study precluded investigating whether the network effects varied by gender. Subsequent research on the relationship among social relations, occupational background and use of contacts during the start-up process showed a significant difference between males and females regarding the average number of family members in the network (Greve, 1995). Women entrepreneurs had an average of 1.32 family members in their network whereas that of male entrepreneurs was only 0.54.

More recent studies have examined the composition of networks. In a study of the impact of gender on entrepreneurial networks (Foss and Bye, 2002) women were shown to have a higher (though not significant) share of social contacts than men, and education was shown to moderate the share effect.[1] At lower education levels women had a higher share of social contacts than men. Despite expectations however, men did not have a higher network range than women, and the moderating effect of education was contrary to the expected direction.[2] At low education levels women had a considerably larger network than men. For men, education had a strong impact; for women it was much smaller.

On the basis of these results it would appear that women are more able to use their social contacts in establishing a business and in taking advantage of wide-ranging networks. This pattern seems to prevail for women in general, regardless of education level. Conversely, for men, a low degree of education appears to make them more isolated. Qualitative parts of the interview material from the study show that women and men gave different rationales for how they construct their networks. They differed with regard to motives for networking, how their networks affect others, and how they are perceived by others in their network. Men's rationale was more utility-focused and instrumental, whereas women, in addition to the needs of running the business, were concerned about the social, symmetric aspects of networks. Due to the sample size it is difficult to generalize the results. However, the study appears to support previous findings on gender differences in networks (Greve, 1995) and the notion that women use more social contacts in their entrepreneurship careers.

Greve and Salaff (2003) extend the earlier anecdotal evidence (Greve, 1995) in an elaborate study of network activities of entrepreneurs during three phases of establishing firms in four countries. Results from the larger study show that kin play a more important role in networks of Norwegian and Italian entrepreneurs than for entrepreneurs in the US and Sweden. This was especially true for females whose parents are self-employed. The authors suggest that the findings in differences between the ways males and females relate to their families when establishing a firm argues for additional research on how women and men develop and use their networks.

Our conclusion is that research concerning gender and social networks among entrepreneurs indicate that Norwegian women tend to include more family/kin and social contacts in their network.

Human Capital

With regard to general human capital (Becker, 1975) Norwegian women, like their Danish counterparts, are generally well educated. Between 1996 and 2000 the proportion of women who applied to study at the public colleges increased from 59.2 percent to 63.9 percent (Statistics Norway, 2001c). Of all students completing higher education in 1999/2000 in colleges and universities, 64.6 percent were women and 34.5 percent men (Statistics Norway, 2001d).

How does education among self-employed differ from that of total employment in Norway? Table 7.4 shows total employment and self-employment according to gender and education level. The proportion on each education level for men and women is shown under the 'Percent' columns.

Table 7.4   Total employment and self-employment distributed on gender and educational level (percent and total)

Education	Total employment			Self-employed		
	Percent			Percent		
	Women	Men	Total	Women	Men	Total
Total	47	53	2275000	25	75	191660
Primary and lower secondary education (level 1–2)	45	55	249645	18	82	21728
Upper secondary education (level 3–5)	45	55	1350728	24	76	104695
Tertiary education, four years or less (level 6)	56	44	496181	34	66	36774
Tertiary education, more than four years (level 7–8)	32	68	142334	25	75	22415
Other	42	58	36112	23	77	6048

Source: Statistics Norway, Structure and business register, Table 05215 and Statistics Norway, Labor market survey: Employment and education, Table: 03373.

At a low level of human capital (level 1–2), there is a negative impact on women's self-employment. Also at a high level (level 7–8), the impact on women's self-employment is negative. It seems like tertiary education (level 6) has the most positive impact on women's self-employment. The reasons for this can be that self-employment for less well-educated and highly educated women implies higher costs in terms of insecurity and amount of work hours. As an example, many women lawyers prefer to work in the public sector rather than working in private law firms with excessive working hours. For men, low human capital seems to trigger self-employment, whereas tertiary education (level 6) seems to have a negative impact on men's self-employment. It may be that men with low human capital see more possibilities within self-employment than in being employed.

The gendered education and labor market in Norway seem to produce different knowledge and competence between men and women. The sort of human capital that is produced through education and work experience therefore ends up as gender-specific through the orientation in work and education undertaken earlier in life. Norwegian women's work in the public sector deprives them of certain knowledge, for example, market experience.

The scarcity of data on entrepreneurial education and work experience in Norway means that research into Norwegian entrepreneurs' human capital is very limited. In a study of start-up in an emerging industry Foss (1994) found that five out of eight human capital variables had a strong direct impact on the likelihood of start-up among nascent entrepreneurs once the effect of resources obtained through networks was controlled. The data gave more support to the human capital model than to the conceptual model, where human capital was hypothesized to only affect start-up indirectly through its effect on social networks. The direct effect of human capital was greater than its indirect impact. The emerging industry of cod farming was the empirical case in this study. Nascent entrepreneurs with more formal schooling in terms of business education and education diversity seemed to be more risk-averse in not using the licenses to start cod farming. Special human capital in terms of technical and industrial experience had a positive impact on the likelihood for start-up. Nascent entrepreneurs with experience from related technology in fish farming and from related work experience (fishing and fish processing) had a positive effect on the probability for start-up. Hence, in the case of an emerging industry, general human capital in terms of education seems to make people risk-averse, and special human capital seem to make people likely to start a firm close to prior experience they have before. If we relate that to Kolvereid's (1992) general entrepreneurial survey, education seemed to make entrepreneurs growth ambitious, whereas general human capital in terms of general work experience did not seem to make people want to grow their business fast. Seeing these studies together, it appears as though education sharpens the underlying competence when deciding whether to proceed with a business idea to start-up, when to start up, and when determining an expansion of the business.

Personal Goals

The motives for women to become self-employed are complex. In a study where women entrepreneurs were asked about their motivations to start up a business, Pettersen et al. (1999) found that the need for self-fulfillment and the need to pursue a good business idea scored high. The need for income was seen as only moderately important, a finding supported by the fact that entrepreneurs in Norway are opportunity-driven rather than necessity-driven (GEM, 2004). Berg (1994) found three reasons for business start-up among women: to create a job, to achieve more freedom regarding their work situation, and to be able to take care of the family. According to Ljunggren (2005) the combination of personal goals and self-fulfillment and considerations regarding the household's needs of income, time consumption and reproduction tasks seems to be underestimated when studying reasons for self-employment.

Using Brush's (1992) integrative perspective on personal goals for entrepreneurship Aslesen (2002) developed four archetypes showing different ways for adjusting family and career and timing the start-up: 1) the career entrepreneur, characterizing entrepreneurs with a low family priority and a high career priority; 2) the combination entrepreneur, with high family priority and a high career priority; 3) the caring entrepreneur, with a high family priority and a low career priority; and 4) the senior entrepreneur, who has a successive priority over time, with family first and then career. Important choices regarding start-up of a business seem to be closely related to these entrepreneurs' family circumstances and their life course.

Industrial Sectors

There are few industrial sectors in Norway where female entrepreneurs dominate. In a study with data from 1997 to 1999, women started 21 percent of new businesses, and men 79 percent (Spilling, 2002). The highest female percentage within the various industrial sectors is within the textile industry (80 percent), a small industry counting for less than 1 percent of all new enterprises. The second largest share is social services where women account for 50 percent. Women have also a relatively high percentage in personal services (42.6 percent), mineral-based products (that is, glass and ceramics) (39.2 percent), retailing (38.1 percent), hotels and restaurants (30.2 percent).

However, men dominate in most sectors and account for 90 percent of new enterprises in construction and building, fishing, electricity and water supply, metal products, transport and chemical enterprises. It appears as though entrepreneurs' choice of industry reflects the gendered patterns we find in educational choices. The general pattern is that women tend to start businesses in trade, hotel and restaurants, agriculture and personal and private services. Men establish firms in industry, construction and building. This pattern is similar to that of female and male managers (Spilling, 2002).

More recent data from 2004 is presented in Table 7.5 below, where self-employment is distributed by gender and industrial sector. Percentages in parentheses.

Table 7.5 shows that men own 74.6 percent of all firms in 2004, whereas women own 25.4 percent. There are three sectors where women own more than 50 percent of the firms: health and social work, other community social and personal services, paid domestic work. These sectors, however, constitute a small share of the total firm portfolio. Paid domestic work constitutes just 1 percent, active membership of organizations 14.8 percent and other community service 13.4 percent. These statistics reinforce the argument made above: self-employment among women in Norway is concentrated in a few industries, which reflects the gender-segregated education and labor market, and that seems to reinforce the classical female skills: social nursing/services and health. When updating this statistic with recent statistics on all new establishments from 2003 the pattern looks very much the same (Statistics Norway, Structure and business register, Table 05188), so we may conclude that the picture from 2001 does not seem to have changed in either direction.

D.   SUPPLY-SIDE ISSUES FOR WOMEN ENTREPRENEURS IN NORWAY

The supply side of venture capital in Norway can be classified according to three different types: *privately-owned*, *semi-privately-owned* and *government-owned*. The private new venture capital (NVC) companies consist of business angles and private and semi-privately-owned venture capital funding businesses. This chapter includes only private and semi-privately-owned venture capital businesses as well as government-owned institutions, and is based on various studies (Ljunggren and Foss, 2004; Wassum Investment Consulting, 2003; Pettersen et al., 1999). The data on venture capital organizations, which actually consists of government-owned funds at different organizational levels (municipality, county and ministry), are empirically based on an evaluation of this system (Pettersen et al., 1999). Empirical

Table 7.5 *Distribution by industrial sectors and gender for all firms in Norway 2004*

Sector	Men	Women	Total	Men	Women
Mining	342 (86.6)	53 (13.4)	395	0.2	0.1
Manufacturing	9386 (77.3)	2754 (22.7)	12140	6.6	5.7
Power and water supply	94 (90.4)	10 (9.6)	104	0.1	0.0
Construction and building	28004 (98.5)	426 (1.5)	28430	19.7	0.9
Trade	21438 (69.1)	9583 (30.9)	31021	15.0	19.7
Hotel and restaurants	3655 (60.3)	2408 (39.7)	6063	2.6	5.0
Transport and communication	16499 (91.1)	1609 (8.9)	18108	11.6	3.3
Financial and insurance	351 (88.4)	46 (11.6)	397	0.2	0.1
Real estate, renting and other business activities	34509 (76.1)	10826 (23.9)	45335	24.2	22.3
IT	7279 (90.4)	771 (9.6)	8050	5.1	1.6
Research and development	85 (84.2)	16 (15.8)	101	0.1	0.0
Education	2053 (62.3)	1240 (37.7)	3293	1.4	2.6
Health and social work	8456 (49.8)	8519 (50.2)	16975	5.9	17.5
Activities of membership organization, recreational, culture and sport activities	8836 (68.0)	4164 (32.0)	13000	6.2	8.6
Other community, social and personal service	1320 (17.8)	6094 (82.2)	7414	0.9	12.5
Paid homework	34 (45.3)	41 (54.7)	75	0.0	0.1
Missing	158 (88.3)	21 (11.7)	179	0.1	0.0
Total	142499 (74.6)	48581 (25.4)	191080	100.0	100.0

Source: Statistics Norway. Norwegian business enterprise sector. Structure and business register. Table 05186.

evidence on the two other types of venture capital firms is found in primary and secondary data, presented in a pilot study by Ljunggren and Foss (2004). The primary data on these firms is a random sample of privately-owned venture capital firms where data was assembled from the companies' homepages. They were also investigated by using secondary data (other reports, newspaper articles, etc.). The topic of new venture capital firms has, to our knowledge, hardly been investigated in Norway. Access to data and research findings is therefore limited.[3]

The division of NVC firms into private and government firms seems to indicate different funding profiles – or a labor division between the two sectors. The data indicates that privately-owned firms prioritize growth, that is, firms already established, while government organizations mainly finance new firms, that is, establishment of new firms.

Private and Semi-private New Venture Capital Funding in Norway

There are several private and semi-privately-owned NVC funds in Norway. A count on the Web showed 30 different private and semi-private companies, but the total is probably 45 to 50 according to the European Venture Capital Association (EVCA, 2001). The private NVC firms are owned by quite large firms and to a lesser degree (if at all) by individuals with private assets. As indicated, the semi-private companies are owned by private investors, mainly larger firms and government funds.[4] The investment profiles of all these companies are focused on different types of technology development/ innovation within space technology, electronics, energy technology, biotechnology and ICT, for example.

Private new venture capital firms

The private NVC firms invest in types of projects often claimed to be high-risk, high-tech, and at an early stage. These types of projects are mainly found in fairly large technological firms. Knowing that female business owners (like most business owners in Norway – regardless of gender) run micro-businesses, an unsophisticated deduction would claim that few women-owned businesses are financed by these firms. As shown above, industries in Norway are gender-segregated where women's businesses are mainly found within the service sector – and knowing that the NVC are not targeting this sector we conclude that female-owned businesses are not a target group for the NVC companies.

Also, the private and semi-private NVC funding could be said to have a geographical skewness, although the semi-private funds are bound to have a geographical dispersion. The private NVC funds are mainly located – and invest in industries – around the capital Oslo. An evaluation of the semi-private funds showed that three out of five of these firms invested in firms within 50 km (30 miles) of the head office (Wassum Investment Consulting, 2003).

Table 7.6 presents an overview of seven of the 45 (approximately) privately-owned venture capital firms in Norway. The industries that are prioritized in these companies are quite similar to each other, and comprise industries that are often regarded as the future innovative industries, hence having the largest growth and profit potential. But these industries are also industries with a low level of women employees, entrepreneurs and owners. The composition of the partners, the advisory boards and boards of directors also tells us something about what kind of competence is emphasized. The data show that most persons in these positions either have a masters degree in science/technology or in business administration; some have a law degree. Partners, advisory boards and boards of directors have hardly any women members, which reflects the general situation among the top management and boards of directors in Norwegian limited companies. The seven NVC firms listed in Table 7.6 have a funding capital of approximately 2612 million NOK, which, compared with the government funds (396 million NOK), is a substantial amount.

A woman business owner in Norway aiming at business growth and wanting to finance this by private or semi-private new venture capital funding needs to have a large technology firm localized close to the capital source. Firms meeting these requirements are extremely rare. In spite of scarce empirical evidence we therefore believe that the amount of money NVCs invest in women-owned firms is negligible.

Semi-private new venture capital firms[5]

In Norway there are six 'seed capital' funds (*Såkorninvest fond*) where the government provides subordinated loan capital, while the stock capital is provided by private investors. The funds are assigned to different regions, except for one (the START fund), which is nationwide. An important part of the funds' assignment is to transfer know-how to their client firms. This is mainly achieved by the NVCs appointing individuals to join the board of directors in the businesses receiving venture capital. These persons are individuals working in the administration of the funds or in the funds' board of directors and their networks. At present we do not have an overview of the competence or gender composition of these funds, but as the government is involved in these firms there is a law requiring that 40 percent of the board of directors of companies with a public ownership are women.

Table 7.7 shows the funds' total investments since they were established in 1997/98. The types of industry in which these funds invest is highly gender-divided. The findings from the Wassum report (2003) show that 42 percent of the investment is made in the ICT industry; biotechnology represents 17 percent, the marine sector 8 percent, off-shore 6 percent, and a group of 'others' totaling 27 percent of the investments. It is not stated what this group of 'others' comprises.

In addition to these funds we were able to identify seven other locally founded venture capital firms of the mixed-ownership type. We do not have much information about these companies but some of them have local private investors in conjunction with local (municipality) government funding. Lastly we identified Argentum, which is a government-owned fund-in-fund, meaning that Argentum invests in other venture capital funds.

Governmental new venture capital funding in Norway[6]

In Norway, bodies at different government levels are appointed to support entrepreneurs economically. The highest governmental body is at the ministry level: the Ministry of Local Government and Regional Development (KRD). The ministry distributes funds to local government authorities; to the county administrations and local municipalities for this purpose. Also, the Norwegian Industrial and Regional Development Fund, 'Innovation Norway', is a main actor. This organization is financed by several ministries (Fisheries and Coastal Affairs, Agriculture and Food, Trade and Industry, Local Government and Regional Development, and The Environment). The 'bias' with the governmental system is the claim of these funds to enhance a policy of some kind, for example, regional policy. But as the new public governance implies that the public sector needs to be more 'businesslike' Innovation Norway now seems to be more concerned about making a higher demand for return on investments than filling regional policy goals.

Innovation Norway administers and distributes establishment grants for businesses and entrepreneurs. The amounts range from NOK 50000 to maximum NOK 400000 (6200–50000 euros).[7] The grants are intended to be used during the early phases of the entrepreneurial process, either during the preparatory stages (developing the business idea) and/or in the entering phase (investments, income support); 40 percent of the grants are intended to be allocated to women. During the period 1994–98 the total amount of establishment grants was 138 million NOK (17.25 million euros), and the total number of grants was 5899. Of these grants, female entrepreneurs received 25 percent of the total amount and 31 percent of the grants, while male entrepreneurs received 59 percent of the amount and 65 percent of the grants. After the 40 percent quotation rule was introduced in 1998 the proportion of grants to women increased.

Innovation Norway also has regional development grants aimed at businesses. These are divided into an investment grant and a business development grant.[8] The regional aspect is highlighted and small firms are

Table 7.6 An overview of parts of the privately-owned Norwegian NVC firms

Venture company[a]	Size of fund in million NOK and in million euros		Industries the NVCs prioritize	Gender composition among partners (P), in the Advisory Board (AB) and in the Board of directors (BoD)	Ownership
Capman	1000	125	Nordic firms, ICT	P: nine males and one female AB: eight males	Finnish-owned with some ownership from a Norwegian government-owned investment company (Argentum)
Northzone Ventures Est. 1994	670	83.75	Scandinavian ICT and telecommunications companies	P: nine males BoD: six males	
Teknoinvest Est. 1984	450	56.25		P: 11 males AB: five males	
Four Seasons Venture Est. 1985	125	15.63	ICT mainly		Different Norwegian companies

Selvaag Venture Capital	100	12.5	Biotechnology, ITC and telecommunications	P: two males	A part of Selvaag Invest. Est. 1984. BoD: three men and one woman. Size of fund 700 million NOK
Alliance Venture	40	5	Companies within ITC, telecom, Internet and media technology with an international potential	P: five males BoD: five males AB: seven males	Asset Management,[b] Storebrand, KLP, Vesta, Vital and the Staff-group
Viking Venture	227	28.38	ICT, medical and biotechnology, marine technology and energy and environmental	P: four males BoD: seven males	Norwegian companies
Total	2.612	326.51			

Notes:
[a] The information in this table is collected from *Dagens Naeringsliv* 21 April 2004 and from the companies' homepages.
[b] A US-owned company.

Table 7.7 Overview of the semi-privately owned investment funds

Fund	Totally invested capital in million NOK/million euros		Other information	No. of firms invested in	Average invested amount in million NOK/euros	
The Start fund Technology-based firms are prioritized	227	28.38	BoD: Six men and two women Team: Four men and one woman	22	10.3	1290000
The Inland fund Såkorninvest Innlandet	28.7	3.59		15	1.9	240000
The Southern fund Såkorninvest Sør	21.4	2.68		15	1.4	180000
The Western fund Såkorninvest	36.1	4.51		13	2.8	350000
The Mid-Norwegian fund Såkorninvest Midt-Norge	53.1	6.64		53	1.0	130000
The Northern fund Såkorninvest Nord	29.4	3.68	BoD: four men and one woman Team: one man	22	1.4	180000
Total	396	49.5		140	2.8	350000

given priority. In the period 1994–98, 4.1 billion NOK (5125 million euros) were distributed. Of this, 3.1 percent, equivalent to 126 million NOK (15.75 million euros) was allocated to 'women's projects' – that is, projects either envisaged or managed by, or targeting, women.

The local municipalities received funding from the Ministry of Local Government and Regional Development to administer a local business development fund allocating start-up grants and business loans. During the period 1994–98 these locally administered funds distributed 787 million NOK (98 million euros) of which 210 million NOK (26.25 million euros) was given to projects benefiting women's businesses. During 1999 this funding was removed from the state budget and the financing of the local business funds became dependent on the local municipalities' priorities in their budgets. This scheme has, however, recently been reinstated as part of the state budget.

In this section we have seen that the supply side of NVC in Norway seems to be gender-biased, women being in disfavor. This is in accordance with US findings, showing that businesses owned by women receiving venture capital have stayed extremely low in numbers during the period 1957–98 (Brush et al., 2001).

E.   GROWTH OF WOMEN'S ENTREPRENEURSHIP EMBEDDED IN COUNTRY CONTEXT

In this chapter the labor force review, profile of women's entrepreneurship, the demand- and the supply-side issues of women's entrepreneurship in Norway leave us with one question: is women entrepreneurship in Norway sort of special? In this section we will relate the lack of growth of women's entrepreneurship to what we may call the national and historical context in which the entrepreneurs are embedded.

The lack of growth of women's entrepreneurship in Norway is due to several factors. We have already pointed to the fact that a gender-segregated labor market conforms to the division of gender, with few women pursuing entrepreneurship. One feature of the history of the Norwegian labor market has been that the development from unpaid family work to paid work in the welfare state after World War II, has shaped an occupational narrowness that reproduces traditional values (Foss, 2005). The rapid conversion of housewives into wage-earners in the public sector during only a decade or so, necessarily 'forced' women to choose an occupation that fitted their qualifications; qualifications acquired through unpaid work in the private sphere, such as childcare, care of the elderly and service work. The fact that Norwegian women and men choose different occupations – as was the case some 20 years ago – indicates the reproduction of labor market participation and traditional gender roles.

Concerning entrepreneurship, we believe that this historical picture explains some elements in the socialization process that has had effect between the generations. According to Astin (1985) childhood socialization and early childhood experiences are important in shaping occupational interests. In a study among youth in northern Norway Karlsen (2001) demonstrates that gender is the most significant factor explaining differences in work preferences among youths. This supports an earlier study by Roalsø (1994) who found that while many girls emphasize human values and cherish close contact with other people, most boys tend to emphasize safety and comfort issues and career-related issues. The transition from unpaid to paid work in traditional female occupations seems to have had a reinforcing effect on the next generation. Our argument is that traditional gender roles for girls have led to gender-segregated educational and occupational choices as adults. In this picture self-employment is likely to come out as a masculine choice and a too risky business for women.

We also claim that another issue contributes to the slow development of female entrepreneurs: Noway has been unsuccessful in creating equal opportunities for men and women in the private sector as has been done in the public sector. The private sector has not only been lagging behind in creating equal opportunities; the attitudes here are rather conservative when it comes to gender equality.[9] The Norwegian Federation of Employers has also been against quotas for women on the boards of private companies; a principle that has applied to the public sector for many years. According to a poll carried out by Statistics Norway, examining the attitudes toward equality among 1700 Norwegian top managers, half were positive towards quotas for women on the boards of private companies. Managers in the private sector, however, were clearly more ambivalent than the rest, as only 20 percent were in favor. The employer organizations were also ambivalent, with only 25 percent favoring the proposition. In contrast, the majority of top managers in the public sector and politicians were in favor of quotas for women. This illustrates the difference between the public and private sector attitudes in Norway. Whereas the former has been on the frontier with regard to gender equality, the latter has been far more ambivalent.[10]

The private sector also distinguishes itself in how it implements the work–family rights developed as part of Norway's official family policy. Norway's advanced welfare system includes unemployment benefit, sickness allowance/payment and paid maternity leave, etc. A comparison of labor market and social welfare developments in Norway and Great Britain between 1980 to 1990 shows that the benefits are far more extensive in Norway, and that both welfare state employment and welfare expenditure have increased in

Norway, whereas it has decreased in Great Britain (Hansen, 1995). From the entrepreneurs' point of view this increase does not help very much, because the self-employed are not fully included in these welfare services if they have a business with legal status as sole proprietorship – as is the most common legal status among the self-employed. Parental leave is generally more generous in the public than the private sector (Ellingsæter, 1999). In the former, mothers receive full wage compensation in connection with paid leave, in addition to being entitled to extra unpaid leave (of up to three years) before the child reaches 12 years of age. Smaller firms, and self-employed people in particular, seldom have the financial ability to implement these arrangements. With regard to paid maternity leave there are some limited rights for the self-employed, but less than those of employed persons (Ljunggren, 1999). There are no rights to unemployment benefit and with regard to sick pay, the self-employed need to purchase insurance, which usually does not cover the first 14 days of sickness. To be included in the welfare system, self-employed persons have to purchase expensive insurance.

Whereas the 'father quota' is compensated for in full within the public sector, it is only partly compensated for in the private sector. Compensation beyond a certain level depends on negotiations with the employer. Another difference between the sectors, which is also related to family policy is that women in the public sector are entitled to spend up to two hours each day breastfeeding until the child is six months. This arrangement does not apply in the private sector. This implies that women entrepreneurs having parental leave are left with a less generous package compared with their colleagues in the public sector.

We conclude that Norway, with emphasis on a dual-earner policy and the development of the welfare state, has created a labor market where women are drawn to the public sector, leaving self-employment as an untraditional and risky career. According to the GEM studies Norwegian entrepreneurs are opportunity driven, and not, as in countries with poorer welfare regimes, necessity driven.

F. FUTURE CHALLENGES IN POLICY AND RESEARCH

Summary of Critical Issues in Norway

This country report points to several critical issues with regard to the low number of women entrepreneurs in Norway. We have highlighted the gender-segregated labor market and education system. The low number of women entrepreneurs seems to follow other trends such as few women in top managerial positions and in boardrooms. The private sector does not seem as appealing to women as the public sector. With regard to the private sector, women entrepreneurs are in the minority in most firms in this sector. Female entrepreneurs are in the majority in a few industries, like health and social services. Women seem to start in industries where they have prior experience and knowledge, often related to service and healthcare. Women's businesses in Norway are smaller than those of men and research into the growth of female businesses has been limited in Norway. Reviews of studies lead us to conclude that there are both structural and individual reasons for the lack of growth. On the demand side we have seen that women put little equity into their business. Studies of social networks show that female networks contain more kin than female entrepreneurs in other nations. Qualitative data suggest that women behave differently in networks than men. Future research needs to address the pros and cons of these two issues.

On the supply side our report shows that different funding profiles emerge when we classify NVC firms according to private and government firms. Privately-owned firms seem to prioritize growth (already established firms) whereas governmental organizations seem to finance the establishment of new firms. Female-owned businesses do not seem to be the target of the former. The private NVC funds also invest in industries in the Oslo region, in high-tech and innovative firms that have a low level of female employees, entrepreneurs and owners. The semi-private NVC firms also seem to be gender-segregated – as their investment is also in male-dominated businesses (ICT industry, biotechnology, marine sector, offshore, etc.). With regard to the governmental NVC funding, our analysis shows that also here women receive much lower establishment grants than men for businesses and in regional development grants.

Policy Recommendations

Policy recommendations have been discussed in Norwegian entrepreneurship research (see Alsos and Ljunggren, 2002; Pettersen et al., 1999; Ljunggren, 2002; Spilling and Foss, 2002; Alsos and Kolvereid, 2005). The suggestions have raised a broad front of issues, which include both special attention towards women and lowering structural hurdles to entrepreneurship in general. Our approach is that policy recommendations need to be embedded in the more structural problem in Norway's gender-segregation in both education and worklife. We advocate the 'double strategy'; having a special entrepreneurship policy to support women entrepreneurs and an integrated policy pursuing both men and women to become entrepreneurs. The policies also need to address issues concerning young people's educational choices. Entrepreneurship still has the flavor of 'being different' in Norway, and like pursuing top management jobs, women entrepreneurship is still viewed as a 'male thing'. We need to increase the desire among youth to pursue innovative educational strategies. This desire is formed early on and is based on values and norms that are produced early in childhood and adulthood. To support children and young people's ideas and to pursue innovative actions has not been seen as a pedagogical task in the Norwegian school system. Norway has more tradition of educating workers rather than entrepreneurs.

The initiative on entrepreneurship in education is shown to support entrepreneurship in general (Luktvasslimo, 2003). According to her, 5000 pupils at high-school level establish businesses each year, and surprisingly girls are the more active parties in these 'youth enterprises' (*ungdomsbedrifter*). The youth enterprises are positive in several ways: they show that entrepreneurship is something everyone can pursue and this is important as the level of entrepreneurship in Norway also needs to be increased among young men. We also believe that role models are important, showing that women can succeed in business life and as self-employed persons. We need more visible women in Norwegian business life. A TV show, *The Apprentice*, is an example of how this can be done.

Research Recommendations

The supply side

Our research recommendations on the supply side is that further studies on women and new venture capital funding in Norway are necessary. The lack of substantial knowledge is striking, especially when it comes to private NVC companies. A more thorough study would include the funding profile of private NVC firms with regard to gender, size and age of the firms, size of investment and type of know-how offered, geographical diffusion, etc. As the types of projects these NVC firms want to invest in are said to be high-risk, high-tech and in an early stage of development, it would be interesting to see whether there are any gender differences in this regard. Knowing that female business owners (like most business owners in Norway, regardless of gender) run micro-businesses, an unsophisticated hypothesis would claim that few women-owned businesses are financed by these firms. So far we do not have any information on banks and business angels funding profile regarding gender. This theme should be further investigated. One problem with the semi-private NVC funds is said to be their high demand on equity ratio; as very few firms can meet them, large parts of the VC funds are not invested. This needs to be investigated to be verified.

Also, the private and semi-private NVC funding could be said to have a geographical skewness, although the semi-private funds are bound to have a geographical dispersion. The private NVC funds are mainly located and invested in industries around the capital (Oslo). Will this have any implications for women business owners? We have indications on the different profiles in investment between the different ownership types. We also know that the government needs to follow equality law on this matter to a larger extent than for private stakeholders. This fact calls for further studies.

One possible question is: what are the factors on both the supply and demand sides affecting the availability and the need for NVC in Norway? Several researchers (Mason and Harrison, 1999) point to the need for research on the demand side. We need to take into consideration that barriers on the demand side can be both structural and individual/motivational. We are specifically concerned with the mental models held by actors in the venture capital business as well as women's own reflections on the need for capital and growth of their business. This challenges us to use new theoretical and methodological approaches.

The demand side
In order to gain knowledge on women's entrepreneurship in Norway we have to move beyond describing the fact that men and women have different educational and worklife experiences and therefore enter entrepreneurship in different ways. When, how, where, to what extent and why (to borrow Ellingsæter's labor market terminology) are questions we need to consider. Newer research on labor market, citizenship and entrepreneurship in Norway suggests aiming for a more comprehensive and differentiated view on gender and employment, women's political integration and the distinction between masculinity and femininity (Skjeie and Siim, 2000; Foss, 2002). Concerning the entrepreneurship field this leads us to broaden our research approaches to include a more comparative view, introducing life-course approaches, and the findings of pedagogic and sociological research. We maintain that a variety of theoretical and methodological approaches are needed to understand the dynamic transition taking place in Norway with regard to education and work. This chapter has indicated that the problem concerning women entrepreneurship very likely appears before adulthood. This moves the focus on to socialization, parenting, role modeling and teaching.

NOTES

1. Social contacts are defined as partner, parents, siblings, relatives, close friends and previous colleagues. The share of social contacts is a weighted measure: the number of social contacts divided by the number of business contacts, multiplied by network range.

2. Range is defined as the number of different actors (out of a total of 17) in the network, with whom the entrepreneur has daily, weekly or monthly contact.
3. The topic of business angles has, however, been studied, see for example Sørheim, 2002; Erikson et al., 2003.
4. Each of these firms has a capital of 20 million NOK (approximately 2.5 million euros).
5. Data in this part of the chapter is based on a report written for the Norwegian Ministry of Trade and Industry: *Evaluering av Såkornordningen*, by Wassum Investment Consulting (2003), and on information provided by the homepages of the companies.
6. All numbers referred to in this paragraph are taken from Pettersen et al., 1999.
7. One euro is at present (2005) approximately 8 NOK.
8. Investment grants are to be used in specific investments in establishing new firms, expansion of a firm or product/production development. Business development grants are given to single firms or groups of firms (networks) and are intended to be used to train employees, marketing, etc.
9. In 1978, when the Gender Equality Act was passed, the Norwegian Federation of Employers (NHO) was firmly against any kind of government regulation. On the 20 years' anniversary of this act in 1999, NHO's director admitted: 'In 1978 we did not agree that there was a need for a law on gender equality. We put more trust in agreements and arguments than in formal legislation. Today hardly anyone would have gone against the act'.
10. This can also be illustrated by the fact that the Norwegian Minister of Trade and Industry has declared that he is tired of the 'old boy's network' in private enterprises. Accordingly, he has proposed that – as a rule – there should be 40 percent women in all boardrooms, full gender equality in all companies owned by the state. He has, furthermore, 'threatened' the private sector with mandatory quotas for women lest it comes up with better female representation. He put the problem like this: 'The women have got the education and the experience, but not the positions'.

REFERENCES

Alsos, G.A. and Kolvereid, L. (2005), 'Entrepreneurship among women in Norway', in E.S. Hauge and P.A. Havnes (eds), *Women Entrepreneurs: Theory, Research and Policy Implications*, Kristiansand: Høyskoleforlaget AS.

Alsos, G.A. and Ljunggren, E. (2002), 'Betydningen av kjønn i etableringsprosessen' ('The meaning of gender in the entrepreneurial process'), in N.G. Berg (ed.), *Entreprenørskap: Kjønn, livsløp og sted* (*Entrepreneurship: Gender, life-course and place*), Oslo: Abstrakt, pp. 109–23.

Anna, A.L., Chandler, G.N., Jansen, E. and Mero, N.P. (1999), 'Women business owners in traditional and non-traditional industries', *Journal of Business Venturing*, **15**, 279–303.

Aslesen, S. (2002), 'Entreprenørskap – med basis i familiestatus' ('Entrepreneurship and family status'), in N.G. Berg and L. Foss (eds), *Entreprenørskap: Kjønn, livsløp og sted* (*Entrepreneurship: Gender, life-course and place*), Oslo: Abstrakt, pp. 153–70.

Astin, H.S. (1985), 'The meaning of work in women's lives: A sociopsychological model of career choice and work behaviour', *The Counselling Psychologist*, **12**, 117–26.

Becker, G.S. (1975), *Human Capital*, New York: National Bureau of Economic Research.

Berg, N.G. (1994), 'Servicelokalisering og entreprenørskap' ('Service location and entrepreneurship'), PhD thesis, Geografisk Institutt, Trondheim: UNIT-AVH.

Berg, N.G. and Foss, L. (eds) (2002), *Entreprenørskap: Kjønn, livsløp og sted* (*Entrepreneurship: Gender, life-course and place*), Abstrakt forlag.

Brun, C. (1998), 'Kjønn og entreprenørskap' ('Gender and entrepreneurs'), in O.R. Spilling (ed.), *Entreprenørskap på norsk* (*Entrepreneurship in Norway*), Bergen: Fagbokforlaget.

Brush, C.G. (1992), 'Research on women business owners: Past trends, a new perspective and future directions', *Entrepreneurship Theory and Practice*, Summer, 5–30.

Brush, C.G., Carter, N., Gatewood, E., Greene, P.G. and Hart, M.M. (2001), 'An investigation of women-led firms and venture capital investment', Paper presented for US Small Business Administration, Office of Advocacy National Women's Business Council.

Burt, R. (1997), 'The contingent value of social capital', *Administrative Science Quarterly*, **42**, 339–65.

Catalyst Inc. (2002), 'Census of women corporate top officers and top earners', (http://www.catalystwomen.org/knowledge/titles/title.php?page=cen_WOTE02).

Clark, T. and James, F. (1992), 'Women-owned businesses: Dimensions and policy issues', *Economic Development Quarterly*, **6**(1), 25–40.

Colbjørnsen, T. (2004), *Leaders and Leadership*, Bergen: Fagbokforlaget.

Dagens Næringsliv (2004), 21 April.

Devine, T.J. (1994), 'Characteristics of self-employed women in the United States', *Monthly Labor Review*, **117**(3), 20–34.

Ellingsæter, A.E. (1999), 'Dual breadwinners between state and the market', in R. Crompton (eds), *Restructuring Gender Relations and Employment. The Decline of the Male Breadwinner*, Oxford: Oxford University Press, pp. 40–60.

Erikson, T., Sørheim, R. and Reitan, B. (2003), 'Family angels vs. other informal investors', *Family Business Review*, **16**(3), 163–71.

EVCA (2001), *Annual Report*, The European Private Equity and Venture Capital Association.

Fortune 500, List of the Fortune 500, http://www.fortune.com/fortune/.

Foss, L. (1994), 'Entrepreneurship: The impact of human capital, social network and business resource on start-up', PhD thesis, Bergen: The Norwegian School of Economics and Business Administration.

Foss, L. (2002), 'Oppsummering og forslag til nye perspektiver og metoder' ('Summary and suggestions for new perspectives and methods'), in N.G. Berg and L. Foss (eds), *Entreprenørskap: Kjønn, livsløp og sted* (*Entrepreneurship: Gender, life-course and place*), Oslo: Abstrakt, pp. 299–323.

Foss, L. (2005), 'The Norwegian Paradox: World champion in gender equality – loser in female management recruitment', in Fuglseth, A.M. and A.I. Kleppe (2005), *Anthology for Kjell Grønhaug in his Celebration of his 70th Birthday*, Bergen: Fagbokforlaget.

Foss, L. and Bye, P. (2002), 'Betyr kjønn noe for etablereres nettverk?' ('Does gender matter for entrepreneurs' network?'), in N.G. Berg and L. Foss (eds), *Entreprenørskap: Kjønn, livsløp og sted* (*Entrepreneurship: Gender, life-course and place*), Oslo: Abstrakt, pp. 219–43.

Global Entrepreneurship Monitoring (GEM) (2004), http://www.gemconsortium.org/.

Greve, A. (1995), 'Networks and entrepreneurship – an analysis of social relations, occupational background, and use of contacts during the establishment process', *Scandinavian Journal of Management*, **11**(1), 1–24.

Greve, A. and Salaff, J.W. (2003), 'Social networks and entrepreneurship', *Entrepreneurship Theory and Practice*, Fall, 1–22.

Hansen, M.N. (1995), The vicious circle of the welfare state? Women's labor market situation in Norway and Great Britain', *Comparative Social Research*, **15**, 1–34.

http://www.allianceventure.com/index.html.

http://www.fsv.no/pages/about.htm.

http://www.northzone.com/.

http://www.selvaag.no/showChannel.asp?channelID=406.

http://www.startfondet.no/.

http://www.teknoinvest.com/index.html.

http://www.vikingventure.no/.

Isaksen, E. and Kolvereid, L. (2005), 'Growth objectives in Norwegian start-up businesses', *International Journal of Entrepreneurship and Small Business*, **2**(1), 17–26.

Jensen, R.S. (2005), *Women Towards Ownership, in Business and Agriculture: National Report*, Oslo: ISF.

Karlsen, U.D. (2001), 'Some things never change: Youth and occupational preferences', *Acta Sociologica*, **44**, 201–80.

Kolvereid, L. (1992), 'Growth aspirations among Norwegian entrepreneurs', *Journal of Business Venturing*, **7**, 209–22.

Kolvereid, L., Alsos, G.A. and Amo, B.W. (2004), 'Entreprenørskap i Norge 2004' ('Entrepreneurship in Norway 2004'), *Global Entrepreneurship Monitor*, Bodø: Handelshøgskolen i Bodø.

Kolvereid, L., Shane, S. and Westhead, P. (1991), 'National environment, product strategy and performance: A three country survey of new ventures', Working Paper/Bodø Graduate School of Business, 14104/91.

Kolvereid, L., Shane, S. and Westhead, P. (1993), 'Is it equally difficult for female entrepreneurs to start businesses in all countries?', *Journal of Small Business Management*, **31**(4), 43–51.

Ljunggren, E. (1998), *The New Business Formation Process: Why Are There so Few Women Entrepreneurs in Norway?*, FE-publikationer 1998:159, Umeå School of Business, Umeå: University of Umeå.

Ljunggren, E. (1999), 'Hvorfor er det så få kvinnelige etablerere i Norge? En kvantitativ studie av entreprenørskap' ('Why are there so few women entrepreneurs in Norway? A quantitative study of entrepreneurship'), *Kvinneforskning*, 4.

Ljunggren, E. (2002), 'Entreprenørskap og kjønn: En kunnskapsreise mellom to perspektiver: fra individ til relasjon' ('Entrepreneurship and gender: A journey of learning: from the individual perspective to the relational perspective'), PhD thesis, Studier i företagsekonomi, serie B, nr. 48, Umeå: Umeå Universitet.

Ljunggren, E. (2005), 'The entrepreneur as social embedded: How does the interaction between the entrepreneur and the household impact on business start-up and business strategy?', Paper presented at the Babson–Kauffman Entrepreneurship Research Conference at Babson College, Wellesley, MA, 8–11 June 2005.

Ljunggren, E. and Foss, L. (2004), 'Women's entrepreneurship in Norway: The need for and access to new venture capital', 13th Nordic Conference on Small Business Research, Tromsø.

Luktvasslimo, M. (2003), *Hva hendte siden? Ungdomsbedrifter i den videregående skolen* (*What happened later? Youth enterprises in high school*), NFT notat 2003:1, Steinkjer: NTF.

Mason, C. and Harrison, R. (1999), 'Venture capital: Rationale, aims and scope', *Venture Capital: An International Journal of Entrepreneurial Finance*, **1**(1), 1–47.

OECD (2000), *Employment Outlook*.

OECD (2001), *Employment Outlook*.

Økonomisk Rapport (1999).

Pettersen, L.T., Alsos, G.A., Anvik, C.H., Gjertsen, A. and Ljunggren, E. (1999), *Blir det arbeidsplasser av dette da, jenter? Evaluering av kvinnesatsing i distriktspolitikken* (*Are you creating any new jobs? An evaluation of the rural policy in Norway*), NF-rapport 13/99.

Roalsø, K.M. (1994), 'Jenters strategier for voksenlivet. En analyse av unge kvinners yrkesaspirasjoner, utdanningsvalg, yrkesmønstre og familie start' ('Young women's strategies for adult life. An analysis of young women's work aspirations, educational choice, work pattern and family start'), Program for ungdomsforskning (Programme for youth research), Oslo: Norges forskningsråd (Norwegian Research Council).

Rosenfeld, R.A. and Birkelund, G.E. (1995), 'Women's part-time work: A cross-national comparison', *European Sociological Review*, **11**, 111–34.

Singh, S.P., Reynolds, R.G. and Muhammad, S. (2001), 'A gender-based performance analysis of micro and small enterprises in Java and Indonesia', *Journal of Small Business Management*, **39**(2), 174–82.

Skjeie, H. and Siim, B. (2000), 'Scandinavian feminist debates on citizenship', in *International Political Science Review*, **21**(4), 345–60.

Skjeie, H. and Teigen, M. (2003), 'Menn i mellom. Mannsdominans og likestillingspolitikk' ('Between men. Male dominance and policy for equal opportunities'), Makt-og demokratiutredningen (Power and Democracy Study), 1998–2003, Gyldendal Akademisk.

Spilling, O.R. (2002), 'Kjønn, entreprenørskap og foretaksledelse i norsk næringsliv' ('Gender, entrepreneurship and business management in Norwegian business'), in N.G. Berg and L. Foss (eds), *Entreprenørskap: Kjønn, livsløp og sted* (*Entrepreneurship: Gender, life-course and place*), pp. 83–108. Oslo: Abstrakt forlag.

Spilling, O.R. and Foss, L. (2002), 'Kjønn, entreprenørskap og politikk' ('Gender, entrepreneurship and politics'), in N.G. Berg and L. Foss (eds), *Entreprenørskap: Kjønn, livsløp og sted* (*Entrepreneurship: Gender, life-course and place*), pp. 265–98. Oslo: Abstrakt.

Sørheim, R. (2002), 'The pre-investment behaviour of business angels: a social capital approach', *Venture Capital: An International Journal of Entrepreneurial Finance*, **5**(4), 337–64.

Statistics Norway (2000), 'Arbeidskraftundersøkelsen. Yrkesfordeling. Sysselsatte, etter yrke i privat/ofentlig sektor. Årsgjennomsnitt 2000', 1000 ('Labour force survey – data on occupations. Employed persons by occupation annual average 2000'). www.ssb.no/emner/06/01/yrkeaku/arkiv/tab-2001-02-01-08.html.

Statistics Norway (various years), Structure and business register.

Statistics Norway (2001a), Population statistics.

Statistics Norway (2001b), Labor force participation.

Statistics Norway (2001c), 'Opptak til statlige høgskoler, etter kjønn og utdanning, 1996–2000' (Admissions to state college by gender and type of education, 1996–2000'), www.ssb.no/emner/04/utdanning_as/200106/t-2-3.html.

Statistics Norway (2001d), 'Antall fullførte utdanninger, etter kjønn, studiåret 1999/2000' ('Number of completed educations after gender study year 1999/2000'), www.ssb.no/emner/04/utdanning_as/200108/vedltab%203.html.

Statistics Norway (2002), 'Arbeidskraftundersøkelsen. Yrkesfordeling. Sysselsatte etter yrke privat/offentlig sektor' ('Labour force survey. Data on occupations. Employed persons by occupations in private/public sector'), Årsgjennomsnitt 2001.
Statistics Norway (2004), *Befolkningsundersøkelsen*.
Wassum Investment Consulting (2003), *Evaluering av Såkornordningen*.

8. Women's entrepreneurship in the United States

Candida G. Brush, Nancy M. Carter, Elizabeth J. Gatewood, Patricia G. Greene and Myra M. Hart

OVERALL ENTREPRENEURIAL ACTIVITY IN THE US

The participation of United States women in entrepreneurial activity is best considered within the context of the overall US (and world) entrepreneurial sector. There are approximately 23 million small firms in the US economy, representing over 99 percent of all US firms. Small firms employ half of all private sector employees and generate over 44 percent of private payroll in the US – and approximately 50 percent of private, gross domestic product. In addition, small firms are responsible for 60–80 percent of net new jobs for the US economy in any year (SBA Office of Advocacy, 2004).

The US population is almost 300 million people, approximately 180 million are between the ages of 18 years and 64, and of this group, over 11 percent are involved in starting a new business or own or manage a business that is less than 42 months old, which means that in 2004 more than 20 million people in the US were involved in entrepreneurial activity. The 2004 US total entrepreneurial activity (TEA) (Hancock and Fitzsimons, 2004) is the highest among G7 countries, and the fourth highest of developed countries, lagging behind New Zealand (14.67 percent), Israel (13.57 percent), and Australia (13.38 percent).

WOMEN'S ENTREPRENEURSHIP

Growth in Numbers and Impact

Entrepreneurial activity

In 2004 US men were still more entrepreneurially active than US women, however the gap has narrowed and is not statistically significant (Minniti et al., 2004). Approximately 11.98 percent of men aged 18–64 are actively involved in starting a business or own or manage a business that is less than 42 months old. Women's entrepreneurial activity rate is 10.69 percent (for every 1 woman there are 1.12 men). From 2000 through 2003, the average participation ratio of US men to women was 1.8 men for every woman.

The participation of women in entrepreneurship varies significantly across the 34 countries participating in the 2004 GEM study, ranging from 39.1 percent in Peru, 25.5 percent in Uganda, and 24.4 percent in Ecuador, to 1.2 percent in Japan and 1.6 percent in Hong Kong and Slovenia. There is no country where women are more active than men, although in a few countries (Ecuador, Finland, Hungary, Japan, South Africa), such as the United States, the gender gap in not statistically significant. On average, participation rates for men tend to be 50 to 60 percent higher than those of women, a result that has been fairly consistent over several years in a row (Minniti and Bygrave, 2003; Minniti et al., 2004). For developed countries, US women's entrepreneurial activity ranks third behind New Zealand (12.09 percent) and Australia (11.03 percent).

Ownership

Women business owners are an important and growing force in the United States economy, both in terms of the number of participants and the gross revenues and employment they represent. The number of women-owned businesses continues to grow at twice the rate of all US firms and one in 18 women in the US is a business owner (Center for Women's Business Research, 2004).

The estimates for 2004 (extrapolated from the 1997 Census) continue to document the impact of women entrepreneurs in the US economy. In 2004, there were a projected 10.6 million privately-held businesses in which a woman or women owned at least 50 percent. The majority women-owned firms were projected to be 30 percent of all businesses, some 6.7 million businesses, while equally-owned firms represented another 18 percent of all firms. The 10.6 million women-owned and equally-owned firms employed 19.1 million people and generated $2.46 trillion in revenue (Center for Women's Business Research, 2004).

The growth of women ownership continues to exceed the national averages for all firms. From 1997 to 2004, the number of women-owned firms grew at a rate of 17 percent. They registered revenue increases of 39 percent. This was in comparison to a 9 percent growth in the number of firms overall and a 34 percent increase in revenues (Center for Women's Business Research, 2004).

Disparity in Size

Although women owners are a growing force in the US economy, and almost reaching parity with men in trying to start businesses, women-owned businesses are, on average, smaller than those owned by men (Kalleberg and Leicht, 1991; Fischer et al., 1993; Chaganti and Parasuraman, 1996).

Despite the fact that women-owned firms were 26 percent of all firms, they only represented 4 percent of all revenues for US businesses. Equally-owned firms (17 percent) added another 5 percent in revenues, but the fact remains that firms with a significant women ownership only represent 9 percent of US revenues. Men-owned businesses are also a smaller share of the total firm revenues than their sheer number would lead us to expect. Men-owned, privately-held firms, constituting 55 percent of the number of firms overall, produce 36 percent of all revenues. In the US economy, 55 percent of revenues are produced by 2 percent of the publicly-held and or foreign-owned firms, or non-profits (US Census Bureau, 2001). The impact of this difference can be seen when we compare average receipts of women- and men-owned firms.

In 1997, women-owned firms had average revenues of $151 130, while equally-owned firms averaged $259 236 and men-owned firms $582 450. The average for all firms was $891 040. The average revenues for women-owned firms with employees was $847 419 – significantly larger than the $22 080 of revenues for women-owned firms without employees. However, men-owned firms with employees averaged $1 985 950 (without employees $45 161), while all firms with employees averaged $3 382 047. Interestingly the average of equally-owned firms with employees was $805 043, smaller than that of women-owned firms with employees. For the 268 000 publicly traded or foreign-owned firms and non-profits in the US, the average revenues were $37 701 708.

Growth Intentions of Women Entrepreneurs

One explanation frequently offered for size differences of US men- and women-owned businesses is that women didn't want to grow their businesses or they deliberately choose to keep their businesses small or have conservative expansion plans (Kaplan, 1988; Chaganti, 1986). The effect of growth motivations on subsequent growth finds support for a positive relationship (Miner et al., 1992). Owner's willingness to grow the firm seems to be one differentiator between firms that grow and those that grow slowly or not at all (Kim and Mauborgne, 1997; Gundry and Welsch, 2001). However, research on US women nascent entrepreneurs (Matthews and Human, 2000) and women owners in other countries (Kolvereid, 1992; Cliff, 1998) found few differences in growth intentions between men and women.

Recent data shows that the size differences for men and women may start to shrink. The number of women-owned firms with 1 million or more in revenue grew by 32 percent from 1997–2000, exceeding the growth in number of all women-owned firms (14 percent) or of all firms (19 percent) with revenues exceeding $1 million (Center for Women's Business Research, 2001a). It is estimated that in 2002, there were almost 113000 women-owned firms with more than a million dollars in sales (Center for Women's Business Research, (2001b). The growth rate for the largest category of women-owned firms was even more impressive.

The number of women with sales exceeding $10 million grew by 37 percent, exceeding the growth in the number of all women-owned firms (14 percent) or all firms with greater than $10 million in sales (13 percent). It was estimated that in 2002, there were almost 8500 women-owned firms with more than 100 employees with average revenues of $66 million (Center for Women's Business Research, 2001a). The number of women-owned firms employing 500+ employees grew by a staggering 124 percent – nine times the rate for women-owned firms in general and nearly triple (46 percent) for all firms in this employment category.

What are some of the differences between these larger women-owned firms and their smaller contemporaries? One difference is that younger women head these firms. In fact 44 percent of women owners of high-growth firms were under 45 years of age compared with only 26 percent of non-high-growth women owners. This new generation of US women business owners is very different from the older generation of women owners. These younger generation women owners are more highly educated and have gained more managerial experience than their older counterparts. They are more likely to start firms in wholesale trade, transportation, communications and utilities. Some 250000 women-owned firms are now in these sectors. The younger women owners are also more likely to express a wish to grow their firms into large enterprises, have a broader range of markets, and use different strategies for expansion.

DEMAND-SIDE ISSUES FOR WOMEN ENTREPRENEURS IN THE UNITED STATES: DO THE DIFFERENCES OF MEN AND WOMEN ENTREPRENEURS IMPACT THEIR SURVIVAL AND GROWTH?

If growth intentions are not an explanatory variable for the difference in size of men- and women-owned businesses, what other factors may impact the growth of women-owned businesses? Some researchers have argued that human, social or financial capital could be important, as well as personal goals and strategic choices (Brush et al., 2003).

Human Capital

A recurring theme in the entrepreneurship literature is the importance of human capital for entrepreneurial success. If women and men come to business ownership from different human capital backgrounds, some of those differences may impact the success of their ventures (Brush, 1992). Human capital takes many different forms: education, experience derived from paid employment or managerial responsibilities, industry experience related to the venture, prior self-employment or start-up experience.

Education
Although education may be important for success, there is no definitive answer concerning educational differences for men and women entrepreneurs. In an early study (Stevenson, 1986) women entrepreneurs were more likely to have completed high school and university than men entrepreneurs. However, a more recent study (Boden and Nucci, 2000) found that women business owners were less likely to have four or more years of college than their male counterparts. In a large sample of men and women owners, Fischer et al. (1993) found few differences in educational levels in a large sample of women and men owners, other than men owners had more production-related business education.

Some studies have shown a link between educational attainment and size or growth, while others have not. Fischer et al. (1993) found no relationship between education and size of the business as measured by sales for men or women owners. Begley and Boyd (1986) found that education attainment of entrepreneurs was not related to growth of the venture (but was related to profitability). However, in one study, US high-growth, women business owners were found to have greater educational attainment than their slower growing women contemporaries (National Foundation of Women Business Owners, 2001).

Experience
Research has not demonstrated a clear difference in educational levels of US men and women entrepreneurs, nor a clear tie to performance, but research has identified differences in experiences that men and women bring to their ventures, and for some types of experience, an impact on success.

Women have less paid employee experience (Boden and Nucci, 2000) and this may impact survival rates. Boden and Nucci found that survival rates for businesses with owners (male or female) that had at least 10 years of prior paid employee experience were higher than for those with less experience. However, they also found that the impact was not a direct one of experience but an indirect one related to start-up capital. Years of paid employment is positively correlated with the amount of capital owners used to start or acquire their businesses; and survival rates are higher for businesses that were started or acquired with $5000 or more in capital.

Although women's work experience is more often in areas that have been considered less helpful to the success of their organizations, for example in teaching, retail sales, office administration, or secretarial areas (Hisrich and Brush, 1983; Scott, 1986; Neider, 1987) than managerial experience (Fischer et al., 1993; Boden and Nucci, 2000), prior management experience was found to have no significant impact on survival rates (Bates, 1990; Boden and Nucci, 2000). And in fact, Fischer et al. (1993) found that although men had more experience managing people, experience was negatively related to sales growth.

Women also have less previous experience in self-employment (Kalleberg and Leicht, 1991) or from starting or owning prior businesses (Fischer et al., 1993), however, the lack of prior start-up experience did not appear to impact the survival of women-owned businesses (Carter et al., 1997).

Finally, US women entrepreneurs have less prior experience in the industry of their start-ups or in similar firms (Fischer et al., 1993; Carter et al., 1997), and most research has found a positive relationship between entrepreneurs' prior experience in the industry and the success of the firm (Van de Ven et al., 1984; Carter et al., 1994). Industry experience of the entrepreneur appears to differentiate higher growing firms from slower ones (Brush and Hisrich, 1991). Fischer et al. (1993) found that experience in similar firms did contribute to the differential sales growth of men-owned businesses over women-owned ones, concluding, however, that educational and experience differences in men and women account for a negligible amount of the variance in performance between men- and women-owned firms.

Social Capital

In the women's entrepreneurship literature, researchers (for example, Aldrich, 1989) have questioned whether women participated fully in the appropriate networks, spending sufficient time and effort in building diverse networks and using them appropriately. However, empirical studies have shown that US men and women entrepreneurs have more similarities than differences in building social capital. Reese (Renzulli et al., 2000) found that women and men were equally aggressive in searching for and obtaining advice and assistance through their networks. Renzulli et al. (2000) found that men and women nascent entrepreneurs had equally-sized (the vast majority of men and women mentioned five people that they used for business discussions) and diverse networks (the probability that each contact in the network will have a different relationship with the nascent than with other contacts in the network).

Although there are many similarities in the networks of men and women, there are some key differences. Renzulli et al. (2000) reported a higher proportion of kin in the networks of women nascents and women business owners. What is also interesting is that men entrepreneurs (nascent and owners) report that they predominantly have men in their network, while women nascent and owners report they have more gender-balanced networks (Aldrich et al., 1989; Renzulli et al., 2000).

Although Renzulli et al. (2000) showed that being female or having females in networks did not affect start-up outcomes, network heterogeneity significantly increased the odds of starting a business, while high proportions of kin in the network decreased the odds. Kin ties are less likely than non-kin ties to be useful in accessing information and resources – key components in successful venture creation (Fischer and Oliker, 1983; Moore, 1990; Renzulli et al., 2000).

Social capital is important in the pre-start-up phase as it can be a significant source of information about opportunities and provide social support that affects entrepreneurial career path choices (Campbell et al., 1986; Campbell, 1988; Renzulli et al., 2000). But social capital is also, maybe even more, important through the growth stages, especially for high-potential businesses. Social and business relationships of the entrepreneur provide information and resources that shape the entrepreneur's and investor's definitions and expectations for the new venture and venture financing (Sargent and Young, 1991). In particular, networks facilitate efficient access to financial capital and prove effective for tapping into professional direction and support offered by venture capital firms (Aldrich, 1989).

Financial Capital

The size differential between men- and women-owned businesses may be a function of the resources available at the start-up and through the growth phases of the businesses. Personal financial resources and the ability to access the resources of others may make the difference between successful starting and growing a business (Headd, 2003). Lack of capital at initial stages can delay or preclude start-up and may have a long-term impact on the firm. Carter and Allen (1997) show that undercapitalization at firm founding has a long-term negative effect on the performance of women-owned firms.

US women use less capital in starting or acquiring their businesses than men (Brush, 1992; Carter et al., 1997). Because the majority of businesses are started with personal savings of the founders (Bhide, 1992), normally accumulated over time, women may be handicapped because of the differential in pay structures between men and women. They are less likely to have high incomes and more likely to have very low incomes than men (Minniti and Bygrave, 2003).

Women are not only more likely to start their businesses on a shoestring but also more likely to operate on a shoestring. Some research shows that men and women use different financing strategies that may affect women entrepreneurs' ability to grow their businesses. US women were less likely to use debt capital in running their businesses (Scherr et al., 1993). And even when using debt financing, it appears that US women and men entrepreneurs used different strategies. Haynes and Haynes (1999) reported that women-owned businesses were more likely to borrow from family and friends and to have a higher proportion of their total debt from friends and family than men-owned businesses – again a strategy that may limit their ability to grow their companies.

There are some contradictory findings about the whether men and women are as likely to use lending institutions for financing their businesses. Carter et al. (1997) found that men and women they surveyed were just as likely to use formal lending institutions for starting their businesses, while Cole and Wolken (1995) found that women were less likely to use banks as a source of capital. The US Small Business Administration (2004) reports that 82.5 percent of all small businesses, but only 78.2 of women-owned firms, use some form of credit. Traditional credit sources were used by 55 percent of businesses but only 46 percent of women-owned ones, business credit cards were used by 34 percent of all and 29 percent of women-owned businesses, while 48 percent of women and 46 percent of all businesses used personal credit cards as financing sources. Coleman and Carsky (1996) found that women were less likely to have bank loans but that the finding was more a function of size and age of the businesses than gender of the owner. There is also some evidence that women use less trade credit and fewer non-depository financial services (Cole and Wolken, 1995) than their male counterparts.

Entrepreneurial firms frequently experience a funding gap when financing growth (Wetzel, 1987). Hisrich and Brush (1987) found that financing challenges decreased in importance as firms developed a track record, however, higher-growth firms, owned by men or women, have a greater need for capital than lower-growth firms. If business owners can't find sources for funding growth, the performance of those businesses will be affected. Carter and Allen (1997) found that access to capital had a greater impact on the size of the business than intentions to grow the business. Carter and Williams (2003) found that access to formal sources of financing significantly affected sales growth, while for example, type of strategies adopted by firms did not.

Although no correlation has been shown for the amount of debt a business carries and its financial success (Haynes and Haynes, 1999), there is a likely effect because of the potential impact on profitability. Without bank financing, women owners may have to resort to other more costly forms of financing. Even the type of funding may have a differential effect, for example, use of bank funding at start-up for men and women had a significant and positive effect on future sales levels in one study (Haynes and Helms, 2000). And as one might imagine, soliciting funds from family and friends can be fraught with problems (Haynes and Haynes, 1999).

According to the National Foundation of Women Business Owners (2001) high-growth business owners use a wider array of financial sources than lower-growth owners. Gundry and Welsch (2001) also found that high-growth women owners used a wider array of financing options: family, friends and relatives, personal savings and leasing to start businesses and SBA loans for expansion than their lower-growth women counterparts.

Personal Goals

Much of the early research in the field of women's entrepreneurship described the motivations for women's entrepreneurial career choices (Schwartz, 1976; Scott, 1986; Neider, 1987; Hisrich and Brush, 1985) and particular attention has been paid to women's attempts to use entrepreneurial careers to balance work and family needs.

Reasons

Carter et al. (2003) explored the reasons that US nascent entrepreneurs offered for their work and career choices and compared these responses to the reasons given by a group of non-entrepreneurs. The researchers found six separate factors related to career choice: independence, financial success, self-realization, recognition, innovation and roles. There was a small but significant difference between men and women (nascent entrepreneurs and non-nascents) for financial success and innovation. US male nascents scored financial success and innovation higher than US female nascents.

In a sample of 468 US women business owners, Brush and Hisrich (1991) reported that few of the owners reported that their businesses were based on a product innovation or entering new markets with distinctively new inventions, however they also reported that the businesses ranged from very innovative to traditionally 'female' businesses. Kalleberg and Leicht (1991) found that women were as likely to report business innovations as men were, and Sexton and Bowman-Upton (1990) reported that women scored higher on the value placed on change.

Although there were few differences of motivations of men and women nascents for starting a business, women's motivations may have an impact on subsequent performance. Gatewood et al. (1995) found that nascent women entrepreneurs who offered internal (I want to be independent) rather than external (I saw a market need) motivations for wanting to start a business were more successful in actually achieving a successful start in the year following. However, motivations for being successful in starting the business may differ from those that will be useful to survival and growth. Brush and Hisrich (1991) found a positive relationship between market opportunity motivation and survival of the business for women entrepreneurs. They found a negative relationship between independence motivation and growth of women-owned business.

Finally, although innovation is usually seen as essential to small business growth (Wilkens, 1987), innovation was unrelated to survival for women's businesses and unrelated to earnings growth for women- and men-owned businesses (Kalleberg and Leicht, 1991).

Family–work balance

It would appear that women entrepreneurs in general are not as motivated by financial rewards as the ability to balance family and work needs. We could only find one research study that demonstrated that women had a higher financial motivation (Fischer et al., 1993), although the authors concluded this difference (along with differences in education and experience) accounted for a negligible variance in performance between men and women.

Women tend to deal with career issues and family simultaneously (Helgesen, 1990). In fact, Caputo and Dolinsky (1998) found that the presence of children in women entrepreneur's households significantly increased the likelihood of women being self-employed. Researchers have found that women choose entrepreneurship because of the flexibility it provides them for balancing work and family demands. DeMartino and Barbato (2003), in a study of entrepreneurs with MBAs found that women entrepreneurs preferred a career that gave them flexibility and allowed them to balance their career and family obligations, while men preferred careers that would allow them to build wealth.

Some strategies that women may adopt to handle the challenges of work and family may impact the performance of the business. One common strategy is part-time self-employment (Longstreth et al., 1987). Devine (1994) found that approximately 55 percent of self-employed women work less than a full week. Obviously this will impact the performance (both size and profits) of their businesses. Women owners of larger businesses work more hours and put greater emphasis on the financial performance of their businesses (Carter and Allen, 1997).

Risk

Another explanation for the differences in growth rates between men and women entrepreneurs is that preferences for risk may impact performance. Sex differences in attitudes toward risk and risk-related behaviors have been found for men and women, in general (Hudgens and Fatkin, 1985), although there have been some contradictory findings (Kogan and Wallach, 1964). Bellu (1993) found women entrepreneurs more willing to accept risk than their male counterparts, while others found no gender differences in risk propensity (Masters and Meier, 1988). Sexton and Bowman-Upton (1990) found that female entrepreneurs scored significantly lower than male entrepreneurs on risk-taking, but female entrepreneur scores were still high relative to published norms for the general population. Although the risk-taking scales they were using were designed to measure four facets of risk (monetary, physical, social, ethical), they correlate most highly with monetary risk.

It may be that women entrepreneurs are less interested in accepting risk purely for monetary gain. Differences and preferences could be tied to motivation (Schneider and Lopes, 1986). Men may demonstrate a greater preference for risk because of a greater preference for economic return. If women have lower risk preference when it comes to economic gains, this could have an impact on the size and growth of their businesses, although increasing the survival rate of their businesses (Sharpe, 1975).

Strategic Choice

Many of the strategic choices that women make affect the viability and performance of their ventures: particularly important may be the choice of industry in which to compete. Companies in the service and trade industries generally have lower growth rates and lower profitability (Kalleberg and Leicht, 1991) because of the amount of competition in their product markets (Humphreys and McClung, 1981), and competition decreases the survival rate for women (Kalleberg and Leicht, 1991).

Women-owned businesses are over-represented in the service sector and under-represented in manufacturing (Hisrich and Brush, 1983; Cuba et al., 1983; Neider, 1987; Anna et al., 2000). In 1997, 55 percent of women-owned businesses were in the services, 17 percent were retail trade, 9 percent in finance, insurance and real estate, 3 percent in construction, while only 2 percent were in manufacturing. This compares, respectively, for all businesses, with 34 percent services, 14 percent retail trade, 9 percent finance, insurance and real estate, 11 percent construction and 3 percent manufacturing (US Census Bureau, 2001). However, women-owned firms continue to diversify across industries. The fastest growth rates are in 'non-traditional' industries: construction (57 percent growth), agricultural services (44 percent), transportation, communications and public utilities (38 percent) (Center for Women's Business Research, 2004).

A number of explanations have been offered for women entrepreneurs' industry choices. It may be that women select these industries because they are easier to enter. Their lack of resources may actually necessitate starting certain types of businesses that don't require equity financing or extensive business experience but also don't hold high financial potential (Ehlers and Main, 1998). Women may find it particularly challenging to raise money for their businesses, may have to pay higher interest rates, or pledge more collateral. Hisrich and O'Brien (1982) proposed that limited access to financial resources may be more a function of the types of businesses that women own than their educational levels and experience.

Alternatively the choice of these industries may be because women 'see' these industries as appropriate or they have previous experience in these industries. Women may want to draw on their past experience but if that experience was gained in a 'feminine' industry that may limit their growth potential because many 'female' industries are highly competitive with lower sales growth and earnings potential.

Institutional and Cultural Barriers

Financial barriers

Although Brophy (1989) wrote that women face significant difficulties in financing their businesses because of the attitudes held by male-dominated institutions, many researchers have concluded that there is little overt discrimination for women owners (Buttner and Rosen; 1992). Carter et al. (1997) reported that women were no less likely than men to have access to credit from banks and suppliers. Haynes (1995) found that women did not appear to pay higher loan process fees or have more stringent collateral requirements.

Other researchers have noted some differences in credit terms for men and women. For example, Coleman (2000) found women were charged higher interest, and although he found no difference in collateral requirements in general, women-owned service firms (the largest percentage by industry of women-owned firms) were more likely to have pledged collateral than men-owned service firms.

There are a number of studies that show that the gender of the borrower may not be as important as characteristics of the business. Coleman's (1998, 2000) data reveals that banks do not discriminate on the basis of gender but on the basis of size of the company. However, since women-owned businesses are typically smaller, younger and in industries that are less promising, they indirectly face challenges when it comes to bank lending.

Buttner and Rosen (1989) noted that although there was no appearance of overt discrimination by banks, women complained of discrimination. The banking relationship for women may be less satisfying because women owners may feel patronized in their interactions with lending officers. Buttner and Rosen found that bank managers may associate entrepreneurial characteristics more closely with men than women.

There also appear to be structural barriers for women entrepreneurs in equity markets. The historically male composition of the equity capital community suggests that the existence of network gaps may present serious access challenges for women trying to grow their businesses with equity capital (Aldrich, 1989). In 1995 and 2000, less than 10 percent of decision-makers in the VC industry were female, and they were twice as likely to leave the industry between 1995 and 2000 as their male colleagues. Without women decision-makers in the VC industry, it is unlikely that women will have the important connections to shepherd them to the bargaining table for an equity investment (Brush et al., 2003).

Cultural barriers

Equally important as barriers in the financial markets are the subtle and not so subtle cultural barriers women face in their careers. Although cultural barriers may have a negative impact on some women's choice to become entrepreneurs (Birley, 1989), a higher number of women may decide to pursue entrepreneurship because of the barriers they encounter in paid employment (Brush, 1992). For many women the decision to pursue entrepreneurship results from experiencing the 'glass ceiling' effect, lack of promotion or lack of salary increases. Entrepreneurship may also be a coping mechanism for women whose careers have been interrupted by childbearing (Vinnicombe, 1987) or when they desire more flexibility in their childbearing years (Matthews and Moser, 1996).

Although women may choose entrepreneurship to avoid the 'glass ceiling' effect in paid employment, they may run into the same cultural constraints as entrepreneurs. The traditional male-centered business model is assumed to be the 'normal' model for entrepreneurship (Baker et al., 1997). This often leads to stereotypes and expectations about how men and women should act, what roles they should assume and how they should perform. A male-centered model may not allow room for a female entrepreneur to operate as comfortably as her male colleagues, and may not provide the women entrepreneur with the legitimacy she deserves. This may be especially challenging when it come to raising financing for growth.

PROGNOSIS FOR THE FUTURE

Women business owners are an important and growing force in the United States economy, both in terms of the number of participants and the gross revenues and employment they represent. The growth of women ownership continues to exceed the national averages for all firms, and the US gender gap for entrepreneurially active men and women has narrowed and was not statistically significant in 2003. This portends an even more important role for US women in the entrepreneurial economy.

Although there are signs that the size differential between men- and women-owned businesses may be narrowing, the reality is that women-owned businesses are, on average, still smaller than those owned by men. In this chapter, we summarized available research for possible explanations for the size differential. One explanation frequently offered has been that women choose to keep their businesses small; they prefer not to grow.

The majority of women-owned businesses in the US, and around the world, are small, probably due to lifestyle choices. But the reality is that the majority of men-owned businesses are small for the same reasons. Growth is not everyone's choice, most women, and men, choose to keep their businesses small (Davidsson, 1989). But not all women prefer to own small, lifestyle businesses with low-growth intentions. There is a growing number of women who seek to start and grow high-potential businesses. And many of these women will encounter greater challenges than men in their pursuit of their dreams.

The tremendous surge in women's entrepreneurship has not been without its challenges. Women have far more control of their destinies when they decide to start or own a business, than when they work for someone else, but they can encounter new barriers when doing so. Women may encounter greater challenges than their male colleagues in establishing partnerships with customers, suppliers and most importantly with financial providers (Brush et al., 2004). Without financial capital, they cannot expand their product lines, open new markets or add additional sales people. They are forced to limit growth.

We know that US women are more likely to start and operate their businesses on a shoestring and have different strategies for financing their businesses than men, and this can have a long-term negative effect on the performance of their firms. They are more likely to borrow from friends and families, and this can limit the amount of capital available to them, as well as bring other problems. The reliance on friends and family may be a result of women's less diverse networks. If diverse networks are linked to entrepreneurial success, women need to broaden their contacts (especially equity contacts) for entrepreneurial success. And participants in the financial markets need to have a better understanding of the myths that exist about women's entrepreneurial capabilities and goals.

There is some evidence that in general women and men may make different decisions about financing and growth, although those differences may be narrowing. Some of these choices are pre-conditioned by differences in educational preparation and business experience. Others are a function of motivations and ambitions for their enterprises. Still others may be related to social and cultural expectations reinforced by structural barriers. But the reality is that there are women who have the right educational backgrounds and experience, the financial savvy, and the desire to grow high-potential businesses. Financial providers need to expand their networks to seek out these women.

Some specific steps that should be considered to encourage women's entrepreneurship in the US:

1. Encourage and educate women to develop an understanding of the growth process and the role that financing plays in that process. It is through an understanding of the entrepreneurial process that informed choices about business ownership and growth can be made.
2. Develop programs that link successful women owners with women aspiring to start and grow businesses. Women need diverse role models representing the spectrum of choices that women make when building an entrepreneurial career.
3. Encourage financial providers to seek out and consider investments in women-led ventures. This may require broadening their networks, and possibly their management, to reach beyond their traditional contacts.

REFERENCES

Aldrich, H. (1989), 'Networking among women entrepreneurs', in O. Hagan, C. Rivchun and D. Sexton (eds), *Women-owned Businesses*, New York: Praeger, pp. 103–32.

Aldrich, H., Reese, P.R., Dubini, P., Rosen, B. and Woodward, B. (1989), 'Women on the verge of a breakthrough?: Networking among entrepreneurs in the United States and Italy', in R.H. Brockhaus, Sr, N.C. Churchill, J.A. Katz, B.A. Kirchhoff, K.H. Vesper and W.E. Wetzel, Jr (eds), *Frontiers of Entrepreneurship Research*, Boston, MA: Babson College, pp. 560–74).

Anna, A.L., Chandler, G.N., Jansen, E. and Mero, N.P. (2000), 'Women business owners in traditional and non-traditional industries', *Journal of Business Venturing*, **15**, 279–303.

Baker, T., Aldrich, H.E. and Liou, N. (1997), 'Invisible entrepreneurs: The neglect of women business owners by mass media and scholarly journals in the USA', *Entrepreneurship & Regional Development*, **9**, 221–38.

Bates, T. (1990), 'Entrepreneurial human capital inputs and small business longevity', *Review of Economics and Statistics*, **72**(4): 551–9.

Begley, T.M. and Boyd, D.P. (1986), 'Executive and corporate correlates of financial performance in smaller business firms', *Journal of Small Business Management*, **24** (April), 8–15.

Bellu, R.R. (1993), 'Task role motivation and attributional style as predictors of entrepreneurial performance: Female sample findings', *Entrepreneurship & Regional Development*, **5**, 331–44.

Bhide, A. (1992), 'Bootstrap finance: The art of start-ups', *Harvard Business Review*, **70**(6), 109–12.

Birley, S. (1989), 'Female entrepreneurs: Are they really any different?', *Journal of Small Business Management*, **27**(1), 32–7.

Boden, Jr, R.J. and Nucci, A. (2000), 'On the survival prospects of men's and women's new business ventures', *Journal of Business Venturing*, **15**(4), 347–62.

Brophy, D.J. (1989), 'Financing women owned entrepreneurial firms', in O. Hagan, C. Rivchun and D. Sexton (eds), *Women Owned Businesses*, New York: Praeger, pp. 55–76.

Brush, C.G. (1992), 'Research on women business owners: Past trends, a new perspective and future directions', *Entrepreneurship Theory and Practice*, **16**(4), 5–30.

Brush, C.G. and Hisrich, R.D. (1991), 'Antecedent influences on women-owned businesses', *Journal of Managerial Psychology*, **6**(2), 9–16.

Brush, C., Carter, N., Gatewood, E., Greene, P. and Hart, M. (2003), *Gatekeepers of Venture Growth: A Diana Project Report on the Role and Participation of Women in the Venture Capital Industry*, Kansas City, KC: Kauffman Foundation.

Brush, C.G., Carter, N., Gatewood, E., Greene, P. and Hart, M. (2004), *Clearing the Hurdles: Women Building High-Growth Businesses*, Upper Saddle River, NJ: Financial Times Prentice Hall.

Buttner, E.H. and Rosen, B. (1989), 'Funding new business ventures: Are decision makers biased against women entrepreneurs?', *Journal of Business Venturing*, **4**(4), 249–61.

Buttner, E.H., and Rosen, B. (1992), 'Rejection in the loan application process: Male and female entrepreneurs' perceptions and subsequent intentions', *Journal of Small Business Management*, **30**(1), 58–65.

Campbell, K.E. (1988), 'Gender differences in job-related networks', *Work and Occupations*, **15**(2), 179–200.

Caputo, R.K. and Dolinsky, A. (1998), 'Women's choice to pursue self-employment: The role of financial and human capital of household members', *Journal of Small Business Management*, **36**(3), 8–17.

Carter, N.M. and Allen, K.R. (1997), 'Size determinants of women-owned businesses: Choice or barriers to resources?', *Entrepreneurship & Regional Development*, **9**, 211–20.

Carter, N.M. and Williams, M. (2003), 'Comparing social feminism and liberal feminism: The case of new firm growth', in J.E. Butler (ed.), *New Perspectives on Women Entrepreneurs: Research in Entrepreneurship and Management*, vol. 3, pp. 25–50.

Carter, N.M., Williams, M. and Reynolds, P.D. (1997), 'Discontinuance among new firms in retail: The influence of initial resources, strategy, and gender', *Journal of Business Venturing*, **12**, 125–45.

Carter, N.M., Gartner, W.B., Shaver, K.G. and Gatewood, E.J. (2003), 'The career reasons of nascent entrepreneurs', *Journal of Business Venturing*, **18**(1), 13–39.

Carter, N.M., Stearns, T.M., Reynolds, P.D. and Miller, B. (1994), 'New venture strategies: Theory development with an empirical base', *Strategic Mangement Journal*, **15**(1), 21–41.

Center for Women's Business Research (2001a), *Removing the Boundaries: The Continued Progress and Achievement of Women-Owned Enterprises*.

Center for Women's Business Research (2001b), *Women-Owned Businesses in 2002: Trends in the US and the 50 States*.

Center for Women's Business Research (2004), *Capturing the Impact: Women-Owned Businesses in the United States*.

Chaganti, R. (1986), 'Management in women-owned enterprises', *Journal of Small Business Management*, **24**(4), 18–29.

Chaganti, R. and Parasuraman, S. (1996), 'A study of the impacts of gender on business performance and management patterns in small businesses', *Entrepreneurship: Theory and Practice*, **21**(2), 73–5.

Cliff, J.E. (1998), 'Does one size fit all? Exploring the relationship between attitudes towards growth, gender, and business size', *Journal of Business Venturing*, **13**(6), 523–42.

Cole, R.A. and Wolken, J.D. (1995), 'Financial services used by small businesses: Evidence from the 1993 National Survey of Small Business Finance', *Federal Reserve Bulletin*, **81**(7), 629–67.

Coleman, S. (1998), 'Access to capital: A comparison of men- and women-owned small businesses', in P.D. Reynolds, W.D. Bygrave, N.M. Carter, S. Manigart, C.M. Mason, G.D. Meyer, K.G. Shaver (eds), *Frontiers of Entrepreneurial Research*, Boston, MA: Babson College, pp. 154–64.

Coleman, S. (2000), 'Access to capital and terms of credit: A comparison of men- and women-owned small businesses', *Journal of Small Business Management*, **38**(3), 37–52.

Coleman, S. and Carsky, M. (1996), 'Understanding the market of women-owned small businesses', *Journal of Retail Banking Services*, **18**(2), 47–9.

Cuba, R., Decenzo D. and Anish, A. (1983), 'Management practices of successful female business owners', *American Journal of Small Business*, **8**(2), 40–45.

DeMartino, R. and Barbato, R. (2003), 'Differences between women and men MBA entrepreneurs: Exploring family flexibility and wealth creation as career motivators', *Journal of Business Venturing*, **18**, 815–32.

Davidsson, P. (1989), 'Entrepreneurship and after? A study of growth willingness in small firms', *Journal of Business Venturing*, **4**(3), 211–60.

Devine, T.J. (1994), 'Characteristics of self-employed women in the United States', *Monthly Labor Review*, **117**(3), 20–34.

Ehlers, T.B. and Main, K. (1998), 'Women and false promise of micro-enterprise', *Gender and Society*, **12**(4), 424–40.

Fischer, C.S. and Oliker, S.J. (1983), 'A research note on friendship, gender, and the life cycle', *Social Forces*, **62**(1), 124–33.

Fischer, E.M., Rueber, A.R and Dyke, L.S. (1993), 'A theoretical overview and extension of research on sex, gender, and entrepreneurship', *Journal of Business Venturing*, **8**(2), 151–68.

Gatewood, E.J., Shaver, K.G. and Gartner, W.B. (1995), 'A longitudinal study of cognitive factors influencing start-up behaviors and success at venture creation', *Journal of Business Venturing*, **10**(5), 371–91.

Gundry, L.K. and Welsch, H.P. (2001), 'The ambitious entrepreneur: High growth strategies of women-owned enterprises', *Journal of Business Venturing*, **16**(5), 453–70.

Hancock, M. and Fitzsimons, P. (2004), *Global Entrepreneurship Monitor: 2004 National and Regional Summaries*, Boston, MA: Babson College.

Haynes, G.W. (1995), 'Executive summary: Financial structure of women-owned businesses', Small Business Administration, Washington, DC: US Government Printing Offices.

Haynes, G.W. and Haynes, D.C. (1999), 'The debt structure of small business owned by women in 1987 and 1993', *Journal of Small Business Management*, **37**(2), 1–19.

Haynes, P.J. and Helms, M.M. (2000, May), 'A profile of the growing female entrepreneur segment', *Bank Marketing*, 29–35.

Headd, B. (2003), 'Redefining business success: Distinguishing between closure and failure', *Small Business Economics*, **21**, 52–61.

Helgesen, S. (1990), *The Female Advantage: Women's Ways of Leadership*, New York: Doubleday.

Hisrich, R.D. and Brush, C.G. (1983), 'The woman entrepreneur: Implications of family educational, and occupational experience', in J.A. Hornaday, J.A. Timmons and K.H. Vesper (eds), *Frontiers of Entrepreneurial Research*, Boston, MA: Babson College, pp. 255–70.

Hisrich, R.D. and Brush, C.G. (1985), 'Women and minority entrepreneurs', in J.A. Hornaday, E.B. Shils, J.A. Timmons and K.H. Vesper (eds), *Frontiers of Entrepreneurial Research*, Boston, MA: Babson College, pp. 566–87.

Hisrich, R.D. and Brush, C.G. (1987), 'Women entrepreneurs: A longitudinal study', in N.C. Churchill, J.A. Hornaday, B.A. Kirchhoff, O.J. Krasner, K.H. Vesper (eds), *Frontiers of Entrepreneurial Research*, Boston, MA: Babson College, pp. 187–99.

Hisrich, R.D. and O'Brien, M. (1982), 'The woman entrepreneur as a reflection of the type of business', in K.H. Vesper (ed.), *Frontiers of Entrepreneurial Research*, Boston, MA: Babson College, pp. 54–67.

Hudgens, G.A. and Fatkin, L.T. (1985), 'Sex differences in risk taking: Repeated sessions on a computer-simulated task', *Journal of Psychology*, **119**(3), 197–207.

Humphreys, M.A. and McClung, H. (1984), 'Women entrepreneurs in Oklahoma', *Review of Regional Economics and Business*, **6**(2), 13–20.

Kalleberg, A.L. and Leicht, K.T. (1991), 'Gender and organizational performance: Determinants of small business survival and success', *Academy of Management Journal*, **34**(1), 136–61.

Kaplan, E. (1988), 'Women entrepreneurs: Constructing a framework to examine venture success and failure', in B.A. Kirchhoff, W.A. Long, W.E. McMullan, K.H. Vesper and W.E. Wetzel, Jr (eds), *Frontiers of Entrepreneurial Research*, Boston, MA: Babson College, pp. 643–53.

Kim, W.C. and Mauborgne, R. (1997), 'Value innovation: The strategic logic of high growth', *Harvard Business Review*, **75**(1), 102–12.

Kogan, N. and Wallach, M.A. (1964), *Risk Taking: A Study in Cognition and Personality*, New York, Holt, Rinehart & Winston.

Kolvereid, L. (1992), 'Growth aspirations among Norwegian entrepreneurs', *Journal of Business Venturing*, **7**(3), 209–22.

Longstreth, M., Stafford, K. and Mauldin, T. (1987), 'Self-employed women and their families: Time use and socioeconomic characteristics', *Journal of Small Business Management*, **25**(3), 30–37.

Masters, R. and Meier, R. (1988), 'Sex differences and risk-taking propensity of entrepreneurs', *Journal of Small Business Management*, **26**(1), 31–5.

Matthews, C.H. and Human, S.E. (2000), 'The little engine that could: Uncertainty and growth expectations', in P.D. Reynolds, E. Autio, C.G. Brush, W.D. Bygrave, S. Manigart, H.J. Sapienza and K.G. Shaver (eds), *Frontiers of Entrepreneurship Research*. Babson Park, MA: Babson College.

Matthews, C.H. and Moser, S.B. (1996), 'A longitudinal investigation of the impact of family background and gender on interest in small firm ownership', *Journal of Small Business Management*, **34**(2), 29–43.

Miner, J.B., Smith, N.R. and Bracker, J.S. (1992), 'Predicting firm survival from a knowledge of entrepreneurial task motivation', *Entrepreneurship & Regional Development*, **4**, 145–53.

Minniti, M. and Bygrave, W.D. (2003), *National Entrepreneurship Assessment: United States of America Executive Report*, Kansas City, KC: Kauffman Foundation.

Minniti, M., Arenius, P. and Langowitz, N. (2004), *Global Entrepreneurship Monitor: 2004 Report on Women and Entrepreneurship*, Boston, MA: Babson College.

Moore, G. (1990), 'Structural determinants of men's and women's personal networks', *American Sociological Review*, **55**(5), 726–35.

National Foundation of Women Business Owners (2001), *Entrepreneurial Vision in Action: Exploring Growth Among Women and Men-owned Firms*.

Neider, L. (1987), 'A preliminary investigation of female entrepreneurs in Florida', *Journal of Small Business Management*, **25**(3), 22–9.

Renzulli, L.A., Aldrich, H. and Moody, J. (2000, December), 'Family matters: Gender, networks, and entrepreneurial outcomes', *Social Forces*, **79**(2), 523–46.

Sargent, M. and Young, J.E. (1991), 'The entrepreneurial search for capital: A behavioral science perspective', *Entrepreneurship & Regional Development*, **3**, 237–52.

SBA Office of Advocacy (2004), *A Voice for Small Business*, Washington DC: United States Small Business Administration.

Scherr, F.C., Sugrue, T.F. and Ward, J.B. (1993), 'Financing the small firm start-up: Determinants of debt use', *Journal of Small Business Finance*, **3**(1), 17–36.

Schneider, S.L. and Lopes, L.L. (1986), 'Reflection in preferences under risk: Who and when may suggest why', *Journal of Experimental Psychology: Human Perception and Performance*, **12**(4), 535–48.

Schwartz, E. (1976), 'Entrepreneurship: A new female frontier', *Journal of Contemporary Business*, **5**(1), 47–76.

Scott, C.E. (1986), 'Why more women are becoming entrepreneurs', *Journal of Small Business Management*, **24**(4), 37–44.

Sexton, D.L. and Bowman-Upton, N. (1990), 'Female and male entrepreneurs: Psychological characteristics and their role in gender-related discrimination', *Journal of Business Venturing*, **5**(1), 29–36.

Sharpe, W.F. (1975), 'Adjusting for risk in portfolio performance measurement', *Journal of Portfolio Management*, **1**(2), 29–34.

Stevenson, L.A. (1986), 'Against all odds: The entrepreneurship of women', *Journal of Small Business Management*, **24**(4), 30–36.

US Census Bureau (2001), *Women Owned Businesses: 1997 Economic Census Survey of Women-Owned Business Enterprises*.

US Small Business Administration (2004), *Tabulation from Survey of Small Business Finances, 1998*, Federal Reserve Board.

Van de Ven, A., Hudson, R. and Schroeder, D. (1984), 'Designing new business start-ups: Entrepreneurial, organizational, and ecological considerations', *Journal of Management*, **10**(1), 87–107.

Vinnicombe, S. (1987), 'Drawing out the differences between male and female working styles', *Women in Management Review*, **7**(2), 5–16.

Wetzel, W.E., Jr (1987), 'The informal venture capital market: Aspects of scale and market efficiency', *Journal of Business Venturing*, **2**(4), 299–313.

Wilkens, J. (1987), *Her Own Business: Success Secrets of Entrepreneurial Women*, New York: McGraw-Hill.

PART TWO

Research Topics on the Growth of
Women-owned Businesses

9. Comparing the growth and external funding of male- and female-controlled SMEs in Australia

John Watson, Rick Newby and Ann Mahuka

INTRODUCTION

'Understanding how firms grow ..., especially small firms, is an important issue' (Carpenter and Petersen, 2002, p. 298) because small and medium enterprises (SMEs) provide the 'engine of economic growth' for many countries (Berger and Udell, 1998, p. 613). However, 'despite a recent revival in research, comparatively little is known about firm growth or its determinants' (Carpenter and Petersen, 2002, p. 298).

Winborg and Landstrom (2001) argued that financial problems (lack of funds) constrained the development and growth of SMEs because many SMEs are unable to access the same kinds of growth funding (particularly equity raisings) often available to large businesses. This view has been supported by a number of researchers, for example: Berger and Udell (1998); Becchetti and Trovato (2002) and Carter et al. (2003). Further, it has been suggested that the lack of funding options is even more acute for female-owned SMEs (Riding and Swift, 1990; Breen et al., 1995; Brush et al., 2001).

However, in a national survey of US small businesses, Levenson and Willard (2000) found that only about 2 percent of firms did not obtain the funding for which they had applied. As this figure included both creditworthy and non-creditworthy firms, Levenson and Willard concluded that the number of credit-constrained firms in the US was quite small. Levenson and Willard also reported that approximately 4 percent of firms are discouraged from applying for funding because they expected a financial institution would turn down their request. It would appear, therefore, that twice as many firms are discouraged from applying for funding as are denied funding.

Kon and Storey (2003) subsequently provided a theoretical explanation for this 'discouraged' borrower phenomenon. They showed that, when there are positive application costs and imperfect screening by banks, some good borrowers may not apply for a bank loan because they believe they will be rejected.[1] Kon and Storey's (2003) application costs included financial (for example, paying others to provide information required by the bank), in-kind (for example, the owner's time in undertaking the loan process), and psychic (for example, the discomfort the owner may feel in passing on private information). Although not specifically referred to by Kon and Storey, psychic costs could also include the potential for reduced (loss of) control that might accompany a bank loan. Cressy (1995) noted that for owners to experience a loss of control does not require the bank to take a stake in the firm, but might, for example, take the form of monitoring activities imposed on the firm. Cressy (p. 293) further argued that the consequent trade-off between borrowing and control implies that firms will borrow less than 'the amount that maximises profits'. Indeed, if 'owner preferences against control are strong enough equilibrium may involve a corner solution with the business being entirely self-funding' (Cressy, 1995, p. 293). To the extent that application costs differ between various groups of owners (for example, men and women) we might, therefore, expect to observe differences in their funding strategies and, consequently, in their demand for external finance.

Given that SMEs are responsible for significant levels of employment, innovation and productivity, it is important that policy-makers and advisers are well informed about the various demand-side issues surrounding the provision of growth funding for SMEs. To date, however, 'only a limited amount of research has focused on small, growing entrepreneurial companies and the factors affecting the capital structure of these firms' (Michaelas et al., 1999, p. 114), particularly female-controlled SMEs (Brush et al., 2001). Michaelas et al. (1999, p. 127) suggested that findings from research on this topic could lead to important 'fiscal policies, probably in the form of tax allowances, that will provide incentives to retain profits and encourage investment in growth-oriented strategies. Only if such an initiative is introduced will the SME sector be enabled to provide the maximum possible contribution to economic performance'. The main aim of the current study, therefore, is to gain a better understanding of the demand-side issues relating to external sources of funding for growth-oriented SMEs and to determine if there are any notable differences between male and female owners.

COUNTRY CONTEXT

As indicated in Table 9.1, there were an estimated 1 179 300 SMEs in Australia as of June 2003. A majority (55 percent) of these businesses were controlled (operated) by either a male or by predominantly males (Australian Bureau of Statistics, 2004). Less than half (44 percent) of all Australian SMEs employed

Table 9.1   Estimated number of Australian SMEs as at June 2003

	Number	%
Age of Business		
– Less Than One Year	152700	13
– One to Less Than Five Years	398500	34
– Five to Less Than Ten Years	239200	20
– Ten or More Years	388900	33
Total	1179300	100
Ownership Details		
– Male or Predominantly Male-owned	649600	55
– Female or Predominantly Female-owned	230200	20
– Equal Number of Male and Female Owners	299500	25
Total	1179300	100
Employing Businesses		
– Male or Predominantly Male-owned	265800	23
– Female or Predominantly Female-owned	57100	5
– Equal Number of Male and Female Owners	190300	16
Total	513100	44
Non-employing Businesses		
– Male or Predominantly Male-owned	383800	33
– Female or Predominantly Female-owned	173100	15
– Equal Number of Male and Female Owners	109300	9
Total	666200	56

staff and female-controlled (predominantly female-controlled) SMEs were the least likely to employ staff. Table 9.2 indicates that there were an estimated 1591500 business owners (operators) controlling these 1179300 Australian SMEs (Australian Bureau of Statistics, 2004). Of these owners about two-thirds were male and one-third female. The female owners were slightly over-represented in the age groups up to 50 years old and under-represented in the age group over 50 years old. The females were also substantially over-represented in the part-time category in terms of the hours they spent working in the business.

Although not available in the latest information release from the Australian Bureau of Statistics (2004), previous evidence for employing businesses suggests that females are over-represented in SMEs up to ten years old and under-represented in SMEs over ten years old (Watson, 2001). Similarly, previous evidence suggests that females are over-represented in the retail and

Table 9.2 Estimated number of Australian SME owners (operators) as at June 2003

	Male		Female		Total	
	Number	(%)	Number	(%)	Number	(%)
Number of SME Owners	1063000	(67)	528500	(33)	1591500	(100)
Age of Owners (Years)						
– Less than 30	97400	(9)	52200	(10)	149600	(9)
– 30–50	597600	(56)	319700	(60)	917300	(58)
– Over 50	368000	(35)	156600	(30)	524600	(33)
Total	1063000	(100)	528500	(100)	1591500	(100)
Owners Working Hours						
– Full-time (> 35 Hours)	857600	(81)	198900	(38)	1056500	(66)
– Part-time (< 35 Hours)	205400	(19)	329600	(62)	535000	(34)
Total	1063000	(100)	528500	(100)	1591500	(100)

service sectors and under-represented in mining, manufacturing, construction and wholesale trade (Watson, 2001).

Contrary to many studies in other countries, the Australian evidence suggests that male- and female-controlled SMEs are similar in terms of their performance. After controlling for key demographic differences (for example, age and industry), male- and female-controlled SMEs in Australia have similar: failure rates (Watson, 2003); return on equity (Watson, 2002); return on assets (Watson, 2002); and risk-adjusted returns (Watson and Robinson, 2003). One interesting finding (reported by Watson and Robinson, 2003) was the lower risk levels exhibited by the female-controlled compared with the male-controlled SMEs. If females are more risk-averse, this might have consequences with respect to their desire for rapid growth and, therefore, their desire for external funding. For example, Cliff (1998, p. 524) noted 'that many female business owners deliberately choose to keep their companies small'.

To shed further light on this issue, a brief examination was conducted comparing the average annual growth in total income and the levels of bank debt for male- and female-controlled Australian SMEs using the database described in Watson and Robinson (2003). It should be emphasized that this database is of employing businesses only. Table 9.3 reports the average annual

Table 9.3   Average annual growth in total income for male- and female-controlled SMEs

Age of Business	Average Annual Growth in Total Income (%)			
	Sex	N	Mean	Median
< 5 Years	Male	136	48	6
	Female	14	16	8
5 Years to < 10 Years	Male	545	11	6
	Female	44	11	5
10 Years to < 20 Years	Male	826	9	4
	Female	44	6	8
20 Years	Male	690	6	3
	Female	27	22	8**
All	Male	2197	11	4
	Female	129	12	6

Notes:
** Significantly different from male growth rate at 5%.
The significant test used was the t-test for means and the Mann-Whitney U test for medians.

growth in total income for the four years commencing in 1994/95 and ending in 1997/98 for male- and female-controlled SMEs.[2] As can be seen, there were few notable differences between the male- and female-controlled SMEs in terms of either their mean or median growth rates; except for firms aged 20 years and older where the female-controlled firms achieved a significantly higher median growth rate. What does this all mean? Well, it would appear that Australian SMEs controlled by women experience the same growth rates as those controlled by men; despite the evidence suggesting that females are more risk-averse than males. However, in the absence of reliable data and given there are significantly more male- than female-controlled SMEs (see Table 9.1), it is possible that anecdotal evidence might lead to the conclusion that female-controlled firms don't grow as fast as male-controlled firms. It would be interesting to see what the experience has been in other countries, where reliable data exists.

Table 9.4 reports the total bank debt and the ratio of total bank debt to total assets (leverage) at the end of 1997/98 for the male- and female-controlled SMEs.[3] It can be seen that for firms less than five years old there is little difference between the male- and female-controlled firms in terms of either their total levels of bank debt or their proportion of bank debt to total assets (leverage). This suggests that if SMEs do experience funding constraints, it applies equally to both men and women. Beyond the first five years, however, it is noticeable that the women were more inclined (than the men) to repay their bank debt rather than to extend their level of borrowing. While the reasons for this contrasting behavior are not known, it might reflect attitudes to risk (leverage) and control. These two issues are, therefore, explored in some detail in the remainder of this chapter.

THEORY

To date, the majority of research concerned with the funding of SMEs has concentrated on supply-side issues. There have been many studies that have examined the factors that influence the investment decisions by suppliers of finance, particularly venture capitalists (MacMillan et al., 1985; DeSarbo et al., 1987; Khan, 1987; Hisrich and Jankowicz, 1990; Hall and Hofer, 1993; Fried and Hisrich, 1994; Knight, 1994; Zacharakis and Meyer, 1998; Shepherd, 1999; Shepherd et al., 2000; Romano et al., 2001). Fried and Hisrich (1988) noted that future research should also look at demand-side issues where the available evidence is far more limited.

Carpenter and Petersen (2002) examined more than 1600 US small manufacturing firms and found that the growth of these firms appeared to be constrained by the lack of internal finance. Similarly, Bruno and Tyebjee

Table 9.4   Total bank debt and debt to asset ratio (leverage) for male- and female-controlled SMEs

Age of Business	Total Bank Debt ('000s)			
	Sex	N	Mean	Median
< 5 Years	Male	136	293	0
	Female	14	258	0
5 Years to < 10 Years	Male	545	393	14
	Female	44	89*	0*
10 Years to < 20 Years	Male	826	1266	13
	Female	44	44**	0*
20 Years	Male	690	1381	70
	Female	27	200***	0**
All	Male	2197	1025	20
	Female	129	115*	0*

Age of Business	Bank Debt to Total Assets (%)			
	Sex	N	Mean	Median
< 5 Years	Male	136	24	0
	Female	14	22	0
5 Years to < 10 Years	Male	545	33	4
	Female	44	12**	0*
10 Years to < 20 Years	Male	826	20	3
	Female	44	13***	0**
20 Years	Male	690	18	7
	Female	27	12	0**
All	Male	2197	23	4
	Female	129	13*	0*

Notes:
*, **, *** Significantly different from male growth rate at 1%, 5% and 10% respectively.
The significant test used was the t-test for means and the Mann-Whitney U test for medians.

(1985) found that ventures that had received external capital achieved statistically significantly higher sales and employment growth compared with ventures without external capital. With respect to women-owned businesses, Carter and Allen (1997) noted that the availability of financial resources was the major influence on their growth. Clearly there appears to be a strong link between the availability of finance and SME growth and this has led to the notion of an 'equity (finance) gap' implying that 'there may be major barriers preventing an owner-manager's access to equity' (Hutchinson, 1995, p. 231). These barriers are generally believed to result from deficiencies in capital markets and would include instances where owners are 'discouraged' from applying for external funds because they believe their application will be rejected (Kon and Storey, 2003). However, it is possible that many SME owners might consciously decide they do not want to access external funding given the financial risks involved and/or the potential for them to lose control of their firms (Barton and Matthews, 1989; Cressy, 1995; Hamilton and Fox, 1998). Indeed Cressy (1995, p. 293) developed 'a model in which non-borrowing and non-growth are regarded as optimal ... solutions to the problem of conflict between the productiveness of financial capital and the desire for business independence from outsiders'. Finally, it is also possible that some businesses 'are not aware of opportunities offered by alternative sources of funding' (Romano et al., 2001, p. 304).

Berger and Udell (1998) suggested that the capital structure of SMEs was dependent on their stage of development within a financial growth cycle. They argued that younger, smaller SMEs with less information available about them would generally rely more on insider (owners' funds) and angel finance compared with SMEs that were older, larger and less informationally opaque. Furthermore, larger, older firms with a track record would normally rely more on public equity and debt for expansion and growth. The results reported in Table 9.4 generally support this proposition for male-controlled firms given that both the mean and median levels of bank debt for this group grew with age of firm. Similarly, the ratio of bank debt to assets grew for this group from the first five years to the second five years, although not thereafter. For the female-controlled SMEs, however, the picture is quite different. It seems that the female-owners significantly reduced their levels of bank debt after the first five years; from about 20 percent of total assets to about 10 percent of total assets. As these businesses had all survived their first five years, it would seem that this reduction in the level of external funding might be the result of personal choice on the part of the owner(s) rather than a bank requirement.

Using structured equation modeling on a sample of Swedish SMEs, Berggren et al. (2000) sought to determine the relative impact of five factors (the size of the firm, its degree of technological development, the perceived need to grow to survive, the amount of internally generated funds, and the owner-operator's aversion to losing control) on a firm's decision to apply for a bank loan. They found that the strength of the owner-operators' desire to maintain control of their firms was the principal determinant in their decision to (not to) apply for bank finance, although this was significantly moderated by the need for technological development (a proxy for industry) and the size of the firm. This finding with respect to control is consistent with the argument advanced by Cressy (1995, p. 292) that the 'Changes in management structure required by successful growth may not therefore be taken on board by owner managers who prefer to have a smaller organisation and a "finger in every pie" rather than a larger, fast-growth organisation with increasingly devolved control'. For female SME owners, maintaining control of their business might be a highly desirable objective. This is supported by Mukhtar's (2002) finding that, in terms of their management styles, women had a significantly greater need (compared with men) to be in control of all aspects of their business. However, as the results reported in Table 9.3 for Australian SMEs indicate that female-controlled firms achieved similar growth rates to their male counterparts, it seems that if women do have a different management style this does not appear to impede the growth of their ventures.

Based on a large sample of New Zealand SMEs, Hamilton and Fox (1998) concluded that debt levels in small firms reflected demand-side decisions and were not just the result of supply-side deficiencies. They argued that managerial beliefs and desires played an important role in determining the capital structure of SMEs and that a deeper appreciation of these issues would lead to a better understanding of the capital structure policies of individual SMEs. Chaganti et al. (1996) also found that the major determinant of SME capital structure was owner goals, as these assisted in predicting debt versus equity and internal versus external funding. These findings might be particularly relevant for female-controlled SMEs because, as Buttner and Moore (1997, p. 34) noted, female entrepreneurs measure success in terms of 'self-fulfillment and goal achievement. Profits and business growth, while important, were less substantial measures of their success'.

Hutchinson (1995, p. 238) suggested that 'when the owner-manager's attitude is risk-averse and is accompanied by a desire to retain control of the firm in some form, he may actively place limits on the use and growth of equity'. This could result in some SME owner-managers deliberately choosing low (no) growth options and might be particularly relevant for female-owned SMEs because:

> female entrepreneurs are more likely to establish maximum business size thresholds beyond which they would prefer not to expand, and that these thresholds are smaller than those set by their male counterparts. Female entrepreneurs also seem to be

more concerned than male entrepreneurs about the risks of fast-paced growth and tend to deliberately adopt a slow and steady rate of expansion. (Cliff, 1998, p. 523)

However, it is again worth noting that the results reported in Table 9.3 for Australian SMEs do not indicate any significant differences in the growth rates for male- and female-controlled firms. What the Australian evidence does indicate (see Table 9.4) is that female-controlled SMEs seem to prefer to repay (minimize) debt. This would reduce both the risk and profitability of their ventures compared with their male counterparts because leverage increases both risk and profitability; provided the owner can earn a return on the borrowed funds that exceeds the after tax interest cost of those funds.

In summary, therefore, it would appear that the existing theories on the determinants of a firm's capital structure (primarily developed from studies of listed companies) might require modification to include 'the many factors that are a part of the small firm financing decision process, among them: goals, risk aversion, and internal constraints' (Barton and Matthews, 1989, p. 1). Based on the above literature review, the following issues/questions were identified for further investigation in this research project:

1. What are the potential obstacles SME owners face in wanting to substantially grow their businesses?
2. What external sources of funding are SME owners aware of?
3. Why might SME owners choose not to seek external funding?
4. What do SME owners see as the main disadvantages of debt funding?
5. What do SME owners believe are the main reasons for banks refusing loans?
6. How strongly do SME owners feel about maintaining control of their firms?
7. Do male and female SME owners share similar views?
8. What factors are likely to influence an individual SME owner's decision to access external sources of funding?

METHOD

Our understanding of SMEs is largely derived from prior research using survey (mail and/or telephone) methodology (Newby et al., 2003). Cooper (1993) suggested that differing research methodologies might be needed to gain a more complete understanding of the processes that determine SME performance. We decided, therefore, to use a focus group methodology for this project. Focus groups are a popular way to elicit views and perceptions from a potentially diverse group of individuals. There is no 'ideal size' for a focus group, but it is generally accepted that eight to 12 is an effective number (Fern, 1982). Blackburn and Stokes (2000) noted that focus groups can be used in any situation where people's perceptions, or views, are of interest. One of the primary benefits attributed to focus groups is the additional insights that can be gained from the interaction of group members (Newby et al., 2003). It has also been suggested that participants might feel more comfortable about sharing their feelings and experiences within a group of peers than in a one-on-one interview with a researcher (Blackburn and Stokes, 2000).

Recently, Newby et al. (2003) suggested that using Group Support System (GSS) technology in focus group sessions could have a number of potential benefits.[4] First, it allows each group member to input 'top of mind' information early in the process and before any individual is able to dominate the discussion. This ensures that all participants have an equal opportunity to have their ideas recorded and considered by the group. As a result, prior studies have suggested that using a GSS approach generally results in more ideas being captured than with a traditional focus group approach. Second, the highly structured nature of GSS focus groups also seems to generate more 'useable' information because unimportant sidetracks are more easily avoided and it is easier to keep participants focused on the task (Sweeney et al., 1997). Third, using the GSS technology in focus group sessions can be helpful in situations where the researchers are interested in participants' rankings (ratings) of ideas generated by the group during a session. The main disadvantage of using the GSS technology is that it might inhibit a free-flowing discussion. However, Newby et al. (2003) noted that using GSS technology does not prohibit researchers from also using a traditional focus group approach for discussing those issues where a deeper understanding is desired.

Consequently, we used a combination of both the GSS and traditional approaches to capture the ideas generated by our focus group participants. For example, we had a number of questions (such as, what sources of external funding are available to business owners wanting to substantially grow their businesses?) where we asked the focus group participants to enter their responses directly into a computer terminal. The GSS technology then allowed us to capture these responses in the form of a tabular report for subsequent discussion by the group. These discussions, as well as the participants' responses to two additional questions that we wanted to pursue in a more free-flowing manner (rather than using the GSS technology), were captured on audio and video tapes. Analysis of the GSS responses (and the audio and video tapes) was conducted in accordance with normal practice. Initially, two members of the research team separately coded the participants' responses to the various questions. These researchers then met to discuss and to agree on the coding categories that would be used to group participants' responses.

Inter-rater reliability was assessed by the degree to which the two researchers arrived at the same inferences (Griggs, 1987) using the kappa statistic K (Siegel and Castellan, 1988). For all questions and across all groups, the observed K was substantially greater than the value that would be expected by chance at a 1 percent level of significance. Where there were any differences in the coding by the two researchers that could not be resolved, the third member of the research team was called in and the final coding decision was decided by a majority vote.

DATA

A market research company was used to recruit a sample of 30 Western Australian metropolitan SME owner-operators who had considered (within the prior two to five years) a major expansion of their business that required significant external funding.[5] We planned to run three separate focus groups with ten participants in each, constituted as follows:

1. 'discouraged' borrowers – those who had ultimately decided not to seek external funding;[6]
2. 'unsuccessful' borrowers – those who had been unsuccessful in their attempt(s) to seek external funding; and
3. 'successful' borrowers – those who had been successful in their attempt(s) to seek external funding.

However, the market research company had great difficulty recruiting participants for the second group and, therefore, this group ended up with seven successful and two unsuccessful participants (both males). Given the often-argued existence of a 'finance gap', this surprised us somewhat, but confirmed the results reported by Levenson and Willard (2000) indicating that the number of credit constrained firms might be quite small, and suggests that the so-called 'finance gap' might be more 'myth' than 'reality'. Table 9.5 provides some brief demographic information about our focus group participants. Note that the majority of participants required less than $100000 in funding. The initial sample contained one person who required more than $500000 but that person failed to turn up for their focus group session.

FINDINGS

Tables 9.6 to 9.11 set out the results from our first six questions where the particpants' responses were captured using the GSS technology. Tables 9.12

Table 9.5 Demographics for focus group participants

			Amount of Funding Required	
Industry	Male	Female	<100000	100–500000
Air Conditioning	1		1	
Appliance Services	1		1	
Beauty		1	1	
Bookbinder	1			1
Builder		1	1	
Carpet Cleaning	1		1	
Clothing Wholesaler		1	1	
Diesel Engines	1		1	
Finance	1		1	
Hardware	1		1	
Health	1		1	
Landscaping Supplies		1	1	
Limousine Tours	1			1
Manufacturer		1		1
Manufacturer		1		1
Mechanical Repairs		1		1
Mechanical Services	1		1	
Motorcycle Sales		1	1	
Physiotherapy	1			1
Plant Hire	1		1	
Printing	1		1	
Scrap Metal	1		1	
Settlement Agent		1	1	
Travel	1		1	
Unknown	1		1	
Unknown	1		1	
Total	17	9	20	6

and 9.13 present a summary of the participants' responses (captured on audio and video tapes) concerning our final two questions where we wanted to have a more free-flowing discussion. For the purposes of presenting our results we have combined the responses from our second (n = 9) and third (n = 9) focus groups and we have labeled this combined group 'successful'. This combined ('successful') group included responses from two 'unsuccessful' applicants and, therefore, we acknowledge this as a limitation.[7] There were eight

Table 9.6   Potential obstacles to growth

Obstacles Faced	Discouraged N = 8		Successful N = 18		Total N = 26	
	No.	(%)	No.	(%)	No.	(%)
Operational Issues – lack of appropriate staff, facilities, time, supplies and expertise/ knowledge in assessing strategy, market size, competition and how to go about growing the business	18	(39)	60	(59)	78	(53)*
Funding Issues – lack of internal cashflow or external funds at reasonable rates and terms	11	(24)	24	(24)	35	(24)
Government Regulation – intrusion, lack of support, fees and taxes	15	(33)	7	(7)	22	(15)*
Fear of Failure/Unsure of Benefits	1	(2)	9	(9)	10	(7)
Other	1	(2)	1	(1)	2	(1)
Total	46	(100)	101	(100)	147	(100)

Note: * 'Discouraged' group significantly different from 'successful' group at 1% (using Chi Square test).

participants in our first focus group comprising our 'discouraged' borrowers.

The first issue we wanted our focus group participants to address was the major obstacles an SME owner might potentially encounter if they wanted to substantially grow their business. Table 9.6 summarizes the participants' responses.[8] Our results indicate that the majority (53 percent) of obstacles identified related to operational issues (such as the lack of appropriate staff, facilities, time and expertise). Next were concerns about funding (24 percent); government regulation (15 percent); fear of failure (7 percent); and other (1 percent).

What was particularly interesting, however, were some of the notable differences between our group of 'discouraged' borrowers and our 'successful' borrowers. Compared with the 'successful' borrowers, the 'discouraged' borrowers were much more likely to list government regulation

Table 9.7   Sources of external funding

Funding Sources	Discouraged N = 8		Successful N = 18		Total N = 26	
	No.	(%)	No.	(%)	No.	(%)
Bank/Financial Institution (Loans/Overdraft/Credit Card)	6	(21)	26	(30)	32	(28)
Equity Issue – new partner, employees, suppliers, listing	4	(14)	23	(26)	27	(23)
Leasing/Hire-Purchase/Loan Sharks	5	(18)	11	(13)	16	(14)
Government – grants or guaranteed loans	3	(11)	5	(6)	8	(7)
Brokers/Financial Advisers	3	(11)	5	(6)	8	(7)
Factoring Debtors	1	(4)	4	(5)	5	(4)
Suppliers (credit)/Customers (up front payments)	1	(4)	4	(5)	5	(4)
Venture Capital	1	(4)	2	(2)	3	(3)
Family/Friends (Business Angels)	1	(4)	2	(2)	3	(3)
Offshore Financing	1	(4)	1	(1)	2	(2)
Franchising	1	(4)	0	0	1	(1)
Self-funded Superannuation Fund	1	(4)	0	0	1	(1)
Business Migrants	0	0	1	(1)	1	(1)
Other/Unknown	0	0	3	(3)	3	(3)
Total	28	(100)	87	(100)	115	(100)

as a major obstacle and much less likely to acknowledge potential operational problems. There were no significant differences across the two groups in terms of the frequency with which the remaining concerns were listed, particularly the financial issues.

When asked about potential sources of funds, most participants noted the three common sources that are grouped in Table 9.7 under the broad headings of banks, equity issues and leasing. However, there were a number of other potential sources of funds that many of the participants were either not aware of or had not thought of (for example: various government schemes; approaching suppliers and/or customers and venture capital). Interestingly, our 'successful' group seemed to identify proportionately more sources of external funding than did the 'discouraged' group. This could possibly indicate that these owners had been more serious about expanding their firms and,

Table 9.8   Reasons SME owners might choose not to seek external funding

Reason	Discouraged N = 8		Successful N = 18		Total N = 26	
	No.	(%)	No.	(%)	No.	(%)
Adequate Internal Funds	4	(15)	18	(28)	22	(24)
Risk/Uncertainty About Future/ Potential to Lose Control/ Fear of Failure	5	(19)	11	(17)	16	(17)
Burden (don't want)/Can't Service More Debt	5	(19)	9	(14)	14	(15)
Terms Unacceptable – interest rates/security/etc.	3	(11)	10	(15)	13	(14)
Expand (don't want to)/Can't Cope/Too Many Hassles/ Lack Confidence	7	(26)	1	(2)	8	(9)*
Time and Aggravation of Trying to Get a Bank Loan	2	(7)	6	(9)	8	(9)
Unavailable Because of Poor/ No Credit Rating	1	(4)	4	(6)	5	(5)
Other	0	0	6	(9)	6	(7)
Total	27	(100)	65	(100)	92	(100)

Note: *'Discouraged' group significantly different from 'successful' group at 1% (using Chi Square test).

therefore, had spent more time and energy researching possible sources of external funding.

Table 9.8 summarizes the responses from our participants when asked to list the reasons why SME owners might not seek external funding. As expected, and consistent with the 'pecking order' hypothesis (Jensen and Meckling, 1976), the most common reason given was because there were sufficient internal funds available. Other major reasons included: the risk involved; not wanting the burden of having to service additional debt; and the terms of the funding might be unacceptable. The contrast between our 'discouraged' group and our 'successful' group was again of some interest. The 'discouraged' group was much more concerned about the work/hassles involved with

Table 9.9   Main disadvantages of debt funding

Reason	Discouraged N = 8		Successful N = 18		Total N = 26	
	No.	(%)	No.	(%)	No.	(%)
Risk – interest rate changes, can't repay debt, spend too much	12	(43)	26	(47)	38	(46)
Burden/Worry/Work/Stress/Paperwork	4	(14)	12	(22)	16	(19)
Dislike of Financial Institutions/Terms/Fees Disclosures	4	(14)	4	(7)	8	(10)
Control May Be Lost – dependence on others is increased	4	(14)	2	(4)	6	(7)*
Costs	0	(0)	5	(9)	5	(6)
Other	4	(14)	6	(11)	10	(12)
Total	28	(100)	55	(100)	83	(100)

Note: * 'Discouraged' group significantly different from 'successful' group at 1% (using Chi Square test).

expansion than were the members of the 'successful' group. This suggests that the members of the 'discouraged' group might have been 'discouraged' for primarily 'internal' reasons rather than because they thought their loan application would be turned down.

The groups were then asked to specifically consider the disadvantages of debt funding; their responses are presented in Table 9.9. Both groups agreed that the major issue centered around the risks involved. These risks included the obvious concern about the potential for interest rate rises, but many participants also raised a (perhaps less obvious) concern that having easy access to funds (particularly credit cards) might cause the business owner to spend unnecessarily (for example, on new equipment). For many of the participants, the additional burden and stress involved with repaying the debt was also of concern. Comparing the 'discouraged' and 'successful' group indicates that the potential for loss of control seemed to be of much greater concern to the 'discouraged' group. This finding is consistent with Cressy's (1995) argument that where an owner's desire for control is strong enough

Table 9.10   Reasons for bank refusing a loan application

Reason	Discouraged N = 8		Successful N = 18		Total N = 26	
	No.	(%)	No.	(%)	No.	(%)
Business Plan – don't have one or not convincing or bank doesn't understand	12	(31)	23	(29)	35	(29)
Track Record – poor credit rating or don't have one	9	(23)	19	(24)	28	(24)
Risk – too high	8	(21)	11	(14)	19	(16)
Lack of Equity/Security	4	(10)	15	(19)	19	(16)
Other	6	(15)	12	(15)	18	(15)
Total	39	(100)	80	(100)	119	(100)

their business will be entirely self-funded. Again, this indicates the importance of 'internal' factors when SME owners consider growth options.

Table 9.10 sets out the participants' responses when asked to list the reasons why a bank might refuse a loan application. The majority of reasons provided by the participants can be grouped under two broad headings: perceived inadequacies in the owner's business acumen (business plan and track record) and the perceived risks (including lack of security). This suggests that business owners need to ensure they have a credible business plan that is easily understood, so that the bank manager can properly assess the risks involved. There might be an important role for external advisors in this regard, particularly for inexperienced owners and/or owners without the necessary skills to complete the task. For this question there were no significant differences between the 'discouraged' and 'successful' groups. There was also nothing in the responses to suggest that the banks routinely made 'screening errors' (Kon and Storey, 2003, p. 37) and, therefore, our focus group results suggest that the 'discouraged borrower' syndrome, as described by Kon and Storey (2003), might be relatively trivial. This is not to say that owners are not 'discouraged' from borrowing funds for growth, but rather the causes of their discouragement might have more to do with the owners themselves (for example, their desire to maintain control and their risk aversion) rather than with deficiencies in the banking sector or the existence of a 'finance gap'.

Table 9.11 confirms just how important maintaining control was for the

Table 9.11 *Importance of maintaining control (1 = very important,*
7 = unimportant)

Rating	Discouraged N = 8		Successful N = 18		Total N = 26	
	No.	(%)	No.	(%)	No.	(%)
1	9	(100)	13	(76)	22	(85)
2			2	(12)	2	(8)
3			1	(6)	1	(4)
4						
5						
6						
7			1	(6)	1	(4)
Mean	1.00		1.67		1.38	
Std Dev	0.00		1.59		1.24	

majority of the focus group participants. In the 'discouraged' group, all participants rated the importance of maintaining control as a '1' (very important). In the 'successful' group there was a little more dispersion in the ratings. However, the majority of the group still attached a very high level of importance to maintaining control. The one exception was a female participant who indicated that, for her, maintaining control was unimportant.[9] The findings reported in Table 9.11, together with the results in Table 9.4 showing that the median (particularly female-controlled) Australian SME has little or no bank debt, are again consistent with the argument advanced by Cressy (1995) that where owners' preferences against control are strong enough their businesses will be entirely self-funded.

The last two tables summarize the responses from the focus group participants to our final two 'general' questions captured using audio and video tapes rather than the GSS technology. We decided for these questions it would be preferable for the participants to have a free-ranging discussion not inhibited by the requirement to enter their thoughts into a computer terminal. This also allowed us to explore gender differences, which was not possible using the GSS technology (where participants provided their responses anonymously). Interestingly, although more time was spent by each of the groups on these last two questions than was spent on any of the other questions, fewer ideas seemed to be generated. This was the result of the conversation being dominated by a few individuals such that the remainder of the participants had limited opportunity to speak and to express their thoughts

Table 9.12   Comparing male and female SME owners' attitudes to risk*

Attitude to Risk	Males	Females	Total
Women more conservative	4	3	7
Depends on personality	2	1	3
No difference	0	2	2
Men more conservative	0	1	1
Total	6	7	13

Note: *In this table, where a participant spoke on more than one occasion, their view was only recorded once.

(this is consistent with the arguments presented in Newby et al., 2003). It should also be noted that the difficulties with transcribing, and then interpreting, the 'traditional' focus group discussions should not be under-estimated by researchers contemplating using that methodology.

Table 9.12 reports the views of the group with respect to the risk-taking propensity of men and women. The responses for the male and female focus group participants are shown separately. Note that for this table, each person's view was recorded only once, although they may have commented on more than one occasion. Interestingly, over half the participants (mainly the males) did not express a view on this issue. The consensus of those who spoke was that women were likely to be more conservative (risk-averse), although a significant number of participants believed that either there was no difference, or that it depended on the personality of the individual owner rather than their sex. This finding may help to explain the results in Table 9.4 showing that the Australian female-controlled SMEs seem to display a greater aversion to using bank finance compared with their male counterparts.

Finally, Table 9.13 sets out the key thoughts/ideas expressed by the participants concerning the factors (issues) that might influence an SME owner's decision to access external funding sources. Although this question overlaps a number of earlier questions, it gave the participants the opportunity to elaborate on issues they might previously have recorded using the GSS technology. Two main thoughts emerged from this discussion. First, that growth for growth's sake, without a growth in profit, was not worthwhile. Second, owners who were planning to exit the firm were unlikely to want to raise additional funding for fear of over-capitalizing the business. In terms of funding sources, we found it interesting that the few negative comments made about banks (for example: banks will only lend you money when you don't need/want it; and banks won't lend to businesses they don't understand) came only from the 'discouraged' group. It is difficult to know on what basis they formed their views. Perhaps it was from their previous experiences or,

Table 9.13   Factors likely to influence an SME owner's decision to access external funding sources

Key Thoughts (Ideas)	No. of times mentioned
Growth:	
Without profit it isn't worth it	4
Can't just decide to grow – there are competitors	2
Business conditions:	
Less likely to borrow if business is volatile and control could be lost	2
If firm is failing you might borrow to try and save the business	2
Exiting the firm:	
Additional funding isn't needed if you are planning to exit the firm	4
Unless you want to build the business up ready for sale	1
Or have someone (who you trust) willing to buy in	1
Although finding that trustworthy person isn't easy	2
I would prefer to sell the business to my staff	1
I would be prepared to offer key personnel a stake in the business	1
I am planning to hand the business over to my kids	1
Accessing debt funding:	
As you get older it is harder to get a loan (repayments)	1
As you get older it is easier to get a loan (security)	1
As you get older you may not want to borrow	1
Age makes no difference	2
Being married helps when you borrow	1
But for women the husband must often co-sign	1
Banks want security	2
Banks don't lend to businesses they don't understand	2
Banks will lend you money when you don't need/want it	1
Bigger firms find it easier to borrow	1
Bigger loans attract lower interest rates	1
More likely to borrow to modernize equipment	1
But over-capitalizing isn't helpful	1
Total	37

alternatively, from hearing about the experiences of others, but clearly these views were not shared by the participants in the 'successful' group. However, the comment that banks don't lend to businesses they don't understand raises two important issues. First, it suggests that banks should not discount the importance of relationship (compared with transactions-based) lending for the SME sector. 'Relationship lending is generally associated with the collection of "soft" information over time through relationships with the firm, the owner, and the local community' (Berger and Udell, 2002, p. F38). By way of contrast, transactions-based lending is 'generally associated with the use of "hard" information' (Berger and Udell, 2002, p. F38), such as financial ratios, and may not be appropriate for many SMEs, particularly if the business is not routine. Second, it is important that SME owners seeking external funding ensure they have a clearly articulated business plan that makes it as easy as possible for a loan officer to understand the nature of their business and the risks involved. SME owners with limited expertise in this area should consider obtaining professional help.

CONCLUSIONS AND DIRECTIONS FOR FUTURE RESEARCH

Previous research has suggested that a lack of external funding opportunities may be inhibiting the growth of many SMEs, particularly female-owned SMEs. Because smaller firms 'are often so informationally opaque ... potential providers of external finance cannot readily verify that the firm has access to a quality project (adverse selection problem) or ensure that the funds will not be diverted to fund an alternative project (moral hazard problem)' (Berger and Udell, 2002, p. F32). This has led to the belief that there is a 'finance gap' within the SME sector. Further, Kon and Storey (2003) argued that, in some cases, owners' perceptions (beliefs) might contribute to this 'finance gap'. That is, some owners might believe that, even though they have a good project, the bank would be unlikely to lend to them and, therefore, they don't bother to apply for a loan. Kon and Storey (2003) referred to these owners as 'discouraged' borrowers.

However, the evidence from this study suggests that the significance of any 'finance gap' for Australian SMEs might be quite small, if it exists at all. We base this conclusion on two observations. First, the market research company we employed to find our focus group participants had great difficulty recruiting any business owners who had tried unsuccessfully to raise external funding to expand their businesses. Second, the results from our focus group discussions did not give us any reason to believe there was a significant 'finance gap' caused by deficiencies in the capital markets. Indeed, it would appear from our results that many SME owners deliberately choose not to expand their business because of the extra workload involved, rather than because of a lack of available funding options.

Further, our results suggest that an SME owner's decision to access external funding depends heavily on the owner's attitude to risk and control, as these were the two key themes to emerge from our focus group sessions. It seems that the majority of participants were acutely aware of the various risks involved in business ownership and this was foremost in their minds when they considered the merits of seeking external funds to expand their business. In terms of gender differences, the majority (both men and women) felt that female business owners were more risk-averse than their male counterparts. There was, however, one female participant who strongly believed that her male partner was much more risk-averse than she was. There were also a number of participants who felt that either there was no difference between men and women or, alternatively, it was a personality attribute not related to the sex of the owner. Watson and Newby (2004) also argued that risk aversion might be a function of an individual's gender role (sex role inventory) rather than their biological sex.

The potential to lose control of their firm was the second major issue at the 'top of the mind' for the majority of our focus group participants. For many participants, it seemed that this concern was a major inhibiting factor when it came to raising external funds. The one notable exception was a male who had two business partners (both male). He felt that having three partners involved in all major decision-making prevented any one of them from taking actions potentially detrimental to the viability of the business. This participant felt, therefore, that relinquishing some degree of control was beneficial for the survival prospects of the firm. Interestingly, a number of the male focus group participants who were in partnerships with their spouses expressed similar sentiments. While they believed that their spouse was more conservative, they saw this as a good thing because it prevented them (the males) from taking unnecessary risks. Again, relinquishing some level of control, albeit to a spouse, was seen as beneficial for the survival prospects of the firm. The importance to SME owners of maintaining control has significant implications for SME growth because, as noted by Cressy (1995), fast-growth organizations often require increasingly devolved control. Owners who are unable to share/devolve control are unlikely to be able to grow rapidly.

With respect to gender differences, the results from this study suggest that, contrary to much of the previous literature, there are no differences between male- and female-controlled Australian SMEs in terms of their average growth rates. There does, however, appear to be a significant difference in terms of their risk-taking propensities. Compared with men, women seem to be less inclined to use bank (external) funding and, where they do, they are more inclined to repay their debts as soon as possible. This reduced (or lack of) leverage for female-controlled SMEs means that, on average, they will be both less profitable and less risky than male-controlled SMEs. However, while the business might have a lower level of risk this does not necessarily mean that the individual SME owner's risk has been minimized. For many SME owners, the majority of their wealth is tied up in their business; it represents their superannuation. There might, therefore, be more effective ways individual SME owners could reduce their risk exposure – for example, by using funds that might otherwise have been used for the early repayment of debt to invest in a managed superannuation fund. This is an area that future research could usefully explore.

We believe that the results of our three focus group sessions have helped us to better understand the way SME owners view both growth and the external funding required to facilitate that growth. A better understanding of SME owners' views with regard to growing their businesses and the use of external funding for this purpose, should be helpful to both policy-makers and business advisors who act as intermediaries between SME owners (demand side) and the providers of external funding (supply side). The next stage in this research project is to develop a survey instrument to further probe the issues raised in our focus groups with a larger representative sample of Australian SME owners.

NOTES

1. Note that Kon and Storey's (2003) definition of a 'discouraged' borrower is limited to creditworthy firms.
2. The growth rate for each firm for each year was calculated as: (total income in current year/total income in previous year) – 1. Note that fewer firms were included in this analysis than in the study by Watson and Robinson (2003) because firms with zero or negative total income in any year were removed from the sample.
3. Note that calculating the total bank debt and the ratio of total bank debt to assets for the 1994/95 period produced similar results.
4. GSS technology requires each focus group participant to input answers to a series of questions directly into a computer terminal with limited discussion taking place. After all responses have been entered, the researchers can display (if they wish) a listing of the responses for discussion and comment by the group.
5. We did not specify the amount of funding that we would consider significant – this was left up to the SME owner. However, we did ask the SME owners to indicate, within broad ranges, the amount of finance they required.
6. Note that our definition of a 'discouraged' borrower is wider than that proposed by Kon and Storey (2003). Our definition includes not only SME owners who might believe that they would be turned down by a bank, but also SME owners who decide not to seek external funds for other more 'internal' reasons, such as: the risk of losing control of their business or the extra work that might be involved in running a larger business.
7. As the GSS software was set up to ensure participants' responses were anonymous, the responses from the two 'unsuccessful' applicants could not be excluded.

8. Note that we did not ask the participants what obstacles they personally might face but, rather, what obstacles SME owners in general might be likely to encounter. We hoped that by asking our questions in this reflective manner we would elicit more responses.
9. In the discussion that followed, however, it was clear that this participant was referring to control in terms of delegating responsibility to her staff rather than control in terms of having external finance providers potentially having a say in the running of the business.

REFERENCES

Australian Bureau of Statistics (2004), *Characteristics of Small Business, Australia (8127.0)*, Canberra: Australian Bureau of Statistics.

Barton, S.L. and Matthews, C.H. (1989), 'Small Firm Financing: Implications From a Strategic Management Perspective', *Journal of Small Business Management*, **27**(1), 1–7.

Becchetti, L. and Trovato, G. (2002), 'The Determinants of Growth for Small and Medium Sized Firms: The Role of the Availability of External Finance', *Small Business Economics*, **19**(4), 291–306.

Berger, A.N. and Udell, G.F. (1998), 'The Economics of Small Business Finance: The Roles of Private Equity and Debt Markets in the Financial Growth Cycle', *Journal of Banking and Finance*, **22**(6–8), 613–73.

Berger, A.N. and Udell, G.F. (2002), 'Small Business Credit Availability and Relationship Lending: The Importance of Bank Organizational Structure', *The Economic Journal*, **112**(477), F32–F55.

Berggren, B., Olofsson, C. and Silver, L. (2000), 'Control Aversion and the Search for External Financing in Swedish SMEs', *Small Business Economics*, **15**(3), 233–42.

Blackburn, R. and Stokes, D. (2000), 'Breaking Down the Barriers: Using Focus Groups to Research Small and Medium-Sized Enterprises', *International Small Business Journal*, **19**(1), 44–67.

Breen, J., Calvert, C. and Oliver, J. (1995), 'Female Entrepreneurs in Australia: An Investigation of Financial and Family Issues', *Journal of Enterprising Culture*, **3**(4), 445–61.

Bruno, A.V. and Tyebjee, T.T. (1985), 'The Entrepreneur's Search For Capital', *Journal of Business Venturing*, **1**(1), 61–74.

Brush, C.G., Carter, N., Gatewood, E., Greene, P.G. and Hart, M.M. (2001), *An Investigation of Women-Led Firms and Venture Capital Investment: A Report for the U.S. Small Business Administration, Office of Advocacy, and the National Women's Business Council*, Washington, DC.

Buttner, E.H. and Moore, D.P. (1997), 'Women's Organizational Exodus to Entrepreneurship: Self-Reported Motivations and Correlates with Success', *Journal of Small Business Management*, **35**(1), 34–46.

Carpenter, R.E. and Petersen, B.C. (2002), 'Is the Growth of Small Firms Constrained by Internal Finance?', *The Review of Economics and Statistics*, **84**(2), 298–309.

Carter, N.M. and Allen, K.R. (1997), 'Size-Determinants of Women-Owned Businesses: Choice or Barriers to Resources', *Entrepreneurship and Regional Development*, **9**(3), 211–20.

Carter, N.M., Brush, C.G., Gatewood, E.J., Greene, P.G. and Hart, M.M. (2003), 'Financing High-Growth Enterprise: Is Gender an Issue?', in N.M. Carter et al. (eds), *Critical Junctures in Women's Economic Lives; A Collection of Symposium Papers*, Minneapolis, MN: The Centre for Economic Progress, pp. 45–51.

Chaganti, R., DeCarolis, D. and Deeds, D. (1996), 'Predictors of Capital Structure in Small Ventures', *Entrepreneurship Theory and Practice*, **20**(2), 7–18.

Cliff, J.E. (1998), 'Does One Size Fit All? Exploring the Relationship Between Attitudes Towards Growth, Gender, and Business Size', *Journal of Business Venturing*, **13**(6), 523–42.

Cooper, A.C. (1993), 'Challenges in Predicting New Firm Performance', *Journal of Business Venturing*, **8**(3), 241–53.

Cressy, R. (1995), 'Business Borrowing and Control: A Theory of Entrepreneurial Types', *Small Business Economics*, **7**(4), 291–300.

DeSarbo, W., MacMillan, I. and Day, D. (1987), 'Criteria For Corporate Venturing: Importance Assigned By Managers', *Journal of Business Venturing*, **2**(4), 329–50.

Fern, E.F. (1982), 'The Use of Focus Groups for Idea Generation: The Effects of Group Size, Acquaintanceship, and Moderator on Response Quantity and Quality', *Journal of Marketing Research*, **19**(1), 1–13.

Fried, V.H. and Hisrich, R.D. (1988), 'Venture Capital Research: Past, Present and Future', *Entrepreneurship Theory and Practice*, **13**(1), 15–28.

Fried, V.H. and Hisrich, R.D. (1994), 'Toward a Model of Venture Capital Investment Decision Making', *Financial Management*, **23**(3), 28–37.

Griggs, S. (1987), 'Analysing Qualitative Data', *Journal of the Market Research Society*, **29**(1), 15–34.

Hall, J. and Hofer, C. (1993), 'Venture Capitalists' Decision Criteria in New Venture Evaluation', *Journal of Business Venturing*, **8**(1), 25–42.

Hamilton, R.T. and Fox, M.A. (1998), 'The Financing Preferences of Small Firm Owners', *International Journal of Entrepreneurial Behaviour and Research*, **4**(3), 239–48.

Hisrich, R.D. and Jankowicz, A.D. (1990), 'Intuition in Venture Capital Decisions: An Exploratory Study Using a New Technique', *Journal of Business Venturing*, **5**(1), 49–62.

Hutchinson, R.W. (1995), 'The Capital Structure and Investment Decisions of the Small Owner-Managed Firm: Some Exploratory Issues', *Small Business Economics*, **7**(3), 231–9.

Jensen, M. and Meckling, W. (1976), 'Theory of the Firm: Managerial Behavior, Agency Costs and Ownership Structure', *Journal of Financial Economics*, **3**(October), 305–60.

Khan, A.M. (1987), 'Assessing Venture Capital Investments With Noncompensatory Behavioral Decision Models', *Journal of Business Venturing*, **2**(3), 193–205.

Knight, R.M. (1994), 'Criteria Used by Venture Capitalists: A Cross Cultural Analysis', *International Small Business Journal*, **13**(1), 26–37.

Kon, Y. and Storey, D.J. (2003), 'A Theory of Discouraged Borrowers', *Small Business Economics*, **21**(1), 37–49.

Levenson, A.R. and Willard, K.L. (2000), 'Do Firms Get the Financing They Want? Measuring Credit Rationing Experienced by Small Businesses in the US', *Small Business Economics*, **14**(2), 83–94.

MacMillan, I.C., Siegel, R. and Narasimha, S. (1985), 'Criteria Used By Venture Capitalists To Evaluate New Venture Proposals', *Journal of Business Venturing*, **1**(1), 119–28.

Michaelas, N., Chittenden, F. and Poutziouris, P. (1999), 'Financial Policy and Capital Structure Choice in UK SMEs: Empirical Evidence from Company Panel Data', *Small Business Economics*, **12**(2), 113–30.

Mukhtar, S.-M. (2002), 'Differences in Male and Female Management Characteristics: A Study of Owner-manager Businesses', *Small Business Economics*, **18**(4), 289–311.

Newby, R., Soutar, G. and Watson, J. (2003), 'Comparing Traditional Focus Groups With a Group Support System (GSS) Approach for Use in SME Research', *International Small Business Journal*, **21**(4), 421–33.

Riding, A. and Swift, C.S. (1990), 'Women Business Owners and Terms of Credit: Some Empirical Findings of the Canadian Experience', *Journal of Business Venturing*, **5**(5), 327–40.

Romano, C.A., Tanewski, G.A. and Smyrnios, K.X. (2001), 'Capital Structure Decision Making: A Model for Family Business', *Journal of Business Venturing*, **16**(3), 285–310.

Shepherd, D. (1999), 'Venture Capitalists' Introspection: A Comparison of "In Use" and "Espoused" Decision Policies', *Journal of Small Business Management*, **37**(2), 76–87.

Shepherd, D.A., Ettenson, R. and Crouch, A. (2000), 'New Venture Strategy and Profitability: A Venture Capitalist's Assessment', *Journal of Business Venturing*, **15**(5–6), 449–67.

Siegel, S. and Castellan, J.N. (1988), *Nonparametric Statistics for the Behavioral Sciences*, New York: McGraw-Hill.

Sweeney, J.C., Soutar, G.N., Hausknecht, D.R., Dallin, R.F. and Johnson, L.W. (1997), 'Collecting Information From Groups: A Comparison of Two Methods', *Journal of the Market Research Society*, **39**(2), 397–411.

Watson, J. (2001), 'Examining the Impact on Performance of Demographic Differences Between Male and Female Controlled SMEs', *Small Enterprise Research*, **9**(2), 55–70.

Watson, J. (2002), 'Comparing the Performance of Male- and Female-Controlled Businesses: Relating Outputs to Inputs', *Entrepreneurship Theory and Practice*, **26**(3), 91–100.

Watson, J. (2003), 'Failure Rates for Female Controlled Businesses: Are They Any Different?', *Journal of Small Business Management*, **41**(3), 262–77.

Watson, J. and Newby, R. (2004), 'Are Sex-Roles Better than Sex?', Presented at the Babson-Kauffman Entrepreneurship Research Conference 2004, University of Strathclyde.

Watson, J. and Robinson, S. (2003), 'Adjusting for Risk in Comparing the Performances of Male- and Female-Controlled SMEs', *Journal of Business Venturing*, **18**(6), 773–88.

Winborg, J. and Landstrom, H. (2001), 'Financial Bootstrapping in Small Businesses: Examining Small Business Managers' Resource Acquisition Behaviors', *Journal of Business Venturing*, **16**(3), 235–54.

Zacharakis, A.L. and Meyer, G.D. (1998), 'A Lack of Insight: Do Venture Capitalists Really Understand Their Own Decision Process?', *Journal of Business Venturing*, **13**(1), 57–76.

10. Builders and leaders: six case studies of men and women small proprietors in the Bulgarian construction industry

Tatiana S. Manolova*

INTRODUCTION

Economies in transition have lately seen a rapid rise in entrepreneurship. During the 1990s, about 5 percent of the adult working population in these countries has attempted to start a new business or become self-employed, a figure very similar to the percentage of nascent entrepreneurs in the United States or Western Europe (Peng, 2001). Prolific as the rate of new business formation is, private businesses in transition economies are usually less growth-oriented than their Western counterparts. Reasons for the low growth orientation of entrepreneurial ventures in transition economies include personal autonomy rather than business growth motivations (Scase, 1997), resource scarcity, environmental uncertainty and weak institutional endorsement (Tan, 1996, 2002; Tsang, 1996), as well as prevailing cultural tendencies (Lee and Peterson, 2000; Verheulet al., 2004).

Women-led entrepreneurial businesses in transition economies, in particular, have shown a lower propensity to grow and a higher propensity to exit under unfavorable industry and competitive conditions. This finding is replicated by studies in Uzbekistan (Welter et al., 2003), Slovenia (Tominc, 2003), Russia (Izyumov and Razumnova, 2000); Poland (Bliss and Garratt, 2001), and Hungary (Hisrich and Fulop, 1994; Szerb and Pinter, 2003). Two recent surveys in Bulgaria reveal lower expectations among women entrepreneurs for growth and development of their ventures (Agency for Small and Medium-Sized Enterprises (ASME), 2002; Stoyanovska et al., 2000). Thus, only one-third of the women entrepreneurs surveyed stated they intended to grow their businesses compared with 50 percent of the men entrepreneurs (ASME, 2002).

The lower growth propensity of women-owned entrepreneurial ventures in transition economies is thought-provoking, because it is in contrast to the socialist legacy of utilizing women's economic potential through promotion of emancipation (Welter et al., 2003). Statistical data from Bulgaria, in particular, show that women constitute about half of the workforce in the country and on average are more highly educated than men (National Statistical Institute (NSI), 2002). In addition, in a recent survey of women business owners, 84 percent of women entrepreneurs believed there were no gender-specific problems in business start-up and initial performance and only 1 percent reported they encountered problems stemming from gender discrimination (Stoyanovska et al., 2000). The contradiction between potential for entrepreneurship and entrepreneurial outcomes provokes the question: if women entrepreneurs have the necessary educational and professional background and if they operate in an institutional environment prima facie supportive of gender equality, why are their businesses showing a lower propensity to grow?

It is important to note that a low propensity to grow may be a function of low growth aspirations, industry and other competitive influences, as well as company-specific impediments to growth. These three influences will be briefly reviewed below.

One explanation for the lower growth propensity of women entrepreneurs' ventures in a transition economy may be that women have ex-ante lower growth aspirations for their ventures. Women's entrepreneurship in transition economies may be predominantly necessity-driven (Reynolds et al., 2002), which is determined by a lack of better work alternatives and an urgent need to earn money and sustain families. Gender-based horizontal and vertical market segregation influence the number and type of labor opportunities for women (OECD, 2002; Verheul et al., 2004). Women typically occupy the service sector and the manufacturing sectors hit most seriously by the economic restructuring in transition economies such as food processing, electronics and textiles (Stoyanovska et al., 2000). Indeed, statistical data suggest unemployment among Bulgarian women is 3–4 percent higher than among men and 62 percent of unemployed women are considered 'long-term unemployed' (NSI, 2002). Not surprisingly, the desire to increase income is the primary motivation to start a business, as reported by 37 percent of the Bulgarian women business owners surveyed by Stoyanovska et al. (2000). Necessity-based entrepreneurs tend to establish lifestyle ventures, which achieve only modest growth due to the nature of the business, objective of the owner and the firm's limited investment in research and development (Lerner and Almor, 2002; Scase, 1997).

A second explanation – also emanating from labor market segregation – may lie in industrial sector differences. Businesses owned by women are concentrated in retail sales and in personal and educational service industries, the so-called female ghetto (Carter, 1989; Kalleberg and Leicht, 1991; Anna et al., 1999; Lerner and Almor, 2002; Verheul et al., 2004). The service and trade industries, characterized by high labor intensity and low barriers to entry and imitation, are highly contested industrial sectors, which in turn leads to lower profit and growth potential (Kalleberg and Leicht, 1991).

A third explanation for the lower growth propensity of women entrepreneurs' ventures in a transition economy, and one that serves as the foundation for this study, may be that women have fewer resources for business expansion (Cliff, 1998). Scarcity of resources is identified as a major impediment to entrepreneurship in transition economies in general (Tan, 1996, 2002; World Bank, 2000), but women may face significantly higher obstacles securing resources for business growth than men do.

To account for the effect of lower a priori growth aspirations and industry differences, this study looks at entrepreneurial experiences in the construction industry, which is not commonly pursued by female entrepreneurs (Carter, 1989: Anna et al., 1999). Construction is traditionally considered a male-type industry, alongside manufacturing and the high-technology sector (Kalleberg and Leicht, 1991; Chell, 2002). In Bulgaria as well, construction is considered a male-dominated industry by 81 percent of the women entrepreneurs working in this sector (Stoyanovska et al., 2000). Prior research suggests women entrepreneurs in non-traditional business sectors tend to have higher aspirations, be more achievement-oriented and view entrepreneurship as a long-term career option (Carter, 1989). For these women entrepreneurs, higher career expectations of autonomy and higher venture efficacy towards planning are positively associated with venture success (Anna et al., 1999). In sum, the choice of a non-traditional business sector allows focus to be placed on the entrepreneurial experiences of women who are more likely to have ex-ante higher growth aspirations and thus to flesh out the subsequent effect of critical resources for business expansion.

The case study reported in this chapter is grounded in the resource-based view of the firm (Penrose, 1959) and prior conceptual and empirical work on women entrepreneurs' access to growth financing for their ventures (Carter et al., 2003). The study explores gender-based differences in three critical resources for business growth: human capital, social capital and financial capital. The importance of human, social and financial capital for the survival and growth of new ventures is well established in entrepreneurship research (Cooper et al., 1994; Davidsson and Honig, 2003; Florin et al., 2003; Wilklund and Shepherd, 2003). Human and social capital are the building blocks that mold the character of a new venture's strategic orientation (Brush et al., 2001). In addition, human and financial capital endowments buffer against the liabilities of newness (Stinchcombe, 1965) and allow the new venture to engage in the process of entrepreneurial experimentation (Cooper et al., 1994).

The chapter is organized as follows. After a brief review of the theoretical argument that forms the conceptual foundation of the study, I present the research context, method and the cases. I then report the findings from the case studies and discuss their theoretical, managerial and public policy implications.

THEORETICAL BACKGROUND

The Resource Base and Growth Potential of Entrepreneurial Ventures

The resource-based view of the firm suggests that heterogeneous sets of resources give each firm its unique character (Penrose, 1959; Wernerfelt, 1984). The growth trajectory of the firm, in turn, is a function of the creative use of under-utilized resources in new productive applications (Penrose, 1959). Achieving superior performance and growth on the basis of unique and inimitable resources is a challenging strategic dilemma for new and small ventures, which are most often resource poor. Young age and small size exposes these players to the double liability of newness and smallness and an increased probability of organizational failure. Survival is problematic for new and small companies because of their difficulties in building organizational legitimacy, raising capital, dealing with government regulations, as well as in competing for and adequately training labor (Aldrich and Auster, 1986; Stinchcombe, 1965). The insufficient or inaccessible resources limit the range of new and small firms' feasible strategic alternatives (Hofer and Sandberg, 1987). In addition, these businesses usually compete in highly populated and contested industrial sectors and are often unable to differentiate their strategies because of low barriers of entry or imitation. In these cases, entrepreneurial resources, rather than distinct small firm strategies may have a direct impact on small business performance (Brush and Chaganti, 1998).

Human Capital and Growth Potential

The entrepreneur's human capital is an intangible asset that reflects the degree of development of managerial know-how and capability.[1] These unique capabilities may later enable the firm to generate rents from a resource advantage (Hitt and Ireland, 1985). The knowledge stock of the entrepreneur serves as the foundation on which the 'knowing ability' and hence intellectual capital of the organization is built through exchange and recombination (Nahapiet and Ghoshal, 1998). Better educated small business owners are more likely to secure financing and create sustainable high-growth business in the long run (Bates, 1990; Florin et al., 2003; Carter et al., 2003). Wilklund and Shepherd (2003) found that growth increases with growth aspirations at a faster rate for entrepreneurs with higher levels of education or experience. Research on entrepreneurship as a process of opportunity discovery and exploitation suggests that the exploitation of entrepreneurial opportunities is greater when individuals have resources (Shane and Venkataraman, 2000), and entrepreneurs' human capital is an important factor for obtaining financial resources (Florin et al., 2003). Human capital is particularly important for small business in an environment characterized by rapid change (Honig, 2001). Entrepreneurs with stronger preparation or those who can tap into the experience of others are more likely to be able to deal with the problems that arise as their ventures grow and develop (Cooper et al., 1994).

Empirical evidence from transition economies suggests human capital attributes, and managerial competencies in particular, are related to new and small business performance, growth and success. Peng (2001) suggests that the professional entrepreneurs who previously held positions characterized as professional, enhance the technology, professionalism and legitimacy of the private sector. In a cross-sectional survey study of nearly 400 small Bulgarian firms, Bartlett and Rangelova (1997) report that managerial skills were ranked as the most important factor contributing to firm success.

Social Capital and Growth Potential

Social capital, or small business owners' degree of development of social contacts, determine the strength of institutional endorsement and support for the entrepreneurial initiative and improve survival prospects (Stinchcombe, 1965). The wider the social acceptance of the small business owner, the stronger the belief that the business venture s/he represents would behave in a desirable or appropriate manner within the socially constructed system (Suchman, 1995). In other words, the social acceptance of the business owner reflects on the social acceptance, or legitimacy of the new and small venture. A study of the liability of newness of young voluntary social service organizations found that external legitimacy, rather than internal coordination, improved the survival chances of these organizations (Singh et al., 1986). In addition, social capital is instrumental in defining appropriate response to uncertainties (Oliver, 1991), fostering of information exchange (Miner and Haunschild, 1995), recognition of mutual interests and facilitating credible commitments (McKendrick and Carroll, 2001), or enabling collective action (Ingram and Simons, 2000). In short, social capital facilitates both resource acquisition and resource exploitation through engaging the new and small venture in the social web of exchange (Nahapiet and Ghoshal, 1998). The degree of development of social capital shapes potential investors' assessments of the quality of young companies, and thus affects those firms' ability to obtain scarce resources needed to operate (Stuart et al., 1999). Even controlling for other factors, social capital is likely to influence the growth and profitability of entrepreneurial ventures positively and durably (Florin et al., 2003).

Social capital may be even more critical to the performance of new and small companies in the context of transition economies. Recent research on entrepreneurs in transition economies has documented their ability to create personal connections or join informal networks (Peng and Heath, 1996; Xin and Pearce, 1996). In transition economies, networks are necessitated by the resource scarcity and the unpredictable institutional environment (Peng, 2001; Puffer and McCarthy, 2001). In an unstable and weakly structured environment, informal networks often countervail constraints imposed by highly bureaucratic structures and often openly hostile officials (Smallbone and Welter, 2001). In a study on the role of social capital for entrepreneurial performance in Russia, Batjargal (2003) suggested that the resource embeddedness of entrepreneurs' networks, or the degree to which network contacts possess valuable and mobilizable resources, becomes an important determinant of performance. Some researchers posit that entrepreneurs in transition economies weigh their relevant 'intangible' or social resources more heavily than the merits of the business opportunity per se (Manolova and Yan, 2002). Manev et al. (2003) find social capital is positively associated with the entrepreneurial orientation and growth of new and small business ventures in Bulgaria. Danis and Lyles (2004) suggest managerial networking behavior appears to be a stronger predictor of firm performance early in transition but this influence wanes over time as competitive methods based on traditional conceptualizations of firm strategy become increasingly important.

Financial Capital and Growth Potential

The amount of financial capital available to a new venture is positively associated with its survival and growth prospects. The amount of initial financial capital is related to the initial competitive strategy that a new venture can follow in terms of the scope of products/services offered, or scope of market(s) served (Cooper et al., 1994). Higher initial financial capital also buys time, while the entrepreneur learns or overcomes problems (Cooper et al., 1994). Financial capital provides a buffer against the liabilities of newness and smallness and allows entrepreneurs to engage in a process of exploration and experimentation, for example, to fund the development of new products, services and technologies. In addition, financial capital is an instrumental resource, which is flexible and can be used to acquire other resources, such as personnel or equipment (Brush et al., 2001). Wilklund and Shepherd (2003) find access to financial capital has a direct effect on new venture growth. In sum, the link between amount of capital raised and the survival and growth prospects of entrepreneurial ventures is well supported by the literature, although some researchers caution that financial capital per se is not a productive resource: having it does not ensure commercial success. Rather, its productive potential is determined through its interaction with social resources (Florin et al., 2003).

Lack of financial capital is among the critical impediments to entrepreneurial growth in transition economies (Tan, 1996; Tsang, 1996; World Bank, 2000). A survey of the business environment for entrepreneurial development in Bulgaria revealed that the inefficient debt market and the non-existent equity capital market is the second most important impediment to the operational activities of small and medium-sized enterprises in the country[2] (ASME, 2002).

To summarize, conceptual development and empirical research in the entrepreneurship area have established the positive effect of human, social and financial capital on the survival and growth prospects of entrepreneurial ventures. This exploratory study is set to investigate if there are any gender-based differences in the access to and/or role of these resources and their relationship to entrepreneurial start-up and growth experiences. Figure 10.1 summarizes the theoretical framework that guides the subsequent exploration.

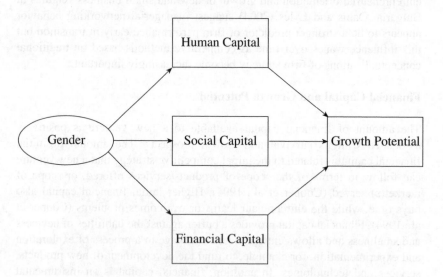

Figure 10.1   Gender-based differences in the role of human, social and financial capital and their effect on growth: a theoretical framework

RESEARCH CONTEXT

Small and Medium-sized Businesses in the Bulgarian Economy

Bulgaria is a lower-middle-income country in Eastern Europe. Socialist central planning virtually eliminated the private sector of the economy for more than 40 years (from the late 40s to 1989). Large-scale institutional and economic reforms started after the fall of the Berlin Wall (1989) and the country set on a road of democratization and market liberalization.

Bulgaria's transition economy is in the mid-stage of its market and institutional reforms. Private businesses became legal in 1988 and have grown rapidly since then. The World Bank estimates that the growth of private business formation in Bulgaria outstripped the rates in countries such as Hungary or Poland (World Bank, 2000). Today small and medium-sized enterprises constitute around 99 percent of all enterprises in the country (ASME, 2004a) and in 2002 accounted for 18.8 percent of the total gross value added and for as much as 27.3 percent of the employment in the economy (ASME, 2004b). Table 10.1 illustrates the role of the small and medium-sized enterprises in the Bulgarian economy.

The overwhelming majority of small businesses in Bulgaria, however, are very small in size. A recent business demographic study revealed that more than 70 percent employed only two or less people, and over 90 percent had less than 10 employees (Doudeva, 2001). These are predominantly lifestyle businesses, funded from personal or family sources, and engaged predominantly (48 percent) in trade or services. Only 4.1 percent of the private ventures are started in construction (ASME, 2004b). Survey data revealed that only 16 percent of small business owners considered their companies a vehicle for capital accumulation (*Pari Weekly*, 1996). As a consequence, less than 10 percent of the small and medium-sized enterprises invested in fixed assets in 1994 (Doudeva, 2001).

Women Entrepreneurs in Bulgaria[3]

Women account for about a quarter of the newly established entrepreneurial ventures in Bulgaria. Women-owned businesses are concentrated in retail, services and textile manufacturing (62 percent). Less than 5 percent of women-owned businesses are started in construction. In other words, women-owned businesses in construction account for slightly over 1 percent of the entrepreneurial ventures in the country.

The main sources of start-up capital are savings, followed by loans from friends and family, similar to the country averages. Only 7 percent of those firms received a bank credit to start their businesses, a percentage not

Table 10.1 Sales revenue by sector and enterprise size in 2000 ('000 BGL)*

Industrial sectors	All enterprises	Micro enterprises (10 or less employees)	Small enterprises (11–50 employees)	Medium-sized enterprises (51–100 employees)	Enterprises with 101–250 employees	Large enterprises (over 250 employees)
State sector	10725903	58931	520097	363968	684441	9098466
Private sector	49136342	15174360	10448190	3503475	6845632	13164685
Total	59862245	15174360	10448190	3503475	6845632	13164685
Change from 1999 (%)	32.16	28.39	36.93	8.71	35.95	30.70

Source: National Statistical Institute, *The Report on Small and Medium Sized Enterprises, 1996–99 and 2000–2002*.

Note: *Size breakdown as per the Law on the Small and Medium-sized Enterprises (*State Gazette*, 1999).

significantly different from their male counterparts. No gender-based barriers to bank financing were reported in the ASME's 2001 survey.

Fifty-nine percent of women entrepreneurs cite as a major reason to start their businesses the lack of an alternative avenue for professional realization. In comparison, the main motive to start a business identified by men is economic independence. About one-fifth of women entrepreneurs were unemployed before they launched their own business, a percentage twice higher than for male entrepreneurs.

The financial results of men- and women-owned businesses are not significantly different, but their growth rates are. Only 18 percent of women-owned businesses registered growth in 2001, compared with 33 percent of men-owned businesses. Fifty-nine percent of women-owned businesses saw a decrease in sales revenue, compared with 40 percent of men-owned businesses.

As a whole, women entrepreneurs in Bulgaria are young and well-educated. Over 80 percent are less than 49 years old, and 55 percent hold college degrees, with an additional 33 percent holding professional diplomas from vocational schools. Education notwithstanding, women consider public opinion with regard to their businesses to be more likely negative. About 40 percent believe people are envious of their accomplishments and try to impede their activities, compared with 30 percent among male entrepreneurs.

Family and children are the most important values for Bulgarian women entrepreneurs. A recent survey by the National Statistical Institute reveals taking care of the household and bringing up children are tasks that the prevailing part of women entrepreneurs manage alone. Barely 2.1 percent of women entrepreneurs use domestic services (NSI, 2004). Self-assessment of their way of life is greatly dependent on matrimonial satisfaction, well ahead of material or job satisfaction. The National Statistical Institute's survey concludes that 'from an emotional-psychological perspective, women entrepreneurs in Bulgaria are first and foremost women, and only after that – entrepreneurs' (NSI, 2004).

RESEARCH METHOD AND THE CASES

Research Method

I chose case study methodology for this exploratory study. Case study methodology is especially appropriate when investigators desire to 1) define topics broadly and not narrowly; 2) cover contextual conditions and not just the phenomena of study; and 3) rely on multiple and not singular sources of evidence (Yin, 1993). Exploratory case studies, in particular, are undertaken prior to the final definition of study questions and hypotheses and try to discover theory by directly observing a phenomenon of interest in its 'raw' form (Glaser and Strauss, 1967).

Case Selection

As is customary in qualitative case study research, non-probability sampling was implemented (Judd et al., 1991). To control for extraneous variation (Eisenhardt, 1989), I chose six private companies operating in the same industry (construction) and in the same location (a major industrial center in Bulgaria). The construction industry provides an appropriate setting for this exploratory research because, as the preceding overview of women's entrepreneurship in Bulgaria suggested, this is not a typical industrial sector where women choose to launch a business. It was expected, therefore, that it would provide a clearer representation of theoretically relevant drivers of entrepreneurial growth and success such as human, social and financial capital.

I applied theoretical sampling, in which theoretically important cases are selected based on a 'matched pair' logic. More specifically, three pairs of female- and male-owned businesses, matched for business age and products/services offered, were selected. The justification for a matched pairs approach is that many factors other than gender may explain observed differences between the experiences of male and female entrepreneurs. This approach is used in other qualitative gender studies in the entrepreneurship area (for example Read, 1994). The sample size was deemed acceptable according to Eisenhardt's recommendation for a 4–10 company case study sample. Access to the companies was garnered through the sponsorship of the local chamber of the Bulgarian Construction Industry Association.

Data Collection and Analysis

Interviews with the company owners provided the major source of data. For each of the companies, the interviews were complemented by site visits. The interviews lasted between one and one-and-a-half hours and were semi-structured, allowing for a lot of open-ended questions. Open-ended interviews allow assessment of the informants' thought process and gathering of new information where little previously existed (Khavul, 2001).

I used method triangulation (Neuman, 2003) to enhance the reliability of the findings. Method triangulation involves a combination of primary and secondary data collection. In particular, primary data collected through the interviews and site observations were complemented by secondary research, including data collected through government publications and the national business press. In view of the project's objective to cover contextual conditions and not just the phenomena of study, I also conducted five interviews with representatives of important players in private entrepreneurs' task and institutional environments. More specifically, I interviewed the chairperson of the local Construction Industry Chamber, two loan officers at local retail banks, a senior expert in the Agency for Small and Medium-sized Enterprises with the Bulgarian Council of Ministers, and a project manager with the Foundation for Entrepreneurship Development – a non-government organization. In addition, reliability of the findings was enhanced through the use of a case study protocol. The protocol helps ensure that the same procedures are followed in multiple cases (Yin, 1993: 40).

The interview protocol consisted of five sets of questions: 1) key company characteristics, history and business transactions; 2) background information of the owner/founder and his/her most important personal/business goals; 3) history of the company's founding and sources of start-up financing; 4) role of human, social and financial capital for new venture development; 5) satisfaction with venture performance and plans for the future.

As is typical in inductive studies, individual case notes were initially written about each firm and then the data were compared across notes to develop insights and derive themes (Eisenhardt, 1989; Edelman, 2000). To aid in data consistency across cases, the interview data were coded based on typical content analysis procedures (Miles and Huberman, 1984) into each of the following coding categories: 1) role of human capital; 2) role of social capital; 3) role of financial capital; 4) role of gender, and 5) performance implications. The results of this analysis revealed some strong cross-case agreement with respect to certain dimensions, such as the severely restricted access to bank financing. Yet cross-case differences were evident with respect to other variables, such as the role of social capital for new venture performance.

The Cases

Company profiles are presented in Table 10.2, whereas entrepreneur profiles are presented in Table 10.3. I used a fictitious name for both the entrepreneur and his/her company in order to preserve confidentiality.

MM EOOD

MM's main line of business is roofing and production of metal profiles for construction. The owner, Emil K., started the company in 1989 together with his father-in-law in a small village in the suburbs of Plovdiv. Emil was afraid of losing his job at the time and decided to make his own living. He holds a degree in woodcarving. In 1991 his father-in-law perceived the business to be too risky and pulled out his capital. Emil became a sole proprietor of the firm

Table 10.2 Company profiles

Company, year established	Entrepreneur	Main line of business	Sources of start-up capital	Changes in ownership/ governance*	Legal form	Number of employees
MM EOOD, 1989	Emil K.	Roofing and metal constructions	Family savings	Started as a partnership with father-in-law; since 1991 sole proprietor	Limited liability company with a sole owner	30
TT EOOD, 1994	Tania M.	Retail: bath fixtures and tiles	Savings, short-term bank loan secured by real estate	Started as a partnership with another lady, partner pulled out of the company	Limited liability company with a sole owner	8
MD OOD, 1996	Mima D.	Finishing work in construction	Savings, loans from friends	–	Limited liability company	15
IP OOD, 1991	Elisaveta T.	Furnace building and insulation	Inherited company from father in 2000	–	Limited liability company	25
KM ET, 1991	Vasil A.	Construction	Savings	–	Sole proprietor	160
IV OOD, 1991	Vasil V.	Distributor: construction materials	Savings, supplier credit	–	Limited liability company	30

Note: *All companies are 100% privately owned.

244

Table 10.3 Entrepreneur profiles

Entrepreneur	Gender	Marital status	Education	Number of ventures started	Number of companies owned
Emil K.	Male	Married	Vocational school, wood carving	1	1
Tania M.	Female	Married, two children	BS in Chemistry	1	1
Mima D.	Female	Married, two children	Vocational school, construction; BS Management in the Construction Industry	2	2
Elisaveta T.	Female	Married, two children	BS in Engineering	—	1
Vasil A.	Male	Married, two children	Vocational school, construction	1	1
Vasil V.	Male	Single	BS in Electronics	2	1

245

that year. He had to place his apartment as a collateral with the bank to take out a loan in 1991. His ambitions when he started the business were to make a better living for his family and himself. His ambitions nowadays are to buy his own land and build permanent buildings where he can run his business and be able to work year round. Currently his business is very much seasonal due to the nature of the work. He had tried to take a loan from different banks to finance his project but says it is very hard to take long-term loans from the banks nowadays. The collateral needed to cover this kind of loan ranges from 150 percent (Union Bank) to 300 percent (Bulbank). Emil is currently working on building a three-storey house in a suburb of Plovdiv, which he hopes to finish soon and put as collateral with a bank to take a loan.

TT EOOD

TT is a wholesale and retail firm that sells bath fixtures and tiles. Tania M. started TT EOOD in 1994. She holds a degree in Chemistry and was employed as an inspector at the local Hygiene and Epidemics Institute[4] at the time. Then, a single mother with a three-year-old son, she decided to start her own business. She had worked with the largest manufacturer of tiles in Bulgaria and knew a lot of people at the company, which helped her get the first order from the factory and open the store. She is among the few women in the business in Bulgaria. In 2001 she embarked on a joint venture with another woman in the business and took a short-term loan from a bank, which was secured by her real estate. Unfortunately, the joint venture did not work out and Tania was left having to pay back the loan. She complains that when appraising the real estate the bank used an appraisal a lot lower than the Fair Market Value of the estate. TT EOOD currently employs eight people. Tania foresees the business growing in the future. She perceives low-cost and low-quality competitive goods from Turkey and Spain as a major threat to the business. She wants to grow the business and plans to take a loan from the bank by securing it with her house.

MD OOD

Mima D. is the owner of two firms. MG ET was founded in 1992 and deals with retail sales of building materials. MD OOD was founded in 1996 and deals with finishing work in the construction business. Mima says that it is good for women to work in this segment of construction because their aesthetic taste towards the beautiful helps them to be successful. Otherwise, she says it was very hard for her in the beginning. She is proud of what she has done and that the business has done extremely well. She started the business with loans from friends and did not have to take a loan from a bank. She foresees that her businesses would be able to generate enough earnings to finance future growth.

Mima finished a vocational high school with a license in construction and holds a degree in Management in the construction industry. Mima is married and has a daughter and a son, 21- and 18-years-old. She is grateful to her husband for putting a lot of work into the household and taking over the leading role there while Mima deals with the business.

IP OOD

Elisaveta T. and her sister inherited their father's business in 2000. Elisaveta had been working in the firm since her father opened the business in 1991. IP OOD builds and insulates furnaces and has 25 full-time employees. Elisaveta holds a degree in Engineering and was working at the local factory for the manufacturing of memory devices before the company closed down. She says that whenever the firm needs money, they could secure a loan with a bank with their property in a village nearby. Elisaveta has two grown up children and says that sometimes it could be difficult to divide up time between the family and the business.

KM ET

Vasil A. started KM ET in 1991 and employed three people at the time. Today the company has 160 full-time employees and is looking into the future with great optimism. Vasil A. decided to start his own business because in 1991 he was afraid of being laid off and unemployed. He started the business without having to borrow money from a bank. He says he was lucky to get a project that did not require any upfront money. He does not have a problem borrowing from the banks nowadays because he has enough real estate to put as collateral.

Vasil A. is married with two children. He says that the roles in his family are clearly defined and his wife takes care of the kids and the home while he is responsible for the financial support of the family.

IV OOD

Vasil V. graduated from Plovdiv Institute of Technology in 1990 with a degree in Electronics and was out in the market looking for a job. He found Ceresit Bautechnik, a German company that was looking for a distributor of its products in Bulgaria. In 1991 he founded IV OOD and became a distributor of construction materials. At the time of the interview the company employed 30 people. He had to take a loan from a bank in 1995 and had to put up 400 percent collateral to back up the loan. He is not happy with the high requirements the banks have when they lend money to businesses.

Vasil is single. He says he likes his job and works long hours but he likes having fun outside work as well.

CASE FINDINGS

The case findings are organized so as to highlight gender-based differences across the main constructs of interest to the study, namely human capital, social capital, financial capital and their role for the growth potential of the entrepreneurial venture.

Gender-based Differences in Human Capital

The female participants in the case studies appear to be as well, if not more highly educated than their male counterparts. All of the women entrepreneurs have college diplomas. In addition, two of the three have industry-specific training: Mima D. holds a degree in Management in the construction industry, while Elisaveta T. holds a degree in Engineering. This is in contrast to the three male participants in the study, two of which hold secondary education (vocational school) diplomas. At the same time, while all of the male participants in the study had industry-specific training (at the vocational school or college level), one of the female participants (Tania M.) holds a degree in Chemistry, which suggests her education is not directly related to the business opportunity pursued.

In terms of prior industry experience, there is a variability of experiences across the study participants. While one of the women entrepreneurs (Elisaveta T.) worked in the same sector/company before assuming a managerial role (she inherited the business from her father), another (Tania M.) was employed in an unrelated field (sanitary inspection). Tania M. appears to have substituted social for human capital in this instance as she decided to start her company to leverage 'contacts and acquaintances' she had with a tile manufacturing facility. The third female participant (Mima D.) launched a business in the finishing stage of construction, which allows her to turn women's 'aesthetic taste towards the beautiful' into a source of competitive advantage. Across the male participants, one (Vasil V.) started the business fresh out of college, without any prior professional or industry experience, whereas the other two launched their ventures more out of necessity (both of them feared they would become unemployed). In contrast (and in keeping with the choice of a non-traditional industry for women's entrepreneurship), two of the women entrepreneurs appear to be opportunity-driven, whereas one is a 'hierarchical' entrepreneur, having inherited, through her family, a business and a tradition of self-employment (Carter, 1989).

Work-family roles may impact women entrepreneurs' ability to realize their human capital in transition economies (Welter et al., 2003). In this regard the female participants in the study provided experiences quite representative of the average trends for women entrepreneurs in Bulgaria. All of them are married with two children (average for female entrepreneurs and above the country average). They combine the worker-mother roles and rely on help from husband/parents in order to juggle the double burden. Tania M.'s comment is indicative:

> I apologize for being late for the meeting. My son is sick and I had to call a friend to sit in so I can make it to work today. It's challenging to be the mother of two sons and run a business ... I'm grateful to my husband who helps take care of the kids and the housework. My greatest regret is that I never had enough time to spend with my elder son when he was growing up.

These attitudes are echoed by the other two female participants in the study. Mima D. was also grateful to her husband 'for putting a lot of work in the household'. Similarly, Elisaveta T. shared that 'sometimes it could be difficult to divide up time between the family and the business'.

In contrast, one of the male participants (Vasil A.) shared that 'the functions in his family are clearly defined and his wife takes care of the kids and the home while he is responsible for the financial support of the family'.

Gender-based Differences in Financial Capital

Across all cases (male and female entrepreneurs), the ventures were started with own savings, supplemental financing by friends, family, supplier credit and (in the case of TT EOOD and IV OOD) a short-term bank loan. All of the participants lamented the restrictive lending requirements towards new and small private businesses. In particular, entrepreneurs were not happy that banks accept only real estate as an acceptable loan collateral, and that the collateral needed to cover the loan ranges from 150 percent to 300 percent (MM EOOD's experience) to as high as 400 percent (IV OOD's experience). Four of the six entrepreneurs interviewed (Emil K., Tania M., Elisaveta T. and Vasil A.) looked on their real estate property as collateral to use in order to secure bank financing. While none of the respondents was happy with the restrictive bank procedures, none suggested any gender discrimination, either. The effect of the restricted access to debt financing is well summarized by Vasil A., who remarked 'he was lucky his first project did not need any money upfront'. As far as growth financing is concerned, Mima D.'s comment is indicative of attitudes across participants. When asked if she foresaw any use of external financing, she said she would grow as much as her internally generated capital would allow.

Gender-based Differences in Social Capital

Study participants revealed a variety of experiences in terms of the role of social capital in the growth and success of their businesses. Both Tania M. and Elisaveta T. used contacts garnered outside or through previous professional experience in order to launch and manage their ventures. All of the participants were members of the local chamber of the construction industry, which reflects their recognition of the importance of industry contacts and institutional endorsement for the development of their businesses. At the same time, women entrepreneurs reflected on some gender-based impediments to building a network of referrals and contacts. Tania M.'s comment is indicative: 'It is hard being a woman in the construction business. Some of the deals are made when men go out hunting or horse racing; events that women are not invited to attend'. Mima D.'s experience provides an additional insight: 'It was very hard for me in the beginning. Most of the competitors in the business are men and in the beginning they looked at me with contempt and some were even making fun of me. It took me a long time to prove myself and earn the respect of men in the business'.

Apparently women entrepreneurs feel they are not taking advantage of all opportunities that formal and informal networks can offer for business growth and success.

Performance and Growth

One of the goals in this study was to explore gender-based differences in entrepreneurial performance and growth in the context of a transition economy. The interview data revealed some interesting yet unexpected findings. It is obvious that most of the firms involved in this study are still in the middle of serious struggles and none of them is a high performer according to Western performance standards.

On the other hand, on the longevity criterion (a critical measure of entrepreneurial success), all of the interviewees' firms fared quite well, having been around for over eight years (15 years in MM EOOD's case). In terms of employment, with the exception of TT EOOD, the firms have stepped up from the volatile 'micro-enterprise' category into the more stable 'small enterprise' category, and one of the ventures (KM ET) falls between the medium-size and large-size category. In addition, a feeling of various levels of success clearly surfaced in the interviews of both male and female entrepreneurs. Mima D. stated that she is 'very proud of what she has done and the business has done extremely well', while Vasil V. stated that 'he liked his job and put long hours into it' and shared that he was 'looking into the future with great optimism'.

Three of the six interviewees had specific growth plans for their businesses. In two of the cases (MM EOOD and TT EOOD) the entrepreneurs were considering bank loans to finance their growth, whereas Mima D. was only relying on internally generated resources. Overall, the growth plans and financing schemes appeared to be quite deliberate and conservative.

Table 10.4 summarizes the case findings with respect to the role of human capital, social capital, financial capital and performance/growth.

Table 10.4 Gender, resources and growth potential: a summary

Entrepreneur	Gender	Human capital*	Social capital**	Financial capital	Growth potential
Emil K.	Male	Medium		Restricted	Plans to grow and use debt financing
Tania M.	Female	Medium	–	Restricted	Plans to grow and use debt financing
Mima D.	Female	High	–	Restricted	Plans to grow and use internally generated resources
Elisaveta T.	Female	High		***	No specific growth plans
Vasil A.	Male	Medium		Restricted	Medium/large business
Vasil V.	Male	High		Restricted	No specific growth plans

Notes:
  *Reflects educational level and industry specific experience.
  **Reflects self-reported constrained access to industry networks.
  ***Did not discuss specifically, financial capital may be less of an issue since business is inherited.

DISCUSSION AND CONCLUSIONS

The original interest in this study lay in the discrepancy between the empirically observed lower growth propensity of women-owned businesses and the professed gender equality in the institutional environment of transition economies. I started with the initial premise that the lower growth propensity of women's entrepreneurial ventures in transition economies may be the result of gender-based differences in the access to resources critical to the survival, performance and growth of entrepreneurial ventures. More specifically, I explored the role of human, social and financial capital based on the experiences of three men and three women entrepreneurs in the construction industry in Bulgaria. The insights gleaned through the case studies generally support previous research on the role of human and financial capital and suggest that additional research is well warranted on the role of social capital for women's entrepreneurship in transition economies. In addition, more research is needed on the growth attitudes among both male and female entrepreneurs. These three findings will be discussed next.

The Role of Human and Financial Capital

The findings from the case studies generally confirm prior empirical work on women entrepreneurs in transition economies (World Bank, 2000; ASME, 2002; Welter et al., 2003; Tominc, 2003; Szerb and Pinter, 2003). Women entrepreneurs appear to be better educated than their male counterparts and cognizant of the role of the entrepreneur's knowledge, training and experience for the success of a business venture. In the case when they feel they do not have the necessary industry and professional knowledge, they take care to compensate the deficiency by utilizing contacts, references and other advantages social capital affords them. The specific context of the study may have provided a clearer representation on the role of human capital, since the construction industry is not a traditionally popular industrial sector for women-led entrepreneurial ventures. In this respect, it may be that only those women who feel they have the necessary training, experience and education (or else, valuable contacts) are likely to enter this industry.

With respect to the role of financial capital, this study provided another example of the restricted scope of financing alternatives for entrepreneurial ventures in transition economies. Savings provided the major source of start-up capital, whereas internally generated company funds provided the major source of growth capital. Even companies that had been in business for over ten years could count not more than a couple of instances of using bank financing, invariably with a negative assessment of the procedure and prohibitive terms of financing. Perhaps more importantly, there appears to be no gender-based differences in the access to financing. In other words, financing is equally difficult to obtain for all entrepreneurs in transition economies.

The Role of Social Capital

This study's findings suggest that women appear to be at a disadvantage in terms of the development of their social capital. The subtle point of distinction is that, while not formally restricted in their access to male-dominated industry networks, women appear to be at a disadvantage in utilizing the opportunities these networks present for business development and growth. Indeed, all three of the women business owners were members of the local chamber of the construction industry that sponsored the study. The interview with the chairperson of the local chamber revealed 17 percent of the members were female. Yet, women felt they were excluded from male-only events and thus prevented from important venues for socialization. This finding resonates with recurrent findings from the literature on women's entrepreneurship in the Western economies (Brush at al., 2001) and calls for future research on the role of formal and informal networks on men's and women's entrepreneurial ventures in transition economies.

This finding has important managerial and public policy implications as well, because social capital is critically important for the survival and continued success of entrepreneurial ventures in transition economies (Xin and Pearce, 1996; Batjargal, 2003). New and small players, who are extremely vulnerable because of environmental turbulence and less than ubiquitous institutional endorsement, need to develop a strong tie network that provides support and legitimacy (Manev et al., 2003). The question then arises if women entrepreneurs should be encouraged to persist in gaining access to male-dominated networks, or if they would be better served by forming parallel women-dominated networks. Apparently the role of social capital for women entrepreneurs in transition economies is well worthy of further exploration.

Growth Attitudes

This study revealed that both men and women entrepreneurs took a deliberate and cautious approach to business growth, and that women were perhaps even more cautious than men were. While research has established that people start and operate their businesses for a variety of reasons other than profit maximization or growth (Wilklund et al., 2003), it appears growth attitudes differ between entrepreneurs from Western and transition economies, and between men and women entrepreneurs within the context of transition economies. The reasons for this divergence need to be further explored. One reason, as suggested by some researchers, may be that in the turbulent institutional environment of transition economies, entrepreneurs are more concerned with business stability than business growth (Tan, 1996, 2002). Another reason may be that entrepreneurs in transition economies show a lower risk propensity compared with their Western counterparts. With regard to differences between men and women entrepreneurs in transition economies, it could be that women place a higher value on their personal goals of independence and self-fulfillment and on their family roles than on the growth of their ventures (NSI, 2004; Cliff, 1998).

This finding has important managerial and public policy implications. It affects the planning and resource allocation approaches of new ventures, as well as the appropriate focus of central and local government initiatives to foster entrepreneurship in general and women's entrepreneurship in particular.

In conclusion, this case-based research contributes to managerial theory and practice in two important ways. First, it expands the paradigm boundary by studying the link between women's entrepreneurial venture resources and their growth potential in the environment of a non-traditional industry in a transforming economy. Second, it offers several implications for future conceptual refinement and empirical testing of the effects of human capital, social capital, financial capital and entrepreneurial growth. On the basis of the theoretical arguments, implications are also drawn for women entrepreneurs and policy-makers.

The study findings suggest that entrepreneurship provides unique opportunities to realize the human capital potential of women in transition economies. Although developing on a smaller scale and at a more cautious pace than high-performing ventures in the developed Western economies, these women-led entrepreneurial ventures show remarkable stability and resilience in light of the resource scarcity and environmental turbulence of the competitive and institutional environment in which they operate. A greater focus on social capital development on the part of women entrepreneurs and public policy-makers would further enhance the growth and performance prospects of women's entrepreneurial ventures in transition economies.

NOTES

*   The author wishes to thank the participants at the 2nd Diana International Research Conference on Growth Financing for Women Entrepreneurs (Stockholm, 28–30 May, 2004) for their thoughtful comments on a previous version of this chapter and Galina Anguelova for her able research assistance.
1.   The discussion of the role of human and social capital for entrepreneurs in transitional economies follows Manev et al. (2003).
2.   The biggest impediment to the fast launch of operational activities was cited to be the cumbersome registration and licensing procedure.
3.   This section is based on the *Report on the Small and Medium-sized Enterprises, 2000-2002* (ASME, 2002: 69–70).
4.   The Hygiene and Epidemics Institute (HEI) and its local branches oversee compliance with state and local health and sanitary codes.

REFERENCES

Agency for Small and Medium-sized Enterprises (ASME) (2002), *Report on the Small and Medium-Sized Enterprises, 2000–2002*, Sofia, Bulgaria: ASME.

Agency for Small and Medium-Sized Enterprises (ASME) (2004a), 'ASME – A state institution for implementation of the state policy for support of SMEs in Bulgaria', Accessed at http://www.asme.bg.

Agency for Small and Medium-Sized Enterprises (ASME) (2004b), *Report on the Small and Medium-Sized Enterprises, 2002–2003*, Sofia, Bulgaria: ASME.

Aldrich, H.E. and Auster, E.R. (1986), 'Even dwarfs started small: Liabilities of age and size and their strategic implications', *Research in Organizational Behavior*, **8**, 165–98.

Anna, A.L., Chandler, G.N., Jansen, E. and Mero, N.P. (1999), 'Women business owners in traditional and non-traditional industries', *Journal of Business Venturing*, **15**, 279–303.

Bartlett, W. and Rangelova, R. (1997), 'Small firms and economic transformation in Bulgaria', *Small Business Economics*, **9**(4), 319–33.

Bates, T. (1990), 'Entrepreneur human capital inputs and small business longevity', *The Review of Economics and Statistics*, **72**, 551–9.

Batjargal, B. (2003), 'Social capital and entrepreneurial performance in Russia: A longitudinal study', *Organization Studies*, **24**(4), 534–56.

Becker, G.S. (1993), *Human Capital: A Theoretical and Empirical Analysis with Specific Reference to Education*, Chicago: University of Chicago Press.

Bliss, R.T. and Garratt, N.L. (2001), 'Supporting women entrepreneurs in transitioning economies', *Journal of Small Business Management*, **39**(4), 336–44.

Brush, C.G. and Chaganti, R. (1998), 'Business without glamour: An analysis of resources on performance by size and age in small service and retail firms', *Journal of Business Venturing*, **14**(3), 223–58.

Brush, C.G., Greene, P.G. and Hart, M.M. (2001), 'From initial idea to unique advantage: The entrepreneurial challenge of constructing a resource base', *Academy of Management Executive*, **14**(3), 223–58.

Carter, S. (1989), 'The dynamics and performance of female-owned entrepreneurial firms in London, Glasgow, and Nottingham', *Journal of Organizational Change Management*, **2**(3), 54–64.

Carter, N.M., Brush, C.G., Greene, P.G., Gatewood, E. and Hart, M.M. (2003), 'Women entrepreneurs who break thorough to equity financing: The influence of human, social and financial capital', *Venture Capital*, **5**(1), 1–28.

Chell, E. (2002), 'Women in science enterprise: An exploration of the issues, some policy implications and research agenda', Paper presented at the Gender Research Forum, Women and Equality Unit, London. Accessed at Elizabeth.chell@umist.ac.uk.

Cliff, J.E. (1998), 'Does one size fit all? Exploring the relationship between attitudes towards growth, gender, and business size', *Journal of Business Venturing*, **13**(6), 523–42.

Cooper, A.C., Gimeno-Gascon, F.L. and Woo, C.Y. (1994), 'Initial human and financial capital as predictors of new venture performance', *Journal of Business Venturing*, **9**(5), 371–95.

Danis, W.M. and Lyles, M.A. (2004), 'A longitudinal study of entrepreneurs in a transition economy: When does competitive strategy matter most?', Paper submitted to the JIBS/AIB Paper Development Workshop at the Academy of International Business Annual Meeting, Stockholm, Sweden.

Davidsson, P. and Honig, B. (2003), 'The role of human and social capital among nascent entrepreneurs', *Journal of Business Venturing*, **18**(3), 301–31.

Doudeva, L. (2001), *Demography of the Small and Medium-Sized Enterprises in Bulgaria within the period 1995–1999. Mapping the Changes in Business Enterprises in Bulgaria*, Sofia, Bulgaria: Center for Economic Development (CED).

Edelman, L.F. (2000), *Facilitators and Impediments to the Internal Transfer of Team-Embodied Competencies in Firms Operating in Dynamic Environments*, Unpublished doctoral dissertation, Boston University.

Eisenhardt, K. (1989), 'Building theory from case study research', *Academy of Management Review*, **14**(4), 532–50.

Florin. J., Lubatkin, M. and Schulze, W. (2003), 'A social capital model of high growth ventures', *Academy of Management Journal*, **46**(3), 374–84.

Glaser, B.G. and Strauss, A.L. (1967), *The Discovery of Grounded Theory: Strategies for Qualitative Research*, New York: Aldine de Gruyeter.

Hisrich, R.D. and Fulop, G. (1994), 'The role of women entrepreneurs in Hungary's transition economy', *International Studies of Management and Organization*, **24**(4), 100–17.

Hitt, M.A. and Ireland, R.D. (1985), 'Corporate distinctive competence, strategy, industry, and performance', *Strategic Management Journal*, **6**, 273–93.

Hofer, C.W. and Sandberg, W. (1987), 'Improving new venture performance: Some guidelines for success', *American Journal of Small Business*, **12**(1), 11–25.

Honig, B. (2001), 'Human capital and structural upheaval: A study of manufacturing firms in the West Bank', *Journal of Business Venturing*, **16**(6), 575–94.

Ingram, P. and Simons, T. (2000), 'State formation, ideological competition, and the ecology of Israeli workers' cooperatives 1920–1993', *Administrative Science Quarterly*, **31**, 25–53.

Izyumov, A., and Razumnova, I. (2000), 'Women entrepreneurs in Russia: Learning to survive the market', *Journal of Developmental Entrepreneurship*, **5**(1), 1–20.

Judd, C.M., Smith, E.R. and Kidder, L.H. (1991), *Research Methods in Social Relations*, 6th edn, Forth Worth, TX: Harcourt Brace Jovanovich College Publishers.

Kalleberg, A.L. and Leicht, K.T. (1991), 'Gender and organizational performance: Determinants of small business survival and success', *Academy of Management Journal*, **34**(1), 136–61.

Khavul, S. (2001), *Money and Knowledge: Sources of Seed Capital and the Performance of High-Technology Start-Ups*, Unpublished doctoral dissertation, Boston University.

Lee, S.M. and Peterson, S.J. (2000), 'Culture, entrepreneurial orientation, and global competitiveness', *Journal of World Business*, **35**(4), 401–16.

Lerner, M. and Almor, T. (2002), 'Relationships among strategic capabilities and the performance of women-owned small ventures', *Journal of Small Business Management*, **40**(2), 109–25.

Manev, I.M., Gyoshev, B.S. and Manolova, T.S. (2003), 'The role of human and social capital and entrepreneurial orientation for small business performance in a transition economy', Paper presented at the Academy of Management Meeting, Seattle, WA.

Manolova, T.S. and Yan, A. (2002), 'Institutional constraints and entrepreneurial responses in a transforming economy: The case of Bulgaria', *International Small Business Journal*, **20**(2), 163–84.

McKendrick, D.C. and Carroll, G.R. (2001), 'On the genesis of organizational forms: Evidence from the market for disk arrays', *Organization Science*, **12**(6), 661–82.

Miles, M.B. and Huberman, A.M. (1984), *Qualitative Data Analysis*, Newbury Park, CA: Sage.

Miner, A.S. and Haunschild, P.R. (1995), 'Population level learning', in L.L. Cummings, B.M. Staw (eds), *Research in Organizational Behavior (Vol. 17)*, Greenwich, CT: JAI Press, pp. 115–66.

Nahapiet, J. and Ghoshal, S. (1998), 'Social capital, intellectual capital, and the organizational advantage', *Academy of Management Review*, **23**(2), 242–66.

National Statistical Institute (NSI) (2002), *Men and Women in the Republic of Bulgaria*, Sofia, Bulgaria: National Statistical Institute.

National Statistical Institute (NSI) (2004), *Small and Medium-sized Enterprises in the Republic of Bulgaria*, Report published on January 29, 2004. Accessed at http://www.nsi.bg.

Neuman, W.L. (2003), *Social Research Methods: Qualitative and Quantitative Approaches*, 5th edn, Boston, MA: Allyn & Bacon.

Oliver, C. (1991), 'Strategic responses to institutional processes', *Academy of Management Review*, **16**(1), 145–79.

Organisation for Economic Cooperation and Development (OECD) (2002), *OECD Employment Outlook: July 2002*, Paris, OECD.

Pari Weekly (1996), 'The financial loop is tightening around the small entrepreneur', 6 June, 13–19.

Peng, M.W. (2001), 'How entrepreneurs create wealth in transition economies', *Academy of Management Executive*, **15**(4), 24–38.

Peng, M.W. and Heath, P.S. (1996), 'The growth of the firm in planned economies in transformation: Institutions, organizations and strategic choice', *Academy of Management Review*, **21**, 492–528.

Penrose, E.T. (1959), *The Theory of the Growth of the Firm*, New York: John Wiley.

Puffer, S.M. and McCarthy, D.J. (2001), 'Navigating the hostile maze: A framework for Russian entrepreneurship', *Academy of Management Executive*, **15**(4), 24–38.

Read, L.H. (1994), 'Raising finance from banks: A comparative study of the experiences of male and female entrepreneurs', *Frontiers of Entrepreneurship Research*, Wellesley, MA: Babson College.

Reynolds, P.D., Bygrave, W.D., Autio, E., Cox, L.W. and May, M. (2002), 'Global Entrepreneurship Monitor: 2002 Executive Report', Babson College, London Business School and Kauffman Foundation.

Scase, R. (1997), 'The role of small business in the economic transformation of Eastern Europe: Real but relatively unimportant?', *International Small Business Journal*, **16**(1), 13–21.

Shane, S. and Venkataraman, S. (2000), 'The promise of entrepreneurship as a field of research', *Academy of Management Review*, **25**(1), 217–26.

Singh, J.V., Tucker, D.J. and House, R.J. (1986), 'Organizational legitimacy and the liability of newness', *Administrative Science Quarterly*, **31**, 171–93.

Smallbone, D. and Welter, F. (2001), 'The distinctiveness of entrepreneurship in transition economies', *Small Business Economics*, **16**(4), 249–62.

Stinchcombe, A.L. (1965), 'Social structures and organizations', in March, J.G. (ed.), *Handbook of Organizations*, pp. 142–93. Chicago: Rand McNally.

Stoyanovska, A., Karamocheva, G., Tisheva, G., Krustenova, E., Velkova, Y., Vladimirova, K., Indjeva, R. and Hadjimitova, S. (2000), *A Survey of Women's Entrepreneurship and the Role of Women in the Economic Transformation in Bulgaria*, Sofia, Bulgaria: International Labor Organization.

Stuart, T.E., Hoang, H. and Hybels, R.C. (1999), 'Organizational endorsements and the performance of entrepreneurial ventures', *Administrative Science Quarterly*, **44**, 315–49.

Suchman, M.C. (1995), 'Managing legitimacy: Strategic and institutional approaches', *Academy of Management Review*, **20**(3), 571–610.

Szerb, L. and Pinter, E. (2003), 'Women entrepreneurship in Hungary', Paper presented to the First Research Symposium on Growth Financing for Women Owned Businesses, Stockholm, Sweden.

Tan, J. (1996), 'Regulatory environment and strategic orientation in a transforming economy: A study of Chinese private enterprise', *Entrepreneurship Theory and Practice*, **21**(1), 31–46.

Tan, J. (2002) 'Culture, nation, and entrepreneurial strategic orientations: Implications for an emerging economy', *Entrepreneurship Theory and Practice*, **21**(1), 31–46.

Tominc, P. (2003), 'Status of women's entrepreneurship and access to financing, and finance strategies in Slovenia', Paper presented to the First Research Symposium on Growth Financing for Women Owned Businesses, Stockholm, Sweden.

Tsang, E.W.K. (1996), 'In search of legitimacy: The private entrepreneur in China', *Entrepreneurship Theory and Practice*, **21**(1), 21–30.

Verheul, I., van Stel, A. and Thurik, R. (2004), 'Explaining female and male entrepreneurship across 29 countries', SCALES-paper N 200403. Accessed at www.eim.nl/smes-and-entrepreneurship.

Wilklund, J. and Shepherd, D. (2003), 'Aspiring for, and achieving growth: The moderating role of resources and opportunities', *Journal of Management Studies*, **40**(8), 1919–41.

Wilklund, J., Davidsson, P. and Delmar, F. (2003), 'What do they think and feel about growth? An expectancy-value approach to small business managers' attitudes toward growth', *Entrepreneurship Theory and Practice*, Spring, 247–70.

World Bank (The) (2000), *The Role of SMEs in the Bulgarian Economy*, Sofia, Bulgaria: The World Bank.

Welter, F., Smallbone, D. and Schakirova, N. (2003), *Women Entrepreneurs in Transition Economies: Necessity or Opportunity Driven?*, RENT XVI, Lodz, Poland.

Wernerfelt, B. (1984), 'A resource-based view of the firm', *Strategic Management Journal*, **5**, 171–80.

Xin, K.R. and Pearce, J.L. (1996), 'Quanxi: Connections as substitutes for formal institutional support', *Academy of Management Journal*, **39**(6), 1641–58.

Yin, R.K. (1993), *Case Study Research*, 2nd edn, Newbury Park, CA: Sage.

11. Access to finance for women entrepreneurs in Ireland: a supply-side perspective

Colette Henry, Kate Johnston and Angela Hamouda

I. INTRODUCTION

One of the main constraints on the level of entrepreneurship and business creation is the difficulty encountered in obtaining finance (Bates, 1997; Lumme et al., 1998; Fischer and Massey, 2000; Cooper, 2002). According to Drucker (1995), the lack of capital is 'the most crippling ailment of infant enterprises' (Drucker, as cited in Hindle and Rushworth, 1999, p. 2). De Bruin and Dupuis (2003) concur, stating that, 'as well as being of considerable importance at start-up, economic [financial] capital is an ongoing issue and is also sometimes implicated in the closure of businesses' (De Bruin and Dupuis, 2003, p. 61).

National and international researchers have highlighted the negative impact of financial constraints on new firm formation, as well as the harmful impact on economic growth and job creation (Egeln et al., 1997; Manigart and Struyf, 1997; Becchetti and Trovato, 2002; Small Business Service, 2003). Moreover, recent studies suggest that financial constraints are more acute with regard to women-led ventures (Carter and Rosa, 1998; Verheul and Thurik, 2001; Carter et al., 2002; Canadian Prime Minister's Task Force, 2003). In the case of Ireland, the evidence, although limited, suggests that both nascent and established women entrepreneurs have experienced greater difficulties in accessing funding for their business ventures than their male counterparts (Bray, 2001; Henry and Kennedy, 2003; Gender Equality Unit, 2003).

This chapter presents the results of a major study into availability and access to finance for women-owned/led businesses in Ireland. The study involved 24 funding organizations, representing 80 per cent of the total funding supply population. The aim of the study is to extend our understanding of why women entrepreneurs lag behind men in securing funding. In this regard, the research seeks to address a number of specific questions, namely:

- How active are banks, venture capital companies (VCs) and support agencies in funding business creation and development in Ireland?
- What are the most important factors funding agencies look for in evaluating a business funding application?
- How successful are female business owners in securing funding as compared with their male counterparts?
- Are funding agencies aware of the barriers facing female entrepreneurs in accessing funding in Ireland?

The chapter proceeds as follows. The next section (section II) provides context to the current study and examines the state of entrepreneurship and, in particular, women's entrepreneurship in Ireland. Relevant demographic, economic and social statistics tracing the development and growth of women in the Irish economy are presented. Section III outlines the theoretical background to the study and examines the financial environment as well as the sources and type of funding available to entrepreneurs in Ireland. The methodology, data collection and details of the sample employed are discussed in section IV, the key findings in section V, and a discussion of the results in section VI. The chapter closes with a summary of the main policy implications and recommendations to emerge from the study in section VII.

II. COUNTRY CONTEXT

The Economic Picture

During the last ten years, Ireland has undergone a phenomenal transformation. Traditionally an agricultural-based economy, through a series of aggressive policies designed to attract multinational firms, Ireland has evolved into a modern, high-value successful economy. Today Ireland is among the fastest-growing economies in the developed world. As reported in Table 11.1 below, between 1994 and 2000, the Irish economy grew by an annual rate of 9 per cent, compared with 2 per cent between the periods 1981 and 1986.[1] Today, economic growth averages 5 per cent, with strong economic growth forecast in the coming years.

With this unprecedented economic growth came a dramatic fall in unemployment. During the mid- to late 1990s, the unemployment rate

Table 11.1   Measures of Ireland's economic performance (1981–2000)

	1981–86	1987–93	1994–2000	2004
Real GDP	2.1	4.8	9.0	5.6
Real GNP	0.1	4.1	8.4	4.9
Unemployment Rate	13.8	15.2	9.5	4.6
Consumer Prices	10.8	2.9	2.5	2.4

Source: Burham (2003); OECD 1999, 2001a; Central Statistics Office.

fell from a high of 15 per cent to under 5 per cent in 2004. In EU terms, Ireland now has one of the lowest unemployment rates in the European Union, currently 4.6 per cent, compared to an EU average of 8.3 per cent.[2]

Surprisingly, it was not until the 1980s that the importance of entrepreneurship and indigenous start-ups was officially recognized. Traditionally, Ireland had little or no enterprise tradition or culture (Garavan et al., 1997). As noted by McKeon et al. (2004), economic policies during this time were deliberately focused on inward foreign direct investment, typically in the high-technology sectors. This policy, while highly successful in reducing unemployment, resulted in Ireland becoming dependent on multinational corporations as a source of employment and economic growth.

Like most modern economies, the small to medium business sector is vital to the Irish economy; SMEs account for over 99.5 per cent of all Irish enterprises and collectively employ approximately 47 per cent of the total workforce. This combined with the fact that Ireland is a small, open, highly trade-dependent economy with a highly educated young workforce, has led to significant resources committed to fostering a spirit of enterprise development. According to recent government reports, Ireland's future economic success is now firmly linked to the successful development and growth of its indigenous start-ups and small firms sector.

To date, this policy of direct intervention has been relatively successful. Recent reports suggest that entrepreneurship activity in Ireland is notably higher than that in most other EU countries. The 2003 GEM Report (GEM, 2003), estimates a total entrepreneurial activity index (TEA) for Ireland of 8.1 per cent compared with an EU average of 6 per cent. However, while Ireland compares well with, for example, Italy (4 per cent), France (2.5 per cent) and Germany (5 per cent), Ireland, along with the rest of Europe, continues to lag behind the USA, Canada, Australia and New Zealand in entrepreneurship activity. This is the case both in terms of total entrepreneurship activity, and particularly female entrepreneurship.

Profile of Women's Entrepreneurship In Ireland

Historical context

The Irish situation with regard to female entrepreneurship is particularly interesting when considered in a historical context. As in most other parts of the world, the traditional role of women in Irish society was very much that of homemaker, which typically included sole responsibility for children and other family dependents. Although, throughout Europe, women started to play an active role in the workforce in the 1940s, laws establishing equality only became an issue in the 1970s. In Ireland, the 'Marriage Bar' – a law requiring women to retire from employment in the civil service upon marriage (Civil Service Regulations Act, 1956) was not abolished until 1973. However, even then, only widows or married women who were not supported by their husbands could apply for reinstatement to the Civil Service. These requirements have since been held to be discriminatory, but it was not until the late 1990s that the act was repealed (*Murdoch's Irish Legal Companion, 2003*).

During the 1990s, the combined impact of legal, economic and social changes led to a dramatic rise in the number of women joining the labour force. According to the Labour Force Survey (2003), women currently account for over 40 per cent of the labour force (FÁS, 1998), with twice as many women in the labour force today, as there were 50 years ago. Today, Ireland has one of the fastest-growing labour forces within the European Union, due, in part, to the increasing number of women working in the economy.

However, despite the positive gains, women continue to be employed in low-status, low-pay occupations and sub-sectors (United Nations Statistics Division, 2000). Women tend to be under-represented in the high-value productive sector activities (Goodbody Economic Consultants, 2002), and are more likely to be employed part-time in the education, health and services sectors (QUB, 2003). Similarly, in terms of occupations, women account for less than a third of all persons employed as managers and administrators, with nearly three-quarters of women holding posts defined as clerical and secretarial staff.

The Extent and Nature of Women's Entrepreneurship in Ireland

There would appear to be some controversy over the actual number of women entrepreneurs/business owners in Ireland. The common lack of statistical data, differences in defining female entrepreneurs, as well as variations in the types of survey methodologies used, have led to confusion over Ireland's stock of women entrepreneurs. In 2000, for example, the European Observatory estimated that females accounted for only 28 per cent of business owners in Ireland. In contrast, by 2001, the OECD estimated that 15 per cent of Ireland's entrepreneurs were female (OECD, 1999; Women's Unit, UK, 2001; OECD, 2001a). In contrast, GEM (2002), reported that the level of female entrepreneurship in Ireland was in fact even lower at only 7.5 per cent, a figure, the report states, that compares well with other EU countries! (GEM, 2001). The most recent GEM report estimates that women account for just over a third of all the entrepreneurs in Ireland, currently 36 per cent.

What do we know so far?

Until recently, research into female entrepreneurship in Ireland was severely limited. Indeed, this lack of knowledge concerning women entrepreneurs contrasted starkly with that of their male counterparts, where considerable research efforts and knowledge was accumulated, dating back as far as the 1980s. To date, research into female entrepreneurship has followed international studies, focusing on both motivational issues and barriers facing female entrepreneurs. Issues examined to date include: barriers facing women's entrepreneurs in the border regions (Henry and Kennedy, 2003); networking strategies of women entrepreneurs (McGowan and McGeady, 2002; Hamouda et al., 2003a); comparisons between men and women as entrepreneurs (Gender Equality Unit, 2003); growth aspirations of women entrepreneurs (Henry et al., 2004), and typical business profile/sectors of women entrepreneurs in particular regions (Browne et al., 2004; Bray, 2004).

A review of the existing literature points to a number of interesting findings:

- Men are twice as likely to start a business in Ireland as women. On average, nearly two-thirds (64 per cent) of entrepreneurs in Ireland are men, with women accounting for just over a third (36 per cent) (GEM, 2004). While this level has held steady for several years, the gap appears to be widening. The number of nascent and new established women entrepreneurs declined by 50 per cent between 2001–3. In contrast, male entrepreneurial activity over the same period declined by less than a fifth (20 per cent).
- Although there is no specific government strategy on women's entrepreneurship, a number of support agencies, including Enterprise Ireland, County Enterprise Boards and Local County Partnerships currently offer supports for female entrepreneurs, including 'women in enterprise' programmes, along with mentoring, financial and accounting supports. These are generally offered on a regional basis, to specific targeted groups.[3]

- Women choose entrepreneurship for a variety of reasons, including a lack of good employment opportunities in their particular field and the desire for greater independence.
- Female business owners in Ireland are highly educated, and are typically in the age bracket 35 to 40 years (Henry and Kennedy, 2003; Bray, 2004; Browne et al., 2004).
- Female entrepreneurs often limit firm growth in order to maintain control over the businesses (Henry et al., 2004). Although the extent to which this is internally imposed or externally imposed (due to lack of supports) is unknown.
- Access to finance is increasingly recognised as a main barrier for women entrepreneurs, although the evidence is conflicting. A major bank survey in 1997, for example, identified no explicit barriers facing women entrepreneurs. However, more recent evidence suggests that most women entrepreneurs use personal savings rather than accessing bank or VC funding (Bray, 2001; Henry and Kennedy, 2003; among others). A recent study by Henry et al. (2004), found that indirect or 'stealth' barriers by some agencies are adversely impacting on the ability of women entrepreneurs to access funding, and hence start their own business.

By way of addressing some of the gaps in the current literature, this chapter presents the findings from a major survey into availability and access to finance for women entrepreneurs in Ireland. The study involves funding agencies across the financial spectrum, including the banking sector, the VC market and the support agencies, along with a micro-funding specialist firm. The remainder of the chapter is organized as follows. Following a discussion on the role of the funding agencies in financing business start-ups and development and the methodology, data collection and details of the sample, the findings from the survey are presented. The results are presented under four key headings and the chapter closes with recommendations aimed at improving the financial environment within which women entrepreneurs operate in Ireland.

III.   THEORETICAL DEVELOPMENT AND RESEARCH CONTEXT

Access to and Availability of Finance for Irish Entrepreneurs

For the majority of Irish entrepreneurs, bank loans are the main source of finance. However, research suggests that for many entrepreneurs, accessing bank funding is a major problem. A survey by the Institute of Small and Medium Enterprise Association (ISME) (1995), concluded that the majority of businesses involved in the survey rated loan negotiations as either 'difficult' or 'very complicated'.[4]

A major theme to emerge in the extant literature is evidence of a 'funding gap' particularly at the early or seed funding stage.[5] This was a particular problem for businesses without collateral or outside the existing designated sectors. The Forfas Report (2002), for example, argued that funding at the seed capital stage would need to be reviewed if 'the aim is to increase the number of successful new business start-ups and to grow an increasing number of medium to large indigenous firms' (p. 10).

In the case of female entrepreneurs, the evidence, although limited, suggests that both nascent and established women entrepreneurs experience greater difficulties in financing their business ventures in comparison to their male counterparts (Bray, 2001; Henry and Kennedy, 2003; Gender Equality Unit, 2003). Moreover, there is a growing recognition that the difficulties of accessing funding severely limit both the creation and growth of women-owned/led businesses.

Finance for Entrepreneurs and Start-up Companies

Bank funding is the main source of funding used by Irish nascent entrepreneurs (GEM, 2003). As presented in Table 11.2 below, just over half of all Irish nascent entrepreneurs plan to access bank funding to set up their business. Other major funding sources, in order of importance, include government programmes and informal investment from family members and personal contacts.

The increasing reliance on government programmes, in the form of public sector guarantees and funding, suggests that the support and enterprise agencies are attempting to bridge the 'funding gap'. These agencies, which operate within specific guidelines, enable firms to access funding at key stages that are often deemed too risky by traditional funding bodies (that is, banks), or access low or no interest loans, often without collateral.

A major discovery to emerge from the GEM study is the scope and scale of informal funding among nascent entrepreneurs in Ireland. As reported in Table 11.2, 'immediate family' was the third most popular source of funding for nascent entrepreneurs. According to the report, if all identifiable sources of informal funding (defined as family, work colleagues, relatives, friends/neighbours and employer) are taken together, informal funding is 'the largest single source of funding in new businesses in Ireland' (p. 28), a fact that is often overlooked by policy-makers.

Table 11.2   Sources of finance for Irish nascent entrepreneurs

Source	Percentages[a]
Banks/Financial Institutions	51
Government Programmes	34
Immediate Family	29
Work Colleagues	14
Other Family/Relatives	9
Friend or Neighbour	9
Employer	6
Other Sources	16

Note: [a]Percentages do not total 100 due to respondents citing more than one source of finance in the Irish GEM research.

Source: GEM (2003), p. 28.

Venture Capital Funding in Ireland

In recent years, the availability of equity finance has significantly increased in most advanced economies, and Ireland is no exception. For example, the EU Seed and Venture Capital Measure under the Operational Programme for Industrial Development 1994–1999 was set up with the objective of establishing VC Funds to provide early stage, small and medium-sized growth-oriented enterprises in Ireland with equity capital. Fifteen VC initiatives were established under this initiative, with ECU 43.9 million being committed. A total of €117 million, a figure that includes both EU and private sector contributions, was invested in 127 companies in the period up to December 2002 (Enterprise Ireland, 2002, p. 20). While the bulk of this investment (71 per cent) was in the software and related sectors, over 40 per cent of the funds went directly to early stage companies.

Under the 2000–2006 Seed and Venture Capital programme, Enterprise Ireland (Ireland's primary state agency for the development of indigenous businesses) has committed €95 million to a total fund of around €400 million, which will be available for investing in Irish businesses. According to Enterprise Ireland (2002, p. 2), these funds will be able to provide smaller investment amounts, have a greater regional perspective, and will specifically target early stage SMEs and sectors that are traditionally difficult to finance. A total of €61 million of these funds have been invested to date, as illustrated in Table 11.3 below.

While access and availability of VC funding has greatly improved in recent years, critics point to a number of weaknesses in the current system, with a

*Table 11.3   Summary of investments (under 2000–2006 programme) –
Ireland*

Fund	Fund Size €'000s	No. of Investments 31/12/02	Total Invested 21/12/02 €'000s
AIB Equity Fund 2002	12 700	2	750
BOI Venture Capital Ltd	18 850	4	3 918
Delta Equity Fund 2 Limited Partnership	90 000	34	17 561
Enterprise Equity Investment Fund Ltd	9 000	3	1 288
Enterprise Equity Seed Capital Investment Fund	7 000	0	–
European BioScience Fund 1	12 700	0	–
EVP Early Stage Technology Fund	5 000	0	–
Guinness Ireland Ulster Bank Equity Fund Limited Partnership	19 000	12	5 085
ICC Regional Venture Capital Fund	25 400	2	1 250
Irish BioScience Venture Capital Fund	19 060	0	–
Kernel Capital Partners Private Equity Fund	19 050	0	–
Mentor Capital Partners Limited Partnership	7 500	0	–
HotOrigin Fund	2 300	0	–
Trinity Venture Fund	138 700	13	31 246
4th Level Ventures University Seed Fund Limited Partnership	8 400	0	–
Totals	394 660	70	61 098

Source: Enterprise Ireland (2002). Seed and Venture Capital Programme 2000–2006 Report, National Development Plan and Enterprise Ireland, p. 4.

clear equity gap both in Northern Ireland and the Irish Republic (InterTradeIreland, 2000; McParland, 2001). According to Knife (2002), during the 1990s, financing for new and growing Irish businesses in the form of seed or venture capital was extremely difficult to find; in many instances, it was easier for entrepreneurs to seek funding from abroad, due to a lack of pioneering funds, and a preference on the part of financiers to stick with traditional types of investment. This has led to concern that the situation is 'quite bleak for a new wave of Irish high-tech entrepreneurs', strongly suggesting that a new approach to funding technology companies at concept stage is needed (Thesing, 2000).

A major barrier to increasing venture investment in Ireland concerns the twin issues of familiarity and risk. Most active investment houses, banks or development agencies lack the means to acquire a good knowledge of the industries they are being asked to invest in, and Ireland lacks a track record of successful indigenous technology ventures (Knife, 2002). Furthermore, studies have suggested that awareness of venture capital firms on the part of entrepreneurs is low, and thus, specialist financial advisers have an important role to play in guiding the flow of proposals to venture capitalists (see for example Robbie and Murray, 1992, among others). This is of particular concern for women entrepreneurs, since research suggests that women entrepreneurs are generally outside formal male networks (Aldrich et al., 1997 and Brush, 1997), hence their potential to access VC capital is potentially limited relative to their male counterparts.

IV. METHODOLOGY

A database representing the 'supply' side of business finance in Ireland, and which comprised banks, venture capital companies and state agencies, was constructed from a combination of the Golden Pages;[6] various business and finance websites, and a venture capital listing in a recent report[7] published by Enterprise Ireland. The database was subsequently adjusted to eliminate the overlap of organizations with sub or regional divisions. This resulted in a final database of 30 funding organizations comprising 16 venture capital organizations, eight banks, five state/semi-state enterprise support organizations and one micro-finance agency.

A structured 33-item questionnaire was developed, comprised of two main parts. Part one focused on the scale of funding currently available to entrepreneurs in Ireland. Issues examined included the types of funding available, and the level of interest among the agencies in financing particular sectors and business ventures (that is, start-ups, growth, etc.). Other issues examined included the number and type of proposal funded in previous years, and the factors most likely to influence the decision to accept or reject a funding application.

The second part of the questionnaire consisted of 18 questions, and focused on the organizations' interest in and experiences of funding women-led/owned businesses. Issues examined included, funding of women-owned/led businesses, differences in the funding requirements between men and women entrepreneurs, and the organization's attitude and interest in promoting female entrepreneurship.

Due to the nature of the questions, as well as difficulties with the availability of some of the proposed interviewees, and time constraints, it was decided to adopt an electronic survey method. Subsequently, the questions were converted to an electronic survey tool, and the 'Survey Monkey'[8] package was used for this purpose. The survey was sent electronically to the relevant contact person, who was normally the investment officer (venture capital organizations); business loan officer (banks), or client executive/ enterprise officer (support organizations), in the various organizations in the sample.

As documented in Table 11.4 below, a total of 24 funding bodies returned completed electronic surveys, consisting of seven banks, 12 venture capitalist organizations, four enterprise support agencies and one specialist in micro-financing.[9]

As reported in Table 11.4, all funding organizations responded well to the questionnaire, with over 87 per cent of banks and 80 per cent of support agencies returning completed questionnaires. Only one bank failed to respond, indicating that the necessary information was deemed too sensitive to reveal.

Table 11.4   Response rates and final sample

Funding Sector	Funding Agencies		
	Contacted No.	Responded Rate No.	Response %
Banks	8	7	87
Venture Capitalists	16	12	75
State/Support Agencies	5	4	80
Micro-financing Specialist	1	1	100
Total	30	24	80

V.   FINDINGS

The findings reported in this section are presented under the following four headings:

- The role of banks, venture capital companies (VCs) and support agencies in funding business development in Ireland;
- The main factors funding agencies consider in evaluating a business application;
- How successful are female business owners in securing funding in Ireland, and how does this compare with their male counterparts?;

- The level of awareness among funding agencies of the barriers and issues facing female entrepreneurs in Ireland.

The Role of Banks, VCs and Support Agencies in Funding Business Development in Ireland

Given the importance of finance to the creation and growth of new businesses (GEM, 2003), and the recent concern over a 'funding gap' for new and growing businesses, each of the funding agencies were asked several questions about the type of financing available, and their level of 'interest' in funding start-up ventures, expansion finance, MBOs and university spin-outs, among others. The level of interest ranged from 'no interest' to 'very strong interest'.

Seed (pre-start-up) financing

Seed or pre-start-up funding is generally not widely available in Ireland. Four of the six banks expressed 'no' or 'moderate' interest in funding this type of business development. Similarly, eight of the 11 VCs were only 'moderately' interested in this type of funding. In contrast, the support agencies expressed a 'strong' to 'very strong interest' in investing at the pre-start-up stage.

Start-up financing

In terms of start-up financing, the picture is somewhat more positive. The majority of agencies expressed an interest in funding this type of business development. Three of the five banks and nearly two-thirds of the VCs expressed a 'strong/very strong' interest in providing start-up finance. Again, the support agencies (n = 3) appear to be active in providing start-up funding, with the majority expressing a 'strong interest' in this type of funding. Only one bank indicated that it had 'no' interest in funding start-up financing.

Early stage expansion and expansion financing for established firms

Growth funding, defined as 'early stage expansion' and 'expansion finance by established businesses' appeared to be the main type of funding available in Ireland. Four of the six banks expressing a 'strong/very strong' interest in this type of funding. Similarly, over three-quarters of the VCs (80 per cent) expressed a 'strong/very strong' interest in expansionary funding. A similar result emerged for the support agencies and the micro-finance company.

Other funding (MBOs, USOs and rescue financing)

All of the funding agencies expressed some interest in funding management buy-outs (MBOs), management buy-ins (MBIs) and university spin-outs (USOs). Although no notable difference emerged between the groups, the VCs appear to be more disposed towards this type of funding. Two-thirds expressed a 'strong/very strong' interest in funding MBOs, MBIs and USOs, compared with just under half of the banks.

In terms of rescue financing, only a small number of agencies expressed any interest in this sort of financing. The majority of the banks (n = 5) and 70 per cent of the VCs expressed 'no' to 'moderate' interest. Of the two support agencies that responded, neither was involved in rescue financing.

Number of investment opportunities received and funded

Each of the funding agencies was asked a series of questions around the investment proposals received and funded in the past financial year. Respondents were also asked to identify, in percentage terms, the organization's current investment portfolio at specific stages of business development. The results suggest that less than one in five of the proposals received were actually funded. In terms of what type of funding was made available, growth financing accounted for the majority of funding allocated by the banking sector, with two-thirds of the banks funding business growth. In contrast, VC funding was evenly divided between start-up and growth funding. In the case of the support agencies, there was a strong focus on pre-start-up and start-up financing, with three of the five agencies providing funding at this stage.

Sectors most likely to receive funding

The IT, Pharmaceutical/Medical and Biotechnology sectors are the top three sectors most likely to attract VC funding in Ireland. Just over a third of the VCs surveyed identified the IT sector as a sector in which they would 'most likely invest'. The pharmaceutical/medical and biotechnology sectors also ranked highly, accounting for 24 per cent and 15 per cent of VC funding respectively.

In contrast, the banks and support agencies are active across a range of sectors. When asked 'In which sectors is your organization most likely to provide funding?', the banks identified services, construction, pharmaceutical/medical and the creative industries as the main sectors of investment (see Figure 11.1 below). Somewhat less important were the IT and biotechnology, accounting for less than 20 per cent of the funding allocated by the banks.

Similarly, support agencies fund a diverse range of sectors reflecting the international investment focus of these agencies towards the high-tech and the internationally traded services sectors.

The Main Factors Funding Agencies Consider in Evaluating a Business Application

According to GEM (2003), a core area of concern among entrepreneurs relates

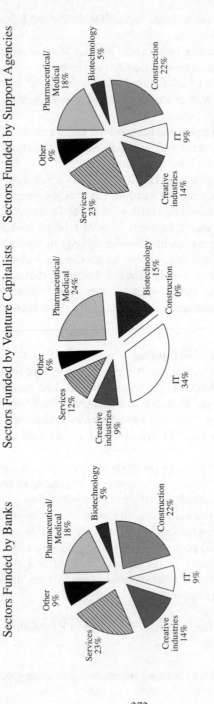

Sectors Funded by Banks

Sectors Funded by Venture Capitalists

Sectors Funded by Support Agencies

Note: Total number of respondents: venture capitalists (10); banks (5) and support agencies (4). *Other includes: aquaculture & fisheries, food, manufacturing, natural resources, social & economic infrastructure, traded services, tourism, manufacturing, internationally traded services.

Figure 11.1 Sectors funded by banks, venture capitalists and support agencies

272

to the attitude of the financial community towards new business ventures suggesting a lack of understanding on the part of entrepreneurs towards the whole funding process. By way of addressing this issue, funders were asked to rank, in order of importance (from one to five, where one equals 'highly important' and five 'not important') a range of entrepreneurial, business and funding characteristics in the decision to accept or reject a funding application. In total, respondents were asked to rank in order of importance 20 factors ranging from the age of the entrepreneur to the export potential of the proposed business idea.

Entrepreneurial characteristics
As reported in Table 11.5, of the seven characteristics listed, previous business experience is the most important entrepreneurial characteristic influencing the funder's financing decision. This is particularly the case for banks and VCs.

Other factors in order of importance are employment and training (mean score 2.05), access to supports (mean score 2.06), and education (mean score 2.4). Age and gender are considered relatively unimportant with an average score of 4. Only the banking sector appears to rate age as an important factor in the funding decision.

Table 11.5   Importance of entrepreneurial characteristics (mean score ratings)*

Entrepreneurial Characteristics	Venture Capitalists n = 12	Banks n = 7	Support Agencies n = 4	Micro-Financial Specialist n = 1	Average Score n = 24
Business Experience	1.25	1.14	2.25	2.00	1.66
Employment and Training	2.42	1.78	2.00	2.00	2.05
Access to Supports	2.83	1.78	1.66	2.00	2.06
Previous Business Failure of Lead Entrepreneurs	2.58	1.88	3.00	4.00	2.86
Education	3.00	2.43	2.00	2.00	2.35
Age	3.50	2.43	5.00	4.00	3.73
Gender	4.67	5.00	5.00	5.00	4.91

Note: *Where 1 = highly important; 2 = important; 3 = undecided; 4 = somewhat important; 5 = not important.

Business characteristics

Business characteristics such as product and market knowledge, growth potential, etc. are clearly very important in evaluating a funding proposal (see Table 11.6). All nine variables have a mean score of 2 or lower, indicating that the factor was important in influencing the funder's decision to accept or reject a business project.

Interestingly, all of the VCs who answered this question rated core business characteristics as very important, an indicated by a mean score of one. The top three business factors influencing VCs funding include, plans to grow, growth potential of the business and uniqueness of the product or service.

Financial characteristics

Realism in financial projections is the single most important financial characteristic in influencing the decision to accept/reject a funding application (see Table 11.7). All of the funding agencies rated this factor as highly

Table 11.6   Importance of business characteristics (mean score ratings)*

Business Characteristics	Venture Capitalists n = 12	Banks n = 7	Support Agencies n = 4	Micro-Financial Specialist n = 1	Average Score n = 24
Adequacy of Market Knowledge	1.33	1.25	1.75	1.00	1.33
Plans for Growth	1.08	1.75	1.00	2.00	1.45
Growth Potential	1.08	2.00	1.00	2.00	1.52
Existence of Development Plan	1.67	1.63	2.00	1.00	1.57
Uniqueness of Product	1.25	1.88	2.00	1.00	1.53
Gaps in Management Structure	1.67	1.50	2.00	2.00	1.79
Stage of Development of Product/Service	2.00	2.00	2.25	2.00	2.06
Export Potential	1.67	3.43	1.00	5.00	2.77
Nature of Ownership/ Legal Structure	2.08	2.38	3.66	2.00	2.53

Note: *Where 1 = highly important; 2 = important; 3 = undecided; 4 = somewhat important; 5 = not important.

Table 11.7   Importance of financial characteristics (mean score ratings)*

Financial Characteristics	Venture Capitalists n = 12	Banks n = 7	Support Agencies n = 4	Micro-Financial Specialist n = 1	Average Score n = 24
Realism of Financial Projections	1.42	1.17	1.33	1.00	1.23
Other Sources of Funding Available/ Obtained	2.00	2.50	2.00	1.00	1.87
Amount of Funding Sought	1.92	1.67	3.75	1.00	2.08
Previous Applications for Funding by Entrepreneurs	3.00	2.67	2.00	2.00	2.41

Note: *Where 1 = highly important; 2 = important; 3 = undecided; 4 = somewhat important; 5 = not important.

important. Less important were other sources of funding available/obtained, the amount of funding sought and whether the entrepreneur had made previous applications to the funder.

Statistical analysis
The data reported in Tables 11.5–11.7 above indicate some differences in the factors viewed as important in accessing funding across the main agencies. The VCs, for example, appear to rate growth and export potential more importantly than the banks, based on mean scores. In contrast, previous failure of the lead entrepreneur, and employment and training, appear to be more important factors for banks than support agencies, based on mean scores. An interesting question to emerge from this analysis is whether funders significantly differ in what factors they consider important in evaluating a funding proposal.

In order to identify any significant differences in the funding criteria, statistical analysis was performed on the data.[10] Consistent with Bible and Brown (1981); Adair et al. (1995) and Dallal (1999), a parametric t-test and non-parametric Mann-Whitney test were employed.[11] The parametric t-test is widely used in the literature to test for significant differences between mean scores (Bible and Brown, 1981). The use of the non-parametric Mann-Whitney test serves to support the parametric analysis, in the event of one or more of the parametric test assumptions not being met (Daniel, 1990).[12] Furthermore, as noted by Chatfield (1988), there is greater credibility attached to the results when the findings of both tests concur.

The statistical analysis revealed differences between the VCs and banks in two important areas. Firstly, the banks appear to place greater importance on access to supports than the venture capitalists, when considering a funding proposal. Secondly, in terms of business characteristics, the two groups differ in three key areas: 'export potential', 'growth potential' and 'plans to grow'. The results suggest that VCs place greater emphasis on export and growth potential in evaluating a funding application. In each case, the results are confirmed by both the parametric and non-parametric tests.

How Successful are Female Business Owners in Securing Funding in Ireland, and How Does This Compare With Their Male Counterparts?

As with previous sections, each of the funding agencies were asked a series of questions to ascertain their views on the funding accessed by female business owners over the last number of years. The aim of this section is to identify any notable trends in the success of women entrepreneurs in accessing funding and to identify any barriers.

Funding allocated to female business owners

Currently, women account for only a small proportion of the funding allocated by the banks, VCs and enterprise support agencies. With the exception of the micro-financing specialist, where women accounted for 42 per cent of the overall projects funded in the past financial year, practically all of the funding agencies reported little or no funding to women-owned/led businesses. Women accounted for only 10 per cent (or an average of €30000) of bank funding. Similarly, of the nine VCs who completed this section, women accounted for less than 5 per cent of the firm's investment portfolio in the previous financial year.

In the case of the support agencies, the results are somewhat more positive. Women-owned/led businesses accounted for between 10 per cent and 25 per cent of funding in the previous financial year.

Funding allocated to female businesses – trends over time

There were mixed views on the success of women entrepreneurs in accessing finance over the last five years. Only one VC reported a slight increase in growth stage investments in women-owned/led businesses. In contrast, both the banks and the support agencies did see a small increase in the number of women successfully accessing funding. When asked to comment on the reasons behind this trend, three key reasons emerged:

- *Nature of the businesses developed by women.* A number of comments were made regarding the businesses being developed by women; that they were largely small in scale, local and predominantly in the services sector, which typically do not lend themselves to attracting grant aid, bank funding or equity financing.
- *Limited pool of proposals.* This was particularly the case for a number of VCs that stressed the limited pool of proposals from women, hence, there was a limited pool of opportunities in which venture capitalists could invest.
- *Sectoral barriers.* This was a point stressed by both the VCs and support agencies. In the case of the support agencies, the current funding policy and guidelines of the enterprise boards regarding which sectors should receive grant funding, makes it 'impossible for them to support and help the growth of women-owned businesses'. Sectors typically receiving funded are outside the sectors where women predominate, that is, the services sector. Similarly, according to the one VC 'we are mandated to invest in early and late stage technology firms. These are very rarely female led'.

The Level of Awareness Among Funding Agencies of the Barriers and Issues Facing Female Entrepreneurs in Ireland

As noted above, institutional and policy barriers have been identified as potentially limiting the ability of women entrepreneurs to successfully access funding. By way of exploring the barriers facing women entrepreneurs, funding agencies were asked a series of questions to ascertain the level of awareness and recognition of the issues facing female entrepreneurs in Ireland. The results suggest a number of positive steps that have been taken by financial institutions, namely:

- Most funding agencies have female funding/investment officers. All the banks and the support agencies and just over half of the VCs have female funding officers. Women hold positions at junior, middle and senior management level across the funding organizations.
- Requests for female funding officers were generally welcomed. While most of the banks would consider such a request, one bank was adamant that this would never happen. '... I don't think the bank would entertain this at all'. In the case of the VCs, of the few women seeking investment from their organizations, none of them ever requested a female investment officer.

However, the study also identified a number of limiting factors:

- Most funding organizations, with the exception of one of the support agencies, have no funding packages specifically for women entrepreneurs.
- Research on women's experience of sourcing and accessing funding is severely limited. None of the VCs or support agencies, and only one of the banks had carried out research on women's entrepreneurship. The micro-financing specialist had recently carried out research in conjunction with Longford Equal Development Partnership, which has led to a special fund being set up to assist women entrepreneurs.

Finally, when asked whether the financial needs of women entrepreneurs in Ireland are adequately met, the majority of the banks and the VCs answered in the affirmative.[13] According to one VC: 'The needs of women are no more adequately or less adequately met than those of men ... gender does not matter' (VC company). In contrast, two of the four support agencies responded 'no' to this question, pointing to the fact that the sectors in which women are setting up businesses fall outside the criteria laid down by the enterprise boards, including Enterprise Ireland and the County Enterprise boards.

VI.   DISCUSSION OF RESULTS

The aim of this study was to extend our understanding of the relationship between female entrepreneurship and access to funding by investigating access to funding by entrepreneurs in Ireland. Based on the evidence presented above, the results point to a number of strengths and weaknesses in the current approach, namely:

Strengths

- *Funding for new and growing businesses is generally widely available in Ireland.* Entrepreneurs and businesses in Ireland have access to a wide range of business funding initiatives, particularly at the start-up and growth stages.
- *Banks are active across the main industrial sectors.* The majority of banks are active in the services, construction, pharmaceutical/medical and the creative industries sectors.
- *Factors important in a funding application are varied, but age and gender are not important.* In assessing funding applications funders focus on core business information, such as growth and export potential,

business planning and management structure. Other key factors include financial projections, business experience, employment, training and access to supports.

- *There are important differences in the funding criteria between banks and VCs.* Statistical analysis indicates a strong focus on growth and export potential by VCs, and a greater focus on access to support among banks.
- *Support agencies are 'bridging the funding gap'.* The enterprise support agencies (including the micro-finance specialist) appear to be a key source of seed funding for many businesses.
- *Funding bodies are active in reducing 'institutional barriers' facing women entrepreneurs.* Most funding agencies have female funding/ investment officers, and requests for female funding officers are generally welcomed.

Weaknesses

- *Seed funding is not a reality for most businesses in Ireland.* There is a notable reluctance on the part of the banks and VCs to engage in seed/pre-start-up financing or rescue funding.
- *Less than 5 per cent of funding applications are actually funded.* Less than a fifth of funding applications received by funding agencies were actually funded in Ireland.
- *Women account for less than 20 per cent of all funding applications.* In the case of VCs, women account for less than 5 per cent of all funding. Lack of business experience, sectoral issues and a limited pool of female business proposals, were identified as key reasons behind the low representation among women-owned/led businesses.
- *No major increase in the proportion of women entrepreneurs seeking or successfully securing funding.* Only one VC reported a slight increase in growth stage investments in women-owned/led businesses. In contrast, both the banks and the support agencies did see some increase in the number of women businesses accessing funding.
- *Research into the funding needs of women entrepreneurs is severely limited.* There appears to be a lack of research informing funding bodies of the actual funding needs of women.
- *Current funding guidelines and policies are severely limiting the potential of women entrepreneurs.* The current lending criteria laid down by the enterprise boards (including Enterprise Ireland and the County Enterprise boards) and the approach adopted by VCs, is severally limiting the extent to which they can support and fund women-owned businesses.

VII. POLICY IMPLICATIONS AND RECOMMENDATIONS

From a policy perspective, the evidence reported above provides further insights into the relationship between financial institutions and women entrepreneurship in Ireland. While the results point to a number of strengths in the current provision, the low level of participation among women entrepreneurs in accessing funding in Ireland gives cause for concern.

By way of policy implications, two key recommendations emerge. Firstly, there is a need to revisit the case for gender-specific funding policies, such as those recently adopted in other countries. Despite the growth of financial provision over the last ten years, funding in Ireland is geared towards entrepreneurs and business in sectors with low female representation. VC funding is primarily focused on three core sectors – IT, pharmaceutical/medical and biotechnology. The current policy of the enterprise agencies on funding high-growth, export-orientated businesses is severely limiting the potential of women entrepreneurs to access this type of funding. The nature and type of businesses established by women entrepreneurs are not traditionally focused on growth and export potential. Hence, from both a policy and practical perspective, this group often falls outside the remit of these funders.

Secondly, there is a need for a concerted effort on the part of government and support agencies to promote research and understanding of the barriers and issues facing female entrepreneurship. Women are now a major economic force within Ireland and a major contributor to Ireland's economic prosperity and growth. However, currently, women-led and women-owned businesses are not on a level playing field with their male counterparts in successfully accessing formal funding. Failure to address the issues and other concerns raised in this study will only serve to perpetuate the low level of female entrepreneurship in Ireland.

NOTES

1. Based on real GDP.
2. Eurostat, 2002.
3. A number of county enterprise boards currently offer training for women entrepreneurs in the particular socio-economic group.
4. Based on a survey of over 150 SMEs in Ireland.
5. Specifically, micro-lending, which typically refers to funding below €25000.
6. The Golden Pages is Ireland's telephone directory of businesses – equivalent to the UK's Yellow Pages.
7. 'Seed and Venture Capital Programme 2000–2006' – 2002 Report, published by Enterprise Ireland, Dublin.
8. See www.surveymonkey.com for further information on the scope and use of this electronic survey tool.

9. In some cases because of the nature of the information required, face-to-face interviews were held with branch managers of banks.
10. Support agencies and micro-finance agencies were not included due to lack of data points.
11. Or alternatively whether the differences are simply due to sampling variation.
12. For further information on both tests, see Adair et al. (1995).
13. Two of the banks felt that the financing needs of women entrepreneurs in Ireland were adequately met, with five of the 12 VCs answering in the affirmative.

REFERENCES

Adair, A.S., Berry, J.N. and McGreal, W.S. (1995), 'Valuation of Residential Property: Analysis of Participant Behaviour', *Journal of Property Valuation and Investment*, **14**(1), 1996, 20–35.

Aldrich, H.E., Elam, A.B. and Reese, P.R. (1997), 'Strong Ties, Weak Ties and Strangers. Do women owners differ from men in their use of networking to obtain assistance?, in S. Birley and I. MacMillan (eds), *Entrepreneurship in a Global Context*, Routledge, London, pp. 1–25.

Bates, T. (1997), 'Financing Small Business Creation: the case of Chinese and Korean immigrant entrepreneurs', *Journal of Business Venturing*, **12**, 109–24.

Beccheti, L. and Trovato, G. (2002), 'The Determinants of Growth for Small and Medium Sized Firms: the role of the availability of external finance', *Small Business Economics*, **19**(4), 291.

Bray, L. (2001), 'Research into Gender Equality in Enterprise Creation in County Louth', Louth Women's Enterprise Project, Louth County Enterprise Board and Louth Leader.

Bray, L. (2004), 'Women in Enterprise in County Louth: Report for Louth County Enterprise Board, Women in Enterprise Programme', Louth Women's Enterprise Project, Louth County Enterprise Board and Louth Leader.

Bible, D.S. and Brown, L.A. (1981), 'Place Utility, Attribute Tradeoff, and Choice Behaviour in an Intra-urban Migration Context', *Socio-economic Planning Sciences*, **15**, 37–44.

Browne, J., Moylan, T. and Scaife, A. (2004), 'Female Entrepreneurs: out of the frying pan – into the fire?', Paper presented at the 27th ISBA Conference, Newcastle, England.

Brush (1997), 'Women's Entrepreneurship', Proceedings of the OECD Conference on Women Entrepreneurs in Small and Medium Enterprises, OECD, Paris.

Burnham, J. (2003), 'Why Ireland Boomed', *The Independent Review*, **7**(4).

Canadian Prime Minister's Task Force (2003), 'Report and Recommendations on Women Entrepreneurs', October, available from the Canadian Embassy, Dublin, www.canada.ie.

Carter, S. and Rosa, P. (1998), 'The Financing of Male and Female-owned Businesses', *Entrepreneurship and Regional Development*, **10**, 225–41.

Carter, N., Brush, C., Gatewood, E., Greene, P. and Hart, M. (2002), 'Does Enhancing Women's Financial Sophistication Promote Entrepreneurial Success?', Proceedings of the Promoting Female Entrepreneurship Research Forum, Dundalk, Ireland, November.

Central Statistics Office available at http://www.cso.ie/.

Chatfield, C. (1988), *Problem Solving: A Statistician's Guide*, London: Chapman and Hall.

Cooper, J. (2002), 'Beyond the Banks', *CMA Management*, **76**(1), 53–5.

Dallal, J. (1999), 'Re: Disadvantages of Nonparametric vs Parametric Tests', Educational Statistics Discussion List (EDSTAT-L), available at edstat-l@jse.stat.ncsu.edu.

Daniel, W.W. (1990), *Applied Nonparametric Statistics*, 2nd edn, Boston, MA: PWS-Kent Publishing Co.

De Bruin, A. and Dupuis, A. (2003), *Entrepreneurship: New Perspectives in a Global Age*, Aldershot: Ashgate.

Drucker, P. (1985), *Innovation and Entrepreneurship*, London: Pan Books Ltd.

Egeln, J., Licht, G. and Steil, F. (1997), 'Firm Foundations and the Role of Financial Constraints', *Small Business Economics*, **9**(2), 137.

Enterprise Ireland (2002), *Seed and Venture Capital Programme 2000–2006 Report*, National Development Plan and Enterprise Ireland.

FÁS (1998), 'Women in the Irish Labour Force', Department of Enterprise and Enterprise Policy 2000–2005, Commission Staff Working Paper, Brussels.

Fischer, M. and Massey, D. (2000), 'Residential Segregation and Ethnic Enterprise in US Metropolitan Areas', *Social Problems*, **47**(3), 410–24.

Garavan, T., O'Cinneide, B. and Fleming, P. (1997), *Enterprise and Business Start-ups in Ireland* (*Volume 1: An Overview*), Dublin: Oak Tree Press.

GEM (The Global Entrepreneurship Monitor) (2001–04), 'The Irish Report – How Entrepreneurial is Ireland', Department of Business Administration, University College Dublin.

Gender Equality Unit (2003), *Women and Men in Ireland as Entrepreneurs and Business Managers*, Department of Justice, Equality and Law Reform, Dublin.

Goodbody Economic Consultants (2002), 'Entrepreneurship in Ireland', available at www.goodbody.ie.

Hamouda, A., Johnston, K. and Henry, C. (2003a), 'State of the Art of Women's Entrepreneurship in Ireland – access to financing and financing strategies – an empirical study', Paper presented at the 2nd International Symposium of Growth Financing for Women Entrepreneurs, Stockholm, 29–31 May.

Hamouda, A., O'Connor, V., Henry, C. and Johnston, K. (2003b), *An Assessment of Women's Participation in the Workforce in Armagh City and District Council Area*, Scoping Study, Queen's University Belfast (Armagh campus), October.

Henry, C. and Kennedy, S. (2003), 'In Search of a New Celtic Tiger: female entrepreneurship in Ireland'. In John Butler (ed.), *New Perspectives on Female Entrepreneurs*, Hong Kong: Information Age Publishing.

Henry, C., Johnston, K. and Watson, J. (2004), 'New Business Creation, Growth and External Funding: A female perspective', Paper presented at the ISBA Conference, Newcastle, November.

Hindle, K. and Rushworth, S. (1999), 'The Demography of Investor Heaven: a synthesis of international research on the characteristics, attitudes and investment behaviour of business angels', Paper presented at the Financing the Future: Small and Medium Enterprise Finance, Corporate Governance and the Legal System conference, Sydney, Australia, 13 December.

InterTradeIreland (2000), *Development of a North/South Equity Funding Programme*, Report, October.

Knife (2002), 'The Status of Seed and Venture Capital in Ireland', Summary report available at: www.knife.ie/SF_Access_SmartVC.htm.

Labour Force Survey (2003), available at http://www.cso.ie/.

Lumme, A., Mason, C. and Suomi, M. (1998), *Informal Venture Capital – Investors, Investments and Policy Issues in Finland*, Boston, MA: Kluwer Academic Publishers.

Manigart, S. and Struyf, C. (1997), 'Financing High Technology Start-ups in Belgium: an explorative study', *Small Business Economics*, **9**(2), 125.

McGowan, P. and McGeady, C. (2002), 'An Investigation of Networking Practices of Female Entrepreneurs as an Aid to their Efforts to Create and Sustain New Ventures', Paper presented at the Promoting Female Entrepreneurship: Implications for Education, Training and Policy Conference, Dundalk Institute of Technology, Ireland, 19 November.

McKeon, H., Johnston, K. and Henry, C. (2004), 'Multinational Companies as a Source of Entrepreneurial Learning – Examples from the IT Sector in Ireland', *Education and Training*, **46**(8–9), 433–43.

McParland, T. (2001), 'Dissemination Report on the Potential for Business Angel Investment and Networks in Europe – Irish Report', Eban website, http://www.europa.eu.int/comm/enterprise/entrepreneurship/financing/docs/benchmarking_ba_en.pdf.

Murdoch's Irish Legal Companion (2003), available at http://milc.lendac.ie.

Organisation for Economic Co-operation and Development (OECD) (1999). Development Assistance Committee (DAC), 'Mainstreaming Gender Equality in the 21st Century: goals on education, health and the environment – a synthesis report of three reference documents', Paris: ref no. DCD/DAC/WID(99)11.

Organisation for Economic Co-operation and Development (OECD) (2001a), *Women Entrepreneurs in SMEs*, Paris.

Organisation for Economic Co-operation and Development (OECD) (2001b), 'Firm-level data in OECD Member Countries: an inventory of existing resources', DSTI/EAS/IND/SWP/AH(2001)2, Paris.

QUB (Queen's University of Belfast Report) (2003), 'An Assessment of Women's Participation in the Workforce in Armagh City and District Council Area', Scoping Study.

Robbie, K. and Murray, G. (1992), 'Venture Capital in the UK', *International Journal of Bank Marketing*, **10**(5), xx.

Small Business Service (2003), 'Bridging the Finance Gap: a consultation on improving access to growth capital for small businesses', HM Treasury, London, available at www.hm-treasury.gov.uk.

United Nations Statistics Division (2000), *United Nations Releases Most Recent Statistics on the World's Women*, The World's Women 2000 Press Release, available at www.un.org/Depts/unsd/ww2000/ww2000pr.htm.

Verheul, I. and Thurik, R. (2001), 'Start-up Capital: does gender matter?', *Small Business Economics*, **16**(4), 329.

Women's Unit UK and Ministry of Industry, Employment and Communications (Sweden) (2001), 'Women as Entrepreneurs in Sweden and the UK', United Kingdom: Cabinet Office.

12. Women entrepreneurs in New Zealand: private capital perspectives

Anne de Bruin and Susan Flint-Hartle*

INTRODUCTION

In New Zealand (NZ), there has been a steady increase in the number of women business owners. Over the 1966 to 2001 census period, both women total employers and women self-employed increased by almost 20 per cent to 29.8 per cent and 31.1 per cent respectively. McGregor and Tweed (2002) claim that 20 women a day start up enterprises, accounting for 40 per cent of all new business start-ups. However despite this growing prominence, there is a paucity of research into many aspects of NZ women's entrepreneurship.

This chapter outlines new research designed to explore the experiences of 'successful' women entrepreneurs, that is, those whose businesses had moved beyond the initiation phase and were commercially viable. As such they were deemed a 'success' either in the popular press or by their industry peers. The research specifically attempts to inform on finance-related issues of women's entrepreneurial activity. It focuses on both the financial capital supply and demand sides. As few studies have explored the women business– external finance issue from the perspective of both the supply and demand (Carter et al., 2004), such a dual approach was considered to be particularly useful in mitigating the lack of information on women entrepreneurs in NZ.

The emphasis of the supply side aspect of our study was the venture capital (VC) industry. Despite being intuitively aware that VC funds catered only to a negligible number of NZ businesses, let alone women-led businesses, we believed, nevertheless, that such a focus would better align our research with that of the earlier Diana Project research, which investigated the reasons for the low share of women businesses in venture and equity capital investment (see, for example, Greene et al., 1999; Gatewood et al., 2003). Importantly, however, it would contribute to an understanding of NZ women-related issues for the sector, especially in light of the greater awareness of the importance of the industry for business financing in NZ and recent government initiatives to support the industry. However, on the advice of a key informant, with whom we conducted a pilot interview and who was associated with the NZ Venture Capital Association (NZVCA), the supply-side scope and terminology used was altered from VC to 'private capital', to encompass a general understanding that private capital in NZ includes venture, private equity and angel finance.

Findings on the following broad research questions are presented. To what extent do venture capitalists invest in women's business ventures and do they perceive women's ventures differently from those of men? What experiences have women entrepreneurs themselves had in seeking financial backing for business growth and expansion? A background to women's entrepreneurial activity and the NZ policy context particularly in relation to the private capital industry is provided. This is followed by a description of the methodological approach. The chapter then highlights the supply-side findings. The demand-side (entrepreneur) perspectives in relation to financial capital are presented next. A case study illustrates avenues for financing in keeping with personal values and changing business needs.

Before proceeding further however, we draw attention to the extremely limited extant literature on gender-related finance issues in NZ. Although solely supply-side focused, studies in the early 1990s by Fay and Williams (1993a, 1993b) are of significance in this respect. The first study revealed bank officers to be less inclined to provide funding assistance to women applicants than men applicants (Fay and Williams, 1993a). Despite suffering methodological weaknesses – the experimental investigation was limited to a single business scenario and one personal history – the results appear 'congruent with the feminist view of sex-role stereotyping and a "male" business culture' (Fay and Williams, 1993b: 71). In fact, a reason for any discrimination suffered could feasibly be laid elsewhere (1993b). It would appear that women applicants failed to conform to loan criteria because they were excluded from male-dominated business networks. They were therefore unable to easily access the necessary skills and knowledge required for loan eligibility. Other NZ research (Duff, 1998; Welsh, 1988) supports this explanation of institutional constraint rather than any deliberate discrimination on the part of bank officers.

COUNTRY CONTEXT

Women's Business Ownership in New Zealand

Women make up 51 per cent of NZ's population of approximately four million and their labour force participation and employment has been steadily growing. In June 2004, the NZ labour force participation rate was 66.7 per cent, with the female rate standing at almost 60 per cent (Statistics NZ, 2004). Interestingly, male labour force participation has declined from 90 per cent to 74 per cent over the 1959–2004 period, while the female rate has doubled over the same period. The decline in male participation has been attributed to both stronger growth of the service-related industries (where employment growth of women has been dominant) relative to the male-dominated manufacturing and agricultural industries, and the increasing childcare responsibilities of men (Department of Labour, 2004).

Although the number of women business owners has steadily increased along with female labour force participation, when self-employment is used as a proxy for entrepreneurial activity, women's entrepreneurship levels are significantly lower than those of men. They make up a relatively small, albeit important, proportion of the total number of employers and self-employed in the country, as shown in Table 12.1.

Table 12.1   Sex and status in employment 2001 (%)

	Paid employee	Self-employed and without employees	Employer	Unpaid family worker
Male	72.3	15.9	10.0	1.8
Female	83.0	9.0	5.1	3.0

Source: Statistics NZ (2001).

Entrepreneurial activity in NZ, as measured by the Global Entrepreneurship Monitor (GEM) indicator of total early-stage activity (TEA)[1] ranks NZ in the top five of participating GEM countries for business start-up opportunities, with 13.9 per cent of the adult population identified as entrepreneurs (Frederick, 2004). The firm-level entrepreneurial activity index (FEA) of existing firms shows that 16.82 per cent are innovative and expect to have job growth – are entrepreneurial firms – placing NZ among the top group (Frederick, 2004: 22). Despite NZ's high TEA and FEA ranking, NZ has a widening 'entrepreneurial gender gap' (the proportion of women entrepreneurs to all entrepreneurs) as evidenced in Table 12.2 below. Between 2001 and 2003, the proportion of female entrepreneurs declined from 43.3 per cent to 36.8 per cent and there appear to be comparatively few women entrepreneurs who have high growth in their businesses (Frederick, 2004: 33–4). Disconcertingly also, the female TEA rate has fallen from 13.56 per cent in 2001 to 9.99 per cent in 2003. By comparison, the TEA rate for men remained relatively stable, averaging around 17.5 per cent over the three-year period.

Table 12.2   Total early-stage activity in New Zealand (%)

Year	Male	Female	Proportion of females to all entrepreneurs
2001	17.77	13.56	43.3
2002	17.45	10.55	37.7
2003	17.19	9.99	36.8

Source: Frederick, 2004, Table 8:32.

Relative to the other GEM countries, NZ women achieved a global ranking of seventh in total female entrepreneurial activity. NZ women lag behind Chinese, Chilean and Venezuelan women whose entrepreneurial activities equal those of their male counterparts (Frederick, 2004). However, in comparison to men, fewer of these women have high-growth businesses (Frederick, 2004). Nevertheless, this statement probably interprets growth aspirations and success in terms of androcentric benchmarks. Our study of women entrepreneurs reported in this chapter was designed to explore success and growth orientation holistically, rather than from any preconceived standpoint. It did not include a male control group. Although the lack of comparison with male entrepreneurs is a criticism that could be levelled against this approach, we felt that such comparisons would not contribute significantly to explaining women's business success.

Policy Framework and the Private Capital Industry

Commencing in 1999, when the first Labour-led centre left coalition government came to power, NZ began a new era in policy reconfiguration and a clear move away from the earlier hands-off industry policy (de Bruin, 2003). Active industry policy and dedicated regional development is now firmly on the agenda, together with continued recognition of the critical importance of small and medium-sized enterprises (SMEs) in the economy. In February 2002, the government announced a policy framework, 'Growing an Innovative New Zealand' (Clark, 2002), to systematically bring NZ back into the top ranks of the OECD group of countries. The Growth and Innovation Framework (GIF) identified three key industry sectors – information and communications technology (ICT), biotechnology and creative industries (especially the screen production and design sectors), to strategically focus government resources and help raise NZ's international competitiveness. Sector-led industry Taskforces for the ICT, biotechnology, screen production and design industries were formed and reported on how to grow and tap the global potential of each of these sectors and develop a framework of action. Funding issues were dealt with in the reports and generally encouragement and stimulation of the VC and private equity industry has now been acknowledged as an important facet in reaping the export potential of these sectors and enhancing New Zealand's innovation system.

It is commonly perceived that the VC sector in NZ is immature and limited in size. A Treasury-commissioned study (Infometrics, 2000) however, found no evidence of a lack of VC. The VC and private equity industry is growing rapidly, though prior to 2002/2003, investment flowed mainly to companies at later stages of development. There was a need therefore to stimulate investment in early stage business. In line with this need, the government set up the NZ Venture Investment Fund (VIF). Incorporated as a Crown Owned Company in July 2002, to accelerate the growth of the NZ VC industry, the VIF has a pool of NZ$100 million in funds to invest. It contracts private sector Fund Managers to manage VIF seed funds to invest in early-stage (seed, start-up and early expansion) high-growth potential, NZ companies.[2] Every one dollar of VIF commitment must be matched by two dollars of private investment capital and the minimum fund size is NZ$30 million. In response to the Biotechnology Taskforce Report, identifying access to capital as a vital factor in developing the industry, the VIF has allocated NZ$25 million for investment in the sector with the 'Biotech Fund'.

The NZ Venture Capital Monitor reports on the state of the VC and private equity sector on the basis of survey responses from the leading VC and private equity companies and provides commentary on initiatives and challenges for industry. The 2003 report underscores that the industry 'came of age in 2003' and that this was 'against a backdrop of growing awareness of the industry and its future' (Ernst and Young, 2004: 2). During 2003, NZ$81.6 million new capital was raised, of which approximately 50 per cent was raised by VIF fund managers. Since 2002, when the survey was first conducted, committed capital has grown by 16 per cent to NZ$1.12 billion at the end of 2003 (Ernst and Young, 2004: 2). With 51 per cent of this capital being available for investment in 2004, the outlook for industry in the near future is bright. An indication of the relatively small size of the overall market in NZ, however, is that in total only 51 deals were conducted in 2003, compared with 39 in 2002 (Ernst and Young, 2004: 3).

Alongside the evolution and growth of the VC market, there has also been a general growth of angel providers and private angel investor networks.[3] Given the predominance of small and medium-sized enterprises (SMEs) in NZ,[4] the key role of the informal capital market, which includes business angel activity, in financing businesses, especially start-ups, must be highlighted (Ernst and Young, 2004; Frederick, 2004; Infometrics, 2004). The GEM NZ 2003/2004 Report points out that 99.2 per cent of total investment in start-ups came from informal sources, stressing that more attention should be paid to the critical role of the '4Fs – family, friends, founders and "foolish" investors' in start-up ventures (Frederick, 2004: 42).

RESEARCH METHODOLOGY

Multiple approaches for data collection were used. As a first step to examining the supply side, we explored the impact of key decision-making in the venture and private equity market, particularly in relation to women-led business issues. We conducted six in-depth interviews with key informants in high-profile private capital investment companies. Only one of these interviewees was a woman but they all belonged to the NZ Venture Capital Association (NZVCA).[5] The majority of these interviewees were CEOs of the VIF Fund Managers and other private equity funds. Utilising a semi-structured interview guide, details were gathered about the core business activity and scope of activities including the range of investment, types and profile of investors and investees and the gender breakdown of the decision-makers in the organization. All the interviews included a question on what initiatives would encourage more women to seek private capital or increase their knowledge of private capital.

An email survey of members of the NZVCA supplemented the six interviews. This survey was sent to 68 members, excluding the six with whom we conducted face-to-face interviews. The survey asked four straightforward questions. How many people were employed at the decision-making level? How many of these were women and what was their role? What was the company's investment range and preference? How many women-led businesses had the company invested in over the last 12 months?

We also interviewed three other key women informants from the supply side. They included the Chief Executive/General Manager of NZVIF Ltd, a leading woman from the banking sector as an expert interviewee on women's business finance strategies and a member of the Biotechnology Taskforce. Choice of the latter informant was in light of the Taskforce specifically identifying access to capital as the major hurdle facing the sector. The biotechnology industry has inherently high research and development costs and long commercialization timeframes, often around three to four times longer than other high-technology sectors (Biotechnology Taskforce, 2003). The Taskforce also called for its own dedicated Biotechnology Investment Fund.

Another component of our study was research into the venture catalyst industry. Venture catalysts are matchmakers between business and sources of private capital. Two in-depth interviews with leading women operators in this market were conducted.

Forty women entrepreneurs comprised the demand-side sample. Of these women 40 per cent were in the 41–45 year age group and 15 per cent each in the 36–40 and 46–50 groups respectively. Overall education levels were high with 65 per cent tertiary university level qualifications, of which 30 per cent were postgraduate. Some 17.5 per cent had trade-related qualifications. Our stratified sample included four Chinese immigrant entrepreneurs. To assist with these interviews the Information Sheet was translated into Chinese and a translator used to help in the interviewing.

A story-telling approach was chosen for the women entrepreneur interviews. It was hoped that the narrative method would produce rich data not only on the reasons for entrepreneurial success of these women, but also on any facets of their entrepreneurial experience that they chose to share and reflect on. In light of the dearth of information on women entrepreneurs in NZ (Dupuis and de Bruin, 2004), it was anticipated that a less rather than a more structured interviewing approach would yield more material to mitigate this knowledge gap. A further rationale was a subsidiary research interest of exploring career trajectories of women entrepreneurs. Choice of method is vitally related to the researcher. Thus, parallel research on copreneurship and an exploration of the 'joint career' concept coupled with desire to promote cross-fertilization between the domains of entrepreneurship and career research (see, for example, de Bruin and Lewis, 2004), played a role in the preference for the narrative interview. In contrast to entrepreneurship study, the use of story-telling in career studies, and in particular with respect to women, is common (see, for example, Mallon and Cohen, 2001; Marshall, 2000). There is, nevertheless, quite an emerging use of the narrative approach in entrepreneurship research (Johansson, 2004). Moreover, since the study was of successful entrepreneurs, it was assumed that these entrepreneurs would not be shy about telling their stories. This assumption has been confirmed as realistic by other researchers. As Johansson points out, 'Successful entrepreneurs have developed a reputation as "raconteurs"' (2004: 283).

The interview dialogue probed experiences with respect to financial resources for the woman's business. Additionally, a single page 'Fact Sheet' was filled in at the conclusion of the interview. This ensured comparable detail from all interviewees in relation to their personal background and business (years in operation, business life cycle stage, export status, ownership structure and employee details). An initial sample was obtained from a list compiled of women who had been profiled in the publication *Her Business*. These women were contacted and some agreed to be interviewed. The snowballing technique was used and interviewees were asked to suggest to us appropriate women entrepreneurs to interview. Thus for instance, one of the large women-led businesses profiled as a case study in the chapter was suggested by a venture capitalist. This woman is presented as a dedicated case study because of her business growth success in the past and her future growth intentions. Moreover, her story illustrated varying financial capital requirements and solutions at different business stages and evolving events in her personal life.

Our purposive sample involved a sector-based approach in choosing entrepreneurs. In light of the government's targeting of the information, communications and technology, biotechnology, screen production and design industries for support within the Growth and Innovation Framework, we sought out women, in the first instance, from these industries. For example, an internet search led us to the *NZ Biotechnology Directory*.[6] This directory, however, yielded only two women-led businesses whose owners we interviewed as entrepreneurs. However, one of our supply-side woman interviewees was also listed in the directory. In total, we interviewed four women entrepreneurs from the biotech industry. All interviews were audiotaped and transcribed. A few lasted as long as 1.5 hours, although the average interview duration was an hour. All these interviews, as well as those conducted for the supply side, were in the period March to early May 2004.

SUPPLY-SIDE PERSPECTIVES

We received 29 replies from the email survey to the broader VC industry, accounting for a 43 per cent response rate. However, we report supply-side findings combining results from both the email survey and the six interviews – 74 contacts and 35 responses in total – a 47 per cent response. These findings indicate that management team size ranged from 12 to one person and 13 of the companies had women in management positions including office manager and accounts manager. Yet only four companies had women in what might be classified as key decision-making roles such as director, principal or partner. There were five leading women in these four companies and one of these companies had two women partners resident overseas. Hence only 11 per cent of VC companies had women as key decision-makers. This percentage moves even lower to 6 per cent, if we exclude the company with the two overseas resident women partners. These figures confirm an initial anecdotal hypothesis that the industry is male-dominated. Respondents had invested in a total of 11 women-led businesses. Although our email survey did not seek to gather data on the total number of venture propositions seeking investment backing (we were advised in our pilot that this could be considered commercially sensitive information and should not be probed as it would reduce the response rate) our in-depth interviews indicated that investment in women-led businesses accounted for only around 3 per cent of the total investment opportunities that arose in the course of the year.

The investment range was generally NZ$100000 to 100 million, though one small company reported a NZ$25000–250000 range. For the majority of companies the median range was from NZ$1 million to 20 million. Overlaying our demand-side interview material we found that this higher range generally failed to capture the finance requirements or aspirations of the women in our sample. There was a perception amongst the women interviewed that VC was for big business and not appropriate for their operations.

The six interviewees from the NZVCA were insistent that gender was not a consideration in the decision to invest in a business. A manager of a VC fund and a private equity fund emphasized that his company was only interested in commercial viability and growth orientation of the business and that the gender of the business owner was not a consideration. In this organization, one out of a decision-making team of eight was a woman. Of 200 applications in 2003, approximately 3 per cent were from women-led businesses. The investment formula for this company was to create relationships with credible people who could execute a growth strategy. Confidence in the person was the crucial first and foremost factor and although the selection team was mainly male, there was little evidence of any predisposition towards gender bias in relation to investment selection.

Another of the interviewees was from a male-only decision-making equity investment company that focused on companies in the manufacturing and tourism sector. This company made equity investments in mid-stage expansion NZ companies that could demonstrate acceptable rates of return – 10–15 per cent after tax. Again, it was emphasized that gender did not play a part in assessment of the viability of the investment. However, it is worth noting that less than 5 per cent of the 100 investment opportunities considered in 2003 were from women-led businesses.

A partner of one of NZ's leading technology VIF fund managers indicated that investments in the technology sector require an active involvement at all stages. It was clearly explained that there is no gender discrimination when committing investment funds. Rather, prior detailed due diligence was conducted to ensure not only return but also the matching of goals, aspirations and abilities of the key players in the venture. As in other instances, of crucial importance was the quality of the relationship between the entrepreneur and the investment company as well as confidence in the venture's potential.

We also interviewed the CEO of the NZ arm of a multinational public company investing substantially in NZ businesses. This organization targeted high-end business expansion and management buy-outs and the number of women-led businesses in their targeted market was minimal. Of 300 applications in 2003, only five were from women but this lack of applications from women could not be adequately explained. It was claimed however, once again, that gender bias was not an issue and that applications from women would be welcomed and evaluated with the same criteria as used for men. It was asserted that any business with growth potential would be looked at favourably if a 20–30 per cent return was potentially feasible. Another company, specializing in expansion equity partnership, based their investment decisions on confidence in the people involved in the ventures, irrespective of gender. This was coupled with recognition of the need to ensure a mutual alignment of objectives between investor and investee.

When questioned about how effective the venture capitalists felt the government VIF scheme had been, there was a general consensus that it had 'a really positive impact' on the accessibility of VC in NZ. This would naturally impact on women. Although possibly a somewhat biased viewpoint as the majority of those interviewed were directly associated with the VIF, it was believed that the VIF was a worthwhile supportive initiative of the government and augured well for future industry growth. One dissenting voice nevertheless maintained that the strict parameters of the VIF criteria could tend to 'a homogenizing effect where investment is made to fit parameters ... true entrepreneurial spirit cannot be pigeonholed'. On the positive side, however, it was believed that the VIF scheme had the potential to increase professionalism and maturity in the industry – again the spin-offs for women, even as a minority group, are obvious.

Interestingly, an interviewee (a man in his thirties) when probed on the question of government initiatives commented that, in general, the way the industry communicated and especially through web sites, was too technical and did not necessarily tell stories of success in a way to which women might easily relate, confirming an earlier point we made on the effect of an androcentric emphasis. Mentioning one government web site for example, he claimed that it totally 'missed' women. He speculated that men set up and maintained these web sites and so they inadvertently appealed to men. However, another interviewee's personal viewpoint was that women in NZ were more advantaged in the business environment than their Australian counterparts in terms of their general acceptance in the business world. It was reiterated that there was no overt gender differentiation in NZ. This interviewee stressed that emphasis should be on developing a greater and more accessible pool of capital for *all* entrepreneurs, as well as mitigating any lack of knowledge in relation to utilizing VC for both men and women.

From our VC industry interviews some recommendations emerged that would assist in growing the non-gender-specific, overall pool of VC and private funds. For instance, it was asserted that the NZ$5 billion dollar NZ Government Superannuation Fund failed to allocate funds for private capital investment and that this contrasted with the Australian situation. Australian superannuation funds, which are relatively bigger due to mandatory employee contributions, channel a significant portion into business expansion. To the contrary, it might be more conservatively argued, however, that VC is not an appropriate use for superannuation funds, which have to meet specific future liabilities and should ideally be free from exposure to risk.

A leading woman from the commercial banking sector was interviewed as an expert informant on financing strategies of women-led businesses. She believed that woman generally tend to seek angel funding mainly from family, or use their own savings or borrow on their credit card. This was borne out in our demand-side findings. Contrary to the majority of successful women entrepreneurs in our sample who were oriented to global markets, she believed that women generally do not have aspirations to grow big and go global. The reasons she gave for this were personal and related to lifestyle rather than any structural or resource deficiency. Her rationale was that women have 'to fit so much more than men into their lives anyway' – she was alluding here to the caring responsibilities and the wider life focus of the majority of women.

A strong thread that emerged from the supply-side interviews was that the potential of the business and the quality of the entrepreneur were the deciding factors for private capital investment. As support for the relative lack of investment in women's ventures, it was asserted that the focus of VC funds was increasingly on the high-technology sector – mainly in the biotechnology, medical and information technology sectors. Women-led, high-growth businesses were not currently prominent in these sectors. Consequently, it would seem that there is little opportunity to remedy the investment gap until this imbalance in participation is addressed.

While the NZ VC industry did not indicate signs of gender discrimination, one of the demand-side interviews provided an interesting insight into how different cultural perspectives of overseas investors could have an impact on women. This interviewee, who was an entrepreneur of long-standing in the biotechnology sector, told of how a VC partner had been taken on for three years and then this VC company was sold into Asian hands. This had 'created big problems because the investors were sexist and their involvement became untenable and was terminated'.

Another demand-side interviewee was in fact an entrepreneur operating in the VC industry so we include her experience in this section as well. Furthermore this example demonstrates that any increase in successful involvement of women in business ventures is likely also to lead to an increase in the migration of women into the VC industry, thus diluting the concentration of men in this industry. This interviewee had sold out of the business she had founded and was now using that money for VC/private equity investment. She had invested in three businesses operating in software, manufacturing and TV sectors and which were all demonstrating positive growth tendencies in the form of exporting. Because of her own similar experiences, she knew she had the ability to help business owners struggling to gain competitive advantage:

> ... I saw it as my investment vehicle ... I would go in and work with people to create ... to turn the business into something and in that case I wanted to put my money where my mouth was, and I knew I wanted a job and I wasn't going to work for someone else.

An interesting part of the supply-side research was a brief excursion into examining the venture catalyst market. This market was termed by one industry interviewee as a 'soft bank model' sourcing private capital from 'seasoned or sophisticated investors'. A woman in the VC industry, however, believed that the venture catalyst term was a very general one. She claimed that the market was crowded with people including investment professionals and was 'in an amorphous state'. Information from leading venture catalyst industry informants indicated that there is a concentration on the IT, retailing and biotech sectors mainly at the start-up stage. However, 'fringe activities' investment in areas like boat building, fashion design and innovative property development opportunities were not precluded. In the catalyst industry contact from women-led business was much higher – estimated at around 50 per cent. Investments ranged from NZ$20000 to 1.5 million. Networking amongst women, for example, the WISE[7] women network was a major source of referrals. An interviewee criticized the VIF initiative in that it focused on growth companies and not true start-ups. A key initiative to enhance women's access to private capital, recommended by one woman venture catalyst, was a privately raised gender-specific fund.

DEMAND-SIDE PERSPECTIVES ON FINANCIAL CAPITAL

Traditionally in NZ across entrepreneurial gender, capital has been sourced from savings, the family, inheritance and the contribution of partners, the bank or some kind of private financier. Overall, there is a tendency to rely on self as well as the 'three F's' of venture funding – friends, family and fools (Hunter and Wilson, 2004). Women in our sample confirmed this tendency, as the most common source of capital was the entrepreneur's own savings. Forty per cent of the women used this type of finance and 12.5 per cent used family and friend finance. Some 22.5 per cent used bank loans and only 2.5 per cent (one entrepreneur) had sought venture capital. There was also a tendency amongst the women to reinvest capital generated internally and 'bootstrapping' (Brush et al., 2004) was evident. In most cases the sector entered, however, presented low entry barriers and could be financed on a relatively small amount of savings. Such small beginnings did not mean that there was low growth potential and aspirations. Twenty-five per cent of the women business owners interviewed now had operations employing over 20 full-time employees and are classified as large firms in NZ. Some 47.5 per cent were currently exporting. A further 30 per cent had intentions of entering the international marketplace.

Research has shown that most women business owners have tended to seek debt capital in the first instance, to facilitate business growth and expansion mainly because this is the most obvious and common avenue available (Hutchinson, 1978; Johns et al., 1976; Dwyer et al., 1985). In our sample, as mentioned previously, bank loans were the primary source of finance for 22.5 per cent. Moreover, a couple of women had revolving credit facilities and had built up strong relationships with their bank, giving them the leeway to expand production at any given time. Knowledge and comfort with using external private capital sources was linked to the expressed desire to grow, especially through exporting. Thus for instance, two women who had no immediate intention to grow their business had not felt the necessity to explore private capital sources, until the need arose.

The type of finance chosen was often related to the high importance placed on preserving control and autonomy. One woman spoke of the 'desire to control her own destiny'. Another entrepreneur illustrated this when commenting about possible government grants: 'This is a private business and there is no government funding whatsoever. We don't want government funding. We don't want strings attached to government funding – we don't need it'. This entrepreneur financed the business (a private education facility) out of personal capital in the first instance. Later as the business grew, she reinvested a major portion of the profits, thereby assuring on-going autonomy. Surpluses achieved during the growth period were immediately ploughed back into the business: 'whenever we get more funding we put it back into the business, put it back into improving facilities, improving the products that we are giving the students'.

Many interviewees believed strongly in growth through retained earnings. Some had a bad experience with borrowed funds in the past, or knowledge of a very similar company 'going under after growing too fast and borrowing too much', and this was often the rationale for self-reliance for financing. Four Chinese entrepreneurs interviewed indicated a strong belief in business financing from their own household savings and re-investment of earnings and profits.

Only one woman entrepreneur had actually been the recipient of VC and her somewhat negative experience was reported in the previous supply-side perspectives section – when the relationship dynamic changed with a change of ownership of the VC funder. Very few of the women, however, were inclined to VC involvement. Those open to VC were, as we expected, the larger-sized firms with further growth aspirations and usually also with a view to greater export growth. Amongst all the women, nevertheless, there was an uneasy feeling that using VC might compromise the passion they felt for their businesses and that external involvement could potentially mean a loss of integrity. The following quote highlights, however, that in addition to financial capital considerations, the need for improving organizational capital went hand-in-hand with business growth:

> I have had approaches (from VCs) and I am in the throes of looking at my business now, so that it can expand to a much greater level, but like all companies that expand quickly, or a lot of companies, I have a lot of structure that is not in place so I have just recently employed a CEO so that he can start putting in some of the structures. We have gone from the seat of our pants onto the next level. We have lots of systems in place, lots of things that work and a whole lot that don't work.

When it came to considering VC there were in some instances a sense of caution and even unease:

> Aren't they also called vulture capitalists? Then you go yes, who do I want to go into business with? ... remembering that I've had a business partner and I want to see the whites of their eyes, I want to talk to them I want to tell them why I am doing this and ok, I understand that this is my passion and it doesn't have to be their passion ... I just don't want to go into business with anybody and so I'm waiting for that person to come along, and we are meeting with venture capital people, absolutely, and I will know when that person comes along that they are right for us and we'll take their money.

There was also a notion that entrepreneurs could fall prey to opportunists in the VC and private equity industry:

> they are very vulnerable and they're open to somebody with the capital coming in and taking that away from them and I heard of that happening a few times and you can see how fragile and how precious an idea is. In those early settling times they do fall prey to people who are not entrepreneurs but opportunists. And I think that opportunism and entrepreneurship are two different things. There are people with money in the bank that go and buy entrepreneurs and I've seen that happen where the hopes would be dashed for what was going to be something that was a dream ... The matrix that power and control comes from an opportunist and a corporate opportunist being superimposed on an entrepreneur doesn't stand up.

On a more positive side, a capital-intensive private company, running a medium-sized business, emphasized that although currently the Board decision was to meet capital expenditure out of cashflow and the company's own borrowings (overdraft), this might not always be the case. VC input was signalled as a possibility in the future as long as the philosophical stance and company integrity was maintained. On the other hand a few of our entrepreneurs had been approached by venture capitalists but remained closed to this proposition as they preferred the independence, control and autonomy of running their own business.

Accessing capital for expansion through factoring was a novel means used by an entrepreneur in the fashion design industry to grow her business. This entrepreneur was rapidly expanding in the global fashion market and was a large-sized business with 60 full-time permanent employees, a further 14 part-time and casual employees and a large pool of contractors of around 600–700 people:

> How I have managed to expand because I have not been back to the bank since that last time which was some time back ... how it works is that you produce your invoices for the goods you are sending and send your goods and then you give ... your invoices are bought by the factoring company and they immediately pay you out 80 per cent of the invoices and then they retain the other 20 per cent until the customer has paid and that is a simplistic view on how it works. ... so factoring ... what that means is that immediately you get 80 per cent of your money back again and then you can use it again and again and again.

Some sectors, namely international language schools and the fashion industry, failed to attract any interest from funders, including banks, in the 1990s. Their entrepreneurial opportunities were unproven or too risky at the time. They could also have been viewed as 'unfashionable' or less 'sexy' investment sectors. As national awareness of their industry, however, had improved in recent years, so too had their ability to access finance. Supportive government grants had also made a positive difference to some entrepreneurs.

Although not necessarily gender-specific, preserving the values and principles of the entrepreneur were important:

> I had values-driven business because everybody ... had to share the same values. ... I had a five-point plan when you joined our business and that was that you had to understand the team came first. ... if the photocopier breaks down it's everybody's problem. ... All rewards were team-based with generous profits sharing so that the focus was on team earnings rather than individual performance.

Similarly, reviving or maintaining family traditions could be an important consideration that overtakes profit as the goal. Thus the business of one of our interviewees involved reviving an original brand that her grandfather had started. Being true to the quality of this brand was a prime consideration: 'I am the custodian of the brand, that's the way I see it.'

Another entrepreneur who now had scaled down her operation from a small-sized to a micro-enterprise employing four full-time staff, was determined to be self-sufficient and not constrained by being 'a process-driven organization'. Her aim was to create 'a client outcome organization' and to focus on and grow her staff. She had also set up a new venture, which clearly illustrates this philosophy. Interestingly, her newest venture is a type of VC investment. She has funded a firm in a different geographic location but in the same core business area and placed two bright young local women at the helm under her guidance. Unlike other VC investments, a minimum return was not required. She was focusing not only on growing the business but also mentoring the two women, thus indulging her passion for watching staff grow.

> It's not about money ... you do everything right and the money will flow ... If you go around flashing that around, it's bad for the staff to see ... it's much better that they get rewarded with bonuses and ... for their team work and the value they bring to the business, not for the fees you are earning ...

This woman had also been approached by multinationals to buy out her business but she had never been 'tempted' because they did not share her values.

Being truthful, courageous and caring underpinned the values of another businesswoman whose high-profile, medium-sized company operates on a project basis and engages a large number of contractors. She said she was advised early in her career to say 'no' more often that 'yes' to potential clients in order to preserve business integrity and her established values: 'It feels quite scary doing that when you first start out because you think gosh who am I to say I don't want to work with you and um that's going to be quite reactive isn't it? ... Most others are willing to give them everything so very quickly.'

Commitment to cultural values was another consideration that entered the picture. A woman in the screen production industry was a case in point. Feeling she was in a position to make a difference, she made a conscious decision to move away from mainstream production. Her focus on producing Maori language children's programmes has now been highly acclaimed.

CASE STUDY: LIVING NATURE, SUZANNE HALL

We include this cosmetics company as a dedicated case as it represents one of only a very few large, internationally competitive, successful women-led NZ businesses. It aptly illustrates the varying financial capital requirements and solutions at different stages of a business and their need to fit with both growth aspirations as well as the entrepreneur's values and evolving personal circumstances.

Living Nature is a private company, employing just under a 100 full-time permanent employees, currently exporting to around 12 countries and with offices in the UK and Germany. It has been operating for 14 years. Our interview with the founder Suzanne Hall[8] provides the main information for this case.

At the initial stage of the business the company received a kick-start from a government Business Development Grant.[9] This $20000 grant had to be matched by an equivalent sum from the business owner. Product development and operating costs meant a growing bank overdraft. In common with many other micro-businesses at the early stage, income from other employment sustained her business: 'I just sort of traded along basically managing by doing other things to fund the business. So I would work a couple of days running a clinic and that would fund the sort of activities of the business.'

Burdened with a large bank overdraft, and driven by personal circumstances – a relationship split-up with her partner whose property had been the security for the overdraft – Suzanne approached the Prometheus Foundation for a loan. Prometheus Ethical Finance[10] lends to socially valuable or environmentally friendly, ecologically beneficial projects throughout NZ. A condition for a loan is personal guarantees as security and also evidence of community support. No one, however, is allowed to be a guarantor for more than NZ$3000 and there have to be twice as many guarantors as the funding. Suzanne went to her customers for these guarantees:

> I had to find NZ$160000 worth of $3000 guarantors so it was horribly humbling ... but it was a really nice exercise and I got a lot of support because a lot of people believe in what we are doing. A lot of the health stores that we were involved with knew about Prometheus and knew the concept of it and thought it was a really good ethical concept and that's how I funded that part of the business.

As her venture grew there was a realization that an injection of more capital was needed, but maintaining control and independence in running the business was important:

> So it got very quickly to a point of thinking I am just not going to grow without having any capital involved and I really thought that I would like a partner and I would like someone who wasn't involved in the business. I had a really bad experience you know with my previous partner that had ended up with a big debt to me and someone interfering with what I was doing and it was pretty scary. So I was a bit scared ... and I left getting a partner involved in the business quite a lot longer than probably was sensible.

After 'specific meditation' on the problem, which was '... the same concept really as writing a business plan but it is slightly more esoteric but it always works', Suzanne had three investment offers, one of which she took up. Her new business partner received a 20 per cent share in the business. Though she believed in the principles and products of the business, she did not want to be directly involved. Some time down the track however, once again personal circumstances, in this instance that of her business partner, forced a re-think of finance. Her seriously ill partner now wished to exit the business, and her share was sold to a trusted mutual friend, who also provided a further capital injection: 'Bill had always helped out and he had always been there to ask advice in the past anyway'. This move also fitted in with Suzanne's growth aspirations for the company: 'I thought, well really I want us to be the world authority on natural skin care, I want us to not be restrained by capital ... I want us to be ready to represent New Zealand in the world and be superb and I'm not going to do that by myself'.

Simultaneously, however, innovative ways of assuring maintenance of control and her company philosophy were devised. Further expertise was also brought formally into the company:

> Bill had been saying to me 'Hey you know we are really keen to have a bigger part' but I was pretty scared in terms of, you know, he has a merchant bank and so I said to him 'Look I'm interested in changing the situation, but you as an individual could invest. Not your bank and not your company and also Peter, who is his analyst, I would really like him to become a shareholder and work part-time in the business and in a set role and coz Peter is incredibly smart in that area and I had a lot of respect for him and thought if he is an investor as well, you know he is in a different role ... I actually changed the whole structure of the business and Bill became a 60 per cent shareholder. I dropped my shares down to 25 per cent and then what we did was we created A shares and B shares. ... the A shares were voting shares only, not profit shares, and then the B shares were all the profits. So I had 25 per cent of the profit shares, Bill had 60 per cent and I had all the A shares which gave me the majority of voting shares so I still got to control the business ... um not that I've ever needed to cause we work together as a team anyway but I had that assurance there.

Four years down the track and with the business growing and more capital required, the A and B share arrangement that had suited the stage of the business in 2000, needed to be re-examined. Once again an innovative solution is being thought through to preserve the philosophical integrity of the business. A covenant in the constitution of the company would ensure this:

> The thing with A and B shares is that the philosophy of the company was maintained and or improved on and the aims of us to be an ecological and ethical business, and you know a lot of that sometimes involved making decisions that are a lot more costly and not as commercial um so that was my concern. ... So I am happy to change the A and B shares things now coz I have a lot of trust in how our relationship has built and how we all work together ... so we are going to covenant into our constitution what are the things that absolutely have to stay in this company Living Nature for it to be who it is. It's um pretty amazing, so it's yeah, so I feel I am going to change it because of that.

Suzanne also confirmed that she saw no barriers for women in business in NZ. In fact she believed being a woman was a definite advantage. As she put it, it is all about ability not gender:

> It is often for me been to my advantage ... I have never really been in an environment where being female has been a disadvantage but then I don't even think that way myself. I don't think of people as a gender. I just think it's important to focus on your capability and to be measured on your capability ... Just get out and do it!

CONCLUDING COMMENTS

NZ has a long history of entrepreneurs who have developed internationally successful and enduring enterprises and few began with large capital input. They tended to rely more on carefully tended relationships between suppliers, customers, staff and markets to develop a company (Hunter and Wilson, 2004). Those who did fail or faced set back, learnt from the experience. The contemporary women entrepreneurs we interviewed were no different. For example, one of the women was made redundant early in her career and set about starting and growing her own company in the same business line as her employer. She now owns one of NZ's most successful international companies. Certainly though, some things have changed for NZ entrepreneurs – increasing globalization and emphasis on new knowledge economy sectors like biotechnology and the information and communications technology sector present different challenges. Women entrepreneurs in this century in new economy sectors are likely to face the need for global growth in order to remain competitive and therefore consideration of less traditional, larger-scale private capital funding becomes more relevant today.

Building the VC and private equity industry and a general awareness of the industry, will undoubtedly enhance the use of these sources of finance by female entrepreneurs. Albeit within the limitations of our sample, there does not appear to be any perception of gender bias on the part of the NZ VC industry and although few in number, there are encouraging trends with some high-profile women in evidence. Overall growth in the size of the VC industry should spill over to increase the share of high-growth-oriented women-led firms being funded through VC/private equity deals. Within the constraints of the current relative immaturity of the VC industry and in light of the small total number of deals conducted, it is difficult however, to provide any robust comment.

One woman entrepreneur in the biotechnology industry who was interviewed in this study did express strong opinions on the 'naivety' of the NZ VC and private equity market, especially in terms of understanding the concepts of intellectual property and global markets. She pointed to financing difficulties encountered by NZ biotechnology industries because of this deficiency. In particular, mention was made of the lack of understanding of scientific ideas and scientists by the financiers. However, we might add that such a suggested shortcoming of the industry could well be mitigated in the future with the dedicated government focus and VC allocation to the 'Biotech Fund'. Moreover in 2003, Health and Biosciences was already the leading sector with 27 per cent of investment by value in 2003 although this was mainly due to a single deal (Ernst & Young, 2004: 4, 8).

Systemic factors such as an expanding high-technology sector in NZ and an education system that produces more high-achieving females in this sector, are integral to increasing both the supply and demand for private capital in relation to women entrepreneurs. For NZ, a 'strategic state' and state entrepreneurship in terms of effectively fulfilling the systemic role of state is thus crucial at this overarching level (de Bruin, 2003). The success of wider government policies such as overall R & D policy, the promotion of growth of SMEs and entrepreneurship and other more specific initiatives, for example, the New Zealand Trade and Enterprise (NZTE) Beachhead Programme[11] to stimulate links with NZ companies and other overseas firms, are all vital to growing private capital for entrepreneurs. Thus, for example, the information, communications and technology industry has utilized the Beachhead scheme to establish an office in Silicon Valley and another office in Wales[12] is being investigated. Such initiatives could hopefully connect NZ ICT businesses not only to global supply chains but also to financial resources including VC. Avnimelech et al. (2004: 44) suggest, 'VC emerged in co-evolution with a start-up culture and specific industries, especially those in the IT sector'. Thus NZ's sector-specific growth initiatives and a wider innovation systems approach in the policy arena could be a fruitful way ahead for providing the foundations for enhancing the fledgling VC and broader private capital industry to the benefit of a strengthened entrepreneurial platform. This is likely to then result in positive spillovers to women entrepreneurs. Government support of the VC industry in Ireland, a country with a population size equivalent to that of NZ, and which initiated a seed and venture capital funding scheme similar to NZ's VIF in the early 1990s, is often quoted (for example, Ernst and Young, 2004) as a model for NZ to emulate. However, we emphasize the prudence of thoroughly researched multi-country experiences to guide the growth policy of the private VC and broader private capital market in NZ. We reiterate that 'carefully planned government policies that draw upon previous mistakes and lessons learned in other nations can have a positive impact on the development of a VC industry' (Avnimelech et al., 2004: 47).

An image of nurturing a child and then letting them go to fend for themselves was used by one of our woman entrepreneur interviewees who had moved from running her own business to being a hands-on venture capitalist. Similar sentiments were expressed by several other women in relation to their businesses. We might therefore speculate that this predilection for nurturing and caring in women, coupled with their increased wealth, could be a driver in stimulating the entry of women into the VC and private equity sector in the future.[13]

We firmly acknowledge that VC and private equity investment is relatively large-scale investment, yet NZ is a nation of SMEs, most with only modest private capital requirements. The informal angel investor market is well suited to the needs of NZ's SMEs. Over the last three years, NZ's ranking in the rate of informal investment in new and growing start-ups has been at the top of the developed country league (Frederick, 2004). Supporting the growth, access and awareness of entrepreneurial finance from informal sources is therefore vital. In this connection, the more holistic approach of the NZVCA to focus on informal investment as well as more formal VC is commendable.[14]

Although female entrepreneurial participation remains at about two-thirds that of men, NZ females nevertheless ranked seventh in total female entrepreneurial activity among the GEM countries, ahead of the United States and Canada and other OECD countries, and slightly ahead of Australia's female TEA of 9.6 per cent (Cruickshank and Eden, 2004). This cross-national data coupled with the findings of our study leads us to believe that the picture and outlook for women-owned business in NZ is promising. For instance, several of our interviewees who had been in business for a fair length of time and in business in less 'enlightened times', felt that conditions for NZ women in business had improved considerably: 'I believe that women in business in terms of their networks and their strengths have grown enormously.'

Finally, we highlight the need for further research on the important area of growth strategies of women entrepreneurs. More detailed sector-specific approaches would be very useful here. We also signal the usefulness of further research on the role of the venture catalyst market in financing women entrepreneurs.

NOTES

*   We are very grateful to all the research participants who gave so generously of their time and expertise. We sincerely thank Suzanne Histen, the manager of the 'Growth Strategies of Women Entrepreneurs Research Project' for her dedication and research support. Thank you also to Judy Zhu, particularly for her assistance with Chinese entrepreneur interviews. We acknowledge funding from the Academy of Business Research, Massey University, which made this research a possibility.
1.   This GEM report renames total entrepreneurial activity (TEA) as total early-stage activity (TEA) to help clarify which entrepreneurial activity was being measured; the acronym remains the same.

2. See www.nzvif.com.
3. See, for example, http://www.mine.org.nz/, which is a New Zealand angel investor network.
4. The definition of SMEs varies across countries and within countries. Differentiation is often on the basis of numbers of full-time equivalent (FTE) employees. In NZ, government agencies often define SMEs as those enterprises with 0–19 FTEs. 'Small' are those with 0–5 FTEs and 'Medium' 6–19 FTEs. Approximately 97 per cent of all New Zealand enterprises are SMEs. See MED and Statistics New Zealand (2004) for further details.
5. The NZVCA's 'mission is to develop a world-best venture capital ("VC") and private equity ("PE") environment for the benefit of investors and entrepreneurs in New Zealand' (http://www.nzvca.co.nz/). Together with Ernst & Young the NZVCA administers the NZ Venture Capital Monitor survey. This survey was sent out to 35 members in the inaugural 2002 year. It is assumed that this number has increased since then. Our database of members was privately sourced.
6. An online Directory based on the 5th edition of the *New Zealand Biotechnology Directory* published in 2000 by the New Zealand Biotechnology Association. A database of New Zealand biotechnology companies, university departments and research institutes, accessed April 2004 but no longer available on the internet. For a current, comprehensive directory see http://www.biospherenz.com/directory/index.asp.
7. WISE – Women in Self-Employment. See McGregor and Tweed (2002) for the most recent research on women's networking in NZ.
8. Suzanne Hall has consented to her name and that of the company being used.
9. Currently New Zealand Trade and Enterprise (NZTE) administers Enterprise Development Grants aimed to assist entrepreneurs and companies with less than 20 full-time equivalent staff to gain additional business skills and obtain external expertise and assistance in developing business projects. http://www.biz.org.nz/public/content.aspx?sectionid= 38&contentid=811 (accessed 10 May 2003).
10. For further details see (accessed 8 May 2004): http://www.med.govt.nz/irdev/ind_dev/ soucap2000/soucap2000-11.html#P2708_109455.
11. The Beachhead Programme is designed to assist with setting up of overseas offices and intended to provide gateways to emerging NZ firms to gain a foothold in overseas markets.
12. See hyperLINK contents: Issue 37, 19 February 2004, http://www.canterburysoftware. org.nz/news04feb19.htm#feature2 (accessed 11 May 2004).
13. Such speculation is particularly reasonable in light of the assertion that in NZ women comprise 58 per cent or more than half of informal investors compared with the international female proportion of 32 per cent (Frederick 2004). Infometrics (2004) however, refutes this GEM Report claim and points to survey results showing that only 5 per cent of those who could be classified as angel investors were female.
14. The NZVCA is looking at ways to build expertise in this area through an angel investor course and educational materials (Ernst and Young, 2004: 13).

REFERENCES

Avnimelech, G., Kenney, M. and Teubal, M. (2004), 'Building Venture Capital Industries: Understanding the U.S. and Israeli Experiences', Berkeley Roundtable on the International Economy, University of California, Berkeley.

Biotechnology Taskforce (2003), *Growing the Biotechnology Sector in New Zealand: A Framework for Action*, Report from the Biotechnology Taskforce, May.

Brush, C., Carter, N., Gatewood, E., Greene, P. and Hart, M. (2004), *Clearing the Hurdles: Women Building High-Growth Businesses*, Englewood Cliffs, NJ: Prentice Hall.

Carter, S., Shaw, E., Wilson, F. and Lam, W. (2004), 'Bank Financing of Entrepreneurs: A Six Stage Qualitative Methodology', Paper presented to the

Qualitative Research in Business Symposium, Massey University, Auckland, 3rd December.

Clark, H. (2002), *Growing an Innovative New Zealand*, http://www.executive. govt.nz/minister/clark/innovate/innovative.pdf, accessed 11 August 2002.

Cruickshank, P. and Eden, S. (2004), 'Widening Entrepreneurial Gender Gap in New Zealand?', Paper Presented at AGSE-Babson Regional Entrepreneurship Research Exchange Forum, Swinburne University of Technology, Melbourne, 24–25 February.

de Bruin, A. (2003), 'State Entrepreneurship', in A. de Bruin and A. Dupuis (eds), *Entrepreneurship: New Perspectives in a Global Age*, Ashgate: Aldershot, pp. 148–68.

de Bruin, A. and Lewis, K. (2004), 'Toward Enriching United Career Theory: Familial Entrepreneurship and Copreneurship', *Career Development International*, **9**(7), 638–46.

Department of Labour (2004), 'The Labour Market Explained: The Labour Force Participation Rate', http://www.dol.govt.nz/PDFs/work-insight-issue-5-ch13.pdf.

Duff, S. (1998), 'The Influence of Bank Loan Officers' Attitudes on Funding Decisions', Palmerston North: Massey University, unpublished research report.

Dupuis, A. and de Bruin, A. (2004), 'Women's Business Ownership and Entrepreneurship', in P. Spoonley, A. Dupuis and A. de Bruin (eds), *Work and Working in Twenty-first Century New Zealand*, Palmerston North: Dunmore Press, pp. 154–79.

Dwyer, M., Rose, D. and Sowman, R. (1985), 'Self Employment and Small Businesses', New Zealand Planning Council, Planning Paper 22.

Ernst & Young (2004), *The NZ Venture Capital Monitor 2003*, NZ Venture Capital Association Inc.

Fay, M. and Williams, L. (1993a), 'Gender Bias and the Availability of Business Loans', *Journal of Small Business Management*, **8**(4), 374–6.

Fay, M. and Williams, L. (1993b), 'Sex of Applicant and the Availability of Business Start up Finance', *Australian Journal of Management*, **16**(1), 65–72.

Frederick, H. (2004), *The Unitec Global Entrepreneurship Monitor 2003/2004: Toward High Growth Enterprise in New Zealand*. Unitec New Zealand's Centre for Innovation & Entrepreneurship Research Report Series, Vol. 3, No. 1, Auckland: Unitec New Zealand.

Gatewood, E.J., Brush, C.G., Carter, N.M., Greene, P.G. and Hart M.M. (2003), *Venture Capital, Women's Entrepreneurship and High Growth Ventures: An Annotated Bibliography*, Stockholm, Sweden: ESBRI.

Greene, P., Brush, C., Hart, M. and Saparito, P. (1999), 'An Exploration of the Venture Capital Industry: Is Gender an Issue?', in P.D. Reynolds, W. Bygrave, S. Manigart, C. Mason, G.D. Meyer, H. Sapienza and K.G. Shaver (eds), *Frontiers of Entrepreneurial Research*, Wellesley, MA: Babson College.

Hunter, I. and Wilson, M. (2004), 'Taping our entrepreneurial heritage', *University of Auckland Business Review*, **5**(1), 1–11. http://www.uabr.auckland.ac.nz/articles/Vol5Issue1/HUNTER.pdf.

Hutchinson, P.J. (1978), 'Financial Assistance to Small Firms: The American experience', *Quarterly Review*, National Westminster Bank, November, 50–62.

Infometrics (2000), 'New Zealand's Venture Capital Market', Treasury Working Paper 00/19, New Zealand Treasury.

Infometrics (2004), *New Zealand's Angel Capital Market – The Supply Side*, A report prepared for the Ministry of Economic Development, New Zealand, June.

Johansson, A.W. (2004), 'Narrating the Entrepreneur', *International Small Business Journal*, **22**(3), 273–93.

Johns, B.L., Dunlop, W.C. and Lamb, K.M. (1976), *Finance for Small Business in Australia: An Assessment of Adequacy*, National Small Business Bureau, Department of Trade and Industry, Canberra.

Mallon. M. and Cohen, L. (2001), 'Time for a Change? Women's Accounts of the Move from Organizational Careers to Self-Employment', *British Journal of Management*, **12**(3), 217–30.

Marshall, J. (2000), 'Living Lives of Change: Examining Facets of Women Managers' Career Stories', in M. Pieperl, M. Arthur, R. Goffee and T. Moris (eds), *Career Frontiers: New Conceptions of Working Lives*, New York, Oxford University Press.

McGregor, J. and Tweed, D. (2002), 'Profiling a New Generation of Female Small Business Owners in New Zealand: Networking, Mentoring and Growth', *Gender, Work and Organization*, **9**(4), 420–39.

Ministry of Economic Development (MED) and Statistics New Zealand (2004), *SMEs in New Zealand: Structure and Dynamics – 2004*, available at http://www.med.govt.nz/irdev/ind_dev/smes/2004/index.html.

Statistics NZ (2001), *Census of Population and Dwellings*.

Statistics NZ (2004), *Household Labour Force Survey*, June 2004 quarter.

Welsh, M. (1988), *The Corporate Enigma: Women Business Owners in New Zealand*, Dunedin: University of Otago, unpublished dissertation.

13. The supply of finance to women-led ventures: the Northern Ireland experience

Claire M. Leitch, Frances Hill and Richard T. Harrison

INTRODUCTION

In Europe, the contribution of women to the entrepreneurial development of economies is worthy of investigation because the growth in presence, size and contribution of women-owned businesses that has occurred in the US over the past ten years has not been matched (Greene et al., 2001; Carter et al., 2001). The progress made by American women in relation to new venture creation has been impressive. For example, in the last two decades, not only have women-owned businesses outpaced the overall growth of businesses by nearly two to one, they have also made a more significant impact upon the economy in terms of employment and revenues generated than the growth in the number of such firms would indicate. Furthermore, predictions have suggested that by 2005 there will be 4.7 million self-employed women in the US, which is an increase of 77 per cent since 1983 – this is in comparison to the 6 per cent increase in the number of self-employed men (United States SBA, 1998; Greene et al., 2001).

On the other hand, in Europe, while there has been an increase in female entrepreneurial activity, the rate of growth has not been so rapid (Carter et al., 2001). For example, in the Netherlands females comprise 34 per cent of all those who are self-employed, while in Finland, Denmark, Spain, Belgium and the UK the percentage is somewhat lower, with figures of around 25 per cent (Duchenaut, 1997; Nilsson, 1997). However, within these European countries disparity in the balance of new ventures created by men and women is evident. For instance, based on the data generated by the GEM (Global Entrepreneurship Monitor) studies in 2002, the UK was found to rank 23rd out of a possible 37 countries in terms of the ratio of female- to male-owned businesses. In 2003, with respect to the gap in the rate of venture creation by men and women, it ranked 7th out of 14 participating G7 and EU countries (Harding et al., 2004).

Furthermore, within the UK itself, differences between the levels of entrepreneurial activity amongst the female population in comparison to the male population, also exist. Regionally, London (6.6 per cent) and the South West (4.6 per cent) had the highest levels of female entrepreneurship in 2003 (Harding and Cowling, 2003), while in Northern Ireland (which is also part of the UK) the total entrepreneurial activity (TEA) is 3.5 per cent in comparison with a figure of 7.1 per cent for male entrepreneurial activity (O'Reilly and Hart, 2003). One aspect of this is a gap between women's self-assessment of their ability to start up in business and that of men (O'Reilly and Hart, 2003), a difference in intentions, self-assessment and aspiration, which has been identified in other studies (Carter and Brush, 2004: 16–17).

In the context of new venture creation a number of differences between men and women have been highlighted, including business and industry choices, financing strategies, growth patterns and governance structures (Greene et al., 2003; Carter et al., 2001). Indeed, Greene et al. (2003) believe these factors provide compelling reasons to study female entrepreneurship, specifically focussing on women-owned/led businesses, the nature of their ventures, their entrepreneurial behaviours, as well as their access to venture capital and private equity capital. The importance of access to finance specifically is most clearly understood from a resource-based theory of the firm perspective. This proposes that in order to be competitive, a firm needs to acquire a stock of tangible and intangible resources that are valuable, rare, inimitable and non-substitutable by other firms. In addition, it requires appropriate capabilities to enable it to coordinate and deploy its resources through organizational processes to achieve this end (Penrose, 1995; Barney, 1991; Pitelis, 2004; Kostopoulos et al., 2004). Finance, in this perspective, is not only a resource in itself, but is instrumental in enabling a firm to acquire other necessary resources and develop appropriate capabilities.

With regard to the study reported in this chapter, since little prior research has been conducted into the financing of new and growing businesses in Northern Ireland, the analysis of gender issues in financing businesses comprises a sub-set of a wider range of issues under investigation. In this chapter, however, the findings reported specifically concern the financing of women-owned/led businesses in the region. In this context, at present, the role that gender plays in relation to the financing of women-owned/led businesses is unclear. While it is known from the GEM data that women's TEA is significantly lower than that of men, and that women make greater use of informal sources of funding than men, there could be several reasons for this. For example, it could be that there is a degree of discrimination even at the unconscious level on the part of funding providers, the product perhaps of structural perspectives such as essentialism or androcentricism (Bem, 1993). Although the evidence is not consistent, there are indications that while women and men (in the US context) have more or less achieved parity in being approved for loans, there are still disparities in terms of interest rates, collateral and guarantees, suggesting that the disparities are seen more in the cost of access to capital than in access itself (Coleman, 2000). Alternatively, or in addition, issues relating to the characteristics and abilities of individual women and/or their businesses, may be significant (Read, 1998).

The findings of the first stage of an ongoing study, which relate to the supply of finance for women-owned/led businesses in Northern Ireland, are presented in this chapter. The research questions below are addressed:

1) To what extent is the finance necessary to start up and grow their businesses available to women?
2) To what extent (if any) does access to capital present a barrier to growth to women-owned/led businesses?
3) Are there any forms of capital that are more difficult than others for women to access?

The chapter is structured as follows. First, the regional economic context is presented. Second, we discuss the low levels of enterprise among females. Third, we examine the sources of finance available for new and growing businesses in the region. Fourth, we summarize the methodology adopted in this research. Fifth, the extent to which there is finance available for women to start up and grow their businesses is explored and an attempt is made to determine if there are any forms of capital that are more difficult than others for women to access. Finally, as this research project is ongoing it is not yet possible to draw definitive conclusions about the experience of women financing and growing their businesses in the region. However, it does raise a number of issues that will be investigated further in the second phase.

THE NORTHERN IRELAND CONTEXT

Northern Ireland is the most westerly region of the UK, with a population of around 1.6 million, of which 51.6 per cent are women. While 48.7 per cent of the workforce are women, only 3.2 per cent of women own a business. Northern Ireland is part of the European Union (EU) and, until 2000, had Objective One status (which entitled it to access a range of funding and support measures to support business development, economic development and social inclusion since its GDP was less than 75 per cent of European average GDP). In relative terms, the economic position of Northern Ireland is particularly weak as it continues to lag behind its European counterparts in relation to economic performance. The per capita GDP for Northern Ireland is one of the lowest in the UK, at only 77 per cent of the UK average (The Ulster Society of Chartered Accountants, 2001: 2). This economic gap is partly attributable to political instability, reliance on public sector employment and the decline of the region's traditional industries. In addition, there are very few public limited companies (only five compared with almost 270 in Scotland, a similarly peripheral regional economy, which is around three times the size of the Northern Ireland economy) and the private sector is dominated by very small, often family-owned, businesses.

In light of this it is acknowledged that growth in the SME sector is a critical stimulant to overall economic growth in the region, and encouraging entrepreneurship is a major focus of economic development policy in the region (Invest Northern Ireland, 2005). However, in Northern Ireland the level of business start-ups is lower than in the rest of the UK (an annual new business creation rate of 6.9 per cent of the stock of current businesses, compared with 11.5 per cent in the UK as a whole). In addition, the level of fast-growing businesses is also low, with only 7 per cent of start-up companies being classified as such (The Ulster Society of Chartered Accountants, 2001: 22). Moreover, despite the assistance provided by government agencies such as Invest Northern Ireland (InvestNI), the region's SMEs appear to have difficulty progressing from start-up to high-growth companies (Harding, 2002; O'Reilly and Hart, 2003). This may be due to the dominant role that the public sector plays in the Northern Ireland economy and which may be associated with a reduction in the level of individual risk-taking. It may also reflect the emphasis placed on pursuing a career in the professions, such as medicine, accountancy and law, for the most able (O'Reilly and Hart, 2003). All of these are perceived as contributory factors to the region's low levels of entrepreneurial activity.

The main economic development organization in Northern Ireland is InvestNI, the aim of which is to 'add value to the economy and create wealth'. It seeks to achieve this by encouraging more people to start a business and by helping companies grow and compete in global markets. Accordingly, it offers a range of start-up programmes contributing, on average, 20 per cent of set-up costs. (Just over 34 per cent of start-ups in Northern Ireland use government grant finance (O'Reilly and Hart, 2003: 41).) However, its aims also include achieving higher levels of growth by indigenous and externally owned businesses. To this end a 'Global Start Team' was recently established and is currently determining its remit. It will target businesses that seek to develop leading edge technologies and that have the potential to trade internationally.

With particular respect to increasing levels of female entrepreneurship within the economy, InvestNI has embarked upon the widely publicized 'Go for It' and 'Investing in Women' initiatives, which seek to improve not only the low levels of female entrepreneurship in the region, but also the quality of start-ups by women. The agency aims to achieve this by attempting to alter the structural and cultural obstacles that traditionally limit female entrepreneurial activity. In addition, they aim to boost the performance of those already in business by providing initiatives targeted directly at this group, such as the development of business networks and the promotion of role models that seek to offer support and encouragement to entrepreneurial women.

WOMEN'S ENTREPRENEURSHIP IN NORTHERN IRELAND

As O'Reilly and Hart (2002: 11) have noted, 'Northern Ireland is a lagging region in terms of entrepreneurial activity' and indeed it ranks alongside the poorest performing regions in the UK. For instance, in comparison with the North East of England, Northern Ireland has roughly similar proportions of potential entrepreneurs and a slightly higher proportion of established entrepreneurs. Both regions, when measured in terms of GDP per capita, are among the poorest areas of the UK (O'Reilly and Hart, 2002). The TEA index for Northern Ireland is 5.2 per cent (3.5 per cent for women and 7.1 per cent for men) (O'Reilly and Hart, 2003), indicating that women in the region are only half as likely as men to engage in business start-up and ownership activities, although female entrepreneurship did increase significantly between 2002 and 2003; in 2002 women were only about one-quarter as likely to start a business as men.[1] Indeed, in comparison to their peers in England and Ireland, females in Northern Ireland are much less likely to be engaged in, or thinking about, enterprise. Interestingly, female necessity entrepreneurship, where women enter self-employment because they perceive that they have no better choices for work, in Northern Ireland is only 16 per cent, compared with around 20 per cent for men (O'Reilly and Hart, 2003).

While there is good information available on the start-up process, a reasonable degree of financial support, and an awareness of equity funding and a strong banking sector (Harding, 2002), it has also been noted that there are low levels of take up of support by females, as well as young people and older entrepreneurs (O'Reilly and Hart, 2002). One reason for this might be the fact that women in Northern Ireland are more likely than women in any other region of the UK to report fear of failure as preventing them from starting a new business venture (O'Reilly and Hart, 2003). Moreover, fewer women in Northern Ireland, relative to the majority of regions elsewhere in the

UK, believe they have the skills to start a business, while similar proportions indicate that they personally know an entrepreneur and that the opportunities for start-up are good. These beliefs are in stark contrast to those held by males. For example, just over half of men, compared with one-third of women, believe that they have the necessary skills to start a business and are less likely to fear failure. Furthermore, more men than women are likely to have personally known an entrepreneur in the past two years as well as believing that the opportunities for initiating new venture creation within the next six months are good (O'Reilly and Hart, 2003).

FINANCE FOR SMALL BUSINESSES IN NORTHERN IRELAND

Traditionally, SMEs in Northern Ireland have relied heavily on owners' equity and retained earnings to finance growth, while venture capital and business angels have played a very limited role in financing SMEs. Furthermore, the major banks have tended to offer only traditional products, primarily secured loans and overdrafts. 'With a few exceptional cases banks have not moved beyond secured lending towards products such as mezzanine finance and debt/equity swaps' (The Ulster Society of Chartered Accountants, 2001: 22). This situation is compounded by the fact that a general lack of unsecured lending appears to dissuade many people from setting up their own businesses in a culture characterized by risk aversion and fear of failure (O'Reilly and Hart, 2003). It is also recognized that there are insufficient venture capital funds available in Northern Ireland to drive business growth, and government appears reluctant to bridge the gap by accepting a higher level of risk.

Concerning those women who do start up businesses, they are less likely than men in Northern Ireland to seek equity finance and a bank overdraft, but are more likely to seek finance from informal investors. Compared with their counterparts in the UK as a whole, Northern Ireland women are more likely to seek unsecured loans and bank overdrafts and are less likely to apply for equity and venture capital finance (O'Reilly and Hart, 2003). This tends to suggest that women's strategies for raising start-up finance in particular, may be difficult for the following reasons. First, Northern Ireland has one of the lowest proportions of informal investors in the UK, although those who are active investors appear to make quite large investments (Harrison et al., 1997b); second, as reported above, unsecured loans are difficult to obtain in Northern Ireland; and third, banks in the region have relied on traditional lending products. The situation is compounded for all entrepreneurs, men and women, by the low level of venture capital funds available.

METHODOLOGICAL APPROACH

The aim of the overall research project from which this chapter is drawn is to investigate the financing of women-owned/led businesses in Northern Ireland, from both the supply and demand sides. On the supply side, the objective is to explore a range of issues that the literature suggests could have an impact on women's ability to raise finance for start-up/growth activity. On the demand side, the objective is to access the experiences of established female entrepreneurs in raising finance for their businesses.

A number of methodological shortcomings of existing research into the financing of women-owned/led business have been identified (Read, 1998; Ahl, 2004). First, there is a general absence of studies that have fully taken into account or controlled for the full range of structural characteristics that may influence a venture's success in raising finance. Second, much of this research, as with research into female entrepreneurship and business ownership more generally, is based on an assumption of entrepreneurship as male entrepreneurship, taking that experience as the benchmark against which to judge female entrepreneurship and, in so doing, both failing to recognize the socially constructed nature of gender and the possibly very different (and appropriate) gendered manifestations of entrepreneurship (Ahl, 2004; Carter and Brush, 2004: 13). Third, while there is a significant body of literature regarding the financing of women-led businesses, relatively few studies have focussed specifically on the demand side of transactions from a female perspective (Amatucci and Sohl, 2004). Fourth, a high proportion of the research that has been conducted tends to be based on the North American experience (see, for example, Gundry et al., 2002; Greene et al., 2003). However, the North American experience is very different from that of many areas of Europe, and especially a very small region such as Northern Ireland, where the financial market and general entrepreneurial activity are unsophisticated in comparison to other areas (The Ulster Society of Chartered Accountants, 2001; O'Reilly and Hart, 2003).

More specifically, in the context of this research relatively little academic research into entrepreneurship in general has been undertaken in Northern Ireland to date, and therefore this study is exploratory in nature. For these reasons, and in the absence of access to major large-scale survey results that would help address the issue of controlling for structural factors, it was decided to adopt a largely qualitative approach in this research (Amatucci and Sohl, 2004). Huse and Landström (1997) have argued that qualitative studies are mainly employed in Europe to generate concepts and models that lead to deeper understanding of problems. Even though there has been much debate within entrepreneurship over the relative merits of qualitative fieldwork versus more quantitative research (Aldrich, 2000), we share the view of Gartner and Birley (2002) that both approaches have a valuable contribution to make in the area of entrepreneurship research.

THE SUPPLY SIDE

Research on the supply side comprised informal, wide-ranging open-ended interviews with representatives from InvestNI (see above). The main aims of these were to explore the agency's role in the financing of start-up and growing enterprises in the province, as well as to determine the range of support programmes available in general, and targeted at women specifically. In addition, semi-structured interviews were conducted with senior representatives from the four main banks (Bank of Ireland, First Trust Bank, Northern Bank and the Ulster Bank) plus two others (the Abbey and HSBC, which have been increasing their presence in business banking in Northern Ireland in recent times). Semi-structured interviews with representatives from three venture capital firms (there are a total of four such organizations in Northern Ireland) were also carried out. To provide as complete a picture as possible, an informal interview was undertaken with the coordinator of the recently established business angel network, formed in March 2004 with a mixture of government and private sector finance. This service was established in response to an equity funding gap identified in the InterTrade Ireland *Report* (2000) and aims to match investors with appropriate investment opportunities. Since it had only just been formally launched at the time fieldwork interviews were being conducted, it proved too early to include this potential source of funding in the research.

Based on a review of literature, as well as the work undertaken by participants in the Diana Project, we designed two similar semi-structured interview schedules, one for representatives of the banks and the other for the representatives of the four venture capital firms. Because gender discrimination in Northern Ireland, as elsewhere in Europe, is unlawful and politically incorrect, and it was anticipated (correctly) that the majority of respondents on the supply side would be male, we deliberately structured the interview schedules so that the first part is ostensibly non-gender-specific, while the second part overtly addresses issues relating to women-owned/led businesses. This was to overcome the tendency of many studies, identified by Read (1998), to sensitize respondents to the issue of gender and discrimination in this area. Table 13.1 outlines the topics covered in the interviews carried out in the banks and venture capital firms. These were very similar in both cases, although specific questions had to be tailored appropriately.

Table 13.1   Interview schedules

Interview Schedule Details

Section I – General Lending/Investment Policy

- preferred type of lending/investment opportunity (e.g., seed, start-up, early stage expansion, etc.)
- availability and range of financial packages for entrepreneurs
- proportion of lending/investment in the preferred types of opportunity
- number of funding applications received in previous financial year and proportions funded
- average amounts of lending and funding given to the different types of opportunity
- requirements for guaranteeing loans (banks)
- preferred industrial sectors for lending/investment
- channels employed to advertise funding opportunities/access investment opportunities
- criteria influencing lending/investment decisions, e.g., characteristics of entrepreneur, characteristics of business, financial information

Section II – Lending/Investment Policy Specific to Women-owned/led Projects

- proportion of women-owned/led projects supported in previous financial year
- industrial sectors in which women-owned/led businesses predominate
- amounts of funding requested by men and women
- availability of packages specifically tailored for women-owned/led businesses
- most effective marketing channels for gaining requests for funding from women/channels for accessing investment opportunities in women-owned/led businesses
- number of female investment officers in institution
- level of seniority of female investment officers in institution
- research undertaken by institution into women's experiences in sourcing and obtaining funding – actual and planned
- perception of extent to which the financing requirements of women-owned/led businesses are met in Northern Ireland

---

FINDINGS

An overview of the banks and venture capital firms included in the study is provided in Tables 13.2 and 13.3 below. It must be noted that as the number of banks and venture capital firms included in the study is small, it is difficult to determine a definite pattern in the responses provided in relation to each theme in the questionnaire. Nevertheless key issues have been highlighted below.

Preferred types of funding opportunity and finance packages available

An issue of particular interest in this context is growth, as studies have indicated that the growth preferences of women may be more modest than those of men (Greene et al., 2003: 16; NDP Gender Equality Unit, 2003; Rosa et al., 1996). Thus, if banks and venture capital firms have a preference for funding growth-oriented companies, this could be to women's disadvantage. From the survey of banks and venture capital firms conducted, the respondents for the banks indicated that with regard to seed and start-up financing the interest of the banks was moderate at best, and preference was expressed for expansion financing for established firms. This is almost certainly a product of the banks' conservative attitude to risk highlighted above. With regard to the venture capital firms, one of these has a particular remit to finance pre-start-up, start-up and early stage expansion. The other two firms had only limited interest in seed and start-up financing and greater preference for early-stage and subsequent expansion financing. As far as finance packages are concerned, the banks prefer to tailor such packages to the specific needs of the individual entrepreneur and their business irrespective of gender. Thus, if women are less interested in growing their businesses than men, these findings suggest that they may be at a disadvantage when seeking finance.

Number of funding applications in past financial year

This section in the questionnaire was designed in an attempt to establish the total number of applications for funding made by both men and women in the previous financial year, and subsequently to try to establish the proportion of applications submitted by women.

With respect to the information obtained from respondents from the banks, it was not possible to gather accurate data on this matter. This is because the main banks in Northern Ireland are subsidiaries of national and international groups and the relevant information is not appropriately disaggregated. Thus it was difficult for respondents to provide meaningful information on the proportion of applications submitted by women. However, it does appear that a relatively high percentage of total applications are successful, with

Table 13.2 Information about the major banks in Northern Ireland

Bank	Year of Establishment	Number of Branches	Number of Employees	Services
Northern (National Australia Group)	1824	96 branches and 12 business centres	2000+	Number of lending products, e.g. specialist term loans and Treasury products
Ulster (Royal Bank of Scotland)	1836	85	1800	Moving towards specialized business centres; specialist advisory service dealing with private and public company acquisitions, disposals, MBO and capital raising
First Trust (AIB UK)	1991	68	1600	Specialist advice and products, including AIB private banking (high net worth, Goodbody's stockbrokers, and AIB Finance
Bank of Ireland	1783	47 local branches and seven regional business centres	1200	Specialist advisory unit (IBI corporate finance) provides expertise on company acquisitions, disposals, MBO and capital raising
Abbey (National PLC)	1944	16 branches in Northern Ireland	25896 (in UK)	Commercial banking including asset financing, commercial lending operations, securities financing and risk management
HSBC	1865	Six branches in Northern Ireland	218000 world wide	Commercial and small business financing, innovation and technology support, specialist venture capital subsidiary

Source: Adapted from The Ulster Society of Chartered Accountants (2001).

Table 13.3   Venture capital activity in Northern Ireland

Date Started	Investment Size	Fund Manager
1984	0–50K	QUBIS[a]
2000	0–50K	University Challenge Fund[b]
2003	0–50K	NITech
2002	50–250K	Viridian Venture Fund
1995	250K–1.5M	Crescent Capital
1985	250K–1.5M	Enterprise Equity
	1.5M+	Dublin & GB Funds

Notes:
[a] QUBIS is the Technology Transfer Office of Queen's University Belfast, which provides start-up support for spin-out companies from the University.
[b] University Challenge Fund provides small amounts of equity for spin-out companies from Queen's University Belfast and University of Ulster.

respondents claiming that 70 per cent or more gained finance. Unfortunately, it is not possible from the results of this analysis to comment on the suggestion that women may have broadly similar success rates as men in gaining offers of finance, but that this may be on less favourable terms (Coleman, 2000; McKechnie et al., 1998; Riding and Swift, 1990).

Regarding the venture capital firms it was easier to gather accurate information. In this case the total number of investment opportunities presented was small in all instances. It should be reported that one fund was only established in 2003 and another that did receive applications was unable to invest because it was engaged in fund-raising. Moreover, in two of the three cases less than 10 per cent of all applications made were successful. This reinforces the point made above, that the sources of venture capital in Northern Ireland are very limited. However, it should be added that the venture capital firms included in the study only invest in Northern Ireland ventures. Moreover, the deal flow for venture capital is also limited irrespective of gender. What is interesting is that only one of the three venture capital firms had invested in women-owned/led businesses, but even in this case such investment amounted to a mere 25 per cent of a total of 30 projects.

Guarantee arrangements required (banks)
There is evidence to suggest that women are less likely than men to seek external finance, preferring to rely on internal financing (Chaganti et al., 1995), and are less likely to risk personal assets or take action that may jeopardize the welfare of the family (Brush, 1992; Read, 1998). Thus if banks,

for example, require the use of personal property to secure a loan, this may deter women from seeking finance from this source (Brown and Segal, 1989). This is important for a number of reasons, not least because banks are virtually the only institutions that provide small business owners with the type of finance they most commonly require, namely short-term finance in the form of overdrafts and term loans (Keasey and Watson, 1993). Moreover, the majority of start-up finance in Northern Ireland and the UK is from banking sources (O'Reilly and Hart, 2003). Perhaps more importantly in relation to growth, research by Cowling and Harding (2004), indicates that businesses with access to short-term debt finance and longer-term secured debt, are more likely to have high growth potential than those that do not.

All the respondents representing the banks stated that they seek security for the funding provided to individuals. However, the types and amounts sought vary from one bank to another. Indeed there are distinct differences. At one extreme a requirement of approximately 90 per cent of the borrowing to be guaranteed by a variety of means, including personal assets, is mandatory. At the other, personal guarantees are considered only as a last option and there is no interest in people's dwellings as collateral. This would suggest that all entrepreneurs should shop around for debt finance in order to minimize their personal risk. Again, however, until systematic information is available from the demand side (or from a more detailed analysis of loan book data to determine the extent to which there are gender-related variations in the conditions attaching to loans) it is impossible to determine the extent to which there are gender-related finance supply issues in this area.

Preferred sector(s) for funding
If there is a mismatch between banks' preferences and the sectors in which women decide to locate their businesses, then clearly women could be disadvantaged. Research by the NDP Gender Equality Unit in Ireland (2003) suggests that women-owned/led businesses predominate in the services sector, for example, wholesale and retail, hotel and restaurants and financial and other business services. With regard to this theme it was particularly difficult to determine a definite pattern. However, out of the 20 industrial sectors covered by the interview schedule, those in which the banks are most likely to provide funding are: energy, media and photography, industrial products and services, manufacturing, retail and services (including professional services and tourism) and medical/health-related. These preferences broadly equate to the importance of these sectors in the economy as a whole, and suggest that at this level of aggregation at least, sector influences underlying the supply of finance by the banks

are relatively unimportant. Given the above, and since the literature suggests that women-owned/led businesses predominate in services and retailing, there seems to be little evidence of disadvantage to women in this respect. A similar picture emerges for the venture capital firms, with all sectors covered by all three firms. Indeed, as the Northern Ireland economy moves away from its traditional manufacturing base in the direction of services, this may be to women's advantage.

Channels used to market funding opportunities (banks); main sources of information on investment opportunities (venture capital firms)

Clearly, if the channels used by banks to market funding opportunities are not available to, accessed, or participated in by women, they may be unaware of funding opportunities available to them. In addition, if the sources of information employed by venture capital firms are male-dominated, then women-owned/led businesses may be excluded as investment opportunities. Of particular relevance in this context is the use of formal and informal networks. The issue of networking and gender is contentious; however, as Carter et al. (2001: 36) note, a number of studies have concluded, 'that there is a great deal of similarity in the networking behaviour of men and women, although the sex composition of networks does vary by gender. Women are more likely to have networks composed entirely of other women, and men are more likely to have networks composed entirely of other men'. From the data obtained during the interviews, it is interesting to note that while the banks between them use a wide range of marketing channels in relation to entrepreneurs and commercial customers, the three channels used by them all are informal networks, formal networks and other intermediaries – especially accountants and lawyers. One bank in particular deals primarily with such intermediaries and actively courts them for business. In relation to informal networks, the same bank sponsors two Irish rugby teams and a Gaelic football team (popular male-dominated sports in Ireland). This is discussed further below.

In relation to the venture capital firms, their sources of information on investment opportunities are varied, but include intermediaries such as accountants, banks and corporate finance houses. This pattern is not surprising and is consistent with the experience of venture capital firms elsewhere. Increasingly venture capitalists will consider investing only in propositions that are referred to them by a trusted source, so again, it is important to be in the right network in order to be referred on to the venture capitalist (Wright and Robbie, 1998; Harrison et al., 1997a). It may be, given that there are gender differences in the basis of network membership and participation, that this places women entrepreneurs at a disadvantage. However, in Northern Ireland such possible disadvantage should be mitigated in part by the fact that two of the venture capital firms are partly funded by the economic development agency, InvestNI, and also receive referrals from that organization. For the venture capital firms included in the research, the best quality investment opportunities arise from referrals from professional advisors such as PriceWaterhouseCoopers and from the incubators/technology transfer offices of the region's two universities. There is no evidence that any particular channels yield more applications for finance from women than from men. However, these findings do demonstrate the importance of entrepreneurs/ small business owners participating in appropriate networks and that, in the case of women, it may not be helpful to confine their activity to those networks dominated by women.

Factors influencing funding decisions (relating to the entrepreneur, the business and funding sought)

There is evidence to suggest that investors and funders may base their funding or investment decisions on a number of relevant criteria including previous experience/track record of founder, plans for growth and strategy, capitalization, plans to export, nature of product/service, financial issues (Gundry et al., 2002). However, the information obtained in this element of the research suggests that both banks and venture capital firms consider each funding application on an individual basis and on its merits. It is noteworthy that the venture capital firms appear less formulaic and more flexible in their attitudes towards the factors in question. For example, they are less likely than the banks to view previous business failure in a negative light, although they do consider relevant circumstances – to illustrate, failure through fraud would be unacceptable. One particularly interesting feature is the differences in attitudes towards export and growth potential between the venture capital firms and the banks. With regard to the former, whose primary aim is to maximize return on investment, they will only invest if proposals exhibit both growth and export potential. However, while they accept proposals on the basis of growth potential, export potential is not a significant factor in the decision-making of the banks. Again, this seems to relate to the banks' attitudes towards risk, and their prime concern with the borrower's ability to service and repay their debt. Another difference between the two groups is that the venture capital firms have investment limits, while the lending activity of the banks is not constrained to the same extent. However, both groups expect the entrepreneur to make a personal investment in their business and in the case of the banks, this can be up to 30 per cent of the total. Such a requirement may have a disproportionate impact on women seeking finance as evidence suggests that they tend to invest less of their own capital in their businesses than men (O'Reilly and Hart, 2003), and may have less access to start-up capital because of lower earnings and lower levels of ownership of property assets to use as collateral (Danes and Olson, 2003; Danes et al., 2005). If US trends are to be followed, even partially, in the UK this may change. One of the factors to which the increase in the rate of formation of women-owned businesses in the US has been attributed is the growth in the divorce rate, which has stimulated women to rethink career and occupational choice options (Jalbert, 2000; Johnson and Skinner, 1986) and, in some cases, has reassigned ownership of assets that can be used to support applications for external funding (Blau, 1998; Lillard and Waite, 2000). It should be noted though, that divorce more generally worsens women's financial (and other) position and that of the businesses in which they are involved (Galbraith, 2003; Amato, 2000).

Women-owned/led projects
As indicated by Table 13.1 above, the main aim of this section was to establish whether or not banks and venture capital firms regard women as a distinct target group. The issues explored included the proportion of overall projects supported, those sectors in which women-owned/led businesses might predominate, specific packages (if any) available for women entrepreneurs and the differences (if any) in levels of funding sought by men and women. With respect to this latter point, the literature suggests that businesswomen are more likely to start their businesses with smaller amounts of finance than their male counterparts (Hisrich and Brush, 1987; Carter and Rosa, 1995; Read, 1998). From the data gathered during the interviews, there was no evidence to suggest that women owners are regarded as a distinct target group by either the banks or venture capital firms. Indeed, no respondents reported that their firms had any specific packages targeted at women. Furthermore, they indicated that there are no differences between men and women in the levels of finance and investment sought. While this seems to run counter to the evidence in the literature, care has to be taken with this interpretation as we cannot actually determine what the application and rejection rates were for the reasons stated above.

Additional topics covered in this section of the questionnaire included determining the gender of existing investment officers in both banks and venture capital firms as well as the amount of research (if any) that has been conducted in either sector on women's experiences in both sourcing and obtaining funding. With respect to the former, all the banks employed female investment officers across all levels of management including director level, while only one of the venture capital firms employed two female investment officers – at middle and senior management levels. Concerning the latter, none of the banks or venture capital firms has conducted research into women's experiences nor has any plans to do so. However, one venture capital company is working in conjunction with InvestNI on this issue.

DISCUSSION AND CONCLUSIONS

While the research is incomplete and it is difficult to draw definitive conclusions, a number of issues have emerged from the work undertaken to date. These are discussed below and will be investigated further in the second stage of the study. Perhaps the most significant in the Northern Ireland context, as reported from the supply side, is that few women appear to actually seek funding from either the banks or venture capital firms. There are a number of possible reasons for this:

- covert gender discrimination on the part of lending/funding officers;
- structural issues relating to hidden societal assumptions about gender;
- women's perceptions that they are unlikely to receive funding from these sources;
- women's strategic decisions relating to the sectoral nature of their businesses;
- lifestyle choices;
- lack of knowledge.

Concerning possible gender discrimination, overt discrimination of this type is both unlawful and politically incorrect in Europe. In this study no evidence of this, either overt or covert, was uncovered. Indeed, all respondents clearly believed that proposals for funding were assessed purely on merit. However, there is some evidence of the influence of societal factors, for example, androcentrism (Bem, 1993). This makes the assumption that the man is both gender neutral and the unspoken norm while the woman is the exception (Ahl, 2004). This is reflected in the comment by a (male) respondent that in relation to marketing, his bank sponsored rugby and Gaelic football matches, both male-dominated sports. The significance of this was clearly lost on him. Moreover, a female bank official, when asked for possible reasons why fewer women than men seek debt finance, suggested that it is easier for women with a family to be employed than self-employed and also that women may not be as entrepreneurial as men. If gender is a social construction (Ahl, 2004) then these attitudes are likely to support the perpetuation of the myth of the 'non-entrepreneurial woman', who, as an exception, represents a higher potential risk (unknown quantity) to potential funders. At a less fundamental level, women's perceptions may be relevant in this respect. If, as stated above, women lack confidence in their own skills and abilities, it is probable that they will be deterred from seeking finance from formal providers and instead rely on informal sources such as family and friends.

Regarding the sectoral nature of women's businesses, as stated above, this research uncovered no significant mismatch, at a relatively high level of aggregation, between the funding preferences of banks and venture capital firms and the sectors in which women decide to establish their businesses. However, choice of sector is important. To illustrate, a number of respondents were hesitant about funding firms in the manufacturing sector, which is in decline (Smith, 2004), preferring applications from service providers and those in the hi-tech sector such as electronics. Furthermore, the main development agency, InvestNI, in its *Draft Corporate Plan 2005–2008*, identifies three important factors for improving competitiveness in Northern Ireland: namely entrepreneurship, innovation and internationalization. These criteria will guide decisions on the provision of support for established and new ventures. Given that there are clear relationships between founding activity and both prior career history and immediate pre-foundation employment (Harrison et al., 2004), the pattern of female employment and labour market participation (part-time, non-managerial employment in the service sector) may represent a significant structural barrier to venture formation and ownership, which in turn will be reflected in differential access to finance (Ahl, 2004).

At a pragmatic level, women's apparent reluctance to seek funding from formal sources may be related to lifestyle choices. For example, women with children and/or other dependants may choose not to grow or develop their businesses, thereby avoiding taking on further responsibility, and thus do not seek finance from formal sources. In this regard it is interesting to note that one bank respondent observed that in Northern Ireland, where there is a high proportion of family-owned firms, men may own the businesses but women run them. In such cases then, it is probable that the men seek the finance. This is consistent with evidence that suggests that one reason for women moving into self-employment is to have flexibility in scheduling consistent with family-related issues (Boden, 1999), and reinforces the importance of understanding the ways in which the connections among gender, occupational choice and organizational structure and performance are differently manifest in male and female business owners (Mirchandani, 1999).

It is clear from the literature that business owners seeking funding from formal sources need to understand how to maximize the probability of being successful. For example, research by Mason and Stark (2004) reveals that the various types of funder consider business plans from different perspectives and emphasize the importance of different aspects. This means that business plans need to be tailored to the interests of the funder and it is important that all applicants understand the necessity of doing this. In addition, as the research reported in this chapter reveals, both banks and venture capital firms actively seek referrals from intermediaries in formal and informal networks. Moreover, Aldrich et al. (1997) identify networking to be a vital aspect in the survival and success of firms. Some commentators have suggested that there are gender differences in the way networks are created and used, particularly in respect of access to finance (Carter and Rosa, 1998). For example, Brush (1992) asserts that women tend to see their businesses as cooperative networks of relationships, while men use networks in a more transactional way. However, others have disputed this view, and Carter et al. (2001) identify this as an under-researched area and highly contentious. Nevertheless, networking is an important mechanism for the exchange of tacit and explicit knowledge in general, and with regard to establishing and growing a business in particular. From the supply side, it is impossible to identify the extent to which there may be network participation issues in women business owners' access to finance, but this remains an important issue, both in terms of the design and use of networks by finance suppliers and in terms of the nature of participation in these networks by male and female entrepreneurs.

Overall, from the supply perspective, women do not appear to be particularly disadvantaged in comparison to men when seeking funding or investment for their businesses. Indeed, respondents expressed the view that the financing needs of women entrepreneurs in Northern Ireland are adequately met, at least in terms of access to debt financing. However, those respondents from the venture capital firms indicated that the overall financing needs of Northern Ireland entrepreneurs in general, are not being met at present. Despite this, the research did uncover some evidence of androcentrism. Further research into the demand for finance, and in particular into the reported experience of the search for capital and the interaction between the experience of seeking finance and providing it, is needed before a full picture of the financing of women-owned businesses in Northern Ireland can be developed.

NOTE

1. However, it should be noted that very little reliance should be placed on year to year variations in these rates derived from the GEM data: evidence from the entire GEM database suggests that for all countries included, entrepreneurial activity rates can vary (in terms of the difference between the lowest and highest rates recorded over the four years) between 10 per cent and 800 per cent (Rosa, 2005, personal communication).

REFERENCES

Ahl, H. (2004), *The Scientific Reproduction of Gender Inequality*, Copenhagen Business School.
Aldrich, H. (2000), 'Learning Together: National Differences in Entrepreneurship Research', in D.L. Sexton and H. Landström (eds), *Handbook of Entrepreneurship*, Oxford: Blackwell Publishers Ltd.

Aldrich, H.E., Elam, A.B. and Reece, P.R. (1997), 'Strong Ties, Weak Ties and Strangers: Do Women Owners Differ from Men in their Use of Networking to Obtain Assistance?', in S. Birley and I.C. MacMillan (eds), *Entrepreneurship in a Global Context*, London: Routledge.

Amato, P.R. (2000), 'The consequences of divorce for adults and children', *Journal of Marriage and the Family*, **62**, 1269–87.

Amatucci, F. and Sohl, J. (2004), 'Women entrepreneurs securing business angel financing: tales from the field', *Venture Capital*, **6**(2/3), 181–96.

Barney, J. (1991), 'Firm resources and sustained competitive advantage', *Journal of Management*, **17**, 99–120.

Bem, S. (1993), *The Lenses of Gender: Transforming the Debate on Sexual Inequality*, New Haven: Yale University Press.

Blau, F.D. (1998), 'Trends in the well-being of American women, 1970–1995', *Journal of Economic Literature*, **36**, 112–65.

Boden, R.J. (1999), 'Flexible working hours, family responsibilities and female self-employment: gender differences in self-employment selection', *American Journal of Economics and Sociology*, **58**, 71–84.

Brown, S.A. and Segal, P. (1989), 'Female entrepreneurs in profile', *Canadian Banker*, **96**(4), 32–4.

Brush, C.G. (1992), 'Research on women business owners: past trends, a new perspective and future directions', *Entrepreneurship Theory and Practice*, **16**(4), 5–30.

Carter, N.M. and Brush, C.G. (2004), 'Gender', in W.B. Gartner, K.G. Shaver, N.M. Carter and P.D. Reynolds (eds), *Handbook of Entrepreneurial Dynamics: The Process of Business Creation*, Thousand Oaks, CA: Sage Publications.

Carter, S. and Rosa, P. (1995), 'The Financing of Male and Female Owned Businesses', paper presented to the ESRC seminar on New Developments in the Finance of New and Small Firms, University of Paisley, Craigie Campus, Ayr (March).

Carter, S. and Rosa, P. (1998), 'The financing of male and female owned businesses', *Entrepreneurship & Regional Development*, **10**, 225–41.

Carter, S., Anderson, S. and Shaw, E. (2001), *Women's Business Ownership: A Review of the Academic, Popular and Internet Literature*, Report to the Small Business Service, Sheffield.

Chaganti, R., DeCarolis, D. and Deeds, D. (1995), 'Predictors of capital structure in small ventures', *Entrepreneurship Theory and Practice*, **20**(2), 7–18.

Coleman, S. (2000), 'Access to capital and terms of credit: a comparison of men- and women-owned small businesses', *Journal of Small Business Management*, **38**(3), 37–52.

Cowling, M. and Harding, R. (2004), Paper presented to the 2nd Diana International Research Conference, Stockholm, May.

Danes, S.M. and Olsen, P.D. (2003), 'Women's role involvement in family businesses, business tensions, and business success', *Family Business Review*, **16**, 53–68.

Danes, S.M., Haberman, H.R. and McTavish, D. (2005), 'Gendered discourse about family business', *Family Relations*, **54**, 116–30.

Duchenaut, B. (1997), *Women Entrepreneurs in SMEs*. Report prepared for the OECD Conference on Women Entrepreneurs in Small and Medium Sized Enterprises: A Major Force for Innovation and Job Creation, Paris, France: OECD.

Galbraith, C.S. (2003), 'Divorce and the financial performance of small family businesses: an exploratory study', *Journal of Small Business Management*, **41**, 296–309.

Gartner, W.B. and Birley, S. (2002), 'Introduction to the special issue on qualitative methods in entrepreneurship research', *Journal of Business Venturing*, **17**(5), 387–95.

Greene, P.G., Brush, C.G., Hart, M.M. and Saparito, P. (2001), 'Patterns of venture capital funding: is gender a factor?', *Venture Capital: An International Journal of Entrepreneurial Finance*, **3**(1), 63–83.

Greene, P.G., Hart, M.M., Gatewood, E.J., Brush, C.G. and Carter, N.M. (2003), *Women Entrepreneurs: Moving Front and Center: An Overview of Research and Theory*, Coleman White Paper.

Gundry, L.K., Ben-Yosef, M. and Posig, M. (2002), 'Status of women's entrepreneurship: pathways to future entrepreneurship development and education', *New England Journal of Entrepreneurship*, Spring, **5**(1), 39–47.

Harding, R. (2002), *Global Entrepreneurship Monitor: Northern Ireland*, London: London Business School.

Harding, R. and Cowling, M. (2003), *Global Entrepreneurship Monitor: London*, London Business School and The Work Foundation: London.

Harding, R., Cowling, M. and Ream, M. (2004), *Achieving the Vision: Female Entrepreneurship*, London: The British Chamber of Commerce.

Harrison, R.T., Cooper, S.Y. and Mason, C.M. (2004), 'Entrepreneurial activity and the dynamics of technology-based cluster development: the case of Ottawa', *Urban Studies*, **41**(5–6), 1045–1070.

Harrison, R.T., Dibben, M. and Mason, C.M. (1997a), 'The role of trust in the informal investor's decision: an exploratory analysis', *Entrepreneurship Theory and Practice*, **21**(4), 63–82.

Harrison, R.T., McIntyre, P. and Mason, C.M. (1997b), 'Informal Investment in Northern Ireland', paper to ISBA Annual Policy and Research Conference, Belfast.

Hisrich, R.D. and Brush, C.G. (1987), 'Women Entrepreneurs: A longitudinal study', in N.C. Churchill, J.A. Hornaday, B.S. Kirchoff, O.J. Krasner and K.H. Vespers (eds), *Frontiers of Entrepreneurial Research*, Boston: Babson College, pp. 187–99.

Huse, M. and Landström, H. (1997), 'European entrepreneurship and small business research: methodological openness and contextual differences', *International Studies of Management and Organization*, **27**(3), pp. 3–12.

Intertrade Ireland (2000), *Report on the Development of a North/South Equity Funding Programme*.

Invest Northern Ireland (2005), *Draft Corporate Plan 2005–2008*, http://www.investni.com.

Jalbert, S.E. (2000), 'Women entrepreneurs in the global economy', www.cipe.org [accessed 28 February 2005].

Johnson, W.R. and Skinner, J. (1986), 'Labor supply and marital separation', *American Economic Review*, **76**, 455–69.

Keasey, K. and Watson, R. (1993), 'Banks and small firms: is conflict inevitable?', *National Westminster Bank Quarterly Review*, May, 30–40.

Kostopoulos, K., Spanos, Y.E. and Prastacos, G.P. (2004), *The Resource-Based View of the Firm and Innovation: Identification of Critical Linkages*, Athens University of Economics and Business.

Lillard, L. and Waite, L. (2000), 'Marriage, Divorce and the Work and Earning Careers of Spouses', *Working Papers*, WP9906, University of Michigan, Michigan Retirement Research Center.

Mason, C. and Stark, M. (2004), 'What do investors look for in a business plan? A comparison of the investment criteria of bankers, venture capitalists and business angels', *International Small Business Journal*, **22**(3), 227–48.

McKechnie, S.A., Ennew, C.T. and Read, L.H. (1998), 'The nature of the banking relationship: a comparison of the experiences of male and female small business owners', *International Small Business Journal*, **16**(3), 39–55.

Mirchandani, K. (1999), 'Feminist insight on gendered work: new directions in research on women and entrepreneurship', *Gender, Work and Organization*, **6**, 224–35.

NDP Gender Equality Unit (2003), *Women and Men in Ireland as Entrepreneurs and as Business Managers*, Department of Justice, Equality and Law Reform Ireland.

Nilsson, P. (1997), 'Business counselling directed towards female entrepreneurs – some legitimacy dilemmas', *Entrepreneurship & Regional Development*, **9**(3), 239–57.

O'Reilly, M. and Hart, M. (2002), *The Household Entrepreneurship Survey: Northern Ireland*, Northern Ireland: Invest NI.

O'Reilly, M. and Hart, M. (2003), *Global Entrepreneurship Monitor, Northern Ireland*, InvestNI and London Business School.

Penrose, E.T. (1995), *The Theory of the Growth of the Firm*, Oxford: Oxford University Press.

Pitelis, C.N. (2004), 'Edith Penrose and the resource-based view of (international) business strategy', *International Business Review*, **13**, 523–32.

Read, L. (1998), *The Financing of Small Business: A Comparative Study of Male and Female Business Owners*, London: Routledge.

Riding, A.L. and Swift, C.S. (1990), 'Women business owners and terms of credit: some empirical findings of the Canadian experience', *Journal of Business Venturing*, **5**, 327–40.

Rosa, P., Carter, S. and Hamilton, D. (1996), 'Gender as a determinant of small business performance: insights from a British study', *Small Business Economics*, **8**, 463–78.

Smith, I.R. (2004), 'Creating New Value in the Supply Chain', paper presented at the Northern Ireland Unlimited Conference, Bangor, 9 June.

The Ulster Society of Chartered Accountants (2001), *Financing for Growth*, Northern Ireland: Industrial Development Board and Local Enterprise Development Unit.

United States Small Business Association (SBA) (1998), *The State of Small Business*, Washington, DC.

Wright, M. and Robbie, K. (1998), 'Venture capital and private equity: a review and synthesis', *Journal of Business Finance and Accounting*, **25**, 521–70.

14. Female entrepreneurial growth aspirations in Slovenia: an unexploited resource

Polona Tominc and Miroslav Rebernik

INTRODUCTION

In most countries the share of men in entrepreneurship is much higher than the share of women. Recent empirical evidence is found in Global Entrepreneurship Monitor (GEM) research report (Acs et al., 2005). GEM is a cross-national research programme, aimed at describing and analysing entrepreneurial process in its early stage (start-up phase) within a wide range of countries. The GEM study for 2004 reports that in general, there are almost twice as many men who are active entrepreneurs than women. These differences are consistent across age groups and in no country are there more women who are active entrepreneurs than men, even though there is a wide variation between countries. The largest gender division occurs within the middle-income countries with a per capita GDP between 10000 and 25000 US$ (like Slovenia, Greece or Spain), where men are on average 75 per cent more likely than women to be active entrepreneurs. The smallest gap appears in the high-income countries with a per capita GDP over 25000 US$ (like USA or Finland), where the percentage difference falls to 33 per cent. In low-income countries with per capita GDP up to 10000 US$ (like Peru, South Africa, Hungary and Ecuador) men are on average 41 per cent more likely to be active in entrepreneurial activity than women.

There is wide evidence of the importance of female entrepreneurs in the economic development of a country, with regard to their contribution to job creation and economic growth, as well as to diversity in the economy. Female and male entrepreneurs differ not only with respect to their participation rates, but also with respect to their personal and business profile: a considerable diversity is found in terms of sectors, products, forms of organization and goals (Brush, 1992; Carter et al., 1997b; Verheul and Thurik, 2001; Wagner, 2004). It is rather surprising that in economic literature there is 'little knowing about precisely why there is less female than male entrepreneurship' (Parker,

2004). Nevertheless, three main groups of factors that influence female and male entrepreneurship can be established in the economic literature (Verheul et al., 2004): factors that determine entrepreneurship in general (Wennekers et al., 2002; Carree et al., 2002, and others), factors that influence female participation in the labour force (Kovalainen et al., 2002; Maume, 1999; Ward and Pampel, 1985, and others), and factors that influence female entrepreneurship (Kovalainen et al., 2002; Charles et al., 2001; Verheul et al., 2004).

The studies mentioned above show that the factors affecting entrepreneurship that would equally apply to both genders and across countries are very difficult to identify. In several studies the perception of good business opportunities is assumed to be important for entrepreneurship for both genders (Eckhardt and Shane, 2003; Shane and Venkataraman, 2000; Reynolds et al., 2003). There is a lack of economic literature investigating gender differences in perception of business opportunities, in both their perception and exploitation, in more detail than just monitoring the number of individuals who own and run their own firm. The present study aims at providing a clearer insight into gender differences on necessity- and opportunity-driven entrepreneurship as well as on gender differences of opportunity perception in Slovenia.

The ability of an individual for entrepreneurship can be regarded as one of the major determinants of entrepreneurship (Davidsson, 1991). Shane (2000) demonstrated the impact of entrepreneurs' competence and knowledge on acting on business opportunities. An entrepreneur is an individual who has the ability to evaluate possibilities and who is motivated to enter and to persist in the entrepreneurship process (Shaver and Scott, 1991). Briefly, the entrepreneur should have *capacity* – the entrepreneurial skills/knowledge and motivation, to turn opportunities into something that creates enduring value. Whether men and women in Slovenia differ regarding their entrepreneurial capacity, is also the research question we try to answer.

Firm's growth is regarded as a key to economic development and to the creation of wealth and employment. Therefore, besides the 'quantity' of entrepreneurship (number of entrepreneurs), the 'quality' of entrepreneurship (value added, contribution to employment, sustainable growth) also matters. Two main streams in the literature can be found. The first is based on longitudinal research designs studying the actual growth (Liao and Welsch, 2003; Gundry and Welsch, 2001), while the second focuses on growth expectations of those entering into the entrepreneurship. The growth subjectively expected by the entrepreneur is objectively constrained by the entrepreneurial capabilities of the entrepreneur and by the business environment and differs in terms of type of business, expected export, competition, etc. (Bager and Schott, 2004; Delmar and Davidsson, 1999). Our chapter is primarily focusing on entrepreneurs who are in the start-up phase of entrepreneurial process and the actual growth cannot be established yet. To get a more detailed insight we also made some comparison of growth expectations of entrepreneurs in established firms, older than three and a half years.

Empirical growth studies researching factors of growth frequently address issues of specific interest to the researcher in a way that makes comparability with other studies difficult. Following the theory that the growth of a firm is, to a certain extent, willed by entrepreneurs and managers who make decisions in the firm (Penrose, 1959, discussion about this in Davidsson and Wiklund, 1999), researchers frequently explore the motivational, behavioural and personal factors that lead to growth. Overall, human capital variables are linked with firm's growth; for example Gundry and Welsh (2001) found out that the entrepreneurial intensity (that is, commitment to the firm's success) differentiates high-growth entrepreneurs from low-growth ones. But studies of gender differences in this topic have yielded contradictory findings (Orser et al., 1998; Kolvereid, 1992). It is not clearly established if growth aspirations of male and female entrepreneurs are statistically different.

The chapter attempts to make four main contributions to the understanding of gender differences in entrepreneurship in Slovenia. The first is to provide a clearer insight into the current state of female entrepreneurship in Slovenia. The second is to explain gender differences in the process of perception of business opportunities of Slovenian male and female entrepreneurs. The third is to provide a clearer insight into gender differences regarding entrepreneurial capacity, while the fourth intended contribution is to enhance the understanding of gender differences in entrepreneurial growth aspirations in Slovenia.

The outcome of our research is expected to contribute to the research results of the Diana Project, which is dedicated to the investigation of the phenomena of female business owners and business growth activities.

COUNTRY CONTEXT

Slovenia, a middle-income developed country of two million inhabitants with per capita GDP of 20274 US$ (in purchasing power parities) joined the European Union in May 2004. Statistical data (*Statistical Yearbook of the Republic of Slovenia, 2003*) show that the basic characteristics of employment in Slovenia are very similar to those in other European countries. Women represent 45.5 per cent of paid employed in Slovenia, but only 38.8 per cent of persons employed in R&D activities. Some 54.7 per cent of all employed in services were women. Regarding unemployment, the ILO unemployment rate for men was 5.7 per cent and 6.3 per cent for women (in the 2nd quarter of

2002). Women in Slovenia have, in general, a similar level of education to men. They represent almost 61 per cent of the population, aged 15 and over, that have no/incomplete/completed basic education; 46.7 per cent of those who have secondary vocational, secondary or post-secondary education, and more than 51 per cent of those with higher and post-graduate education. But this range of completed education does not ensure that women participate equally in legislatorial and managerial positions: only 29.1 per cent of legislators and managers are women (*Statistical Yearbook, 2003*).

People in Slovenia are more than three times less likely to be involved in early-stage entrepreneurial activities than is the average across GEM countries. In 2004 there were on average 2.6 persons per 100 adults between the ages of 18 and 64 years who took some action towards creating a new business in the past year in Slovenia (Rebernik et al., 2005). Gender differences in Slovenian entrepreneurship rates are comparable with other middle-income countries (a per capita GDP between 10000 and 25000 US$). There are on average 44.2 women involved in entrepreneurship per 100 men in 2004 in Slovenia. The most entrepreneurially active age group across all GEM countries consists of people who are between 25 and 34 years old. This also holds true for men in Slovenia, while women in Slovenia are on average most entrepreneurially active between 35 and 44 years of age.

As our prior studies pointed out (Tominc and Rebernik, 2004), the general climate towards female entrepreneurship in Slovenia is in no way negative. But there are several aspects that lead to the conclusion that women in entrepreneurship don't have the same opportunities as men. Within GEM, several aspects of social support for female entrepreneurship were analysed by the opinions of 37 carefully selected national experts (coming from the government, chambers of commerce and business associations, universities and research institutes, etc.). Only six of them were women, therefore gender differences among them were not analysed. The second source of data is the research of the Slovenian Entrepreneurship Observatory where the survey of 442 female and male entrepreneurs was done (Rebernik et al., 2004b).

Both experts and male/female entrepreneurs rated the statement that in Slovenia women are encouraged to self-employ or set up a new venture, very low. They believe that there are only a few promotion programmes that would encourage women to act on business opportunities. Legislative and promotion actions are mainly centred towards the promotion of equality between men and women, but there are only a few such actions that would take into account the specific needs of women and help them in their efforts to participate in entrepreneurial activities. Similar findings were also stated by The European Observatory for SMEs (1996). Support and developmental programmes in some European countries are mainly centred on providing equal opportunities for men and women and do not focus on female entrepreneurship itself.

We also found substantial differences in opinions between female entrepreneurs and experts about women having equal opportunities to men in accessing the same number of good business opportunities. Female entrepreneurs rated this statement statistically significantly lower than experts. On the other hand, there are no significant differences regarding this aspect between experts and male entrepreneurs.

The analysis of the differences in opinions between male and female entrepreneurs leads us to the conclusion that there aren't equal conditions for men and women to access good business opportunities. It emerged that a statistically significant lower average estimate was rated by female entrepreneurs, while male entrepreneurs believe to a greater extent that women have equal opportunities to access good business opportunities as themselves.

There is a variety of reasons why women have more difficulties in accessing good business opportunities than men. The traditional structure of education and employment can certainly be considered one of them. In Slovenia, women are mainly employed in a small number of services and labour-intensive sectors, less suitable for entrepreneurial activities. It is also true (Tominc, 2002) that women have, on average, a higher degree of professional competence than men in jobs with a predominantly male workforce.

Taking into account the fact that women still represent an unexploited source for entrepreneurship since their participation rate still lags behind that of men, it appears that setting up efficient mechanisms for the promotion of female entrepreneurship (educational programmes, the creation of informal connections or networks between female participants, financing of ventures, etc.) could represent a source for entrepreneurial ideas in Slovenia in the future.

HYPOTHESES AND THE RESEARCH MODEL

Individuals participate in entrepreneurial activities for two main reasons: they start a new business to exploit a perceived business opportunity or they are pushed into entrepreneurship because all other options for work are either absent or unsatisfactory. It emerged that 97 per cent of individuals involved in business start-ups are either 'opportunity' or 'necessity' entrepreneurs (Acs et al., 2005). In 2004 a great variability is observed in the balance of opportunity and necessity entrepreneurship. On a world scale, on average about 65 per cent of those involved into entrepreneurial endeavours claim that they are attempting to take advantage of a business opportunity, while 35 per cent state that they are doing so because they have no other viable employment option. In Slovenia, the ratio between opportunity and necessity entrepreneurs is more favourable and accounts for roughly 80 per cent of opportunity and 20 per cent of necessity entrepreneurship (Rebernik et al., 2005).

Our first research question is whether there are gender differences in participation of men and women in Slovenia in the opportunity- and necessity-based entrepreneurship. The following hypothesis H1 is stated:

H1: The participation of men and women in opportunity- and necessity-based entrepreneurship in Slovenia statistically differs.

With the increased attention to the early stages of entrepreneurship process in recent years, the concept of opportunities has been increasingly used in entrepreneurship research (Eckhardt and Shane, 2003; Shane and Venkataraman, 2000; Reynolds et al., 2003). Davidsson (2003) suggests that the opportunity concept is arguable. For example, opportunity is by almost all definitions known to be a favourable situation – it is known to be profitable. From this point of view individuals cannot know whether or not what they pursue is an opportunity – only successful actions can therefore be marked as opportunities. Since our chapter is focused particularly on start-up entrepreneurs, evaluating opportunities in a retrospective way is not possible. This question leads to the concept of *perceived opportunities*, and is adopted in our study. Based on the literature and available data our second research question is whether men and women in Slovenia differ in their perceptions of good business opportunities. The following hypothesis H2 states:

H2: The perception of good business opportunities in Slovenia is statistically different between men and women.

Following the theory of growth set up by Penrose (1959) researchers explored the motivation, behavioural and personal factors that lead to venture creation and its growth. The new venture is viewed as a creation process, performed by an individual (or individuals), who has the ability to perceive and evaluate possibilities and who is motivated to exploit them by his/her preferences and personal and business goals (Shaver and Scott, 1991). A higher degree of motivation for entrepreneurship could be expected in environments where entrepreneurship is socially legitimate and viewed as an acceptable behaviour (Liao and Welsch, 2003), and where the opportunity costs of entering an entrepreneurial career are low (Verheul et al., 2001). Individuals are often attracted to entrepreneurship by the expectation of great material and/or non-material benefits (Hofstede et al., 1998) like social status and respect. However, an individual enters into a process with limited knowledge and skills. Although the entrepreneur will accumulate information and experience during the process (Delmar and Davidsson, 1999), the initial self-confidence into his/her skills and knowledge for entrepreneurship matters. Shane (2000) demonstrated an impact of entrepreneurs' competences and knowledge in acting on business oppor- tunities. The entrepreneur should have capacity – the entrepreneurial skills/ knowledge and motivation, to turn opportunities into something that creates enduring value. Whether men and women differ regarding entrepreneurial capacity is the next research question. The above discussion suggested hypotheses H3 and H4:

H3: Entrepreneurial capacity – motivation of men and women in Slovenia is statistically different.

H4: Entrepreneurial capacity – skills and knowledge of men and women in Slovenia are statistically different.

Several studies have shown that small and medium-sized firms are of great and growing importance to the economy. In particular they are expected to help solve unemployment and economic recession, especially by creation of new jobs (Reynolds et al., 2003; Arenius et al., 2004; Storey, 1994). In a small firm the importance of the owner's/ manager's willingness to grow is likely to be relatively greater than in a large firm. But not all entrepreneurs are willing to grow their business, since they may expect some consequences of growth to be negative and in conflict with their goals (Kolvereid, 1992; Storey, 1994). Our chapter deals with growth expectations of those individuals who are in a start-up phase of entrepreneurial process, and therefore the actual growth cannot yet be measured. The role of gender in a company's growth is vague. Liao and Welsch (2003) report on a study of Norwegian entrepreneurs made by Kolvereid (1992), which found no significant relationship between growth aspirations of entrepreneurs and their experience, gender, location and size of their business. Other researchers claim that gender is an influential feature for a company's growth – being female is supposed to have a negative effect on growth, and female entrepreneurs rarely become 'growth entrepreneurs' (Kjeldsen and Nielsen, 2004). Since it is not clearly established if growth aspirations of male and female entrepreneurs are statistically different, hypothesis H5 is proposed to enhance the understanding on this topic in Slovenia:

H5: The entrepreneurial growth aspirations of men and women in Slovenia are not statistically different.

The frame of our analysis is presented in Figure 14.1.

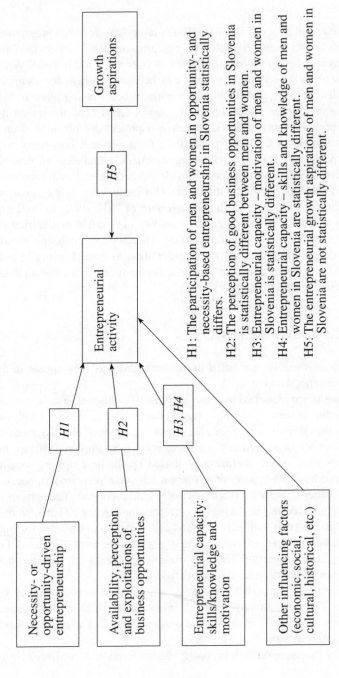

Figure 14.1   Testing for gender differences in entrepreneurial activity

H1: The participation of men and women in opportunity- and necessity-based entrepreneurship in Slovenia statistically differs.

H2: The perception of good business opportunities in Slovenia is statistically different between men and women.

H3: Entrepreneurial capacity – motivation of men and women in Slovenia is statistically different.

H4: Entrepreneurial capacity – skills and knowledge of men and women in Slovenia are statistically different.

H5: The entrepreneurial growth aspirations of men and women in Slovenia are not statistically different.

DATA

The main data source for our study is GEM, a large-scale research programme of entrepreneurship launched with ten countries in 1997. Since then the coverage has widened to 43 countries from all over the world in 2004. While two basic sources of economic growth can be distinguished, for example, major established firms, and the entrepreneurial process taking place in new and growing enterprises (Reynolds et al., 2003), GEM concentrates on the latter. The primary data in the GEM research project are obtained from a survey of a sample of the adult population, from personal interviews with national experts, and from a detailed questionnaire completed by national experts. Secondary data are obtained from established international sources of standardized data like Eurostat, OECD, etc. Our study relies on the survey of adult population in Slovenia, with a sample size of 2012 adults in 2002 and 2030 adults in 2003. The entrepreneurial activity does not shift significantly from one year to another (Acs et al., 2005). Therefore, in analysing growth aspirations of entrepreneurs, individuals identified as entrepreneurs in both 2002 and 2003 research cycles in Slovenia, are included in the consolidated sample, consisting of 357 entrepreneurs.

VARIABLES AND METHODS

Explanations of variables are listed in the same order as they appear in the hypotheses described above.

Entrepreneurs are identified as those individuals, who are, first, personally involved in the creation of the new ventures or who are, second, employed as owners-managers of new firms, less than 42 months old. To measure gender differences in opportunity- or necessity-driven entrepreneurship, the entrepreneurs were asked whether they started up the new venture because they perceived business opportunities (opportunity entrepreneurs), or because they had no better choices for work (necessity entrepreneurs). The number of men/women involved in early stages of entrepreneurship per 100 men/women who are 18 to 64 years old were counted and the proportion rates for both genders and for both motives for starting a new venture were calculated. For both genders the proportions of opportunity and necessity entrepreneurs among all entrepreneurs were also calculated.

The perception of (perceived) business opportunities is measured by the share of adults who are 18 to 64 years old and answered YES to the question: *In the next six months will there be good opportunities for starting a business in the area where you live?*

One part of the entrepreneurial capacity, the motivation, is measured by the share of adults of age 18 to 64 years who answered YES to the question: *Do those successful at starting a new business have a high level of status and respect?*

The other part of the entrepreneurial capacity, the skills and knowledge, is measured by the share of adults who are 18 to 64 years old and answered YES to the question: *Do you have the knowledge, skill and experience required to start a new business?*

Growth aspirations of entrepreneurs can be divided into those that are subjectively stated by the entrepreneur and those that are objectively possible, regarding characteristics of their products/services, expected export, competition, etc. The growth aspirations of entrepreneurs were assessed by taking into account their anticipation of increase in the number of new jobs, while potential of their ventures to grow was estimated upon their opinions about creation of new markets and market expansion with their products/services and export orientation:

1. *degree of growth aspiration – employment*, is found in those male and female entrepreneurs who intend to increase the number of jobs by 20 or more in the next five years;

2. *degree of growth aspiration – employment/market creation*, is found in those male and female entrepreneurs who intend to increase the number of jobs in the next five years by 20 or more or plan some market expansion/creation for their products/services;

3. *degree of growth aspiration – employment/market creation/export*, is found in those male and female entrepreneurs who intend to increase the number of jobs by 20 or more, plan some market expansion/creation for their products/services or export more than 50 per cent of their sales.

Besides gender of respondents, their age as well as the age of the venture were taken into account. While the main focus of our study were gender differences, we also expected that the age of respondents may be important. Regarding the age of their ventures, three groups of entrepreneurs were established. The first are *nascent entrepreneurs* who have taken some action towards creating a new business, the second are *new entrepreneurs* who are employed as owners/managers of new businesses, which have paid wages or salaries for less than 42 months, while *established entrepreneurs* are those who are employed as owners/managers of businesses that have paid wages or salaries for more than 42 months.

The independent samples t-test was used to test gender and age differences on variables described above. The general criteria to accept the hypotheses is that the difference is statistically significant at the 5 per cent level (two-tailed test).

FINDINGS

Table 14.1 reports the results on participation rates of men and women in opportunity and necessity entrepreneurship in Slovenia in 2003, overall for 18 to 64-year-old adults, as well as for five main age groups.

Table 14.1   Number of men/women involved in early stages of entrepreneurship per 100 men/women

	Men	Women	Stat. signif. (2-tailed)
Opportunity			
Overall 18–64 years old	4.95	1.14	0.000
18–24 years old	4.65	0.71	0.047
25–34 years old	10.48	1.49	0.000
35–44 years old	3.31	2.34	0.564
45–54 years old	4.15	0.65	0.023
55–64 years old	0.67	0.00	0.349
Necessity			
Overall 18–64 years old	1.10	1.65	0.175
18–24 years old	0.00	0.00	–
25–34 years old	0.00	0.76	0.240
35–44 years old	1.46	0.00	0.087
45–54 years old	2.40	1.50	0.524
55–64 years old	1.35	0.00	0.195

There are significant differences between men and women participation rates in opportunity-based entrepreneurship if the overall (18–64 years old) participation rates are compared ($p = 0.000$), while regarding age groups separately, significant gender differences are found for those who are 18 to 24 ($p = 0.047$) and 25 to 34 years old ($p = 0.000$). After the age of 34 years gender differences in opportunity-driven entrepreneurship are not significant.

Regarding the necessity-based entrepreneurship, gender differences are not statistically significant, nor are overall participation rates within age groups.

The proportions of opportunity and necessity entrepreneurs among all entrepreneurs are also calculated for both genders. Proportions are reported only for all ages (18–64 years) together. Thus, results should be treated with care. Since a very limited number of entrepreneurs were found in the sample, estimates of proportions are less reliable. Nevertheless, to illustrate this topic, results are reported. On average 30.97 per cent of female entrepreneurs and 17.34 per cent of male entrepreneurs were pushed into entrepreneurship because they had no better option for work (difference is not significant, $p = 0.267$), while 69.03 per cent of female entrepreneurs and 77.81 per cent of male entrepreneurs were exploiting the perceived business opportunity (difference is not significant, $p = 0.504$).

It can be concluded that women are less frequently involved in entrepreneurship because of opportunity than men between the age of 18 to 34 years, while the participation rates of men and women pushed into entrepreneurship out of necessity do not significantly differ. Thus, hypothesis H1 can be partly accepted: on average gender differences in opportunity entrepreneurship are significant (within age groups this holds for younger entrepreneurs who are 18 to 34 years old), while in necessity entrepreneurship they are not.

The study of hypothesis H1 also leads to the question whether gender differences in opportunity perception in Slovenia exist, therefore to the analysis of hypothesis H2. As already mentioned, the perception of (perceived) business opportunities, is measured by the share of adults, who are 18 to 64 years old and answered yes to the question: *In the next six months will there be good opportunities for starting a business in the area where you live?*

Among adults of age 18 and 64 years there are, on average, 32.38 per cent of those who believe that in the area where they live, good business opportunities are likely to appear within the next six months. The percentage of men who believe that such opportunities are likely to appear is higher (34.63 per cent) than that of women (30.15 per cent), but the difference is not significant ($p = 0.204$). We also found that the age of respondents matters. The highest percentage of those who believe that good business opportunities are likely to appear within the next six months belong to the age group between 18 to 24 years, for both genders: men 51.82 per cent and women 46.33 per cent. In all other age groups the proportions are smaller and in addition, in all age groups gender differences are not significant (all $p > 0.05$). This leads us to the following question: if the perception of opportunities is equal for men and women, why are they less frequently exploited by women than by men? We will omit the research into this question as it exceeds the boundaries of this study. Therefore, hypothesis H2, that gender is associated with the perception of good business opportunities in Slovenia cannot be confirmed.

Motivation as a part of entrepreneurial capacity was analysed through the question of whether individuals who successfully established a new company are respected and have a high status in society. The question was responded to positively by, on average, 74.11 per cent of men and 79.90 per cent of women (gender differences are not statistically significant, p = 0.052). In all age groups the proportion of women is higher than that of men, but the highest proportion for both genders appears in the age group of 18–24 years old, where the majority believes that successful founders of new companies are respected in society and enjoy a high social status. On average, it is believed by 82.17 per cent of men and as much as 91.33 per cent of women. Gender differences in all age groups are not statistically significant (all p > 0.05). Gender difference in the motivation for entrepreneurship cannot be confirmed; the hypothesis H3 is rejected.

Following are results of the analysis of the skills and knowledge part of entrepreneurial capacity. On average, almost half of adult males believe (49.93 per cent) that they have such skills and knowledge, whereas only 27.12 per cent of women share this opinion (gender differences are statistically significant at p = 0.000). The lowest proportion of those who believe that they have the necessary skills and knowledge is found within the age group of those who are 18 to 24 years old: 37.95 per cent of men and 10.83 per cent of women (the difference is significant at p = 0.000). In all other age groups the proportions for both men and women are higher, and in all age groups gender differences are significant (p < 0.05); except for those who are 25 to 34 years old (p = 0.392). Therefore gender is an important issue when people regard their knowledge and skills needed for entrepreneurship; hypothesis H4 is accepted.

Table 14.2 reports the results on growth aspirations of male and female entrepreneurs. Regarding the age of their ventures they are divided into nascent/new and established entrepreneurs.

Table 14.2   Entrepreneurial aspirations among nascent/new and established male and female entrepreneurs in Slovenia, GEM 2002 and 2003

	Nascent/new entrepreneurs		Established entrepreneurs	
	Men %	Women %	Men %	Women %
Growth aspirations – employment	23.36	26.32	1.89	5.66
Growth aspirations employment/ market creation	28.97	34.21	1.26	1.89
Growth aspirations employment/ market creation/export	11.21	2.63	1.26	0.00

The percentage points between men and women differ in nascent/new, as well as in established enterprises, but there are no statistically significant differences in growth aspirations across genders. Notably, it cannot be proven ($p > 0.05$) that men have greater growth aspirations than women. In our sample, the percentage of female entrepreneurs with aspirations for employment and employment/market creation is higher than that of male entrepreneurs.

On the basis of data available, we cannot state that in Slovenia men have higher growth aspirations than women; we thus confirm hypothesis H5, but we can conclude that people tend to have higher entrepreneurial aspirations in the beginning of their entrepreneurial endeavour than people who are established entrepreneurs. There are no gender differences in this respect ($p < 0.01$), except in one case: it is also impossible to state that among nascent/new female entrepreneurs there is a significantly higher percentage of those with entrepreneurial aspirations for employment/market creation/export than the percentage found in female established entrepreneurs.

The results are consistent with some other research (for example, Schott and Bager, 2004) showing that entrepreneurial aspirations seem to be higher in nascent entrepreneurs than among the entrepreneurs in new firms and established entrepreneurs. Various explanations can be found in the literature on reasons why entrepreneurial aspirations in nascent/new entrepreneurs are, as a rule, higher than the aspirations of established entrepreneurs (Carter et al., 1997a; Brown and Kirschoff, 1997). To mention just two: survival of ventures and learning. A large number of new ventures do not survive, and it is likely that those who do not survive have the highest and most unreal expectations. It is also very likely that nascent/new entrepreneurs acquire specific knowledge and skills about enterprises and the entrepreneurial environment, which subsequently lowers their expectations.

CONCLUSIONS AND POLICY IMPLICATIONS

Even though there are no formal barriers for Slovenian women to engage in entrepreneurial activities and the social climate regarding female entrepreneurship is seemingly favourable, women in Slovenia are less likely to become entrepreneurially active out of opportunity than men, especially between 18 to 34 years old, which is in general the most entrepreneurially active period all over the world.

Expectations about the availability of good business opportunities do not differ across genders, therefore the question why women less frequently exploit perceived business opportunities is still open. The possible reason could be that women have less self-confidence in their skill, knowledge and experience, as our study pointed out, although statistical data show a similar level of formal education for both men and women in Slovenia. But it is true that women are mainly employed in a small number of services and labour-intensive sectors, less suitable for entrepreneurial activities.

Women also do not differ from men regarding the opinion that successful entrepreneurs in Slovenia are respected in society, but it seems that this fact does not motivate them to the same extent as men.

In the Slovenian GEM study (Rebernik et al., 2004a) it was found that entrepreneurial growth aspirations in Slovenia were much higher than in other European countries. In 2003, there were 13.11 per 100 adults entering entrepreneurship (nascent and new male/female entrepreneurs), aged between 18 and 64 who intended to increase the number of jobs by 20 or more, plan some market expansion/creation for their products/services or export more than 50 per cent of their sales in Slovenia, which places Slovenia far ahead of the rest of Europe (Sweden taking second place with 8.46, and with the average being 5.18 for all 17 European countries). In the present study there was no evidence found for the notion that the entrepreneurial growth aspirations of women are lower than those of men. However, when compared with those who have just started their businesses with established entrepreneurs, both male and female entrepreneurs demonstrated lower growth aspirations.

A detailed insight into female entrepreneurship in Slovenia showed considerable unexploited possibilities. Female entrepreneurs in Slovenia usually do not face prejudice against their entrepreneurial career. There are no legal obstacles that would limit women from owning an enterprise. Recently, appropriate legislation was adopted, which grants equal opportunities for both genders (the Equal Opportunities Act, the Employment Act and the Parental Protection and Family Benefits Act). But women decide to become entrepreneurially active less frequently than men.

Since women remain an unexploited source of entrepreneurship, setting up effective mechanisms for the promotion of female entrepreneurship could become an important source of entrepreneurial ideas in Slovenia. Support and development programmes in some European countries mainly focus on ensuring equality between genders and do not focus on female entrepreneurship itself. Such programmes are rarely adopted to cater for the special needs of female entrepreneurs. The possibilities for setting up specialized programmes for financing start-ups set up by women should be studied, and the necessary infrastructure should be established (governmental and non-governmental bodies), which would help female entrepreneurs in various phases of their companies.

REFERENCES

Acs, Z.J., P. Arenius, M. Hay and M. Minniti (2005), *Global Entrepreneurship Monitor 2004 Executive Report*, Wellesley, MA and London: Babson College and London Business School.

Arenius, P., A. Erkko and A. Kovalainen (2004), *Finland GEM Executive Summary 2003*, Esopoo, Finland: Helsinki University of Technology.

Bager, T. and T. Schott (2004), 'Growth expectations by entrepreneurs in nascent firms, baby businesses and mature firms: analysis of the Global Entrepreneurship Monitor surveys in Denmark 2000–2003', paper presented at 1st GEM Research Conference, Berlin, Germany.

Brown, T.E. and B.A. Kirschoff (1997), 'The effects of resource availability and entrepreneurial orientation on firm growth', *Frontiers of Entrepreneurship Research*, 32–46.

Brush, C.G. (1992), 'Research on women business owners: past trends, a new perspective and future directions', *Entrepreneurship: Theory and Practice*, **16**(4), 5–30.

Carree, M.A., A.J. van Stel, A.R. Thurik and A.R.M. Wennekers (2002), 'Economic development and business ownership: an analysis using data of 23 OECD countries in the period 1976–1996', *Small Business Economics*, **19**(3), 271–90.

Carter, N., W.B. Gartner and P.D. Reynolds (1997a), 'Exploring start-up sequences', *Journal of Business Venturing*, **11**, 151–66.

Carter, N., M. Williams and P.D. Reynolds (1997b), 'Discontinuance among new firms in retail: the influence of initial resources, strategy and gender', *Journal of Business Venturing*, **12**, 125–45.

Charles, M., M. Buchmann, S. Halebsky, L.M. Powers and M.M. Smith (2001), 'The context of women's market careers: a cross national study', *Work and Occupations*, **28**(3), 371–96.

Davidsson, P. (1991), 'Continued entrepreneurship: ability, need and opportunity as determinants of small firm growth', *Journal of Business Venturing*, **6**, 405–29.

Davidsson, P. (2003), 'The domain of entrepreneurship research: some suggestions', in J. Katz and D. Shepherd (eds), *Advances in Entrepreneurship, Firm Emergence and Growth*, Vol. 6, pp. 315–72, Oxford: Elsevier/JAI Press.

Davidsson, P. and J. Wiklund (1999), 'Theoretical and methodological issues in the study of firm growth', JIBS – Jonkoping International Business School Working Paper Series 1999–6, Sweden. http://www.ihh.hj.se/eng/research/publications/wp/jibs_working_paper1999.htm.

Delmar, F. and P. Davidsson (1999), 'Firm size expectations of nascent entrepreneurs', JIBS – Jonkoping International Business School Working Paper Series 1999-7, Sweden, available at http://www.ihh.hj.se/eng/research/publications/wp/jibs_working_paper1999.htm.

Eckhardt, J. and S. Shane (2003), 'The individual-opportunity nexus', in Z.J. Acs and D.B. Audretsch (eds), *Handbook of Entrepreneurship Research*, Dordrecht, NL: Kluwer.

Gundry, L.K. and H.P. Welsch (2001), 'The ambitious entrepreneur: high growth strategies of women-owned enterprises', *Journal of Business Venturing*, **16**, 453–70, New York: Elsevier Science Inc.

Hofstede, G., N.G. Noorderhaven, A.R. Thurik, L.M. Uhlaner, A.R.M. Wennekers and R.E. Wildman (1998), 'Culture's role in entrepreneurship: Self-employment out of dissatisfaction', RIBES – Rotterdam Institute for Business Economic Studies, Working paper 9815, Rotterdam.

Kjeldsen J. and K. Nielsen (2004), 'Growth creating entrepreneurs: what are their characteristics and impact, and can they be created?', in M. Hancock and T. Bager (eds), *Global Entrepreneurship Monitor Denmark 2003*, Denmark: Borsens Forlag.

Kolvereid, L. (1992), 'Growth aspirations among Norwegian entrepreneurs', *Journal of Business Venturing*, **5**, 209–22.

Kovalainen, A., P. Arenius and L. Galloway (2002), 'Entrepreneurial activity of women in the global economy: analysis of data from 29 countries', paper presented at the Babson Kauffman Entrepreneurship Research Conference 2002, Boulder, Colorado.

Liao, J and H. Welsch (2003), 'Social capital and entrepreneurial growth aspiration: a comparison of technology- and non-technology-based nascent entrepreneurs', *Journal of High Technology Management Research*, **14**, 149–70.

Maume, D.J. (1999), 'Glass ceilings and glass escalators. Occupational segregation and race and sex differences in managerial promotions', *Work and Occupations*, **26**(4), 483–509.

Orser, B.J., S. Hogarth-Scott and P. Wright (1998), 'On the growth of small enterprises: the role of intentions, gender and experience', in *Frontier of Entrepreneurship Research*, Wellesley, MA: Babson College, pp. 366–80.

Parker, Simon (2004), *The Economics of Self-employment and Entrepreneurship*, Cambridge University Press, Cambridge.

Penrose, E.T. (1959), *Theory of the Growth of the Firm*, New York: Wiley.

Rebernik, M., P. Tominc and K. Pušnik (2005), *GEM Slovenia 2004 Report*, Institute for Entrepreneurship and Small Business Management, Faculty of Economics and Business, University of Maribor, Maribor.

Rebernik, M., P. Tominc, M. Glas and K. Širec-Rantaša (2004a), *GEM Slovenija 2003: Spodbujati in ohranjati razvojne ambicije*, Institute for Entrepreneurship and Small Business Management, Faculty of Economics and Business, University of Maribor, Maribor.

Rebernik, M., M. Rus, D. Močnik, K. Širec-Rantaša and P. Tominc (2004b), *Slovenski podjetniški observatorij 2004*, Institute for Entrepreneurship and Small Business Management, Faculty of Economics and Business, University of Maribor, Maribor.

Reynolds, P. B. Bygrave and E. Autio (2003), *GEM 2003 Executive Report*, Wellesley, MA and London: Babson College and London Business School, E.M. Kauffman Foundation.

Schott, T. and T. Bager (2004), 'Growth expectations by entrepreneurs in nascent firms, baby businesses and mature firms', in M. Hancock and T. Bager (eds), *Global Entrepreneurship Monitor Denmark 2003*, Denmark: Borsens Forlag.

Shane, S. (2000), 'Prior knowledge and the discovery of entrepreneurial opportunities', *Organization Science*, **11**(4), 448–69.

Shane, S. and S. Venkataraman (2000), 'The promise of entrepreneurship as a field of research', *Academy of Management Review*, **25**(1), 217–26.

Shaver, K.G. and L.R. Scott (1991), 'Person, process, choice: the psychology of new venture creation', *Entrepreneurship: Theory and Practice*, **16**(2), 23–45.

Statistical Yearbook of the Republic of Slovenia, 2003 (2004), Statistical Office of the Republic of Slovenia.

Storey, D. (1994), *Understanding the Small Business Sector*, London and New York: Routledge.

The European Observatory for SMEs, *Fourth Annual Report* (1996), Zoetermeer, The Netherlands: European Network for SME Research.

Tominc, P. (2002), 'Some aspects of the gender wage gap in Slovenia, *Društvena istraživanja (Journal for General Social Issues)*, **11**(6), 879–96.

Tominc, P. and M. Rebernik (2004), 'The scarcity of female entrepreneurship', *Društvena istraživanja (Journal for General Social Issues)*, **13**(4–5), 779–802.

Verheul, I. and A.R. Thurik (2001), 'Start-up capital: does gender matter?', *Small Business Economics*, **16**, 329–45.

Verheul, I., A.J. van Stel and A.R. Thurik (2004), 'Explaining female and male entrepreneurship across 29 countries', paper presented at 1st GEM Research Conference, Berlin.

Verheul, I., S. Wennekers, D. Audretsch and R. Thurik (2001), 'An eclectic theory of entrepreneurship: policies, institutions and culture', Tinbergen Institute Discussion Paper, Tinbergen Institute, Amsterdam.

Wagner, Joachim (2004), 'What a difference a Y makes – female and male nascent entrepreneurs in Germany', IZA Discussion Paper No. 1134, The Institute for the Study of Labor, Bonn (www.iza.org).

Ward, K.B. and F.C. Pampel (1985), 'Structural determinants of female labor force participation in developed nations, 1955–1978', *Social Science Quarterly*, **66**, 654–67.

Wennekers, A.R.M., L.M. Uhlaner and A.R. Thurik (2002), 'Entrepreneurship and its conditions: a macro perspective', *International Journal of Entrepreneurship Education*, **1**(1), 25–64.

15. Spain – the gender gap in small firms' resources and performance: still a reality?

Cristina Díaz and Juan J. Jiménez

INTRODUCTION

The under-capitalization of women-owned firms has been associated with their experiences of gender disadvantage within waged work and is reinforced by women's role in domestic labour. Accordingly, women will see their opportunities to amass financial, human and social capital constrained, which becomes translated into their creating firms that face structural disadvantages – firms in the service and retail sectors, of smaller size and younger (Marlow and Strange, 1994; Chell and Baines, 1998). Also, a lower economic performance has been linked to this initial under-capitalization (Brush, 1992; Boden and Nucci, 2000).

Accruing various forms of capital is crucial for business success, yet access to capital is shaped and influenced by the wider economic and social pressures that are deep-rooted and gender-based (Marlow and Carter, 2004; Breitenbach, 1999), this is to say, the gender belief system – attitudes towards social roles; gender stereotypes – can have an effect on women when attempting to secure resources for their ventures (Eagly and Karau, 2002).

According to the expectancy theory, pursuing growth would be a function of the business-owners' expectancy perceptions that their effort will bring the rewards they look forward to – and this will be influenced by their abilities and skills – together with the perceived value of the reward. Maybe it is not only that women have fewer resources but that they perceive the consequences of growth in a more negative way: more workload that would be incompatible with their family needs, loss of control, interference with other goals such as employees' well-being or quality of the products/services.

This study explores how the gender effect may influence the availability of resources in young and small firms of the service sector[1] that will therefore lead to differences in the performance of these firms. Our thesis is that the effect of the gender system on the under-capitalization and different performance of female-owned firms compared with their male counterparts will persist although to a lesser extent when controlling for structural variables. But, we wonder if women business-owners perceive success and the need for growth in the same way as their male counterparts. We seek to answer the following questions. Have men and women a different level of resources in the initial phase of their firms? Have they different gender roles that influence the time they can devote to them? If this is the case, do they achieve the same performance? And, do they perceive it in the same way?

Following this introduction, we take into account how the Spanish context is highly dependent on self-employment and business ownership. We discuss the theoretical background for this study that supports the methodological approach. The initial results of the study are then commented upon and we draw our conclusions from them.

COUNTRY CONTEXT

Female entrepreneurship in Spain, as in the rest of the world, is undergoing a period of expansion; women's participation in the entrepreneurial sector has tripled: in 1987 female business-owners were 10 per cent of the total and in 2004 they composed 31.28 per cent of this total.

However, from an international perspective, the women/men TEA (total entrepreneurial activity) ratio for 2003 puts Spain in the 21st position of the 31 countries of the GEM sample. This position is relatively low, and indicates that the situation for the Spanish female entrepreneur needs to be given a push forward, as it has been highlighted that the role of these women is important in order to achieve economic convergence with Europe (Coduras et al., 2004).

With respect to the businesses, female-owned ones are concentrated in the wholesale/retail sector followed by the hotel industry,[2] while male-owned firms are concentrated in agriculture, manufacturing, building and transport/communications. The size of the firms (in number of employees) is larger in certain sectors: manufacturing, building and hotel industries, mainly the ones where women are not present or are under-represented.[3]

Looking at owners' characteristics, we can observe that on average, women entrepreneurs are younger than their male counterparts (34 versus 40 years old). This may be a partial explanation of why women business-owners tend to be more highly educated than their male counterparts – the percentage of women with university degrees is nearly double. And women are more likely to work part-time.[4]

In relative terms, the lack of cultural and social support for the female entrepreneur is stronger in Spain – occupying the 27th position – than in other countries in the GEM study with less entrepreneurial tradition. This reality is translated into a comparatively scarce female participation in the business world, which could be explained mainly by the lack of social services that would help them solve the dilemma between professional career and family. More than half of the female panel of experts (55.6 per cent) doubt that entrepreneurship is especially difficult for a woman, but 35.9 per cent thought it was difficult or very difficult. They highlighted as barriers: access to grants, paperwork, and competition obstacles and having primary responsibility for the family (Coduras, 2004).

In Spain there is paucity of research on women entrepreneurs and the studies that have been done to date are descriptive and based on only small female samples. Their conclusions can be summarized as that women have less education, their main strategy being survival (de Luis Carnicer and Urquizu Samper, 1995), their businesses are small and concentrated in personal services, the hotel industry and retail – very female-oriented ones (de Luis Carnicer and Urquizu Samper, 1995; Sánchez-Apellániz, 2000). They pay special attention to their customer service (Belso Martínez, 2003; Chinchilla, 1997; de Luis Carnicer and Urquizu Samper, 1995) and their principal problems are financing the development of their firms and the lack of a viable business plan (Sánchez-Apellániz, 2000).

In Spain there is a great imbalance among employees due to gender. This is to say, the present situation of women is far from the ideal, as gender discrimination persists and is manifested through different quantitative indexes. Table 15.1 shows economic activity of males and females of working age.

Table 15.1   Population of 16 years old and older, classified by sex and economic activity

	Both sexes	Women	Men	% Women's share	% Female quota
Total	34474.3	17738.3	16736.0	51.45	100
Active	19330.4	7997.3	11333.1	41.37	45.08
Employed	17323.3	6846.4	10477.0	39.52	38.59
Unemployed	2007.1	1150.9	856.1	57.34	6.49
Searching for first job	278.4	175.0	103.3	62.86	0.98
Inactive	15143.9	9741.0	5403.0	64.32	54.92

Note: Data in thousands.

Source: Instituto Nacional de Estadística, 2004b.

Spain has the highest female unemployment rate of all European countries (15.8 per cent) and therefore one of the highest differences between female and male unemployment (only equal to Greece), it also has one of the lowest employment rates (35.9 per cent), is superior to only two other EU countries: Italy and Greece (32.9 per cent and 32.7 per cent respectively, the EU average being 43.9 per cent) and it has a higher male rate of 25.1 per cent (EU average 17.1 per cent).

Table 15.2   Average annual wage in euros by employee

	Both sexes	Women	Men	% Wage gap
All occupations	19 802.5	15 767.6	22 169.2	28.88

Source: Wages' Structure Survey, 2002.

There exists nearly a 30 per cent wage gap (see Table 15.2) and the percentage of women in management positions is 6.38 per cent of the female employed population, whereas for men the figure is 8.39 per cent.

Despite changes,[5] the effect of gender (traditional roles, norms, values and other sociological and psychological influences related to it) prevails over economic variables (for example, labour earnings or educational attainments) in the explanation of asymmetric housework allocation within two-earner couples (Alvarez and Miles, 2003).

THEORY

Greene et al. (1997) identified human capital and social capital as critical components of entrepreneurial knowledge and capabilities. Both types of capital are important because they represent initial 'endowments' that provide the basis for acquiring other sorts of resources, like physical, organizational and financial capital (Brush et al., 2001). With respect to social capital, a lot of studies find differences in access to it and the initial capitalization for women-owned and men-owned firms. Also, time is one of the main resources for business management, and more so, for new businesses (Lévesque and MacCrimmon, 1997; Cooper et al., 1997) and women due to their family responsibilities suffer competing demands on their time. Figure 15.1 shows all these components in a representation of the research model. It also depicts the position of our hypothesis – see below.

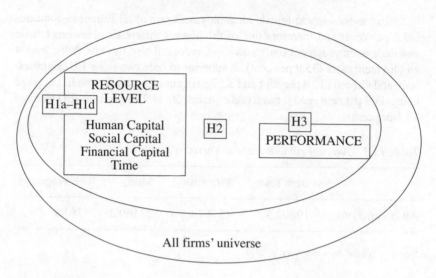

Figure 15.1   Research model

Human Capital

The educational level of women entrepreneurs has been found to be similar to that of men (Birley et al., 1987; Fischer et al., 1993), but women more frequently chose liberal studies over technical, business or engineering ones (Hisrich and Brush, 1983; Neider, 1987; Cliff, 1998). The majority of studies find that women have less industry experience[6] (Belcourt et al., 1991; Fischer et al., 1993; Carter et al., 1997), in helping to start up businesses (Fischer et al., 1993; Carter et al., 1997; Carter and Kolvereid, 1997; Cliff, 1998), and managerial experience (Stevenson, 1986; Fischer et al., 1993; Srinivasan et al., 1994, Marlow and Carter, 2004) because of the 'glass ceiling' that limits their promotion as salaried employees in other organizations and therefore obliges them to acquire this in their own firm.

   Hypothesis 1a: Female business-owners have a lower level of human capital than their male counterparts.

Social Capital

A person's social network is an indicator of his/her social capital (Bordieu, 1986; Casrud et al., 1987). Men devote more time to developing and maintaining their contacts (Cromie and Birley, 1992; Verheul and Thurik, 2000); maybe the family and domestic responsibilities lead women to experience more isolation than men (Moore and Buttner, 1997) as they will have less time to participate in networks of contacts (Mencken and Winfield, 2000).

Women are found to have homogeneity in their networks (Cromie and Birley, 1992; Aldrich et al., 1989; Smeltzer and Fann, 1989) although not more than men (Verheul et al., 2002). But, men and women occupy different positions in the social structures, with men having positions of higher status and less family and domestic responsibilities than women (Mencken and Winfield, 2000). It is probable that men share networks of contacts that have higher social and economic power than do women, which can be of greater assistance for gathering information and other resources during business start-up, as well as important sources of ongoing referrals (Greer and Greene, 2003; Mencken and Winfield, 2000; Uzzi, 1999).

Having a large number of strong redundant ties creates a disadvantage in the business world, as they offer a restricted range of knowledge and experiences beyond that already known by the entrepreneur and those close to him/her (Aldrich, 1989; Renzulli et al., 2000).[7] So, women, including greater proportions of kin in their discussion networks[8] may secure greater social support than men, but at the cost of sacrificing the necessary instrumental support needed for economic achievement (Hulbert, 1991). This led us to hypothesize that:

Hypothesis 1b: Female business-owners have fewer network contacts who can give them instrumental support than their male counterparts.

Financial Capital

Access to capital has been identified as a major challenge to female entrepreneurship (Carter et al., 2001). Previous research has found that women have a lower level of initial capitalization irrespective of sector (Carter and Rosa, 1998; Verheul and Thurik, 2000) and a higher probability of borrowing from family and friends (Haynes and Haynes, 1999) and/or using external financing (Carter and Rosa, 1998). This can be due to the fact that guarantees required are beyond the scope of many women's assets,[9] that they have poorer relationships with lenders[10] and they might have less experience.[11]

Some studies that take into account different structural characteristics find differences in the terms of credit – higher collateral (Riding and Swift, 1990; Coleman, 2000) and interest rates (McKechnie et al., 1998; Coleman, 2000) – or in the satisfaction with their banking experience (Riding and Swift, 1990; Fabowale et al., 1995). Carter et al. (2003) argue that the reason why there are not conclusive results may be due to the fact that the influence of gender is deep and rarely visible, factors from the demand side and from the supply side interact to co-produce the result that women business-owners in general continue to have a lower level of capitalization and a lower proportion of external financing. Therefore, we propose that:

Hypothesis 1c: Female business-owners have a lower level of capitalization and external financing than their male counterparts.

Time

Time-use surveys show that working women still bear primary responsibility for household chores, even when they also work full-time outside the home. Couples' behaviour is much less egalitarian and has changed much less than attitudes. Therefore, those women who choose the self-employment option are not escaping from subordination, still undertaking a dual role as business-owners and as carers (Marlow, 1997). Having to take full responsibility for the household[12] in combination with running a business means that they cannot attend to the business as much as a male entrepreneur – who is not subjected to such expectations by society. Women have to work longer hours to do both jobs and it is uncommon for them to expect support from their partners at home (Ahl, 2002).

The double burden limits the time women business-owners devote to their firm[13] (Loscocco et al., 1991; Tigges and Green, 1992; Rosa et al., 1994; Fasci and Valdez, 1998). And gender not only has a negative direct effect in the number of hours devoted to the business, it also has a negative indirect effect through other explicative variables (Verheul et al., 2004). Therefore, based on empirical results of previous studies, we propose that:

Hypothesis 1d: Female business-owners have a higher level of family responsibility, and this limits the time they devote to their firms, compared with their male counterparts.

Influence of Resources on Performance

Studies find that years of schooling (Robinson and Sexton, 1994), work experience and industry-specific experience (Bruederl et al., 1992; Cooper et al., 1994) can have a positive effect on a firm's performance. Venkataraman and Van den Ven (1998) find evidence that the survival and growth of an entrepreneurial firm depend on its ability to maintain and extend its network of inter-firm relationships. Cooper et al. (1994) argue that financial capital can provide a buffer against random shocks and can allow the pursuit of more capital-intensive strategies, which are better protected from imitation.

Women with families had more problems allocating time between family and business (Longstreth et al., 1987); they have to sacrifice leisure time in order to satisfy capably both roles. Women work fewer hours than desired in their firms: a fact that is significantly related to earnings (Clain, 2000; Fasci and Valdez, 1998; Robinson and Sexton, 1994; Rosa et al., 1994). Family situation affects performance differently depending on the owner's sex (Loscocco and Leicht, 1993).

Taking into account the fact that the majority of studies show that women business-owners seem to have fewer initial resources than their male counterparts, and that this renders new firms vulnerable, we propose that:

Hypothesis 2: Female-owned businesses' lower level of resources contribute to a lower economic performance of their businesses compared with their male counterparts.

Perception of Success

Female owners, on average, may be less concerned with financial rewards than male owners (Du Rietz and Henrekson, 2000; Cliff, 1998; Brush, 1992) and would assign more importance to social values and qualitative success measures (Cliff, 1998; Brush and Hisrich, 2000), such as self-fulfilment and goal achievement (Moore and Buttner, 1997), customer satisfaction and personal flexibility (Fasci and Valdez, 1998; Holmquist and Sundin, 1988).

Davidsson (1989) argues that most existing small firms do not grow to any considerable extent; neither do they have an interest in growth. And Cliff (1998) finds that female business-owners tend to establish maximum performance thresholds after which they do not want to grow more and these thresholds are lower that the ones of their male counterparts. We have to recognize the additional validity of a low-growth, less aggressive approach to earnings, along with the importance of business survival as a criterion of business success (Greer and Greene, 2003).

This is not to say that women do badly on the profit and economic front or that it is always secondary, but they also aspire to other goals, and maybe prioritize them in some moments of their lives. We hypothesize that due to the different influence of the gender system women business-owners would have different business goals and/or the balance needed between them and the personal goals is different for their male counterparts:

Hypothesis 3: Business-owners give different importance to different measures of performance by function of their gender.

METHOD AND DATA

The sample for the study was women and men entrepreneurs from a Spanish region, Castilla-La Mancha, and the data were collected from November 2004 to February 2005. The initial sample was selected from CAMERDATA consisting of new (between one to eight years old), small (with fewer than 100 employees) and from the service sector firms.[14] A questionnaire was sent to 835 firms; 177 of them we were not able to contact or were not in operation at the moment of the survey. A phone call was made to the firms for which we had the phone number, reminding them of the upcoming second mailing of the questionnaire. We received 112 responses,[15] therefore, the final response rate was 17 per cent.

Independent variables include business profile characteristics (firm size and age), gender of the owner/s,[16] resources such as human capital, social capital, financial capital and time. The dependent variables are revenues for 2003 and different types of satisfaction: personal, with their job and with the balance achieved between work and family.

We are going to examine if there are differences between independent variables for female- and male-managed firms with a non-parametric test. Second, the relationship between the different independent and dependent variables is investigated using correlation coefficients. Subsequently, through a series of regression analyses we investigate what independent variables help to explain the dependent ones and in what proportion.

FINDINGS

Non-parametric Tests Between Two Independent Samples

With the Mann-Whitney test we are going to examine if two independent samples (firms managed by a man/male team and firms managed by a

Table 15.3   Human capital

	Education	Sectoral experience	Management experience	Start-up experience	Age
U-Mann-Whitney	214.000	206.000	307.500	262.500	229.000
W Wilcoxon	710.000	641.000	538.500	493.500	482.000
Z	−2.361	−1.993	−0.228	−0.911	−2.190
Asintotic (bil) Sig.	0.018[a]	0.046[a]	0.820	0.362	0.029[a]
Mean rank					
Men	22.90	22.10	26.25	26.13	30.61
Women	33.77	29.20	23.50	23.50	21.91

Note: [a]significant at 0.01 level; [b]significant at 0.05 level; [c]significant at 0.1 level.

woman/female team) come from the same population, this is to say, if there are differences in the variables due to the variable selected to split the sample. Table 15.3 shows the results of the study of human capital.

Hypothesis 1a is not supported as women have a higher level of education and more sectoral experience, maybe because they are traditionally 'female sectors', and female business-owners are significantly younger than their male counterparts. Table 15.4 shows the results of the study of social capital.

Table 15.4   Social capital

	Network size	Time network	Family and friends	Acc./ lawyer	Other business-owner	Customers prov.	Homophi.
U-Mann-Whitney	199.500	215.500	287.000	252.000	224.000	173.500	203.000
W Wilcoxon	352.500	368.500	722.000	687.000	434.000	383.500	413.000
Z	−1.093	−0.712	−0.064	−1.360	−1.509	−2.808	−1.789
Asintotic (bil) Sig.	0.274	0.477	0.949	0.174	0.131[c]	0.005[a]	0.074[b]
Mean rank							
Men	25.12	24.57	24.90	23.69	27.28	24.02	28.00
Women	20.74	21.68	25.15	26.03	21.70	19.18	20.65

Note: [a]significant at 0.01 level; [b]significant at 0.05 level; [c]significant at 0.1 level.

Hypothesis 1b is partially supported as women have less business-owners and less customers/providers in their networks and therefore can have less access to information about opportunities or other resources. Also, we can appreciate

Table 15.5   Financial capital

	Initial capital	Personal funds	Family loans	Bank loans
U-Mann-Whitney	293.500	330.500	303.000	269.000
W Wilcoxon	789.500	826.500	799.000	522.000
Z	−0.023	−0.192	−1.049	−1.351
Asintotic (bil) Sig.	0.982	0.847	0.294	0.177[c]
Mean rank				
Men	25.47	26.66	25.77	29.32
Women	25.55	27.48	28.73	23.73

Note: [a]significant at 0.01 level; [b]significant at 0.05 level; [c]significant at 0.1 level.

that men have significantly more homophilous ties than women in the business world. Table 15.5 shows the results of the study of financial capital.

Hypothesis 1c is not supported as there are no significant differences in the initial capital used for starting up the firm, although in these subsectors this is not a barrier for entrance. But, we can point out that there seems to be a tendency for men to use bank loans more often than their female counterparts. Table 15.6 shows the results of the study of time devoted to the firm.

Table 15.6　Time

	Full-time	Type of income	Waged job	Another firm	Formative activity	Familiar responsib.	Family–work conflict
U-Mann-Whitney	319.500	294.000	115.500	121.000	121.000	118.000	84.500
W Wilcoxon	815.500	547.000	235.500	226.000	292.000	223.000	237.500
Z	–0.508	–0.769	–0.995	–0.842	–0.223	–0.405	–0.595
Asintotic (bil) Sig.	0.611	0.442	0.320	0.400	0.823	0.685	0.552
Mean rank							
Men (N)	26.31 (31)	27.70 (30)	18.08 (18)	18.45 (20)	16.22 (18)	16.94 (18)	13.97 (17)
Women (N)	27.98 (22)	24.86 (22)	15.70 (15)	16.14 (14)	16.86 (14)	15.93 (14)	15.32 (11)

Note: [a]significant at 0.01 level; [b]significant at 0.05 level; [c]significant at 0.1 level.

There is no support also for *hypothesis 1d* as there is no difference in the time devoted to the firm due to the sex of the owner. Women business-owners also consider their firm as a principal source of income for their family. There are no differences in family responsibility between men or women; this may be due to a different rhetoric by which men interpret responsibility as contributing with income. Also, it seems that women do not want to answer these questions maybe because they feel their answers would not fit with the masculine values dominant in the entrepreneurial world.

Correlation Analysis

(See Table 15.7 for the correlation matrix.) Individual women are more likely to use family loans than other types of businesses. And they tend to value their income from the firm as a second source of income for their family, maybe because it is lower than that of their partners.

The individual man has less education and a higher propensity to network with other men; this is a coherent relation with the fact that education and homophily are significantly negatively correlated in the sample.

The firms managed by mixed teams – mostly in the education services – are the largest in number of employees, their owners have a high level of education and they network more than other entrepreneurs with the other sex. Firms where the founding team is a male one – which are prevalent in the cleaning services – are younger, and their owners have a poor sectoral experience, maybe their labour experience has been far from the service sector. And, they are more likely to finance their firms with bank loans than with personal funds.

The size of the firm – measured in number of employees – is related positively and significantly to the education of the owner, whether it is a principal source of income for his/her family, and with the initial capital. Managers of older firms are more likely to have strong ties in their networks (kin, friends) and less start-up experience – although these relations are significant only at the 0.10 level – but these firms have been founded with significantly lower initial capital.

With respect to the characteristics of the owner, education is related in a positive way to management experience – although not very significantly – and negatively with homophily. Having strong ties in the network is positively related with having sectoral experience but negatively with having management experience. It might be because managers with management experience have a significantly larger network – which is negatively related to having a great number of kin in it – mostly composed of other business-owners.

Having accountants and lawyers in the network is negatively related to having other business-owners; maybe if they have mentors or role models in the latter group they do not need to ask for advice from the former. But when they are part of the network the business-owners are more likely to seek bank loans as a financing source than they are to use their personal funds for financing the firm. When business-owners relate to other counterparts it seems that this relation is more likely to occur with people of their own sex, who are working full-time in their firms and who consider their income as a main source of income for their family.

Considering the revenues of the firm as a main income for the family, influences business-owners' willingness to use more initial capital in their firms and from formal sources (bank loans) rather than personal ones (these are negatively related to using family loans and bank loans).

Female teams are less successful in terms of revenues even though their owners seem to be more satisfied in a personal sense than other types of owners. There are some variables that are highly and positively related to revenues. These are: number of employees, education, managerial experience,

Table 15.7   Correlation matrix

	1	2	3	4	5	6	7	8	9	10
1 individual man	1									
2 individual woman	$-.257^b$	1								
3 mixed team	$-.492^a$	$-.492^a$	1							
4 male team	$-.185^c$	$-.185$	$-.289^a$	1						
5 female team	$-.134$	$-.110$	$-.210^b$	$-.079$	1					
6 num. employees	$-.058$	$-.058$	$.223^b$	$-.087$	$-.168$	1				
7 firm age	$-.015$	$.137$	$.025$	$-.177^c$	$-.023$	$.053$	1			
8 education	$-.259^b$	$.090$	$.296^a$	$-.170$	$-.084$	$.260^b$	$.106$	1		
9 sectoral exp.	$-.116$	$.079$	$.150$	$-.231^b$	$.059$	$-.043$	$-.045$	$-.055$	1	
10 management experience	$-.021$	$.065$	$-.034$	$.090$	$-.103$	$.147$	$-.067$	$.178^c$	$-.002$	1
11 margin start-up experience	$-.003$	$-.080$	$-.017$	$.139$	$-.001$	$-.008$	$-.207$	$-.066$	$-.020$	$.209^c$
12 network size	$.158$	$-.144$	$-.007$	$-.018$	$-.040$	$.118$	$-.018$	$-.032$	$.180$	$.266^b$
13 kin-friends	$.076$	$.047$	$-.057$	$-.067$	$-.015$	$-.162$	$.188$	$.035$	$.189^c$	$-.273^b$
14 lawyer-accountant	$-.171$	$.083$	$.034$	$.058$	$.040$	$-.016$	$.055$	$.094$	$.024$	$-.091$
15 business-owner	$.066$	$-.110$	$-.066$	$.170$	$-.017$	$.133$	$-.106$	$.093$	$-.057$	$.222^b$
16 homophily	$.237^b$	$-.081$	$-.242^b$	$.097$	$.076$	$.097$	$.090$	$-.300^a$	$-.018$	$.034$
17 initial capital	$-.021$	$-.011$	$.058$	$-.074$	$.034$	$.306^a$	$-.283^a$	$-.065$	$-.021$	$.090$
18 pers. funds	$.141$	$.062$	$-.024$	$-.225^b$	$-.022$	$-.143$	$-.036$	$.066$	$-.021$	$.139$
19 family loan	$-.074$	$.251^b$	$-.081$	$-.044$	$-.049$	$.070$	$-.066$	$-.024$	$-.016$	$-.083$
20 bank loan	$-.057$	$-.104$	$.010$	$.234^b$	$-.047$	$.091$	$.101$	$-.181^c$	$.087$	$-.103$
21 full time	$-.044$	$.033$	$-.034$	$.044$	$.044$	$.160$	$.158$	$-.061$	$.162^c$	$.189$
22 type of income	$.011$	$-.179^c$	$.121$	$-.023$	$.044$	$.184^c$	$.080$	$-.161$	$.104$	$.062$
23 revenues	$.067$	$-.052$	$.109$	$-.060$	$-.215^b$	$.561^a$	$.142$	$.272^a$	$.138$	$.279^a$
24 job satisfaction	$-.093$	$-.048$	$.087$	$-.065$	$.151$	$.271^a$	$-.013$	$.145$	$.115$	$.095$
25 satisfaction with staff	$-.157$	$-.167$	$-.010$	$-.144$	$.227^b$	$-.099$	$-.173$	$-.009$	$.264^b$	$.098$
26 balance satisfaction	$-.135$	$.121$	$-.094$	$.041$	$.203$	$-.021$	$-.016$	$-.142$	$.145$	$-.030$

Note: [a]Significant at 0.01 level; [b]significant at 0.05 level; [c]significant at 0.1 level.

network size, initial capital and considering the firm as a main source of income for the family. Whereas having a high proportion of kin and friends – strong ties – in the network is related negatively as they commonly facilitate redundant information.

Having sectoral experience is correlated with personal satisfaction as the individual is working in an area where he/she has previous knowledge. And when the family helps the business-owner financially, this may imply that they support him/her and in this sense there is a lower possibility of conflict between family and business ownership. We can see that business-owners in larger firms that have used more initial capitalization seem to be more satisfied with their job.

11	12	13	14	15	16	17	18	19	20	21	22	23	24	25	26

1
-.184 1
-.216ᶜ -.216 1
-.128 .074 -.115 1
.084 .156 -.061 -.234ᵇ 1
-.050 .064 .041 -.134 .202ᶜ 1
-.083 .130 -.002 -.054 .117 .116 1
.285ᵃ -.050 .061 -.238ᵇ .067 -.041 -.194ᶜ 1
-.156 -.013 -.083 .059 -.129 -.035 -.032 -.295ᵃ 1
-.191ᶜ -.001 -.016 .268ᵇ -.097 .096 .194ᶜ -.755ᵃ -.090 1
-.055 .131 -.006 .011 .231ᵇ .312ᶜ .028 -.121 .083 .224ᵇ 1
-.011 .050 -.044 .056 .203ᵇ .260ᵇ .249ᵇ .140 -.092 -.055 .154 1
.007 .310ᵃ -.211ᶜ .082 .040 .112 -.018 .104 .053 -.072 .236ᵇ .207ᵇ 1
-.013 .107 -.042 .098 -.106 .112 .322ᵃ -.046 .102 -.020 .144 .232ᵇ .214ᶜ 1
-.171 .142 -.073 .185ᶜ -.033 -.110 .321ᵃ -.003 .021 -.027 -.014 .178ᶜ -.101 .275ᶜ 1
-.159 .018 -.145 -.028 -.011 -.067 .074 -.115 .202 -.012 .079 .137 -.001 .351 .343 1

Job satisfaction is a 'joker', being related on the one hand to revenues and on the other to satisfaction with staff and satisfaction with the balance achieved between work and family, both of which are correlated.

If we study the correlation between the dependent variables for the subsample of male-managed firms and for the subsample of female-owned firms we find differences (see Table 15.8). We find support for hypothesis 3, as business-owners have different relations between different measures of performance as a function of their gender.

Job satisfaction for men is related to the balance they can achieve between their work and family, whereas for women, job satisfaction is related not only to this variable but also to the revenues they achieve, as this factor may be

Table 15.8   Correlations between dependent variables for subsamples

	Male-owned firms						Female-owned firms					
	R	JS	PS	BS	PS	GI	R	JS	PS	BS	PS	GI
Revenues (R)	1						1					
Job satisfaction (JS)		1					0.459^b	1				
Satisfaction with staff (SS)			1						1			
Balance satisfaction (BS)		0.405^b		1				0.702^b		1		
Profitability satisfaction (PS)	0.460^b		0.494^b	0.433^b	1			0.615^b		0.625^b	1	
Growth intention (GI)						1						1

Note: ^{a}Significant at 0.01 level; ^{b}significant at 0.05 level; ^{c}significant at 0.1 level.

indispensable to achieve credibility and legitimacy in their homes and markets. The satisfaction with profitability achieved is related to revenues, satisfaction with staff and balance satisfaction for male business-owners and with job and balance satisfaction for female ones. The relation with revenues seems to show that male managers' satisfaction with profitability can be more correlated with the real profitability obtained by their firms.

We can also observe differences in the intentions for growth and in the expected consequences of it (see Table 15.9). Women do not intend to grow their firms to the same extent as men, and they highlight all the reasons for not growing to a greater level than men, except that growth can interfere with other goals. The difference is remarkable in that they want to maintain control, that they already devote a reasonable quantity of time and energy to the firm and that they want to balance work and personal lives. Despite this we can point out that a high proportion of women are pursuing growth and that men who do not want to grow are also concerned with family–work balance.

Regression Analysis

To further investigate the influence of gender[17] and the other factors on the firm revenues and other measures of performance, regression analyses are performed. The results of these regression analyses are presented in Tables 15.10 and 15.11. From the correlation matrix (Table 15.7) we have seen that

Table 15.9   Attitude to growth and expected consequences of it

	Men business-owners (%)	Women business-owners (%)
I intend to make the firm grow	83.6	69.7
I do not intend to grow my firm because:		
I have achieved the size in which I manage comfortably	54.5	66.7
I want to maintain control	36.4	62.5
I devote a reasonable quantity of time-energy to my firm	33.3	60.0
I want to balance work and personal life	63.6	90.9
Growth is not important for me	11.1	16.7
Growth can interfere with other goals	36.4	28.6
Environment is not favourable	20.0	37.5

there are important differences between the dependent variables in their relationship with the explanatory variables. The results of the regression analysis also show important differences in the degree to which the selection of explanatory variables can explain the dependent variables, where variance explained is relatively higher for REVENUES ($R^2 = 0.650$), and SATISFACTION WITH STAFF ($R^2 = 0.383$), as compared with the other variables (job satisfaction and satisfaction with work–life balance).

Regarding gender effects on the dependent variables, we see that although not significant, the fact that the firm is female-managed has a negative impact on revenues, but that women seem to have more personal satisfaction – whereas the interaction term for men showed a significant and negative impact on it – and satisfaction with the balance achieved between work and family. Hence hypothesis 2 is rejected as there is no evidence that female-owned businesses' have a lower economic performance compared with their male counterparts, a result that is logical taking into account that we have not found that they have a lower level of resources.

In order to study if the dependent variables are explained by different factors or their strength is different in function of the owner's/s' gender, we performed regressions for the most significant independent variables for the two subsamples.

We can observe that the variables that help to explain the general sample are more helpful for explaining the male sample. For the male-owned firms their size, the network size of the owner/s and his/their/her level of

Table 15.10   Male-owned firms and female-owned firms regression

	Revenues	Job satisfaction	Satisfaction with staff	Balance satisfaction
Male-owned firms				
Number of employees	0.413[b]	0.498[c]	−0.052	−0.026
Education	0.376[c]	0.086	0.142	−0.232
Management experience	−0.422[c]	−0.088	0.424	0.111
Network size	0.494[b]	−0.119	−0.145	−0.112
Kin-friends in the network	−0.309	−0.010	0.216	−0.257
Personal funds	−0.081	0.022	0.300	−0.088
Family loans	0.336	−0.259	−0.029	−0.369
Bank loans	−0.051	−0.149	−0.404	−0.039
Full-time dedication	0.075	−0.038	0.213	0.096
R^2	0.598	0.311	0.258	0.288
Female-owned firms				
Number of employees	0.231	0.084	−0.050	−0.079
Education	0.230	−0.193	−0.526	−0.472
Management experience	0.315	−0.249	0.340	0.237
Network size	0.183	0.465	0.151	−0.016
Kin-friends in the network	−0.177	−0.535	−0.448	−0.395
Personal funds	0.419	−0.060	−0.200	−0.134
Family loans	0.155	−0.030	−0.383	0.257
Bank loans	0.248	−0.307	−0.503	−0.210
Full-time dedication	−0.061	0.188	−0.175	0.355
R^2	0.869	0.578	0.471	0.582

Note: [a]Significant at 0.01 level; [b]significant at 0.05 level; [c]significant at 0.1 level.

education have a significant and positive effect on revenues. Contrary to our expectations management experience has a negative impact, this may be explained by the 'inertia effect', which induces them not to adapt to new techniques of management that are more adequate to the present environment.

For female-owned firms, although not significant, having managerial experience and having invested their own savings in the firm help to obtain higher revenues. Having financial support from the family has a positive effect on not achieving a balance between work and family but other types of support – as having kin in the networks – do not help in this sense.

Table 15.11   Regression results explaining different dependent variables

	Revenues	Job satisfaction	Satisfaction with staff	Balance satisfaction
Number of employees	0.496[a]	0.226	−0.144	−0.172
Firm age	0.211[b]	−0.130	−0.209	0.096
Men-owned firms	0.156	0.083	−0.315[b]	−0.003
Women-owned firms	−0.139	0.098	0.126	0.237
Education	0.174[c]	0.119	−0.026	−0.031
Sectoral experience	0.228[b]	0.140	0.105	0.114
Management experience	0.024	0.082	0.318[c]	0.131
Start-up experience	0.000	−0.051	−0.095	−0.038
Network size	0.200[c]	0.043	0.067	0.012
Kin-friends in the network	−0.237[b]	−0.078	−0.020	−0.223
Lawyer-accountant	0.109	0.087	0.182	−0.105
Business owner	−0.155	−0.282	0.055	0.004
Personal funds	0.150	−0.383	−0.095	−0.303
Family loans	0.089	−0.192	−0.084	0.028
Bank loans	−0.174	−0.412	−0.016	−0.228
Full-time dedication	0.142	0.102	−0.058	−0.080
R^2	0.650	0.208	0.383	0.202

Note: [a]Significant at 0.01 level; [b]significant at 0.05 level; [c]significant at 0.1 level.

CONCLUSIONS

We base our study on the fact that entrepreneurship, as is the labour market, is heavily influenced by the gender system of society, this is to say entrepreneurship is still a male domain. But, due to the fact that we control for some structural variables we find that the differences are minimized or even disappear as the firms have to compete in the same market conditions. So although we find that as a group, women and men business-owners show differences, we also find that there are lot of similarities. It seems that if women do not want to grow more it is not because they have a lower quantity of resources but because they may perceive the expected consequences of growth as more negative.

During the 20th century the social structures have evolved and there has been a progressive advance in women's participation in diverse aspects of social life. Despite this, we observe that the roles ascribed to women and to men are still different, so we can say that their participation in the economic, politic and social fields is not equal.

However, a third of the firms have been created by women, that is, women have not only been incorporated into the labour market but they are creating employment. This is the reason why in the European Conferences the important role that women have in the development of the SMEs has been highlighted. The extent to which the European economy is competitive will depend on the adequate promotion of the women's competences and the balanced participation of men and women in the positions for making decisions.

So, this is a phenomenon that should command greater attention and analysis in our country. And we believe that with further research, a clearer understanding of the role of gender in small business can be reached, and this in turn can lead to more effective social policy goals and practices.

NOTES

1. Structural characteristics of the firms will be controlled, so that the impact of the owner gender trait may be isolated from them, because the other way can lead us to equivocal results. There seems to be a tendency to sustain that women-owned firms have a similar level of success as male-owned ones (Kalleberg and Leicht, 1991; Johnson and Storey, 1993), especially if some structural variables are controlled, such as similar size, sector (Orhan, 2001; Du Rietz and Henkreson, 2000), age and location (Perry, 2002), but some studies control them and still find a disadvantage for women-owned firms (Du Rietz and Henrekson, 2000; Fasci and Valdez, 1998; Rosa et al., 1996; Cooper et al., 1994; Fischer et al., 1993).
2. Others being real estate companies and consulting firms, education, health/veterinary activities and social services.
3. Women managers are the majority in firms without employees (50.18 per cent), only 27.23 per cent of firms with less than ten employees are managed by women and 18.89 per cent of the firms with more than ten employees.
4. Only 6.9 per cent of the owners work part-time, women accounting for 67.28 per cent of them and if the cause is due to family responsibilities the percentage rises to 97.73 (Instituto Nacional de Estadística (2004a)).
5. In Spain, since 1975, the percentage of women with higher education has risen steadily, the female rate of labour force participation has doubled, and women postpone marriage and motherhood due to entry into the labour market and remain in it after these events (Alba, 2000; Carrasco and Rodríguez, 2000).
6. Although some studies find that women tend to create their businesses in industries where they have previous experience (Neider, 1987; Hisrich and Brush, 1984), these are not comparative studies.
7. Whereas weak ties, conversely, act as 'bridges' connecting to non-overlapping resources (Granovetter, 1973) and some studies find no differences in weak-tie networking by women entrepreneurs (Aldrich et al., 1997; Katz and Williams, 1997).
8. Hisrich and O'Brien, 1981; Sexton and Kent, 1981; Nelson, 1987; Cromie and Birley, 1992; Renzulli et al., 2000; Mencken and Winfield, 2000; Greeve and Salaff, 2003.
9. It might be that the wage gap contributes to a lower amount of personal savings (Greer and Greene, 2003).
10. This could be related to their difficulty in entering informal financial networks (Aldrich, 1989).
11. Decreasing their chances of gaining requisite capabilities needed to demonstrate management competence to capital providers.

12. Cliff (1998) finds that women business-owners devote nearly 5.7 hours more to their domestic chores and child care than their male counterparts.
13. Some studies find that men business-owners are more likely to work full-time than their female counterparts (OECD, 1998; Verheul and Thurik, 2000). And when they work part-time more women do so in order to fulfil family and domestic responsibilities, whereas men normally have another firm or waged occupation (Van Uxem and Bais, 1996).
14. Section nine of the IAE – Economic Activities Tax – includes: cleaning services, education, social work, cultural and recreational services, personal services, amusement parks and conference organization.
15. From which 13 were not taken into account because the firms were older than originally established.
16. We divided our sample into the following gender designations: 1) those in which the individual owner or the team members were male ($n^1 = 32$), 2) those in which the individual owner or the team members were female ($n^2 = 22$) and 3) those with mixed ownership ($n^3 = 42$). For having more disaggregate information in the correlation matrix we have distinguished between individual men, individual women, mixed team, male team and female team.
17. We do not include the mixed team in the regression as it generates multicollinearity problems.

REFERENCES

Ahl, H. (2002), 'The making of the female entrepreneur: A discourse analysis of research texts on women's entrepreneurship', *JIBS dissertation series No. 015*, Jönköping International Business School Ltd.

Alba, A. (ed.) (2000), *La Riqueza de las Familias*, Barcelona: Ariel.

Aldrich, H. (1989), 'Networking among women entrepreneurs', in O. Hagan, C. Rivchun and D. Sexton, *Women-owned Business*, NY: Praeger, pp. 103–32.

Aldrich, H.E., Reese, P.R. and Dubini, P. (1989), 'Women on the verge of a breakthrough? Networking among entrepreneurs in the United States and Italy', *Entrepreneurship and Regional Development*, **1**, 339–56.

Aldrich, H., Elam, A. and Reese, P.R. (1997), 'Strong ties, weak ties and strangers: Do women business owners differ from men in their use of networking to obtain assistance?', in Birley, S. and MacMillan, I. (eds), *Entrepreneurship in a Global Context*, Routledge, 1–25.

Alvarez, B. and Miles, D. (2003), 'Gender effect on housework allocation: Evidence from Spanish two-earner couples', *Journal of Population Economics*, **16**, 227–42.

Belcourt, M., Burke, R.J. and Lee-Gosselin, H. (1991), 'The glass box: Women business owners in Canada', background paper, Ottawa, Ontario: Canadian Advisory Council on the Status of Women.

Belso Martínez, J.A. (2003), 'Discriminación de género y fomento de nuevas empresas: Conclusiones a partir de un análisis multivariante sobre las pymes valencianas de reciente creación', *Revista del Ministerio de Trabajo y Asuntos Sociales*, **41**, 15–38.

Birley, S., Moss, C. and Sanders, P. (1987), 'Do women entrepreneurs require different training?', *American Journal of Small Business*, **12**(1), 27–35.

Boden, R.J. Jr and Nucci, A.R. (2000), 'On the survival prospects of men's and women's new business ventures', *Journal of Business Venturing*, **15**(4), 347–362.

Bordieu, P. (1986), 'The forms of capital', in J.G. Richardson (ed.), *Handbook of Theory and Research for the Sociology of Education*, New York: Greenwood Press, pp. 241–58.

Breitenbach, E. (1999), 'Changing gender relations in contemporary Scotland', in G. Hassan and C. Warhust (eds), *A Different Future: A Moderniser's Guide to Scotland*, Glasgow: The Big Issue and Centre for Scottish Public Policy.

Bruederl, J., Preisendorfer, P. and Ziegler, R. (1992), 'Network support and the success of newly founded businesses', *Small Business Economics*, **10**, 213–25.

Brush, C.G. (1992), 'Research on women business owners: Past trends, a new perspective and future directions', *Entrepreneurship: Theory and Practice*, Summer, 5–30.

Brush, C.G. and Hisrich, R.D. (1991), 'Antecedent influences on women-owned businesses', *Journal of Management Psychology*, **6**(2), 9–16.

Brush, C.G. and Hisrich, R.D. (2000), 'Women-owned businesses: An exploratory study comparing factors affecting performance', Working paper from Research Institute for Small and Emerging Businesses, Inc., www.riseb.org.

Brush, C.G., Carter, N.M., Green, P.G., Hart, M.M. and Gatewood, E.J. (2001), 'The Diana Project: Women business-owners and equity capital: the myths dispelled', Kauffman Center for Entrepreneurial Leadership, www.entreworld.org.

Burt, R.S. (1992), *Structural Holes: The Social Structure of Competition*, Cambridge, MA: Harvard University Press.

Carrasco, C. and Rodríguez, A. (2000), 'Women, families, and work in Spain: Structural changes and new demands', *Feminist Economics*, **6**(1), 45–57.

Carter, N.M. and Kolvereid, L. (1997), 'Women starting new businesses: The experience in Norway and the United States', OECD Conference on Women Entrepreneurs in Small and Medium Enterprises: A Major Force in Innovation and Job Creation, Paris, April.

Carter, N.M., Williams, M. and Reynolds, P.D. (1997): 'Discontinuance among new firms in retail: The influence of initial resources, strategy, and gender', *Journal of Business Venturing*, **12**, 125–45.

Carter, S. and Rosa, P. (1998), 'The financing of male- and female-owned businesses', *Entrepreneurship & Regional Development*, **10**, 225–41.

Carter, S., Anderson, S. and Shaw, E. (2001), *Women Business Ownership: A Review of the Academic, Popular and Internet Literature*, Report to the Small Business Service, RR 002/01.

Carter, S., Shaw, E. and Wilson, F. (2003), 'Securing a business loan: How women entrepreneurs view banks and how banks view them', XVII RENT, Poland.

Casrud, A.L., Gaglio, C.M. and Olm, K.W. (1987), 'Women on the verge of a breakthrough? Networking among entrepreneurs in the United States and Italy', *Entrepreneurship and Regional Development*, **1**, 339–56.

Chell, E. and Baines, S. (1998), 'Does gender affect business performance? A study of microbusinesses in services in the UK', *Entrepreneurship & Regional Development*, **10**, 117–35.

Chinchilla, M.N. (1997), '¿Cómo emprenden las mujeres? Motivaciones y competencias distintivas', *Iniciativa Empresarial y Empresa Familiar*, **13**, 11–16.

Clain, S.H. (2000), 'Gender differences in full-time self-employment', *Journal of Economics and Businesses*, **52**(6), 499–513.

Cliff, J.E. (1998), 'Does one size fit all? Exploring the relationship between attitudes towards growth, gender, and business size', *Journal of Business Venturing*, **13**, 523–42.

Coduras, A., López-García, P., Justo, R., de la Vega, I., Catedra Najeti (2004), 'Spain 2003 GEM Report', Mayo, www.gemconsortium.org/document.asp?id=346.

Coleman, S. (2000), 'Access to capital and terms of credit: A comparison of men- and women-owned businesses', *Journal of Small Business Management*, **38**(3), 37–53.

Cooper, A.C., Gimeno-Gascon, F.J. and Woo, C.Y. (1994), 'Initial human and financial capital as predictors of new venture performance', *Journal of Business Venturing*, **9**, 371–95.

Cooper, A., Ramachandran, M. and Schoorman, D. (1997), 'Time allocation patterns of craftsmen and administrative entrepreneurs: Implications for financial performance', *Entrepreneurship Theory and Practice*, Winter, 123–36.

Cromie, S. and Birley, S. (1992), 'Networking by female business owners in Northern Ireland', *Journal of Business Venturing*, **7**(3), 237–51.

Davidsson, P. (1989), 'Entrepreneurship and after? A study of growth willingness in small firms', *Journal of Business Venturing*, **4**, 211–26.

Davidsson, P. (1991), 'Continued entrepreneurship: Ability, need, and opportunity as determinants of small firm growth', *Journal of Business Venturing*, **6**, 405–529.

de Luis Carnicer, P. and Urquizu Samper, P. (1995), 'El sector comercio: ¿un refugio para la mujer empresaria?', *Revista Esic Market*, April–June, Madrid, 167–83.

Du Rietz, A. and Henrekson, M. (2000), 'Testing the female underperformance hypothesis', *Small Business Economics*, **14**, 1–10.

Eagly, A. and Karau, S. (2002), 'Role congruity theory of prejudice toward female leaders', *Psychological Review*, **109**, 573–98.

Fabowale, L., Orser, B. and Riding, A. (1995), 'Gender, structural factors and credit terms between Canadian small businesses and financial institutions', *Entrepreneurship Theory and Practice*, **19**(4), 41–65.

Fasci, M.A. and Valdez, J. (1998), 'A performance contrast of male- and female-owned small accounting practices', *Journal of Small Business Management*, **36**(3), 1–7.

Fay, M. and Williams, L. (1993), 'Sex of applicant and the availability of business "start-up" finance', *Australian Journal of Management*, **16**(1), 65–72.

Fischer, E.M., Reuber, R.A. and Dyke, L.S. (1993), 'A theoretical overview and extension of research on sex, gender, and entrepreneurship', *Journal of Business Venturing*, **8**(2), 151–68.

Granovetter, M. (1973), 'The strength of weak ties', *American Journal of Sociology*, **6**, 1360–80.

Greene, P., Brush, C. and Brown, T. (1997), 'Resources in small firms: An exploratory study', *Journal of Small Business Strategy*, **8**(23), 29–40.

Greer, M.J. and Greene, P.G. (2003), 'Feminist theory and the study of entrepreneurship', in Butler, J.E., *Women Entrepreneurs*, Greenwich, CO: Information Age Publishing, Inc.

Greeve, A. and Salaff, J.W. (2003), 'Social networks and entrepreneurship', *Entrepreneurship Theory and Practice*, **28**(1), 1–22.

Haynes, G.W. and Haynes, D.C. (1999), 'The debt structure of small businesses owned by women in 1987 and 1993', *Journal of Small Business Management*, **37**(2), 1–20.

Hisrich, R.D. and Brush, C.G. (1983), 'The woman entrepreneur: Implications of family, educational, and occupational experience', *Frontiers of Entrepreneurship Research*, Wellesley, MA: Babson College, 255–70.

Hisrich, R.D. and Brush, C.G. (1984), 'The woman entrepreneur: Management skills and business problems', *Journal of Small Business Management*, **22**(1), 30–7.

Hisrich, R.D. and Brush, C.G. (1986), *The Women Entrepreneur: Starting, Financing and Managing a Successful Business*, Lexington Books, Toronto.

Hisrich, R.D. and O'Brien, M. (1981), 'The women entrepreneur from a business and sociological perspective', in K.H. Vesper (ed.), *Frontiers of Entrepreneurship Research*, Wellesley, MA: Babson College, 21–39.

Holmquist, C. and Sundin, E. (1988), 'Women as entrepreneurs in Sweden: Conclusions from a survey', *Frontiers of Entrepreneurship Research*, Wellesley, MA: Babson College, 643–53.

Hulbert, J. (1991), 'Social circle and job satisfaction', *Work and Occupation*, **18**, 415–30.

Instituto Nacional de Estadística (2004a), *Encuesta de Población Activa*, III Trimester, www.ine.es.

Instituto Nacional de Estadística (2004b), *Encuesta de Población Activa*, IV Trimester, www.ine.es.

Instituto Nacional de Estadística (2004c), *Encuesta de Estructura Salarial*, www.ine.es.

Johnson, S. and Storey, D. (1993), 'Male and female entrepreneurs and their businesses: A comparative study', in S. Allen and C. Truman (eds), *Women in Business: Perspectives on Women Entrepreneurs*, London: Routledge Press, pp. 70–85.

Kalleberg, A. and Leicht, K.T. (1991), 'Gender and organizational performance: Determinants of small business survival and success', *Academy of Management Journal*, **34**(1), 136–61.

Katz, J.A. and Williams, P.M. (1997), 'Gender, self-employment and weak-tie networking through formal organizations', *Entrepreneurship & Regional Development*, **9**, 183–97.

Lévesque, M. and MacCrimmon, K.R. (1997), 'On the interaction of time and money in new ventures', *Entrepreneurship Theory and Practice*, Winter, 89–110.

Longstreth, M., Stafford, K. and Mauldin, T. (1987), 'Self-employed women and their families: Time use and socio-economic characteristics', *Journal of Small Business Management*, 30–7.

Loscocco, K.A. and Leicht, K.T. (1993), 'Gender, work–family linkages, and economic success among small business owners', *Journal of Marriage and the Family*, **55**(4), 875–87.

Loscocco, K.A., Robinson, J., Hall, R.H. and Allen, J.K. (1991), 'Gender and small business: An inquiry into women's relative disadvantage', *Social Forces*, **70**, 65–85.

Marlow, S. (1997), 'Self-employed women – new opportunities, old challenges?' *Entrepreneurship & Regional Development*, **9**, 199–210.

Marlow, S. and Carter, S. (2004), 'Accounting for change: Professional status, gender disadvantage and self-employment', *Women in Management Review*, **19**(1), 5–17.

Marlow, S. and Strange, A. (1994), 'Female entrepreneurs: Success by whose standards?', in M. Tanton (ed.), *Women in Management: A Developing Presence*, London, Routledge, 171–84.

McKechnie, S., Ennew, C. and Read, L. (1998), 'The nature of banking relationship: A comparison of experiences between male and female small business owners', *International Small Business Journal*, **16**(3), 39–55.

Mencken, F.C. and Winfield, I. (2000), 'Job search and sex segregation: Does sex of social contact matter?', in *Sex Roles*, Kluwer Academic Publishers.

Moore, D.P. (1999), 'Women entrepreneurs: Approaching a new millennium', in G.N. Powell (ed.), *Handbook of Gender and Work*, Sage Publications.

Moore, D.P. and Buttner, E.H. (1997), 'Women's organizational female business owners: An exploratory study', *Journal of Small Business Management*, July, 18–34.

Neider, L. (1987), 'A preliminary investigation of female entrepreneurs in Florida', *Journal of Small Business Management*, **25**(3), 22–9.

Nelson, G. (1987), 'Information needs of women entrepreneurs', *Journal of Small Business Management*, **25**(1), 38–44.

OECD (Organisation for Economic Co-operation and Development) (1997), 'Women entrepreneurs in SMEs: A major force in innovation and job creation', Synthesis of the OECD Conference, www1.oecd.org.

OECD (1998), *Women Entrepreneurs in Small and Medium Enterprises*, OECD Conference Paris 1997.

OECD (2000), *Women Entrepreneurs: Improving Knowledge and Statistics*, report, Working Party on Small and Medium-sized Enterprises.

Orhan, M. (2001), 'Women business owners in France: The issue of financing discrimination', *Journal of Small Business Management*, **39**(1), 95–102.

Perry, S.C. (2002), 'A comparison of failed and non-failed small businesses in the United States: Do men and women use different planning and decision-making strategies?', *Journal of Developmental Entrepreneurship*, **7**(4), 415–28.

Renzulli, L.A., Aldrich, H. and Moody, J. (2000), 'Family matters: Gender, networks and entrepreneurial outcomes', *Social Forces*, **79**(2), 523–46.

Riding, A. and Swift, C. (1990), 'Women business owners and terms of credit: Some empirical findings of the Canadian experience', *Journal of Business Venturing*, **5**, 327–40.

Robinson, S. and Sexton, E.A. (1994), 'The effect of education and experience on self-employment success', *Journal of Business Venturing*, **9**, 141–56.

Rosa, P., Hamilton, D., Carter, S. and Burns, H. (1994), 'The impact of gender on small business management: Preliminary findings of a British study', *International Small Business Journal*, **12**(3), 25–32.

Rosa, P., Carter, S. and Hamilton, D. (1996), 'Gender as a determinant of small business performance: Insights of a British study', *Small Business Economics*, **8**, 463–78.

Sánchez Apellániz, M. (2000), 'El empresariado femenino en Andalucía', *Boletín Económico Andaluz*, **28–29**, 73–88.

Sexton, D.L. and Kent, C.A. (1981), 'Female executives and entrepreneurs: A preliminary comparison', in *Frontiers in Entrepreneurship Research*, K.H. Vesper (ed.), Wellesley, MA: Babson College, pp. 21–39.

Smeltzer, L. and Fann, G. (1989), 'Gender differences in external networks of small business owners/managers', *Journal of Small Business Management*, **27**(2), 25–32.

Srinivasan, R., Woo, C. and Cooper, A. (1994), 'Performance determinants for male and female entrepreneurs', in W.D. Bygrave, S. Birley, N.C. Churchill, E. Gatewood, F. Hoy, R.H. Keely, W.E. Wetzel, Jr (eds), *Frontiers of Entrepreneurship Research*, Wellesley, MA: Babson College, pp. 43–55.

Stevenson, L.A. (1986), 'Against all odds: The entrepreneurship of women', *Journal of Small Business Management*, **24**(4), 30–36.

Tigges, L.M. and Green, G.P. (1992), 'Small business success among men and women-owned firms', Rural Sociological Society Association Paper.

Uzzi, B. (1999), 'Embeddedness in the making of financial capital: How social relations and networks benefit firms seeking financing', *American Sociological Review*, **64**, 481–505.

Van Uxem, F. and Bais, J. (1996), *Het starten van een bedrijf. Ervaringen van 2000 starters*, EIM Business and Policy Research, Zoetermeer.

Venkataraman, S. and Van den Ven, A. (1998), 'Hostile environmental jolts, transaction set, and new business', *Journal of Business Venturing*, **13**, 231–55.

Verheul, I. and Thurik, A.R. (2000), 'Start-up capital: differences between male and female entrepreneurs: Does gender matter?', *Small Business Economics, **16**(4), 329–45.

Verheul, I., Carree, M. and Thurik, R. (2004), 'Allocation and productivity of the time in new ventures of female and male entrepreneurs', *ERIM Report Series in Management*.

Verheul, I., Risseuw, P. and Bartelse, G. (2002), 'Gender differences in strategy and human resource management: The case of Dutch real estate brokerage', *International Small Business Journal*, **20**(4), 443–76.

16. Gender, entrepreneurship and business finance: investigating the relationship between banks and entrepreneurs in the UK

Sara Carter, Eleanor Shaw, Fiona Wilson and Wing Lam*

INTRODUCTION

An individual's ability to engage in entrepreneurship is predicated on the availability of resources, in particular access to finance. Research that has investigated entrepreneurial finance in the form of equity capital has focused mainly on the supply side (Mason and Harrison, 1999), where the perspective of the venture capitalist or venture capital industry is the central concern (Sapienza, 1992; Wright et al., 1997; Zacharakis and Shepherd, 2001). The demand-side perspective, focusing on the approaches taken by firms seeking external investment, has attracted less research interest, although some researchers have explicitly commented on the need to focus on variations in the ability of some entrepreneurial groups to obtain venture finance (Timmons and Sapienza, 1992; Timmons and Bygrave, 1997).

Women are one of the main entrepreneurial groups that have, so far, notably failed to obtain their share of venture finance. Current estimates suggest that in the USA, less than 5 per cent of the $73 billion venture capital pool is awarded to women-owned firms (Greene et al., 1999; Business Week Online, 2001). Greene et al. (1999) suggested three reasons why women experience difficulties in raising equity capital: firstly, women choose not to seek this type of external investment; secondly, women encounter structural barriers that preclude their access to equity capital; and thirdly, women lack the knowledge and capabilities to obtain equity capital. In addition, it has also been argued that women choose to start their businesses in sectors or locations that do not match the preferences of external lenders (Brush et al., 2001).

In the UK, greater research attention has focused on debt finance, the more widely used method of external finance used to facilitate business start-up and growth. Studies that have compared male-owned and female-owned businesses report a bi-modal profile in funding arrangements, with women using on average only one-third of the starting capital used by men (Carter and Rosa, 1998; Rosa et al., 1994, 1996). Similar findings have emanated from research studies undertaken in a variety of country contexts. However, while research provides unequivocal evidence that women-owned businesses start both with lower levels of overall capitalization and lower ratios of debt finance (Hisrich and Brush, 1984, 1985; Brush, 1992; Carter and Rosa, 1998; Coleman, 2000; Carter and Anderson, 2001), the causes of this are uncertain. Some studies have attributed the causes as being sexual stereotyping and discrimination (Hisrich and Brush, 1984; Buttner and Rosen, 1988), women's lack of personal assets and credit track record (Riding and Swift, 1990), and women's inability to penetrate informal financial networks (Olm et al., 1988; Aldrich, 1989; Greene et al., 1999). Other studies, however, have failed to confirm these propositions (Buttner and Rosen, 1989; Chrisman et al., 1990; Riding and Swift, 1990; Haines et al., 1999; Haynes and Haynes, 1999).

The debate has continued largely because of the methodological difficulties facing researchers in providing clear and unequivocal evidence (Brush, 1992, 1997; Mahoot, 1997). To date, methodologies have relied mainly upon a narrow set of approaches, using telephone and personal interviews or postal questionnaires that depend on self-reported evidence from entrepreneurs. Few studies have developed the more sophisticated methodologies required to tease out the reasons why women fail to gain the volume and ratio of debt finance necessary to start and sustain a high-growth business. Fewer still have explored the issue from the perspective of both the supply side and the demand side by focusing equal attention on banks and entrepreneurs.

This chapter presents details of the methodological approach and interim results from a large-scale, ongoing study exploring the relationship between entrepreneurship, gender and bank lending in the UK. The study takes a social constructionist perspective, focusing on perceptions that are held by male and female entrepreneurs about banks; the perceptions that are held by male and female bank officers about male and female entrepreneurs; the effects of economic, social, human and cultural capital on the ability of entrepreneurs to mobilize financial resources; and the effects of these perceptions on the ability of male and female entrepreneurs to raise bank finance to start and sustain a business. Following this introduction, the chapter briefly outlines the UK country context and considers the theoretical perspectives on gender and business ownership that inform the methodological approach used in this study. The research approach and details of the six-stage methodology are then presented. The chapter then highlights some of the initial results from both supply side (banks) and demand side (entrepreneurs), before drawing tentative conclusions.

COUNTRY CONTEXT

Women's Business Ownership in the UK

There are an estimated four million enterprises in the UK, employing a total of 21.7 million people and with a combined annual turnover of £2200 billion (DTI, 2004). While there are no official statistics that disaggregate enterprise ownership by gender, a series of large-scale surveys collectively suggest that about 15 per cent of UK enterprises are female-owned, 50 per cent are male-owned and 35 per cent are co-owned by males and females (Small Business Service, 2003; Carter et al., 2004).

The popular view of a large-scale expansion in the number of female entrepreneurs in the UK over the past decade, a view perhaps influenced by the range of public policy initiatives designed to increase female self-employment, is not fully upheld by the statistical evidence. Since 1992, there has been a growth in the number of self-employed women in the UK, from 899000 in 1992 (Q1) to 962000 in 2004 (Q1), an increase of 6.5 per cent. The female share of self-employment (26 per cent in 1992 and 26.6 per cent in 2004) has remained largely static (Labour Force Survey, 2004). The proportion of economically active women in self-employment (7 per cent) has also remained static over the same period. This data can be compared with the total (all persons), which shows that UK self-employment grew from 3445000 in 1992 (Q1) to 3613000 in 2004 (Q1), an increase of 4.6 per cent. In 2004, self-employment accounted for 12.16 per cent of the total economically active population, the same proportion as 1992.

The relatively low levels of female self-employment and business ownership in the UK may be best explained by the overall position of women within the labour market. Women's employment is largely concentrated in the retail and services sectors, particularly in non-manual administration and junior managerial positions (Marlow and Carter, 2004). While a growing number of women are apparent within the professions, such as medicine, law and accountancy, women are still under-represented in senior management (Equal Opportunities Commission, 2001). Only 7 per cent of FTSE board directors are female and 39 of the top 100 FTSE companies do not have any female directors (Small Business Service, 2003). Although there is some evidence that the pay-gap is narrowing, women in full-time employment earn, on average, only 82 per cent of that earned by their male counterparts, while women in part-time employment earn just 60 per cent of that earned by their male counterparts (Equal Opportunities Commission, 2004). Research suggests that not only are women less likely to become self-employed, their experience of business ownership differs substantially from that of men; most female self-employment is confined to traditionally female occupational sectors, such as education, health, finance and business services; more than half of self-employed women work part-time (less than 30 hours per week); and over a third of women, compared with 12 per cent of men, use their home as a business base (Small Business Service, 2003).

The proportion of female entrepreneurs in the UK is comparable with other Northern European countries (Holmquist, 1997; Nilsson, 1997), but considerably lower than in the USA, where there are an estimated 10.1 million businesses in which a woman owns at least 50 per cent of the company and women-owned firms account for 28 per cent of all businesses (National Women's Business Council, 2004). Estimates suggest that majority women-owned firms employ 9.2 million workers and generate $1.2 trillion in sales revenue (National Women's Business Council, 2004). While the majority (53 per cent) still operate within the services sectors, there is evidence that women-owned businesses in the USA are moving out of traditionally 'female' sectors such as retailing and low-order services and into construction, production and technology-based sectors (Carter and Allen, 1997; Brush and Hisrich, 1999). This too contrasts with the UK, where female entrepreneurship is still predominantly located within the service economy (Marlow, 1994, 1997; Marlow and Carter, 2004), and 'new economy' businesses, initially believed to present the potential for gender-neutral entrepreneurial action, have emerged as a masculine province; the number of 'new economy' firms owned by men substantially outnumber those owned by women and traditional patterns of gender representation and stereotyping appear to persist (Wilkinson, 2001).

THEORETICAL PERSPECTIVES ON GENDER AND BUSINESS OWNERSHIP

The theoretical position underpinning this research identifies gender as a social structure: it appears natural and accepted, so we rarely 'see' gender structure (Risman, 1998). Gender is a taken-for-granted means of organizing all aspects of our society, including families and work. Bem (1993) used the term 'lenses of gender' to describe the hidden assumptions that produce and reproduce the meaning and salience of gender in society. There are three hidden assumptions: essentialism, androcentrism and gender polarization. Essentialism is the assumption that basic differences in orientation and personality between men and women are rooted in biology and nature. Androcentrism is male-centredness, the belief that males are more valuable than females and that male experience is both gender neutral and the norm for all people. Assuming that work is full-time, life-long and contains no breaks for family commitments, or when 'he' is used to mean he or she, is an androcentric position. Gender polarization is the assumption that not only are women and men different, but this difference is superimposed in so many ways that a link is forged between sex and virtually every aspect of human experience, for example, modes of dress, social roles, ways of expressing emotion. The means to justify androcentrism or essentialism is through gender polarization. This research study is designed to investigate whether this will be found as bank lending officers discuss the topic of bank lending to business owners.

Drawing on Bourdieu's (1990, 1991) conceptual framework with respect to gender symbolism, his roots in structuralism lead him to posit that the social order represents hierarchical relations of difference symbolized in binary opposites: male, female; dominated, dominant; strong, weak. The natural attitude to the gender divide draws heavily on tacitly taken-for-granted assumptions, from the everyday practices in the sexual division of labour and the 'sweet rationale', which explain the 'necessity' for things being as they are. Women are connoted with negative qualities and the masculine with the positive. This contributes to masculine domination. A person's structural position is also determined by capital: economic, social, cultural (which includes educational qualifications) and symbolic (for example, feminine beauty or acquiring masculine traits). Both men and women have formal cultural capital in the form of education and qualifications. However, cultural capital may take the form of a particular combination of educational experiences and family or social connections and interactions with key agents. This could be taken as given or achieved through membership of networks. Alternatively, significant qualities might be recognized like 'drive', the ability to work long unsociable hours or having good social skills that help build an enterprise. These qualities can be viewed as part of what Bourdieu calls the 'habitus', a set of dispositions like attitudes and taste, which people absorb in socialization and contribute toward their practical knowledge and skill in functioning in business. Bourdieu's framework helps us understand how gender hierarchies work, by recognizing the way in which socially constructed ideas of difference (neither neutral nor objective) reflect a hierarchical ordering prevalent in society. The recognition of informal characteristics as constituting cultural capital may help in revealing those virtually invisible social practices that remain difficult to detect and combat. It is possible that the qualities women bring to business ownership may not realize the same value as men's since the dominant ideology and the doxa, or taken-for-granted assumptions are in the hands of the predominantly male elite who make decisions on loans.

A structural perspective on gender was used by Kanter (1977), who showed that when women had access to powerful mentors, interactions with similar people and the possibility for upward mobility, they behaved like others with similar advantages, regardless of sex. Women were less often successful, not because they feared success or had never developed competitive strategies, but because they were more often blocked from network advantages. Men who shared this lack of opportunities also did not advance. Kanter argues persuasively that the properties of the structural system best explain sex differences at work. In this study, we investigate what behaviours are seen to lead to success in business, and how men and women's experiences of networking and other behaviours that are seen to lead to success, compare. There appears, however, in Kanter's work to be an unquestioning acceptance of Weberian notions of bureaucracy: bureaucracy is based on impersonal rules, procedures and hierarchies that work together to produce the most rational and efficient form of organization. An ideal bureaucracy would produce non-discriminatory decisions within the banking system. Within bureaucracy traditional forms of power and discrimination disappear: bureaucracy is in essence gender neutral. This study explores whether this is the case in banking or whether the bureaucracy is found to reflect a specifically male basis of decision-making and way of organizing, mirroring the relationships that women have with men within the broader social relations of patriarchy (Ferguson, 1984; Halford et al., 1997).

This study also explores how men and women as business owners 'do gender' (West and Zimmerman, 1987). A person is expected to 'do gender' and the ease of interaction depends on it. Others' expectations create the self-fulfilling prophecies that lead all of us to 'do gender'. Within this framework, the very belief that biological males and females are essentially different (apart from in terms of reproduction) exists to justify male dominance. Gender difference is primarily a means to justify inequality. Gender is so ubiquitous because unless we see difference, we cannot justify inequality (Lorber, 1994). A key question remains whether those who make decisions on loans perceive differences between men and women that lead to inequalities.

Such a perspective regards social structures as existing outside of individual desires and motives. The structural perspective posits that there is a complex interplay between social structures and human action: human action can, in part, be explained by the constraints and opportunities created by social structures and the outcomes of such action can impact upon and influence the morphology of structures (Giddens, 1984). For the research study, two questions arise: why do bank loan officials and business owners act as they do and what are the taken-for-granted or cognitive image rules that belong to this situation?

Developed as a legitimate framework for replacing structural functionalism, social network theory can provide a more nuanced understanding of this interplay between social structure and human action. In this study, social network theory can provide insight into the complexities and subtleties surrounding access and availability of bank finance and the relationships shared between banks and business owners. This theory is premised on individuals being embedded within and connected to one another by networks of overlapping relationships of different contents and strengths (Granovetter, 1973, 1982; Olm et al., 1988; Aldrich et al., 1989). Individuals are connected by both direct and indirect relationships: by leveraging direct relationships with 'brokers', that is, individuals with whom a direct relationship is shared, individuals are able to access indirect relationships and resources and so widen their social network. Social action and behaviour can be understood by considering both the position individuals hold within networks and the interactions they share. Of particular relevance to this study is the proposition that the relationship shared by any two individuals will be influenced by the other relationships within which they are embedded. This study explores the extent that networks inform business owners about preferred banks and factors that appear to influence loan decisions. Similarly, the study also explores whether networks inform bank loan officials about which businesses are 'viable propositions'.

The analytical strength of social network theory encompasses both structural and interactional dimensions (Aldrich et al., 1989). Structural dimensions refer to the anchorage, density, reachability and range of networks. The wider the range or diversity of an entrepreneur's network, the greater the variety of resources they may access. Interactional dimensions refer to the meanings that individuals attach to the relationships in which they interact, for example, economic transactions, information exchanges or normative expressions of friendship and affection, with stronger relationships containing more than one type of interaction. Networks that are both structurally diverse and interactionally weak tend to be the most valuable in mobilizing a range of entrepreneurial resources (Aldrich et al., 1997; Granovetter, 1973, 1982; Olm et al., 1988). Research has suggested that male networks tend to contain a greater diversity of weak ties, while female networks being both narrower and denser, and consisting primarily of kinship or friendship links, lack the weak ties and relationships with brokers that are necessary to mobilize entrepreneurial resources (Cromie and Birley, 1992; Aldrich and Reece, 1994; Starr and Yudkin, 1996; Aldrich et al., 1997; Katz and Williams, 1997). This study will compare the network structures and interactions of male and female entrepreneurs in an attempt to reveal the effects of these differences on their ability to raise bank finance.

RESEARCH METHODOLOGY AND APPROACH

The study was based on a six-stage methodology that took place sequentially between October 2003 and September 2004. In stages 1–3 data collection focused on the bank lending officers, and in stages 4–6 on the experiences and perceptions of the entrepreneurs. Three specific aspects of the methodology require further discussion.

Firstly, the study used Kelly's (1955) Personal Construct Theory, which provides a methodology for examining cognitive images and processes. This theory suggests that we react to the world as we understand it; we develop personal beliefs about what the world is like, which we then use as a guide for our own actions and responses. These are our personal constructs. Kelly argues that constructs are bipolar in nature: individuals never affirm anything without simultaneously denying something. Sense is made of the world by noting similarity and difference. It is in the contrast that the usefulness of the construct subsists. The repertory grid technique developed by Kelly provides a methodology for examining an individual's construct system. Participants (bank lending officers and entrepreneurs) were asked to name six 'elements' (three male and three female entrepreneurs) of whom they have some reasonable knowledge. The constructs are the qualities that are attributed to people, and are elicited as the participant is presented with three of these elements and are asked to state in which way any two are similar and therefore different from a third. This process is repeated several times with different groups of elements. As many triads of elements are presented as is possible or until the respondent can no longer produce new constructs. The similarities and differences that they identify are taken to be opposite ends of the personal construct the individual uses. The elements are in the columns of a grid, and the bipolar constructs on the horizontal lines. The respondent is then asked to indicate by scoring (1–7) on the grid how each construct applies to each element. This method allows for systematic comparison between people.

Secondly, the study replicated the business plan developed by Fay and Williams (1993) for their analysis of gender discrimination among bank lending officers in New Zealand. This four-page case presents the business plan of an individual, J.S. Jones, seeking bank finance to purchase an ongoing restaurant business. Two amendments were made to the case prior to use in this study. Firstly, the original case identified the applicant's gender by a photograph. The photograph was removed as it was considered a potential source of bias and the sex of the applicant identified by use of a first name. The names given to the case were Emma Jones and Jack Jones, selected as the most popular first names in the UK in the year preceding the study. Secondly, some minor details within the case were changed to reflect the UK context. These modifications were minimal and entailed the substitution of currency signs (NZ$ to UK£), the home address of the applicant (from NZ to UK) and the applicant's alma mater (from University of Otago to University of Manchester).

Finally, a major factor in the uncertainty that surrounds women's access and usage of business finance in the UK has been the reluctance of banks to make public their lending patterns, disaggregated by gender. However, a number of commercial banks have identified women entrepreneurs as an important new market and wish to be seen as more 'woman-friendly'. Data from bank lending officers was drawn from one of the major UK clearing banks. Recent acquisition had fuelled dramatic growth within this organization. As part of its subsequent restructuring programme, which had taken place three years prior to the study, the bank had recruited a new tier of lending staff focused on new business development, and a sample drawn from these new business lending officers formed the basis of the supply side of our study. Because these respondents had all been employed by the bank in the same occupational position at the same time, they shared a broadly similar frame of organizational experience and thus possible bias resulting from variations between individuals in organizational experience and knowledge was minimized. Of the 400 new business development officers recruited into the bank, only 10 per cent were female. One of the bank's concerns was that their female lending officers were under-performing compared with their male counterparts, and the research team were asked to consider the organizational implications of this as an additional research objective.

Stage One: In the first stage of the study, four in-depth interviews were held with bank head office lending and credit control staff. These interviews focused on identifying the current policies, criteria and procedures governing lending decisions. The interviews also focused on the potential changes in lending procedures that had been brought about by new IT systems. Decisions regarding bank lending to businesses are traditionally made through personal representation, but technology-based banking (internet/telephone banking) may be creating a new set of lending criteria, particularly for lower value loan decisions. While algorithms used by banks remained confidential, these initial interviews clarified the systems and criteria used within the bank and their equivalent across the UK banking sector.

Stage Two: In the second stage, six focus groups were held with bank business lending officers, three with male lending staff and three with female lending staff. Broad geographical coverage was attained by holding focus groups in London, Bristol, Manchester and Edinburgh. Prior to the focus group, each participant was given a copy of the Fay and Williams (1993) case study and taped individual interviews recorded their reactions as they discussed the business plan, applying the criteria that they would normally use within the bank. Three of the focus groups used the female case (Emma Jones) and the other three focus groups used the male case (Jack Jones). Following these individual interviews, the focus groups commenced by asking the participants to discuss the case and assess its merits and funding potential.

Thereafter, discussion focused more broadly on the bank's lending criteria, their own personal lending criteria and the characteristics that they look for in potential entrepreneurs, and the procedures that they adhere to in proposing funding decisions. To control moderator bias, the moderator was the same sex (female) for all six groups.

Stage Three: The third stage immediately followed each focus group. This stage consisted of a further round of individual interviews with the bank lending officers who had participated in the focus groups. These interviews used repertory grid techniques to ascertain the individual personal constructs they each held of entrepreneurs.

The demand-side data was drawn from matched pairs of male and female entrepreneurs. While the central concern of the study is women, controlled experimentation requires both sexes. The precise nature of the relationship between banks and women entrepreneurs can only be portrayed by comparison with the male experience. A matched pairs approach has been identified as particularly relevant for the analysis of gender and finance, as many of the factors cited as causal in negative loan decisions may simply be a function of sector and business track-record (Read, 1998).

Stage Four: The fourth stage consisted of telephone interviews with 100 entrepreneurs (50 male, 50 female), who had started businesses in the business services sector within the previous three years. The sample was drawn from the Yellow Pages for central Scotland. Researching new businesses requires particular care in sample construction. Many 'off-the-shelf' business datasets, such as Dun and Bradstreet, have been constructed for credit referencing purposes and consequently exclude a large proportion of new firms (Storey, 1994). National and local government datasets of new firms, however, present difficulties in terms of access and other restrictions. The Yellow Pages gives the most readily available lists of businesses and the highest coverage, while minimizing the main problems (omissions, clusters, foreign elements and duplicate listings) associated with other business sampling frames. Given the relatively low numbers of women in business, initial sample assembly concentrated on building the female sample of firms (advertising agencies, marketing and advertising consultants, management and business consultants). Male businesses, being more prevalent, were then sought to individually match each of the female sample businesses. The telephone interviews focused on the resource acquisition of entrepreneurs, their relative access to and use of different kinds of capital (economic, human, social, cultural) as well as their broad experiences and perceptions of bank lending.

Stage Five: From this initial sample of 100 entrepreneurs, 30 matched pairs (30 men and 30 women) went forward to participate in the last two stages of data collection. The reduction in sample size was the result of an anticipated natural fall-out and the need to more precisely match industry sub-sectoral activities, some of which only became apparent during the course of the initial interview. In the fifth stage, in-depth personal interviews were conducted with each of the 60 business owners. The interview schedule was highly structured and based on a detailed 20-page questionnaire. Many of the questions and scales used were drawn from previous research, including the Diana survey, enabling comparative analysis (Brush et al., 2004).

Stage Six: The final stage followed immediately after the Stage Five personal interviews, and entailed the use of repertory grid techniques to elicit their individual constructs about entrepreneurs. The technique was identical to that used with the bank lending officers in Stage Three.

RESULTS AND ANALYSIS

Initial analysis of the data from both the supply side and the demand side suggest promising insights into the relationship between gender and business finance. The broad results reported below highlight some of the initial findings from both the supply side and the demand side, focusing on Stage Two (individual interviews and focus group discussions with bank lending officers) and Stage Four (telephone interviews with entrepreneurs).

Supply-side Data: Focus Groups with Bank Lending Officers

In the Stage Two pre-focus group individual interviews, bank lending officers were given a copy of the Fay and Williams (1993) case study, which outlined the loan application of an entrepreneur seeking bank finance to buy a middle-market restaurant in a tourist town. In half the interviews, the applicant was described as being female (Emma Jones) while in the other half the applicant was described as male (Jack Jones). The interview protocol asked bank lending officers to read the case and simultaneously articulate their initial reactions to the application. These interviews, half with female lenders and half with male lenders, revealed no gender differences in the likelihood of pursuit. Few lenders even mentioned the gender of the applicant, preferring to consider other personal attributes such as age, education and industry experience. Mostly, lenders' reactions focused on the business idea, the size of the loan, the applicant's financial track record and ability to provide security and their debt to asset ratio. All of the lenders were enthusiastic about the application, specifying that they would be likely to take it forward for serious funding consideration. Each lending officer specified that their next steps would be to meet the applicant and all individually expressed the view that they would not consider funding any application until they had met the individual. An emphasis on meeting the applicant both served the bank's

quality assurance and compliance demands and satisfied their own professional standards.

The focus group discussions enabled a fuller exploration of what 'meeting
the loan applicant' entailed and, in particular, an emphasis on the personal
characteristics they considered desirable and sought in their loan applicants. In
these discussions, lending officers placed emphasis on the personal qualities
of the individual requiring finance, and many spoke of the need for evidence
of 'business acumen'. None of the lending officers could define precisely what
'business acumen' entailed, but spoke instead of industry experience,
management experience, 'c.v. and track record'. Few lending officers
expressed a preference that entrepreneurs should conform to a specific set of
personal characteristics, but age and education were often raised in
discussions. The age of the Fay and Williams' case applicant (32) was seen as
perfect; sufficient experience had been gained, but relative youth brought
energy and drive to the business. Most, however, stated that age was only an
issue at the margins: very young entrepreneurs were unlikely to have gained
sufficient experience to run a successful enterprise, very old entrepreneurs
were unlikely to be successful in a loan application where the debt repayment
period exceeded their own life expectation. Tertiary-level education was seen
as an advantage by the lending officers, but this was tempered in their
discussions by numerous examples of successful entrepreneurs with few
academic qualifications. None of the focus groups considered gender as a
personal quality that was decisive in a loan application: indeed, in some of the
focus groups, the issue of gender was not raised by the lending officers. One
group commented that they would query a female applicant wanting to start a
business in a traditionally male sector, but this was qualified by discussions of
examples of women who had successfully done this. Many of the lending
officers placed emphasis on establishing a personal rapport with the
entrepreneur, but equally they stated that personal dislike would not
necessarily deter a positive decision providing the applicant complied with
other aspects they were seeking.

Throughout the focus groups, there was clear and unambiguous evidence of
individual decision-making by the bank lending officers. Thus, it was possible
for a loan application to be supported by one lending officer and rejected by
another. This element of individualized decision-making is crucial in interpreting the loan application process, and in particular the type of applicants
who are likely to be successful and those likely to fail. When individuals such
as bank lending officers have the ability to make decisions based on personal
judgement, these decisions reflect their individual biases and opinions and the
ordering of the world with which they concur. While individualized decision-
making may reflect the inherent biases of lending officers, it is economically
irrational for banks as a corporate entity to discriminate against women

entrepreneurs by more frequently rejecting their loan applications. Banks seek to do business; the ideal bank bureaucracy is gender neutral and produces non-discriminatory decisions within the banking system. Nevertheless, judgements about loan applications submitted to banks are made by individual employees and their decisions reflect their individual biases.

A more nuanced view of the role of gender within the bank was produced not as a consequence of discussions about female entrepreneurs, but by discussions with women lending officers about their role as bank employees. Many women lending officers were exercised by the effects of gender on their own position within the bank and the denial of personal experience of gender inequality was a recurrent theme within the women's focus groups. Most women lending officers repeatedly denied gender inequalities, others believed that their gender gave them an advantage, and a minority reported anecdotes to support their view that their gender placed them at a professional disadvantage with their male colleagues. While the majority rejected the notion of gender disadvantage, paradoxically they spent a great deal of time discussing it and these discussions of their own gendered experiences were to the exclusion of discussions about the experiences of female entrepreneurs.

One of the differences that emerged from the focus groups was how male and female lending officers 'do business' within the bank. Loan applications are initially screened by lending officers who, if supportive, write a detailed loan proposal that is forwarded to Head Office credit controllers for approval. Discussions about the interactions between male and female lending officers and credit sanction staff were distinctly different. Male lending officers more often actively sought to network with other bank staff, particularly credit controllers, within the bank. There were some acknowledgements that active networking, for example, through socializing at sports events or office parties, could both advance their personal ambitions and also smooth the process of loan application proposals. While this approach was not always successful, there was a specific view expressed by several of the male lending officers that internal bank processes were negotiable. In contrast, the women lending officers were far less instrumental in seeking to influence bank decision-making through networking. Indeed, the prevailing view within the female focus groups was that the internal credit sanctioning process was 'objective'; while they might know the credit sanctioners individually, it was not possible for them to either influence which credit sanctioner would receive their proposal or in any way to influence the credit controller's loan approval decision.

Demand-side Data: Telephone Interviews

The Stage Four telephone interviews were conducted with a sample of 50 male and 50 female entrepreneurs operating in the business services sector in the central belt of Scotland. Previous studies of entrepreneurship and gender have consistently revealed differences in size and performance levels between male- and female-owned enterprises. Even controlling for sector, business age and location, this small survey revealed distinctive gender-based differences. These differences are most apparent in the industry focus, ownership, size and capitalization of firms.

While nominally all of the businesses were drawn from the Business Services sector, this industry sector includes a number of distinct business activities. Respondents were asked to specify their precise sub-sectoral focus and describe their firm's activities. Of the 50 male entrepreneurs, 32 described the nature of their firms as 'Management and Business Consultancy' compared with only 12 female entrepreneurs. In contrast, 22 female entrepreneurs described their firm's activities as 'Business Services', compared with only two male entrepreneurs. These differences are statistically significant ($x^2 29.658$, df = 5, p < 0.000). These results confirm previous observations (see Rosa et al., 1994) of intra-sectoral gender differences in business focus.

Previous studies have also remarked on the greater likelihood of women to start single-person enterprises (Marlow, 1994, 1997). This survey also found that women were more likely to start in business by themselves: 90 per cent of women, but only 66 per cent of men started as sole owners ($x^2 8.39$, df = 1, p < 0.004). While an equally small proportion (10 per cent) of male and female entrepreneurs started in business with a male owner, 20 per cent of male entrepreneurs (and no female entrepreneurs) started with an additional female owner ($x^2 11.111$, df = 5, p < 0.001). Male entrepreneurs were also more likely to both start in business with a co-owning spouse and also to employ their spouse within the firm: 34 per cent of male entrepreneurs, but only 2 per cent of female entrepreneurs, specified that they shared ownership of the firm with their spouse ($x^2 17.344$, df = 1, p < 0.000), while 16 per cent of males, but only 2 per cent of females, employed their spouse within the business ($x^2 5.983$, df = 1, p < 0.015).

Gender differences were also apparent in the overall size of the firms. Despite being started within the same time period, men were more than twice as likely to employ additional staff. In total, 40 per cent of male entrepreneurs, but only 16 per cent of female entrepreneurs, employed additional staff ($x^2 7.143$, df = 1, p < 0.007). Men were also more likely to report higher sales turnover in the previous financial year. The majority of women (60 per cent), but only 24 per cent of men, reported a sales turnover of less than £25000. In contrast, 24 per cent of men, but only 2 per cent of women, reported a sales turnover in excess of £100000 ($x^2 20.487$, df = 9, p < 0.015). Women were also more likely to report static sales figures in the previous year (32 per cent of women, compared with 8 per cent of men), while men were more likely than women to report both increases (64 per cent) and decreases (18 per cent) in sales turnover. Previous studies have suggested that the customer base of female entrepreneurial firms may also be gendered; as women-owned firms tend to be established in sectors, such as services and retail, with both high levels of female employment and high levels of female consumption (Marlow, 1997; Carter and Anderson, 2001). As industry sector was strictly controlled, few differences were predicted within this survey. Nevertheless, women were more likely than men to state that their customer base comprised equal numbers of men and women, while men were more likely to specify that they served companies and could not specify the gender of their customers ($x^2 26.222$, df = 5, p < 0.000).

Previous studies have also suggested that women-owned firms generally start with lower levels of financial capitalization (Carter and Rosa, 1998). Given the low barriers to entry within the business services sector, it was unsurprising that both men and women started in business with relatively small amounts of capital. Even so, gender differences were apparent: 86 per cent of women and 62 per cent of men started in business with initial capital investment of less than £12000, while the remainder (14 per cent of women and 34 per cent of men) started with capital greater than £12000. Levels of personal investment also differed by gender: 88 per cent of women and 70 per cent of men invested less than £10000, while 12 per cent of women and 24 per cent of men personally invested more than £10000. It is likely that the level of personal investment in the new venture is related both to the individual's prior earnings and to total household income. While this was not investigated in Stage Four, the Stage Five in-depth interviews collected detailed information regarding individual earnings and total household income in the year prior to business start-up. Future analysis will explore the degree to which individual earnings and household income levels, either separately or in combination, influence levels of personal financial investment in the business start-up. Interestingly, more women than men had started in business with some external investment: in total, 42 per cent of women but only 10 per cent of men had started in business with external financial investment. For most women, however, the sums contributed by external sources were very small-scale. Of the 21 female entrepreneurs with external investment, 17 reported external capitalization of less than £1000. Of the five male entrepreneurs with external investment, four reported external capitalization in excess of £1000.

CONCLUSIONS

Although the data analysis is still ongoing, the initial analyses of the data suggest that gender continues to be an important, but largely hidden variable in the acquisition of finance for business start-up. The influence of gender can be seen in both demand-side and supply-side factors. From the data that is emerging from this study, it is becoming clear that the influence of gender may be profound, but is rarely overt. Women entrepreneurs in the UK still start businesses with a lower overall level of capitalization and a lower ratio of debt finance than do men. In this respect, gender can be seen to be a determining influence on the demand side of the debt finance process. However, gender effects can also be observed on the supply side. As expected, the results so far suggest that this is not a case of overt discrimination by banks. Rather it is possible that both demand-side and supply-side factors interact at the point of contact to co-produce an outcome. The aspirations and expectations of women entrepreneurs and the perceptions held by bank lending officers of women entrepreneurs and 'female-type' businesses both affect the finance lending decision. While there is no evidence of any intentional discrimination on banks' behalf, indeed it is very clearly not in the interests of a bank to delimit lending to women entrepreneurs, individualized decision-making by bank lending officers allows the possibility of judgements that reflect the lending officers' world view to be negotiated and reproduced.

These emerging results suggest that the multi-stage and complex methodology adopted in this study may prove to be particularly useful in advancing our knowledge of the effects of gender on business finance. The methodology enables researchers to unravel deeply held values and perceptions, ones that might not be forthcoming using conventional, post-hoc survey techniques. By exploring the personal constructs held by bank lending officers and male and female entrepreneurs, this study has started to reveal the role that both sides play in the business lending decision. The co-production of outcomes, the result of supply-side and demand-side interaction, may represent an important advance in our understanding of the influence of gender in acquiring business finance.

NOTE

*   The research team are grateful for the financial support of the Economic and Social Research Council, Award Reference No. RES-000-23-0247.

REFERENCES

Aldrich, H. (1989), 'Networking among Women Entrepreneurs', in O. Hagen, C. Rivchum and D. Sexton (eds), *Women Owned Business*, New York: Praeger.
Aldrich, H. and Reece, R. (1994), 'Gender Gap, Gender Myth: Does Women's Networking Behaviour Differ Significantly from Men's?', Paper presented at the Global Conference on Entrepreneurship, INSEAD, Fontainebleau, France, 9–11 March.

Aldrich H.E., Elam, A.B. and Reece, P.R. (1997), 'Strong Ties, Weak Ties and Strangers: Do Women Owners Differ from Men in their use of Networking to Obtain Assistance?', in S. Birley and I.C. MacMillan (eds), *Entrepreneurship in a Global Context*, London: Routledge.

Aldrich, H., Reese, P. and Dubini, P. (1989), 'Women on the Verge of a Breakthrough? Networking Among Entrepreneurs in the United States and Italy', *Entrepreneurship & Regional Development*, **1**, 339–56.

Bem, S. (1993), *The Lenses of Gender; Transforming the Debate on Sexual Inequality*, New Haven: Yale University Press.

Bourdieu, P. (1990), 'La Domination Masculine', *Actes de la Recherche en Sciences Sociales*, **84**, 2–31.

Bourdieu, P. (1991), *Language and Symbolic Power*, Cambridge: Polity.

Brush, C. (1992), 'Research on Women Business Owners: Past Trends, a New Perspective and Future Directions', *Entrepreneurship Theory and Practice*, **16**(4), 5–30.

Brush, C. (1997), 'A Resource Perspective on Women's Entrepreneurship: Research, Relevance and Recognition', Proceedings of the OECD Conference on Women Entrepreneurs in Small and Medium Enterprises: A Major Force in Innovation and Job Creation, Paris, pp. 155–68.

Brush, C. and Hisrich, R.D. (1999), 'Women-Owned Businesses: Why Do They Matter?, in Z.J. Acs (ed.), *Are Small Firms Important? Their Role and Impact*, Norwell, MA: Kluwer Academic Publishers, pp. 111–27.

Brush, C.G., Carter, N.M., Gatewood, E., Greene, P.G. and Hart, M.M. (2004), 'The Diana International Project: Research on Growth-Oriented Women Entrepreneurs and their Businesses', Insight Report, ESBRI, Stockholm, Sweden.

Brush, C., Carter, N., Greene, P., Gatewood, E. and Hart, M. (2001), 'An Investigation of Women-led Firms and Venture Capital Investment', Report prepared for the US Small Business Administration Office of Advocacy and the National Women's Business Council.

Business Week Online (2001), *Venture Capital, A Gender Gap in Start Up Funding*, 14 December.

Buttner, E.H. and Rosen, B. (1988), 'Bank Loan Officers' Perceptions of the Characteristics of Men, Women and Successful Entrepreneurs', *Journal of Business Venturing*, **3**, 249–58.

Buttner, E.H. and Rosen, B. (1989), 'Funding New Business Ventures: Are Decision-Makers Biased Against Women Entrepreneurs?', *Journal of Business Venturing*, **4**, 249–61.

Carter, N. and Allan, K.R. (1997), 'Size Determinants of Women Owned Businesses: Choice or Barriers to Resources?', *Entrepreneurship & Regional Development*, **9**(3), 211–20.

Carter, S. and Anderson, S. (2001), *On the Move: Women and Men Business Owners in the United Kingdom*, Washington DC: NFWBO and IBM.

Carter, S. and Rosa, P. (1998), 'The Financing of Male and Female-Owned Businesses', *Entrepreneurship & Regional Development*, **10**, 225–41.

Carter, S., Mason, C. and Tagg, S. (2004), *Lifting the Barriers to Business Survival and Growth: The FSB Biennial Survey 2004*, London: Federation of Small Businesses.

Chrisman, J.J., Carsrud, A.L., DeCastro, J. and Herron, L. (1990), 'A Comparison of the Assistance Needs of Male and Female Pre-Venture Entrepreneurs', *Journal of Business Venturing*, **5**, 235–48.

Coleman, S. (2000), 'Access to Capital: A Comparison of Men and Women-Owned Small Businesses', *Journal of Small Business Management*, **38**(3), 37–52.

Cromie, S. and Birley, S. (1992), 'Networking by Female Business Owners in Northern Ireland', *Journal of Business Venturing*, **7**(3), 237–51.

DTI (2004), 'Statistical Press Release: URN 04/92, 26th August 2004', London: Department of Trade and Industry.

Equal Opportunities Commission (2001), *Men and Women at Work*, Manchester: EOC.

Equal Opportunities Commission (2004), *Facts About Women and Men in Great Britain*, Manchester: EOC.

Fay, M. and Williams, L. (1993), 'Gender Bias and the Availability of Business Loans', *Journal of Business Venturing*, **8**(4), 363–76.

Ferguson, K. (1984), *The Feminist Case Against Bureaucracy*, Philadelphia: Temple University Press.

Giddens, A. (1984), *The Constitution of Society: Outline of the Theory of Structuration*, Berkeley: University of California Press.

Granovetter, M. (1973), 'The Strength of Weak Ties', *American Journal of Sociology*, **6**, 1360–80.

Granovetter, M. (1982), 'The Strength of Weak Ties: A Network Theory Revisited', in P. Marsden and N. Lin (eds), *Social Structure and Network Analysis*, Beverly Hills, CA: Sage Publications.

Greene, P., Brush, C., Hart, M. and Saparito, P. (1999), 'An Exploration of the Venture Capital Industry: Is Gender an Issue?', in P.D. Reynolds, W. Bygrave, S. Manigart, C. Mason, G.D. Meyer, H. Sapienza and K.G. Shaver (eds), *Frontiers of Entrepreneurship Research*, Wellesley, MA: Babson College.

Haines, G., Orser, A. and Riding, L. (1999), 'Myths and Realities: An Empirical Study of Banks and the Gender of Small Business Clients, *Canadian Journal of Administrative Sciences*, **16**(4), 291–307.

Halford, S., Savage, M. and Witz, A. (1997), *Gender Careers and Organisations: Current Developments in Banking, Nursing and Local Government*, Basingstoke: Macmillan Press.

Haynes, G.W. and Haynes, D.C. (1999), 'The Debt Structure of Small Businesses Owned by Women in 1987 and 1993', *Journal of Small Business Management*, **37**(2), 1–19.

Hisrich, R. and Brush, C.G. (1984), 'The Woman Entrepreneur: Management Skills and Business Problems', *Journal of Small Business Management*, **22**(1), 30–7.

Hisrich, R. and Brush, C. (1985), 'Women and Minority Entrepreneurs: A Comparative Analysis', *Frontiers in Entrepreneurship Research*, Wellesley, MA: Babson College.

Holmquist, C. (1997), 'The Other Side of the Coin or Another Coin? Women's Entrepreneurship as a Complement or an Alternative?', *Entrepreneurship & Regional Development*, **9**(3), 179–82.

Kanter, R.M. (1977), *Men and Women of the Corporation*, New York: Harper and Row.

Katz, J.A. and Williams, P.M. (1997), 'Gender, Self-Employment and Weak-Tie Networking through Formal Organizations', *Entrepreneurship & Regional Development*, **9**(3), 183–97.

Kelly, G.A. (1955), *The Psychology of Personal Constructs*, New York: W.W. Norton.

Labour Force Survey (2004), *Labour Force Survey: Summary for Regions*, London: Office for National Statistics.

Lorber, J. (1994), *Paradoxes of Gender*, New Haven: Yale University Press.

Mahoot, P. (1997), 'Funding for Women Entrepreneurs: A Real, Though Disputed, Problem', Proceedings of the OECD Conference on Women Entrepreneurs in Small and Medium Enterprises: A Major Force in Innovation and Job Creation, Paris, April, pp. 217–26.

Marlow, S. (1994), *Female Entrepreneurs: Do they Mean Business?*, ESRC Report completed in September and quoted in *Times Higher*, 30 September.

Marlow, S. (1997), 'Self Employed Women – Do They Mean Business?', *Entrepreneurship & Regional Development*, **9**(3), 199–210.

Marlow, S. and Carter, S. (2004), 'Accounting for Change: Professional Status, Gender Disadvantage and Self-employment', *Women in Management Review*, **19**(1), 5–17.

Mason, C. and Harrison, R. (1999), 'Venture Capital: Rationale, Aims and Scope', *Venture Capital*, **1**(1), 1–46.

National Women's Business Council (2004), *Key Facts About Women Business Owners and Their Enterprises*, Washington DC, National Women's Business Council.

Nilsson, P. (1997), 'Business Counselling Services Directed Towards Female Entrepreneurs – Some Legitimacy Dilemmas', *Entrepreneurship & Regional Development*, **9**(3), 239–57.

Olm, K., Carsrud, A. and Alvey, L. (1988), 'The Role of Networks in New Venture Funding for the Female Entrepreneur: A Continuing Analysis', in Kirchoff, B.A., Long, W.A., McMullan, W.E., Vesper, K.H. and Wetzel, W.E. Jr (eds), *Frontiers of Entrepreneurship Research*, Wellesley, MA: Babson College.

Read, L. (1998), *The Financing of Small Business: A Comparative Study of Male and Female Business Owners*, London: Routledge.

Riding, A.L. and Swift, C.S. (1990), 'Women Business Owners and Terms of Credit: Some Empirical Findings of the Canadian Experience', *Journal of Business Venturing*, **5**, 327–40.

Risman, B.J. (1998), *Gender Vertigo: American Families in Transition*, New Haven: Yale University Press.

Rosa, P., Carter, S. and Hamilton, D. (1996), 'Gender as a Determinant of Small Business Performance: Insights from a British Study', *Small Business Economics*, **8**: 463–78.

Rosa, P., Hamilton, D., Carter, S. and Burns, H. (1994), 'The Impact of Gender on Small Business Management: Preliminary Findings of a British Study', *International Small Business Journal*, **12**(4), 25–32.

Sapienza, H. (1992), 'When do Venture Capitalists Add Value?', *Journal of Business Venturing*, **7**(1), 9–28.

Small Business Service (2003), *A Strategic Framework for Women's Enterprise*, London: DTI Small Business.

Starr, J. and Yudkin, M. (1996), *Women Entrepreneurs: A Review of Current Research*, Wellesley, MA: Center for Research on Women.

Storey, D. (1994), *Understanding the Small Business Sector*, London: Routledge.

Timmons, J.A. and Bygrave, W.D. (1997), 'Venture Capital: Reflections and Projections', in D.L. Sexton and R. Smilor (eds), *Entrepreneurship 2000*, Chicago: Upstart Publishing.

Timmons, J.A. and Sapienza, H. (1992), 'Venture Capital: The Decade Ahead', in D.L. Sexton and J. Kasarda (eds), *The State of the Art of Entrepreneurship*, Boston: PWS Kent.

West, C. and Zimmerman, D.H. (1987), 'Doing Gender', *Gender and Society*, **1**(2), 125–51.

Wilkinson, H. (2001), *Dot Bombshell: Women, E-quality and the New Economy*, London: The Industrial Society.

Wright, M., Robbie, K. and Ennew, C. (1997), 'Venture Capitalists and Serial Entrepreneurs', *Journal of Business Venturing*, **12**(3), 227–49.

Zacharakis, A.L. and Shepherd, D.A. (2001), 'The Nature of Information and Over-Confidence on Venture Capitalist's Decision Making', *Journal of Business Venturing* **16**(4), 311–32.

Index